Worlds of Difference

Worlds of Difference

Inequality in the Aging Experience

Third Edition

ELEANOR PALO STOLLER

Case Western Reserve University

ROSE CAMPBELL GIBSON

University of Michigan

PINE FORGE PRESS

Thousand Oaks, California
London ■ *New Delhi*

For information address:

PINE FORGE PRESS
A Sage Publications Company
2455 Teller Road
Thousand Oaks, California 91320
(805) 499-4224
e-mail: sales@pfp.sagepub.com

Sage Publications Ltd.
6 Bonhill Street
London EC2A 4PU
United Kingdom

Sage Publications India Pvt. Ltd.
M-32 Market
Greater Kailash I
New Delhi 110 048 India

Production Editor: Wendy Westgate
Editorial Assistant: Nevair Kebakian
Book Designer: Lisa S. Mirski
Typesetter: Christina M. Hill
Indexer: Molly Hall
Cover Designer: Ravi Balasuriya

Printed in the United States of America

11 12   11 10 9 8 7

Library of Congress Cataloging-in-Publication Data

Stoller, Eleanor Palo.
    Worlds of difference: Inequality in the aging experience / By
Eleanor Palo Stoller and Rose Campbell Gibson. — 3rd ed.
        p. cm.
    Includes bibliographical references and index.
    ISBN 978-0-7619-8664-5 (acid-free paper)
    1. Aging. 2. Gerontology. I. Gibson, Rose Campbell. II. Title.
    HQ1061 .S835 2000
    305.26—dc21   99-6360

About the Authors

Eleanor Palo Stoller is the Selah Chamberlain Professor of Sociology at Case Western Reserve University, where she teaches Sociology of Aging, Sociology of Gender, and Qualitative Methods. She was formerly Professor of Health Policy at the University of Florida and Professor of Sociology and Chair of Women's Studies at the State University of New York–Plattsburgh. She received her undergraduate degree in American studies from Grinnell College and her PhD in sociology from Washington University. Her research on informal networks of older people and on lay care in illness has been funded by the National Institute of Aging and the Administration on Aging. Results of this research have appeared in a number of journals, including *Journal of Marriage and the Family, Journal of Gerontology, The Gerontologist, Journal of Health and Social Behavior, Research on Aging,* and *Medical Care.* She is a member of the editorial boards of *Journal of Aging Studies, The Gerontologist, Journal of Applied Gerontology,* and *Family Issues.*

Rose Campbell Gibson is Professor Emerita at the University of Michigan, where she taught Sociology of Aging and Research Methods. After receiving her PhD from the University of Michigan, she was a Postdoctoral Fellow there in Statistics and Survey Research Design and Methodology on Minority Populations and Faculty Associate at the Institute for Social Research. She is the author of *Blacks in an Aging Society* and of numerous articles and chapters that have appeared in volumes such as *Handbook of the Psychology of Aging, Journal of Gerontology, Milbank Quarterly, The Annals,* and the *Journal of Aging and Health.* She is past Editor-in-Chief of *The Gerontologist* and serves on several other editorial boards in the field of aging. Her research on sociocultural factors in aging has been funded by the National Institute of Aging, the Administration on Aging, and private foundations.

About the Publisher

Pine Forge Press is a new educational publisher dedicated to publishing innovative books and software throughout the social sciences. On this and any other of our publications, we welcome your comments and suggestions.

Please call or write us at:

Pine Forge Press
A Sage Publications Company
2455 Teller Road
Thousand Oaks, CA 91320
(805) 499-4224
e-mail: sales@pfp.sagepub.com

Visit our World Wide Web site, your direct link to a multitude of online resources: http://www.pineforge.com

Contents

PART II

Social and Psychological Contexts of Aging

Cultural Images of Old Age   75

PART IV

Family: Variations on "The American Family"

PART V

Health and Mortality: Inequalities

Preface

We undertook the first edition of *Worlds of Difference* because we believed in the importance of enhancing the inclusiveness of the undergraduate curriculum in social gerontology. We remain committed to this goal for two reasons. First, undergraduate students today represent greater diversity in gender, race, and social class than did undergraduates in previous decades, and pedagogical research has demonstrated that students become engaged in curricula that give voice to their experiences. Second, projected increases in diversity within the elderly population over the coming decades demand that people working in the field of gerontology be knowledgeable about the experiences of people of different genders, races, ethnic groups, and social classes. Designing an inclusive curriculum is not just a matter of fairness or affirmative action; it is a central component of educating people to live and work in the 21st century (Moses, 1992).

In preparing the introductory essays and selecting the readings for the three editions, we have been guided by several principles. First, we believe it is essential to move beyond conceptions of gender, race, and class as attributes of individuals that must be controlled statistically or experimentally (J. S. Jackson, 1989). Instead, we conceptualize these categories as social constructs, as classifications based on social values that influence identity formation, opportunity structures, and adaptive resources. We visualize these social constructs as interlocking hierarchies that create systems of privilege as well as disadvantage. Too often, the experience of people who are disadvantaged along one or more hierarchies is contrasted with the experience of the dominant group, which is presented as the norm. Supported by the ideology of a meritocracy, this approach masks the structural foundations of privilege. Too frequently, it is assumed that only people of color have race, that only women have gender, that only the poor have social class, and that only recent immigrants have ethnicity (Higginbotham, 1989). Our emphasis on the intersections of these multiple systems of inequality is designed to help students understand that older people can experience disadvantage along one dimension but privilege along others. Despite our reliance on the image of intersecting hierarchies, we recognize that people experience race, gender, and class simultaneously—that social structures and social processes "are simultaneously 'gendered,' 'raced,' and 'classed'" (West & Fenstermaker, 1995). As Margaret Andersen and Patricia Hill Collins (1998) explain, "Race, class and gender are part of the whole fabric of experience for all groups, not just women and people of color" (p. xiii).

Second, we have attempted to supplement the "social problems" approach implicit in the multiple jeopardy perspective on gender, race, and class by emphasizing strengths as well as deficits. We selected readings that depict older people as active creators of culture rather than as merely passive victims. We emphasized the adaptive resources people develop across a lifetime of disadvantage and the ways in which these adaptive resources help people cope with the challenge of old age. We minimized simple comparisons (e.g., female versus male, Black versus White) in which the dominant group is an implicit standard against which other groups are compared to see how they differ (Stanford & Yee, 1991). Instead, we explored diversity in the experience of aging along any one dimension. We selected readings to introduce students to Black women who are wealthy as well as others who are poor, and to poor women who are White as well as poor women who are American Indian, Black, and Latina American. As the anthropologist Johnetta Cole (1986) explains, gender is experienced differently depending on one's race and social class, and the experience of race and class is mediated through one's gender.

Third, our exploration in *Worlds of Difference* has been guided by a life course perspective. A number of the readings introduce students to the historical conditions different categories of people experienced at particular chronological ages. People who are elderly today lived through the Great Depression of the 1930s, World War II, postwar prosperity and optimism, and the Civil Rights movement. Elderly Blacks grew up in a legally segregated world that not only limited their economic options but also provided a particular worldview and encouraged special adaptive resources. Exploration of the diversity in the social and historical contexts within which today's cohorts of elderly people experienced significant life course events is essential to understanding their experience of old age. We chose to explore these contexts by providing views of social reality through the eyes of young and middle-aged adults in the 1930s, 1940s, and 1950s, those cohorts that make up the older population today.

The book is organized by topic rather than by group or by dimension of inequality. We want to emphasize diversity in older people's encounters with negative images, in their experience of family, and in their productive activities. We want students to understand that the impact of gender, race, and class cannot be understood in additive terms; we are less concerned that students master a catalog of descriptive characteristics of each particular group. The aging experience of an affluent Black woman and a working-class White woman are very different, even though both are disadvantaged on two hierarchies and privileged on a third. To achieve this understanding, we have chosen readings that give voice to people whose perspectives have been overlooked. The readings emphasize what Johnetta Cole describes as commonalities as well as differences, that is, recognition that the social construction of gender, race, and class involves emphasizing differences and suppressing similarities (Hess, 1990). We also highlighted these issues in the discussion questions at the end of each part and in the test bank, which is available to instructors.

Worlds of Difference reflects the work of more than two people. The idea for this anthology emerged from a roundtable, Innovations in Courses on Aging in the Undergraduate Curriculum, organized by Pine Forge publisher Stephen Rutter during the 1991 meetings of the Gerontological Society of America. We are grateful to Steve for providing the catalyst for the book. Ingrun Lafleur merits our special thanks for introducing one of us to the meaning of an inclusive curriculum. Over the last 5 years of her life, she was a mentor, a colleague, and, most important, a friend. For those who knew Ingie, her influence will be obvious throughout the anthology. Many other people contributed to the project. We are indebted to Penny Dugan for her creative lending library of literary anthologies, an essential resource as we began the first edition. The contributions of Lesa Ball, Amy Stoller, Jeff Stoller, and Charmaine Judon to the earlier editions are still evident. We are especially indebted to Lisa Dobransky and Judy Reardon for the creative thinking and careful reading that facilitated the new edition.

We also appreciate the critical input from our readers, including our students. We thank the reviewers for this edition:

Eileen E. MaloneBeach, *Central Michigan University;*
Alton Clark Dubois, *Concordia University;*
Donna Demster-Mclain, *Cornell University;*
Rosalie Gilford, *California State University, Fullerton;*
Debra McGinnis, *California State University, Long Beach;*
Joyce Burris and Susan Kirk, *California State University, Sacramento;*
Charlene Snowden, *CUNY, Medgar Evers College;*
Robin D. Moremen, *Northern Illinois University;*
Ralph Cherry, *Purdue University, Calumet;*
Andrew Scharlach, *University of California, Berkeley;*
JoAnn Damron-Rodriquez, *University of California, Los Angeles;*
Kathy Williams, *University of Central Oklahoma;*
Share Bane, *University of Missouri, Kansas City;*
Kathleen Grove, *University of San Diego;*
Helen Rosenberg, *University of Wisconsin, Parkside;* and
Judith N. Moore, *Western Michigan University.*

Working together over the past eight years on the three editions of *Worlds*, as we call the project, has taught us the joys of collegial friendships—and the frustrations of deadlines and page limits. We learned from each other and emerge from this collaborative venture with an understanding of aging that is greater than the sum of the knowledge we brought to the project. Most of all, we want to thank our husbands, Michael A. Stoller and Ralph M. Gibson, and our children, Jeffrey Mark Stoller, Kirsten Elin Stoller, Ralph M. Gibson, Jr., and John S. Gibson, for giving us the love and understanding and time we needed to finish all three editions of *Worlds of Difference*.

E.P.S.
R.C.G.

Introduction:
Different Worlds in Aging:
Gender, Race, and Class

Gerontologists have long stressed the heterogeneity of the elderly population. People enter old age with an accumulation of experiences gained over six or seven decades, experiences that influence their attitudes, behaviors, and resources. Some of these experiences, such as wars, economic fluctuations, technological developments, and cultural change, are shared with other people in their age cohort. Others emerge from biographical experiences unique to the individual. The strength of a social gerontological approach to the study of late life is that it enables us to understand the ways in which what is occurring within the larger society shapes the life course of individuals. As the sociologist C. Wright Mills (1959) put it, social gerontology allows us to see the link between history and biography.

Even though older people today have lived through the same historical period, the impact of that history on their individual biographies varies with their position in society. Some characteristics of individuals and of their personal histories may appear unique, but there are also discernible patterns in the experiences of different segments of the older population. These patterns reflect social structural arrangements and cultural blueprints within society, both today and during the decades in which people lived and grew old. In this book, we will examine three dimensions of experience that structure both the distribution of society's resources and the meanings and expectations we associate with old age: gender, race or ethnicity, and social class.

We frequently think of gender, race, and social class as attributes of individuals. In classifying people into categories based on gender, race or ethnicity, and social class, people often emphasize biological characteristics. Clearly, there are biological differences between men and women. We often try to classify people into racial or ethnic groups on the basis of skin color or facial features. Some people have even argued that social class placement is biologically based, reflecting genetically determined differences in intelligence.

Without denying that there are differences among individuals that are grounded in biology, our emphasis will be on gender, race or ethnicity, and social class as *social constructs* or classifications based on social values. The sociologist Beth Hess (1990) describes the process through which the biological category of sex is transformed into the social construct of gender:

Layers of meaning have been wrapped around the distinguishing feature of biological sex to produce a palimpsest of gendered reality—socially constructed systems of thought and action that organize perception, identities, and the allocation of scarce resources. Thus, rather than being a property of the individual, maleness and femaleness are products of the operation of social systems on both the variability and similarities provided by nature. . . . Gender is created by suppressing similarities, and it is maintained by a deep ideological commitment to differences between women and men. The basic process is categorization, the establishment of a gender hierarchy in which a superstructure of social, political, and economic differences have been superimposed on the biological. (pp. 83-84)

This distinction between individual differences and social constructs can be confusing. The sociologist Toni Calasanti (1996) reminds us of the distinction between heterogeneity and diversity. Heterogeneity refers to individual-level variation—differences among elderly people that reflect the complex interaction of genetic inheritance, sociohistorical experience, and unique biographies. Let's consider individual-level biological differences. Some biological differences are important in specific contexts. We classify people according to blood type, but although receiving the wrong type of blood in a transfusion could have serious repercussions, blood type usually has little impact on our lived experience. An opthamologist told one of us that we were lucky not to have been born into a hunting and gathering society, because our poor eyesight would have almost certainly meant early death. But the same opthamologist easily prescribed contact lenses to correct this deficiency. Differences in skin color are biologically based, but so are differences in height and body shape, in the size and shape of teeth, bones, hearts, lungs, and other organs; and in the number of active sweat glands and the pattern and amount of sweat we produce (Cohen, 1998).

In contrast to individual heterogeneity, diversity refers to the interlocking structural positions of groups within a society. As Calasanti (1996) explains, "being sensitive to diversity involves an awareness of lived experience as embedded in power relations: relations that are constituted by both oppressed and privileged groups" (p. 155). Within the context of diversity, race is a social and political category, not a biological category. Within the United States, we use skin color as a defining characteristic of race, despite the fact that the world's population cannot be divided into categories of "white" and "black." Skin color tends to get lighter as one moves north from central Africa to northern Europe or from southern India into central Asia, a pattern not always evident in the United States. As the anthropologist Mark Cohen (1998) explains:

The pattern of graded colors is not so evident to Americans because of a historical accident. After 1492, America was colonized by people from the lightest and darkest ends of the spectrum, so we tend to think in terms of distinct colors. But our vision of separate colors is inaccurate and gives us a false sense of the separateness of human groups. (p. 47)

That categorizing people according to their race, gender, or social class is indeed a social process is evident in the way we apply race or ethnic labels. A child whose mother is Black and whose father is White has been considered Black, whereas a child whose mother is White and whose father is Japanese American has been considered Asian (Cyrus, 1993). Jews have traditionally traced group membership through the mother. A person was considered Jewish if his or her mother was Jewish, regardless of the background of the father. Official tribal enrollment requirements for American Indians vary among tribes, ranging from one-half to one-sixteenth Indian ancestry (Nagel, 1997).

Categorizing people as White also reflects a social construction. The category *White* encompasses people from a range of geographic origins and cultural traditions—people who did not originally think of themselves as White. People who emigrated to the United States from Italy, Poland, or Sweden did not consider themselves White in their countries of origin. Indeed, many identified with a particular region rather than the nation. Immigrants learned to think of themselves as White within a particular geographic and historical context, as they differentiated themselves from Blacks, American Indians, or other so-called non-White groups in their new geographic location (Conzen, Gerber, Morawska, Pozzetta, & Vecoli, 1992). Even today, the social construction of White encompasses a heterogeneous collection of Americans from a range of ancestral origins, some of whom identify strongly with their ethnic heritage and others who know only vaguely of their ancestral heritage (Alba, 1990).

Although labels such as *race* are social constructions, they have real consequences in people's lives. These labels influence more than the way people are counted in social surveys. They also structure the opportunities and constraints people encounter as they move through their life course. They shape our self-concepts and the ways other people respond to us. There is no biological reason for classifying a child according to the racial status of the minority parent rather than the white parent or in determining what percentage of lineage is required for identification with a particular group. These distinctions reflect the social process Hess (1990) described: a process of categorization that superimposes social hierarchies on biological differences. As Mark Cohen (1998, p. 12) argues,

Classifying people by color is very much like classifying cars by color. Those in the same classification look alike, superficially (if you ignore the detailed differences), but the classification tells you nothing about the hidden details of construction or about how the cars or the people will perform.

Our exploration of gender, race, and class as social constructs will emphasize these variables both as labels attached to individuals and properties of hierarchical social structures within which people form identities and through which they realize their life chances (Hess, 1990). We will also investigate the ways in which people's positions along these multiple hierarchies generate diverse views of social reality. This involves listening to descriptions of aging and old age from multiple perspectives, of giving voice to people whose perspectives have been overlooked. Integrating this chorus of voices will enrich our understanding of aging by highlighting common motifs as well as the tonal and rhythmic complexity that characterizes the experience of aging in the contemporary United States.

Our journey through the "worlds of difference" shaped by these social constructs will be guided by several themes. We begin by emphasizing that hierarchies based on gender, race, and class create systems of privilege as well as of disadvantage. When we think about these hierarchies, it is often easier to recognize elements of discrimination. Gerontologists have documented multiple ways in which discrimination throughout the life course translates into an accumulation of disadvantage in old age. We know, for example, that legally segregated school systems and legally sanctioned discriminatory hiring practices limited opportunities of today's elderly Blacks to accumulate financial assets during their younger years. Research has demonstrated how a lifetime of poverty translates into poor health in later life. Other studies have shown how the rules regulating pension benefits increase the financial risks associated with widowhood for older women. The concept of *multiple jeopardy* reminds us that occupying several disadvantaged positions simultaneously compounds our risk of negative outcomes in old age. For example, both Blacks and women face higher risks of being poor in old age than do white men, but the probability of poverty is even higher for elderly Black women. The notion of multiple jeopardy should not imply that either privilege or disadvantage can be considered in additive terms. Being disadvantaged on hierarchies based on race and gender does not "equal" being disadvantaged on gender and social class, for example. Neither is privilege on one dimension canceled or negated by disadvantage on another (Markides, Liang, & Jackson, 1990). As Toni Calisanti (1996) explains, people experience their race-ethnicity, gender, social class, and sexual orientation simultaneously: "I do not experience my gender first, with my race 'added' to this" (p. 149).

An emphasis on disadvantage sometimes masks the ways in which these same hierarchies create systems of privilege. By focusing on discrimination experienced by people at the lower end of these hierarchies, we sometimes overlook the ways in which being White, being male, and being middle or upper class provides unearned advantages. Being able to ignore issues surrounding race is one aspect of privilege, an advantage denied people of color who are constantly reminded of their disadvantaged status. The political scientist Andrew Hacker (1992) reminds us that "what every Black American knows, and whites should try to imagine, is how it feels to have an unfavorable—and unfair—identity imposed on you every waking day" (p. 21). Because White Americans spend most of their time in environments in which being White is taken for granted, they need pay little attention to race. Advantages associated with one's race, class, or gender are taken for granted by members of the dominant group. Hacker suggests a parable to elucidate the often overlooked advantages to being White. He asks his White students to imagine that tonight,

> You will be visited by an official you have never met. He begins by telling you that he is extremely embarrassed. The organization he represents has made a mistake, something that hardly ever happens.
> According to their records, he goes on, you were to have been born black: to another set of parents, far from where you were raised. However, the rules being what they are, this error must be rectified, and as soon as possible. So at midnight tonight, you will become black. And this will mean not simply a darker skin, but the bodily and facial features associated with African ancestry. However, inside you will be the person you always were. Your knowledge and ideas will remain intact. But outwardly you will not be recognizable to anyone you now know.
> Your visitor emphasizes that being born to the wrong parents was in no way your fault. Consequently, his organization is prepared to offer you some reasonable recompense. Would you, he asks, care to name a sum of money you might consider appropriate? He adds that his group is by no means poor. It can be quite generous when the circumstances warrant, as they seem to in your case. He finishes by saying that their records show you are scheduled to live another fifty years—as a black man or woman in America. (pp. 31-32)

How much financial recompense would you request?

Most of Hacker's students report that "it would not be out of place to ask for $50 million, or $1 million for each coming Black year" (p. 32), a calculation he interprets as clear evidence of the value that White people place on their race.

Peggy McIntosh (1998) draws another analogy in illustrating the privilege dimension of systems of inequality. She explains,

> As a white person, I realized that I had been taught about racism as something that puts others at a disadvantage, but had been taught not to see one of its corollary aspects, white privilege, which puts me at an advantage. (p. 4)

She equates White privilege with an "invisible package of unearned assets" and provides a number of illustrations of the ways in which her everyday life is made easier because of her race. For example,

> I can, if I wish, arrange to be in the company of people of my race most of the time. I can avoid spending time with people whom I was trained to mistrust and who have learned to mistrust my kind or me. . . . I can go shopping alone most of the time, fairly well assured that I will not be followed or harassed by store detectives. . . . Whether I use checks, credit cards, or cash, I can count on my skin color not to work against the appearance that I am financially reliable. I did not have to educate my children to be aware of systematic racism for their own daily physical protection. . . . I can do well in a challenging situation without being called a credit to my race. (pp. 8-82)

These advantages or assets are unearned, because access to them is determined by an ascribed rather than an achieved status—by the application of a label that operates as a social construct. They are rendered invisible by the ideology of a meritocracy and a classless society, which teaches us that the United States is a land of equal opportunity where ambition, intelligence, and hard work are responsible for success. This is a comfortable explanation for people who are successful, because it tells them they deserve the advantages they enjoy. Affluent retired people pursuing a life of leisure in the Sunbelt can tell themselves that they earned their piece of "the American Dream," a lifestyle available to anyone with talent, intelligence, and the willingness to work hard. At the same time, this explanation holds less affluent elders responsible for their lack of success. If only they had worked harder or been more clever or intelligent, they would have reaped more rewards. In explaining poverty in old age, it is an example of an explanation that blames the victim.

Sorting out privilege and disadvantage is sometimes complicated, because people can experience disadvantage along one dimension but privilege along others. To assume that all men are privileged over all women or that all Whites are advantaged relative to all people of color is to ignore intersections among multiple hierarchies. A woman who is married to a wealthy industrialist can express dissatisfaction with the expectation that she accommodate her life to the demands of her husband's career, with her unequal voice in family decisions, and with her sole responsibility for managing home and family (Ostrander, 1984), but it is difficult to argue that she is disadvantaged relative to an Black man struggling to escape poverty as a sharecropper in the rural South or a Mexican American agricultural laborer as he follows the seasonal demand for migrant workers. As we explore the impact of gender, race, and class on the experiences of older Americans today, we will look for evidence of these intersections. We will learn that race, gender, and class represent interlocking systems of experience that affect all aspects of human life, not simply separate features of experience that can be understood in additive terms (Andersen & Collins, 1998). Gender is experienced differently depending on one's race and social class (Cole, 1986). Analogously, the constraints or privileges of race and class are mediated through one's gender. Lifetimes of experiences at various points along these hierarchies contribute to diversity in old age, diversity not only in the quantity of resources people have accumulated but also in their relationships, the meanings attached to aging, and their definitions of social reality.

As we explore these worlds of difference, we will emphasize strengths as well as deficits. The "multiple jeopardy" approach to studying inequality in old age has emphasized the negative outcomes of occupying disadvantaged positions along several of these hierarchies. Social gerontologists working from this perspective have documented the accumulation of deficits across the life course that produce poverty, poor health, and inadequate living conditions in old age. Although it is important to recognize the problems faced by older people coping with the effects of disadvantaged status, it is equally important to learn how these elderly Americans create meaning in their lives despite barriers based on gender, race, and class. Sociologists recognize both of these dimensions of inequality when they debate the relative impact of social structure and human agency. Through the readings, we will meet older people who are active creators of culture and not merely passive victims reacting to systems of oppression. We will learn to view social reality from multiple perspectives and discover that particular institutional arrangements can provide protection against oppression in some segments of society while simultaneously reinforcing oppression in others.

To illustrate this seeming contradiction, we will consider the role of religion in the life of elderly Black women. In many respects, religion as an institution appears to reinforce these women's subordinate position in society. Religious doctrines defining women's proper place emphasize their role as mothers and justify their subordination to men. Although Black churches are estimated to be 75% female, and women perform the majority of the work in local congregations (Gilkes, 1985), women are selected for leadership positions less often than men. The African Methodist Episcopal Church, which began ordaining women in 1948, was the first denomination in the United States to accept women into the clergy, but interviews with male clergy reveal continuing prejudice against women in the ministry (Grant, 1982). Some critics have argued that although religion can serve as a coping mechanism for adversity, dependence on prayer can serve as a substitute for direct action (Taylor, 1982). The dominance of European imagery and an emphasis on rewards in the afterlife also have been criticized for reinforcing racism and fostering passive acceptance of inequality in this life.

A more complex view of religion in the life of elderly Black women is provided by the anthropologist Johnetta Cole (1986). Cole describes the Southern A.M.E. congregation in which she grew up and its role in the life of Sister Minnie:

> In this black church where we sang "Jesus will wash me whiter than snow" in Sunday school, the superintendent was my great-grandfather but most of the teachers were women. We looked up at stained glass windows depicting a blond, blue-eyed image of Jesus and showing Mary as a white woman. However, as the choir my mother directed sang "Amazing Grace," Sister Minnie would begin to twitch as the spirits moved her, and she began to speak in tongues and shout and dance in expressions of "getting happy." Her religion, its imagery as Eurocentric and male as it was, also involved the retention of elements of an African religion. And importantly, it was obviously a source of tremendous relief and satisfaction to a woman who somehow had to support herself and several children on the less-than-minimum wages she received as a domestic for a Southern white lady, living in a city where even the water fountains were marked "white" and "colored."
>
> Sister Minnie was never in the pulpit, nor did anyone who shared her gender ever hold forth as a preacher. Yet she and other women were always frying chicken and preparing the potato salad that were essentials for many church suppers. Without defending this division of labor, it is necessary to note that on those Sundays when Sister Minnie's usher board served and she brought men and women to their seats, or even more so, when, with one arm folded behind her back, she brought some of the collection plates to the minister, one saw a woman who in Mt. Olive A.M.E. church was able to play a public role of dignity and consequence denied her in much of the racist, sexist, and elitist southern United States. (pp. 309-310)

For Sister Minnie, the church was a source of recognition and self-esteem. But this is only one way in which churches have provided support in Black communities. The Black church also provided both emotional and material support at a time when these were not available to Blacks through public services (Taylor & Chatters, 1986; Walls & Zarit, 1991). L. Steinitz (1981) concluded that churches served as surrogate families, offering both concrete help and psychological assurance, especially to older people without family nearby. In addition to religious activities and social support, Black churches have had a major role in political mobilization (Walls & Zarit, 1991), providing a strong foundation for the Civil Rights movement that emerged during the 1950s and 1960s.

We will see similar contradictions in our examination of family and of productive activity, including paid employment and unpaid assistance to family and friends. Listening to Sister Minnie and to the voices of other people introduced in the readings will help us begin to answer a question Ralph Ellison (1952) posed almost five decades ago:

> Can a people . . . live and develop for over three hundred years simply by reacting? Are American Negroes simply the creation of white men, or have they at least helped to create themselves out of what they found around them? (pp. 316-317)

Recognizing the adaptive strategies of elders of color, however, should not blind us to the societal arrangements that demanded these strategies. For example, sharing resources across networks of extended kin and fictive kin enhances survival among poor women, but this strategy does not eliminate the economic barriers that maintain economic inequality. The increasing number of elderly people who are assuming the role of surrogate or custodial parents for their grandchildren cannot reduce the prevalence of unemployment, substance abuse, or incarceration in the middle generation. And the ability of families of color to teach children to survive prejudice and discrimination while maintaining their self-esteem does not alter the strains of everyday racism. Nikki Giovanni's (1979) poem, *Nikki Rosa*, illustrates this dynamic process through which families can alleviate the starkest impact of poverty and racism:

> childhood remembrances are always a drag
> if you're Black
> you always remember things like living in Woodlawn
> with no inside toilet
> and if you become famous or something
> they never talk about how happy you were to have
> your mother
> all to yourself and
> how good the water felt when you got your bath
> from one of those
> big tubs that folks in chicago barbecue in
> and somehow when you talk about home
> it never gets across how much you
> understood their feelings
> as the whole family attended meetings about Hollydale
> and even though you remember
> your biographers never understand
> your father's pain as he sells his stock
> and another dream goes
> and though you're poor it isn't poverty that
> concerns you

and though they fought a lot
it isn't your father's drinking that makes any difference
but only that everybody is together and you
and your sister have happy birthdays and very good
Christmasses
and I really hope no white person ever has cause
to write about me
because they never understand
Black love is Black wealth and they'll
probably talk about my hard childhood
and never understand that
all the while I was quite happy.

The sociologists Kathleen Slevin and Ray Wingrove (1998) reported similar experiences in the life stories of the 50 elderly Black professional women whom they interviewed. Their parents taught them the lessons they would need to overcome obstacles, or as one woman put it, to "turn stumbling blocks into stepping stones." At the same time, they had to learn that, "no matter how much education they achieved, their opportunities would still be limited by their race" (p. 12). The themes of survival and resistance that permeate these women's lives highlight the cumulative challenges of racism even among those women who were advantaged by social class. Their stories remind us that in periods of fiscal restraint and political conservatism, gerontologists must work to ensure that these celebrations of strengths are not redefined as rationales for not providing much-needed public services.

In addition to issues of social inequality, we also will explore variations in cultural meanings and the dynamics of aging both among and within different population categories. Often, this requires moving beyond research, which tends to reflect the experiences of the dominant group. Recognizing this limitation in the gerontological literature does not mean that researchers are purposely distorting information or are insensitive to concerns of older women or older people of color. Biases and oversights reflect the fact that knowledge is socially constructed. Gerontologists, like other scientists, approach their research from a specific social location that shapes what they know about the world (Andersen, 1993). The past experiences and current attitudes that researchers bring to their subject shape the questions they ask, what they observe, and how they interpret their observations.

Listening to diverse voices enriches our perspective by giving us new lenses through which to view the multiple social worlds that can exist within a particular setting. Trying on different lenses can bring into focus dimensions of social reality that were overlooked from the perspective of the dominant group. Feminist research on family care of the elderly provides an example of this process. When one of us was in school, she was taught that many traditional functions of the family had been shifted to specialized, bureaucratic institutions. One example used to illustrate this shift was the growth of nursing homes. As she heard about the decline in family care of the elderly and the plight of older people isolated in nursing homes, she watched her own mother struggling to meet the expanding physical and emotional needs of her increasingly frail elderly grandmother. The contradiction between the stereotype of abandonment of older people and the strains experienced by family caregivers is more evident to women than to men. Adult daughters are more likely than adult sons to be providing care to older relatives. Furthermore, they tend to absorb the costs of that care themselves, struggling to meet the demands of their other roles both within and beyond the family. Jane Lewis and B. Meredith (1986) report caregiving daughters' struggle to "keep life as 'normal' as possible for their own family, . . . [which] entailed assuming the whole burden of care themselves and keeping it as unobtrusive as possible" (chap. 6, p. 10). We should not be surprised that male researchers were slower than women to design research projects exploring the burdens and rewards of family care of frail elders. This aspect of the aging experience was less likely to be visible to men than to women. Dorothy Smith (1987) notes that all research is done from a particular standpoint or location in the social system and is shaped by the perspective of the researcher. Throughout this reader, we will introduce examples of the ability of diverse perspectives to yield new insights. We will see, for example, how abandoning definitions of kin based on White families makes visible the richness and complexity of kin and kinlike relationships within Black communities. We will discover how expanding the standard definitions of productivity that are based on the paid employment experience of White men reveals the extensive amount of unpaid productive work performed by people throughout their lives. We will uncover the biases in retirement research that emphasizes pension income, and we will explore a variety of strategies people use in reinterpreting negative stereotypes based on age, gender, race, and class.

A final theme shaping our journey through different worlds of aging is an emphasis on the life course. A life course perspective, which we will explore in detail in the next chapter, highlights the ways in which people's location in the social system, the historical period in which they live, and their unique personal biographies shape the experience of old age. This perspective allows us to explore how occupying different positions along dimensions of gender, race, and class over one's lifetime can lead to different aging experiences. It also reminds us of the importance of the historical period in which people live. People who are the same age experienced particular segments of history at the same stage of life. They experienced life transitions within similar sociohistorical contexts. The intersection of historical trends with hierarchies based on gender, race, and class produce variation both among older people from different population categories and among people of different ages within particular categories. To illustrate this process, consider the historical context experienced by a particular subset of elderly Americans: Blacks who will be 80 years of age in the year 2000 and were born in 1920. Most of these people completed their education in racially segregated schools, many similar to the one Maya Angelou (1969) describes in her autobiographical novel, *I Know Why the Caged Bird Sings*:

> Unlike the white high school, Lafayette County Training School distinguished itself by having neither lawn, nor hedges, nor tennis court, nor climbing ivy. Its two buildings (main classrooms, the grade school and home economics) were set on a dirt hill with no fence to limit its boundaries or those of bordering farms. . . . Rusty hoops on the swaying poles represented the permanent recreational equipment. . . . Only a small percentage [of the graduates] would be continuing on to college—one of the South's A & M (agricultural and mechanical) schools, which trained negro youths to be carpenters, farmers, handymen, masons, maids, cooks, and baby nurses. (p. 163)

In 1954, the U.S. Supreme Court, in *Brown v. Board of Education of Topeka*, declared separate but unequal treatment unconstitutional, overturning segregation laws officially sanctioned since the *Plessy v. Ferguson* ruling in 1896. But these Black elders were 34 years old in 1954, and they had long completed their formal education. Despite the limited opportunities constraining their own youth, many foresaw possibilities of change for their children. Barbara Smith (1983) describes this vision in the introduction to her anthology, *Home Girls*:

> The women in my family, and their friends, worked harder than any people I have known before or since, and despite their objective circumstances, they believed . . . that Beverly and I could have a future beyond theirs, although there was little enough indication in the 40s and 50s that Negro girls would ever have a place to stand. (p. xxi)

Blacks born in 1920 witnessed the Civil Rights movement of the 1950s and 1960s—some were among its leaders—but they witnessed these events as adults in their 30s and 40s. Their childhoods were lived within a racially segregated world, in which they struggled to maintain self-respect while avoiding direct challenges to the rules for "living Jim Crow":

> There were many times when I had to exercise a great deal of ingenuity to keep out of trouble. It is a southern custom that all men must take off their hats when they enter an elevator. And especially did this apply to blacks. One day I stepped into an elevator with my arms full of packages. I was forced to ride with my hat on. Two white men stared at me coldly. Then one of them

very kindly lifted my hat and placed it upon my armful of packages. Now the most accepted response for a Negro to make under such circumstances is to look at the white man out of the corner of his eye and grin. To have said: "Thank you!" would have made the white man think that you thought you were receiving from him a personal service. For such an act I have seen Negroes take a blow in the mouth. Finding the first alternative distasteful, and the second dangerous, I hit upon an acceptable course of action which fell safely between these two poles. I immediately—no sooner than my hat was lifted— pretended that my packages were about to spill, and appeared deeply distressed with keeping them in my arms. In this fashion, I evaded having to acknowledge his service, and, in spite of adverse circumstances, salvaged a slender shred of personal pride. (Wright, 1937/1991, p. 50)

These elderly Americans lived to watch their children become what Henry Louis Gates, Jr. (1994) called "pioneers in cross-race relations" (p.150), yet many found adjusting to integration difficult, particularly those who had gone only to a segregated elementary school. Indeed, Gates argues that for many of the elderly residents of the small West Virginia town in which he grew up, "integration was experienced as a loss. The warmth and nurturance of the womb-like colored world was slowly and inevitably disappearing" (p. 184).

Whereas this composite presents one view of the intersection of history and biography in this cohort of elderly Blacks, the simplified portrait ignores intracohort variation. Indeed, a life course perspective reminds us to expect diversity among today's older population. Although all people celebrating their eightieth birthday at the turn of the century lived through the same segment of history, their experience of this history—the meanings they attach to particular events and the impact of these events on their lives—varies depending on their social location. We have introduced you to some variations in the experience of the past seven decades from the standpoint of an 80-year-old Black. Consider the contrasting life experiences of other people who were also born in 1920: a White woman born on a small farm in rural Mississippi; a Jewish man who escaped the horrors of Nazi Germany as a teenager; the now elderly daughter of a wealthy family from the Mainline in Philadelphia; or the aging son of Polish immigrants who prides himself on his own son's graduation from medical school.

At the same time, a life course perspective sensitizes us to diversity among people of different ages within the same population category. Middle-aged people today who grew up in the middle-class suburbs of the 1950s can be expected to have different attitudes toward saving and spending money than their parents, whose childhoods coincided with the Great Depression of the 1930s. Young-old people whose first experiences with government assistance programs were social security and economic recovery programs of the

1930s may be less reluctant to use public services than will old-old people who associate public assistance with the stigma of welfare. We encourage our readers to exercise their gerontological imaginations as they hypothesize about the effects of (a) increasing rates of women's labor force participation on future retirement decisions, (b) greater knowledge and emphasis on preventive health care on future patterns of morbidity and mortality, and (c) the widening gap between the rich and poor on future income and service needs among older people. The most difficult hurdle we encounter in developing these hypotheses is the interaction among physical changes associated with aging, the historical context in which people have lived, and the social context within which they find themselves in late life. The challenge of a life course perspective is recognizing continuity in the experience of aging within a context of population diversity and social change.

We have emphasized the importance of diversity in enriching our understanding of aging and old age. Others have advocated inclusion of women and minorities on the grounds of fairness and equal treatment. But there is a yet more urgent reason for incorporating a more inclusive approach to our study of aging. Projected increases in diversity within the elderly population over the next decades demand that people working in geriatric and gerontological positions be knowledgeable about the experiences of people of different genders, races or ethnic groups, and social classes. As the anthropologist Yolanda Moses (1992), who is currently president of City College of New York, explains, designing an inclusive curriculum is not just a matter of fairness or affirmative action. It is a central component of educating people to live and work in the 21st century.

The time frame available for achieving this goal is shrinking as population changes demand social policies reflecting concerns of an increasingly diverse older population. In 1995, 89.8% of the population was White, 8.0% were Black, 4.0% were Hispanic, 1.5% were Asian Americans/Pacific Islanders, and 0.4% were American Indians (U.S. Bureau of the Census, 1995). (These percentages do not sum to 100%, because the U.S. Census does not treat Hispanic origin as a racial category. People who identify themselves as Hispanic Americans also identify themselves in terms of one of the racial categories. For example, a person from Chile who identified herself as Hispanic origin and White would be counted twice in these percentages.) By 2025, 15% of the elderly population are projected to be minority, increasing to 20% by the year 2050. By the year 2050, the number of elderly Whites will double, but the number of elderly Blacks will triple, and the number of elderly Asian Americans and Pacific Islanders and the number of elderly Hispanic Americans will increase more than five times (Morgan & Kunkel, 1998).

Increasing diversity in attitudes, behavior, and resources among older people will require reconsideration of policies and programs designed originally for a homogeneous population composed of White, English-speaking elderly people (Wray, 1991). Disadvantaged ethnic minority elderly, like their younger counterparts, are disproportionately represented among people with income below the federal poverty level. Older women, particularly minority women, are more vulnerable to poverty than are older men. Older members of minority groups have a lower life expectancy and poorer health than members of the dominant group, and meager financial resources limit their access to health care (Torres-Gil & Hyde, 1990).

Achieving these policy goals requires sensitivity to the diversity in resources and preferences among older people. Although the concept of color-blind or gender-neutral policies sounds fair and equitable, it is important to remember the sociological maxim that "equal rules applied to unequal situations produce unequal outcomes." Even ostensibly neutral social policies can produce outcomes that are structured by older people's gender, race, and class (Hooyman & Gonyea, 1995).

The readings that follow will explore the themes introduced here. We begin in Part I with an examination of the life course perspective. A life course perspective emphasizes the ways in which people's social location, the historical period in which they live, and their personal biography shape their experience of the aging process. We shall see how particular time periods relegated people to circumscribed roles that limited their life chances, increased the likelihood of experiencing negative life events, and weakened their adaptive resources. The readings also illustrate the ways in which the impact of various events experienced prior to old age are filtered through people's position on the interlocking hierarchies.

In Part II, we explore cultural images of old age and the ways older people respond to them. We will see how these images vary along dimensions of gender, race, and class and explore strategies used by older people for maintaining personal integrity within a context of negative stereotypes.

Part III introduces the world of productivity. Economists have traditionally defined productive activities as those behaviors that add to the stock and flow of valued goods and services. Because productivity has been measured by counting exchanges of money, choices regarding productivity in old age have traditionally been framed as a dichotomy of work versus leisure. Here we will consider unpaid as well as paid activity and consider ways in which productive activity across the life course influences resources in old age. Part IV considers the diversity in family structure and kin relations among older people. We will return to the theme of family care of frail elders. But we will also look beyond ideologies describing "the American Family" to consider the diversity of family experiences today's cohorts of older people have encountered across their lives. Last, in Part V, we will examine gender, race, and social class differences in disease, disability, and mortality in old age. Here, we explore differences in exposure to biomedical, social, and psychological risk factors and in having access to medical care in shaping the health status of older people.

PART I

The Life Course Perspective

Aging in Individual, Sociocultural, and Historical Contexts

Advantages of Using the Life Course Framework in Studying Aging

Here we introduce the life course perspective as a framework for an inclusive approach to the study of aging. As we indicated in the Introduction, a life course perspective emphasizes the ways in which people's location in the social system, the historical period in which they live, and their unique personal biography shape their experience of old age. Our approach to the life course perspective has four main premises, which we will explain and illustrate:

1. The aging process is affected by individuals' personal attributes, their particular life events, and how they adapt to these events.

2. Sociohistorical times shape opportunity structures differently for individuals with specific personal characteristics, such as being in a subordinate position on a social hierarchy. Thus, people's life events, adaptive resources, and aging experiences differ.

3. Membership in a specific birth cohort (i.e., being born in a particular time period) shapes the aging experience. Within cohorts, however, the experience of aging differs depending on one's position in systems of inequality based on gender, race or ethnicity, and class.

4. Sociohistorical periods shape the aging experiences of cohorts. These historical times, however, have different impacts on the experiences of disadvantaged and privileged members of the same cohort.

What Is the Life Course Perspective?

The life course perspective directs our attention to the powerful connection between individual lives and the historical context in which these lives unfold (O'Rand, 1998). Moving away from developmental models of aging that posit universal stages, a life course perspective demonstrates that the combination and sequence of events that comprise our biographies are culturally and historically contingent (Colby, 1998). The historical period in which we grow up and our positions on intersecting systems of inequality shape both the life events we experience and the adaptive resources with which we cope with life's challenges and craft our futures.

Gerontologists explain this intersection between biography and history in several ways. The sociologist Matilda White Riley (1998), a principal architect of the life course perspective, distinguished among age, cohort, and period effects in explaining how the shape of the life course varied depending on year of birth. *Age* refers to chronological age, a marker of biological and developmental time. *Cohort* is defined as an aggregate of persons born at the same time (e.g., 1900-1909) or during the same historical period (e.g., The Great Depression of the 1930s). The concept of cohort captures the socially shared experiences of age peers. *Period* refers to location in time, the distinctive historical and cultural events experienced by persons at a particular point in history. Gerontologists define a *period effect* as the impact of an event on the people who experience it. History creates a period effect when change is relatively uniform across successive birth cohorts (Quadagno, 1999). For example, the oil shortages in the 1970s generated interest in more energy-efficient homes and more fuel-efficient automobiles. In contrast, a *cohort effect* refers to the differential impact of a particular event or experience on members of different cohorts. For example, the second wave of feminism that expanded opportunities for middle-class women in the 1970s and 1980s had a greater effect on women of the baby boom cohort (1946 to 1964) than it did on women of the Depression cohort (born 1930-1939), who had already made decisions regarding work and family earlier in their lives.

As we shall see later, a central tenet of the life course perspective is that the impact of an historical event on our lives is dependent, in part, on how old we are when we experience that event. Riley (1998) suggested an escalator metaphor for understanding the interplay between lives and times. As people age, she explained, they move diagonally upward in age and across time. Each cohort enters society at a specific point in time, and each cohort lives through a unique slice of history. A visual representation of multiple cohorts would consist of a series of roughly parallel escalators, each beginning at a different time (birth) period. However, the picture is somewhat more complicated, because society changes over time. As Riley (1998) explains "Unlike the static floor over which the escalator is moving, the social structures surrounding people's lives—at work, in the home, in the community, and in the society—are themselves continually changing" (p. 39). This metaphor of the escalator, moving successive cohorts of people diagonally across time and age and over a moving floor, captures Riley's Cohort Principle: Because society changes, members of different cohorts grow older in different ways.

A life course perspective reminds us that membership in a specific birth cohort shapes the aging experience. As the sociologist Ann Foner (1986) explains, "Each cohort brings to old age its own unique history, and this past influences the nature of the later years of cohort members" (p. 134). The impact of a particular event varies depending on the age when we experience it. For example, many families lost their land during the farm crisis of the 1980s. Some retired farmers saw their adult children forced to sell land that their parents and grandparents had farmed. But selling the family farm held different meanings for the adult children who had made financial decisions that they perceived as leading to foreclosure than for their elderly parents (Meyer, 1988). The sociologist Glenn Elder (1974) has studied the effect of the Great Depression of the 1930s on different cohorts. His studies of children growing up during the Great Depression of the 1930s demonstrated that younger children were more adversely affected by the Depression than older children. Another study traced the impact of World War II. In a follow-up of the Stanford-Terman Study of Gifted Children, Elder and colleagues (Elder, Shanahan, & Clipp, 1994, 1997) documented the differential impact of World War II on two cohorts of men, all of whom came from privileged backgrounds. Men whose early careers were interrupted by the war attained no more occupational achievement than younger men who launched their careers in the period of economic prosperity following the war, despite the fact that the younger men had lower levels of education. Men who were older when they were mobilized for wartime responsibilities were more likely to suffer family and work disruptions immediately after the war and were more likely to suffer long-term declines in their health. As these studies suggest, events that occur early in life reverberate across the entire life course: "It's not just living through a major historical event that matters but the age at which one experiences that event" (Quadagno, 1999, p. 179).

How Does the Life Course Perspective Help Us Understand Inequality?

The Impact of Historical Time on Subcohorts. In understanding inequality, we need to consider differences within cohorts as well as differences among people born in different historical periods—to disaggregate cohorts into subcohorts characterized by attributes like race or gender (Uhlenberg & Miner, 1996). Subcohort differences are related to differences in life events and differences in the adaptive resources that people develop for coping with life's challenges. For example, before the Civil Rights movement, many opportunities were closed to Blacks. These blocked opportunities produced certain negative events—the effects of racial discrimination. Special adaptive resources were called into play to deal with discrimination, and these resources have affected the aging experience among cohorts of Blacks who are elderly today. Annette Jones White (1991) describes these resources as "living constantly on tiptoe and in a react mode" (p. 190). Harriet McAdoo (1986) characterizes this climate of racism as a

mundane extreme environment: . . . The "extreme" difficulties which White society imposes on Black people by denying their identity, their values, and their economic opportunities are not unusual or extraordinary but "mundane," daily pressures for Blacks. The concept of a mundane extreme environment suggests vividly how racism is a pervasive, daily reality for Black families. (p. 189)

White described learning these adaptive strategies from her mother:

> She taught me how to turn away wrath with a soft answer but
> without letting anybody make me think I was inferior to them. She
> also tried to keep me informed of the dangers I might face so that I
> could avoid situations that would put me in danger. She tried to
> keep me out of situations that could lead to humiliation and
> "incidents." For example, on one of the few times she took me
> downtown, she avoided a confrontation. It was generally known
> that Blacks were supposed to step off the sidewalk if they were
> meeting a group of Whites. To not do so invited several things—a
> tongue lashing, a vicious elbow to the chest or side, or, possibly,
> arrest. As we walked, we approached a group of Whites. My
> mother quickly walked to a store window and we window
> shopped until the Whites passed by. I knew why and she knew I
> knew why, but we never discussed it. That was her way of
> avoiding an incident. (pp. 190-191)

The quote from Richard Wright (1991) in the Introduction provides
another of what Wright described as "lessons in how to live as a
Negro." In neither of these illustrations were the narrators passive
victims of discrimination. They developed adaptive strategies that
enabled them to survive in a social context characterized by racism
but at the same time to maintain their personal integrity. Although
the Civil Rights movement initiated significant improvements in the
lives of cohorts of Blacks moving into old age in the coming
decades, discrimination has not disappeared, even among people
who are privileged by social class. The sociologist Joe Feagin (1991)
has documented continued discrimination against Black Americans
in public settings. One of Feagin's respondents spoke of putting on
"her shield" before leaving home each morning to prepare for
potential discrimination. As another respondent, a retired
psychology professor, explained:

> I don't think White people, generally, understand the full meaning
> of racist discriminatory behaviors directed toward Americans of
> African descent. . . . They forget that in most cases, we live lives of
> quiet desperation generated by a litany of daily large and small
> events that whether or not by design, remind us of our "place" in
> American society. (p. 115)

Feagin's respondents described a litany of discriminatory encounters,
including inordinate waits for service, being seated near the kitchen
in restaurants, being followed by store detectives while shopping,
and watching other pedestrians cross the street as they approach.
Another example of adaptive resources comes from a study of
coping strategies and adaptations to aging among 60 Black women
leaders, aged 60 to 94 at the time of the study. The researchers Hill,

Colby, and Phelps (1983) analyzed oral history transcripts collected for the Black Women's Oral History Project conducted by the Schlesinger Library of Radcliffe College. A major finding of their study was that one specific type of response was significantly related to adaptation to aging—direct instrumental coping. The authors speculated that the use of direct instrumentality when managing life problems, including those relating to racial discrimination, required great personal strength and courage, resources that these women were able to apply in adapting to old age. The following passage from their study provides yet another illustration of an instrumental coping response to the stress of racial discrimination:

> And I have been refused . . . well the first time I ever went to Orlando, my cousin went with me to the airport and the plane was late and we went into the dining room to get a cup of coffee and they made us leave. And when I said I had just come back from a trip around the world for the State Department and I refused to move, they sent a policeman to get me. Yeah, I've had plenty of things happen to me because I was black as a handicap. But I made a speech before they got me out of there. (p. 16)

Patricia Hill Collins (1991) describes the dilemma Black women encountered in teaching their daughters to live within a system of racial discrimination, of maintaining a

> delicate balance between conformity and resistance: . . . To ensure their daughters' physical survival, they must teach their daughters to fit into systems of oppression. . . . And yet mothers know that if daughters fit too well into the limited opportunities offered Black women, they become willing participants in their own subordination. . . . The issue is to build emotional strength, but not at the cost of physical survival. (pp. 53-54)

The adaptive resources of these Black mothers are illustrated in the selection by Alice Walker, "In Search of Our Mothers' Gardens."

As these examples suggest, cohorts are not homogeneous collections of people, despite similarity in age. Cohorts exhibit considerable diversity along dimensions of gender, race, social class, ethnicity, religion, and sexual orientation. Although all members of a cohort experience segments of history at similar chronological ages, the impact of particular events often varies along these other dimensions. One way of sharpening our understanding of the life course perspective and cohort membership is to consider the impact of the same historical events on different cohorts: the Great Depression of the 1930s; World War II in the 1940s; and the Civil Rights movement in the 1950s, 1960s, and 1970s.

The Great Depression of the 1930s. The cohort born between 1931 and 1940 was smaller in size than were cohorts born either before or after. This relatively small size meant that members of this cohort encountered less competition and more opportunities for advancement than members of larger cohorts. They entered the work force during the postwar prosperity of the 1950s, when an expanding economy provided employment opportunities. Many members experienced upward mobility during their life, from relative poverty during the Depression to middle-class status by the 1950s and 1960s. But their relatively small numbers can also bring unique challenges. For example, when their parents encounter poor health and disability, members of this Depression cohort will have fewer siblings with whom to share the responsibility of caring for their parents. They themselves, however, will have a larger number of children on whom to rely for support, as members of this cohort were among the parents of the large post-World-War-II baby boom.

The Depression had a different impact on the cohort born between 1901 and 1910. When the stock market crash of 1929 ushered in the Depression of the 1930s, members of this cohort were entering their early marriage and childbearing years. Because of difficult economic conditions, some delayed marriage and childbearing. Compared to younger and older cohorts, a larger proportion never married, and those who married had smaller families. Rather than individual histories of upward mobility, most members of this cohort experienced a decline in financial resources during the early decades of their life. People in this cohort are the parents of the small Depression-era cohort. Survivors of the 1901-1910 cohort, most of whom are now over 90 years of age, have fewer children on whom to rely for help in coping with disability.

Hard times, such as those experienced during the Depression years, can strengthen as well as weaken adaptive resources. The selection by Elder and Liker, "Hard Times in Women's Lives: Historical Influences Across Forty Years," describes the long-term effects of coping with financial hardship during the Depression among women in this cohort. Their analysis also demonstrates the significance of adaptive resources in coping with negative life events and the ways in which these resources are differentially distributed according to social class.

The World War II Years. The imprint of World War II (WWII) on today's cohorts of older adults also illustrates the differential impact of the same historical event on individuals with different characteristics. For many older men today, WWII involved military service. War meant combat and risks of death or injury, and 291,557 young male members of this cohort never returned from battlefields in Europe, North Africa, or the South Pacific. Wartime also meant geographic mobility, long separation from family, exposure to different people, and the mastery of new skills. For many, WWII was the central experience of their lives. In recalling his wartime experiences, one man mentioned his senior officer's response to the jubilation he and his fellow soldiers expressed at the dismissal and separation from service parade at the end of the war:

> "You just don't understand how big a part of your life this has been," [he told us.] "When you hear a marching band sometime in the future, you'll pick up the beat and you'll be right back here on the parade ground marching again." And he was right. That's the way it's turned out. (Schecter, 1985)

The postwar years provided unprecedented opportunity for returning soldiers. Many purchased homes or pursued college educations with funding provided through the GI Bill. Economic expansion, coupled with entry into the labor force of relatively small cohorts of new workers, generated upward mobility for many members of this cohort, whose lives seemed to capture the essence of the American Dream.

Women also endured wartime separation as husbands, boyfriends, fathers, and brothers were shipped overseas, but for women, the greatest impact of WWII centered on the occupational sphere. Between 1941 and 1944, the number of employed women in the United States increased by almost 5 million, from 14,600,000 to 19,367,000 (Clive, 1987). The composition of the female labor force changed after the war. Earlier in the century, women who worked for wages were disproportionately young, unmarried, and poor. By 1950, the majority of women workers were married and middle aged, with an increasing proportion from the middle and working classes. The occupational distribution of the work force also changed. Women were employed not only in unprecedented numbers but also in unprecedented jobs— "jobs that were well paid, were industrialized, and that gave a new legitimacy and value to the work that women did" (Andersen, 1993, p. 106). Although women were laid off at double the rate of male workers after the war and were resegregated into clerical and service sectors of the work force, their labor force participation rate continued to increase in the decades following WWII.

Expanding economic opportunities accompanying WWII did not extend to all U.S. citizens. Scarcely 4 months after the Japanese attack on Pearl Harbor, the U.S. government posted civilian exclusion orders, requiring the evacuation of 125,000 people of Japanese ancestry living along the Pacific Coast. Of these people, 70% were U.S.-born U.S. citizens. The orders to these Japanese citizens were often terse:

> Dispose of your homes and property. Wind up your businesses. Register the family. One seabag of bedding, two suitcases of clothing allowed per person. People in District #1 must report at 8th and Lane Street, 8 p.m. on April 28.

The selection from *Farewell to Manzanar* by Jeanne Wakatsuki Houston and James D. Houston provides a glimpse of the effect of the relocation orders on one Japanese American family.

Despite the demand for workers, employers were slow to hire Blacks, who remained concentrated in positions with low wages, such as janitors and domestics. But as wartime production continued to expand, employers were forced to forego their prejudices. At the urging of Black labor leader A. Philip Randolph, President Roosevelt issued an executive order banning employment discrimination on the basis of race in all defense industries. For people of color, WWII brought unprecedented employment opportunities and for many, marked the end of the Depression. The selection from Piri Thomas's novel *Down These Mean Streets* illustrates this economic impact of WWII on the life of a Puerto Rican family.

The Civil Rights Movement. Before the Civil Rights movement of the 1950s, 1960s, and 1970s, legally enforced racial segregation existed throughout the United States. This was the social context in which today's cohorts of elderly Blacks lived the first half of their life. Integrated work settings during WWII provided many Americans with their first experiences interacting as coworkers across racial lines. Demands for equal rights grew quickly, then, in the postwar era: Black soldiers confronted the disparity between fighting fascism abroad and confronting racism at home. Political pressure from Black leaders encouraged President Truman to integrate the military and establish a Civil Rights Commission (Bullard, 1989/1993). The Civil Rights movement had begun. The Civil Rights movement expanded opportunities for many Blacks, but it influenced the lives of White Americans as well.

> The 1950s and 1960s bore witness to significant events, which made lasting impressions among many White Americans who, until this time, had been either satisfied with or unconcerned about the institutional and individual discrimination facing Black Americans. . . . Older cohorts were as aware as younger cohorts of these changing norms. (Danigelis & Cutler, 1991, p. 400)

The movement left in its aftermath some changed as well as some unchanged behaviors and some changed as well as some unchanged attitudes. But older Americans were no more resistant to these changes than were younger Americans. The sociologists Nick Danigelis and Steve Cutler found that older cohorts changed their attitudes about race at about the same rate and degree as younger cohorts. A White Chicago restaurant owner interviewed by the writer Studs Terkel (1992) illustrates these changing attitudes and behaviors:

It is different than it was. In the earlier years, I'll admit to a lot of preconceptions based on race. . . . In recent years, with the integration of offices, people are working together. They learn to work with each other. They respect each other a lot more. . . . We are much more liberal than we were back then. I sense it in myself. (pp. 314-315)

Changes in Inequality Over the Life Course: The Impact of Cumulative Advantage and Disadvantage

Diversity among members of a cohort increases over the life course, with inequality higher among people 65 years of age and older than among any other age group (O'Rand, 1996). Gerontologists using the life course perspective attribute this pattern to the theory of cumulative advantage (or disadvantage), and they most often illustrate this explanation with reference to employment experiences. People who are advantaged early in life receive better educations, credentials that enable them to establish careers that offer high salaries, secure employment, and generous fringe benefits. They approach retirement with the maximum social security benefit and adequate pensions bolstered by investment income and other assets accumulated over their working lives. In contrast, people who begin life in disadvantaged positions are more likely to find employment in the secondary labor market, characterized by low wages, few benefits, and high labor turnover. When they reach old age, their lower earnings and irregular work histories, spotted by periods of unemployment, translate into lower social security benefits and limited pension income. As a result of the life course accumulation of advantage or disadvantage, the highest income quintile of the elderly population receives 57% of all pension income, whereas the bottom two quintiles (i.e., bottom 40%) receive only 4.4% of all pension income (Uhlenberg & Miner, 1996). Significantly, women and persons of color are less likely than White men to have had jobs that provide them with pensions when they retire.

The expansion of pension coverage during the decades following WWII has enabled each successive cohort to retire earlier than preceding cohorts, but a change in pension plans may alter this pattern for future cohorts. More and more pensions are designed as defined contribution (DC) rather than as defined benefit (DB) plans. DB plans typically provide a monthly benefit to the retired worker, with the size of the benefit a function of prior earnings, years of service, and age at retirement. In contrast, DC plans specify how much money employers and employees will invest in a retirement account. The pension benefit that workers receive when they retire depends on how much money is in the account when the worker retires, an amount that reflects both the total contribution and the rate of growth of the investment over time. There are two features of DC plans that can accentuate inequality among subcohorts over the life course. First, some DC plans are funded completely or partially by employee contributions. Workers with lower incomes may feel that current demands on their limited income must take precedence over long-term investment. But the impact of compounding returns means that low-wage workers are severely penalized for their inability to begin saving early in life. For example, a 22-year-old worker who invests $100 per month will have a retirement account of $781,969 by age 65, assuming a tax-sheltered 10% rate of return. Workers who do not begin saving $100 a month until age 42 will have only $104,997 in that account when they reach age 65. Assuming a more optimistic rate of return of 13% (not out of line with recent stock market performance), the early saver will have a retirement account of $1,998,001, in comparison to only $162,998 for the later saver.

Second, under DC plans, workers are permitted to borrow on their retirement investment accounts or to receive a lump sum cashout when they change jobs. There is a tax penalty for early withdrawal, but families without resources to pay for unexpected expenses like medical bills or to cover basic living expenses during periods of unemployment may see no alternative. As a result, when these workers grow old, they will have almost no pension income.

The growth of DC pension plans also illustrates the life course perspective's concern with the intersection of individual lives and historical time. Workers who have contributed to DC pension plans and who invested those funds in the stock market have experienced tremendous growth in their pension funds over the past 15 years as the stock market has soared to unprecedented levels. This gain is especially valuable to workers who began their careers at the beginning of the market surge. Even if future decades bring only slow rates of growth, these increases will be compounded on an already large investment account. Let's imagine for a moment that the next 25 years are indeed characterized by slow rates of growth. New workers establishing DC pension accounts can contribute the same amount of money as did the older cohort, but that investment will grow much more slowly. Another upsurge in the stock market 25 years later will add to their investment account, but the younger cohort will never make up for the lower compounding of their initial investment during their earlier years. As this example indicates, historical events, such as stock market upturns and downturns, affect all cohorts, but the magnitude of that impact will vary depending on the age of cohort members when they experience the events.

Key Issues

This discussion and the accompanying readings illustrate several points:

1. The advantages of using a life course perspective when studying the aging process

2. How sociohistorical events shape the aging experiences of different cohorts

3. How position along interlocking systems of inequality based on gender, race or ethnicity, and social class produces differences in the experiences of aging within particular cohorts' aging

4. How the same historical event differently shapes the experiences of individuals who occupy different and unequal statuses within a cohort

The Readings

The reading by Elder and Liker, excerpted from their article, "Hard Times in Women's Lives: Historical Influences Across Forty Years," illustrates the advantage of using a life course perspective and the concept of cohort to study people's lives and their responses to old age. This selection also shows how a particular historical event—the Great Depression—differently shaped the late-life adaptive resources of middle-class and working-class women. Working-class women, who entered the Depression with minimal resources, were more vulnerable to feelings of inadequacy and helplessness when faced with economic hardships that seemed unmanageable. Some middle-class women were sheltered from economic loss, but middle-class women who did experience economic deprivation faced those losses with more cognitive and emotional resources. Successfully managing the challenges of the Depression reinforced feelings of mastery among these deprived middle-class women. As Elder and Liker conclude, "women who experienced particular losses and learned to deal with them are better equipped to manage subsequent events of this type."

Elder and Liker also highlight the point that occupying a disadvantaged position in one system of inequality and a privileged position in another—being women and being middle-class—resulted in Depression experiences that were different from those who were disadvantaged in two systems—being women and lower class. Like the example of the older Black woman described by Hill, Colby, and Phelps, whose coping with racial discrimination was tied to her adaptation to aging, in this study, "The women's effective coping with personal economic loss in the middle years represented valuable preparation for the inevitable losses of old age." One conclusion suggested by these two examples is that smooth sailing in a protected environment may not develop one's adaptive skills.

The remaining selections introduce the social context in which older people from four different race or ethnic groups lived their lives. Each of these readings illustrates the ways in which people in certain historical time periods are relegated to circumscribed roles that narrow their opportunity structure, increase their negative life events, and weaken their adaptive resources. A life course perspective suggests that these factors combine to structure experiences of old age that differ from the experience of the dominant group.

The excerpt from *Farewell to Manzanar* by Jeanne Wakatsuki Houston and James D. Houston recaptures the evacuation and internment experience of today's Japanese American elderly told through the eyes of a young Japanese American girl. Born in 1935, the narrator was a child at the time of the internment. She will celebrate her 65th birthday in the year 2000. Following her father's arrest by U.S. officials, her family moved from Ocean Park [where they had been the only Japanese family in the neighborhood] to Terminal Island, an ethnic ghetto owned by the fish canneries who employed Japanese American workers. Later, the U.S. government moved the family to Manzanar, a relocation center in the desert. This reading about the Wakatsuki family illustrates how the same historical period—WWII—had different impacts on the opportunity structure and adaptive resources (in this case, economic security) of different segments of the population. WWII provided expanded occupational opportunities for many Americans, but for Japanese Americans, the war meant loss of homes and businesses.

The selection by Piri Thomas from his novel *Down These Mean Streets* illustrates the economic function of WWII for a Puerto Rican family in New York City. Thomas, who was born in 1928, was a teenager in El Barrio in Manhattan during WWII. The reading also illustrates the adaptive resources available to disadvantaged members of systems of inequality. In the period before WWII, the family coped with the stressful life events accompanying poverty by using the special resources of family closeness and escape to memories of better times—to Mrs. Thomas's "Isla Verde." Although these adaptive resources did not eliminate problems of poverty, they enabled the family to survive under oppressive economic conditions.

Alice Walker's essay, "In Search of Our Mothers' Gardens," helps us understand the experiences of Black women of Walker's mother's and grandmother's generations who spent their early lives in an era of legalized racial segregation. Walker begins with the question, "What did it mean for a black woman to be an artist in our grandmothers' time?" Clearly, talent and genius were not nourished, yet some of these women found ways of keeping creativity alive, "year after year, century after century," in music, oral history, needlework, or in the case of Walker's mother, gardening. Caught in an oppressive environment, these women "handed on the creative spark, .. the respect for the possibilities—and the will to grasp them." This reading illustrates how the same historical period can have different effects on the lives of people who occupy different and unequal statuses (Black women and White women), even though they are members of the same birth cohort.

The excerpt from *Lame Deer: Seeker of Visions* by John Fire/Lame Deer and Richard Erdoes is the story of a Lakota-Sioux American

Indian born in 1903. His life was influenced by the historical period in which he lived and by his status as an American Indian. A history of broken treaties and misguided federal policies have produced a situation in which today's elderly American Indians have the lowest incomes and highest risk of substandard housing of any segment of the older population. During this century, native peoples lost vast regions of tribal land, their children were educated in boarding schools where speaking their own language was prohibited, and federal policies repeatedly redefined their relationship with the federal government. Many of these policies were guided by a so-called melting-pot model, which assumed that different groups should lose their cultural uniqueness and melt or blend into the dominant culture. In this selection, Lame Deer remembers his encounters with the Bureau of Indian Affairs schools, encounters in which there was insistence on learning the dominant language and culture by throwing over the old ways of the Lakota. This reading illustrates two of the issues in this section: how particular historical events differently shape the opportunity structures of people with certain personal characteristics and how life events, adaptive resources, and aging experiences differ for some individuals in certain sociohistorical times.

The selection from Connie Wu, *Making Waves: World of Our Grandmothers,* chronicles the experiences of Chinese immigrants who arrived in the late 19th century to work on the transcontinental railroads. The struggles to immigrate and struggles to overcome discriminatory barriers in the new country are recounted by a fourth-generation Chinese American woman. The selection illustrates a point made in this section: There are differences within cohorts due to positions along interlocking systems of inequality based on gender and ethnicity. The main characters in this excerpt were Chinese American women who were uniquely affected by the confluence of racial discrimination and U.S. immigration laws in the new country and traditional gender-related cruelties in the old. Wu's narrative also illustrates the impact of distance from the immigration experience and reminds us that, whereas some Asian American families are newcomers to the United States, others have lived in the U.S. for generations.

The impact of the immigration experience is also illustrated in Carolina Hospital's poem "Dear Tía." *Tía* is the Spanish word for "aunt," and Hospital's poem laments lost relationships—and disappearing memories—with relatives separated by geographic distance and political barriers. When Fidel Castro took over Cuba in 1959, many Cubans fled to the United States, particularly Miami, where they were granted political refugee status. The professional and managerial skills many brought with them, as well as the fact that the great majority were Caucasian and did not experience overt racial prejudice, contributed to the ability of this first wave of Cubans to achieve economic success in their new country (Novas, 1994). But the political relationship between the U.S. and Cuba severed relationships with relatives still in Cuba, and Hospital's poem tells of the pain of forgetting people left behind. Cubans who fled to the United States as adults are among today's Latino elders.

1

Hard Times in Women's Lives:
Historical Influences Across Forty Years

Glen H. Elder, Jr.
Jeffrey K. Liker

A recurring theme in the human drama of rapid change centers on the fragmentation of lives and their internal discontinuities in a transformed environment. When such changes occur midway in life, initial purposes and directions lose meaning for the anticipated future. The ends of life may become obscure. Migration from rural to urban areas is one potential source of disjuncture in the life course; economic cycles provide another. Americans who grew up in Depression scarcity soon faced the problems and temptations of prosperity. Now their postwar offspring must cope with a period of retrenchment that calls for the scarcity virtues of thrift and conservation. In various ways, historical change thrusts people into new situations that can challenge the means, pathways, and ends of accustomed life.

An alternative or supplementary account of social change in life experience stresses the preparatory influence of certain historical transitions for subsequent life adaptations. This alternative account can be illustrated by the military and homefront demands of wartime America. Military service in World War II and the Korean War opened up developmental experiences and educational opportunities that improved career prospects for some veterans. Wartime employment opportunities also enabled some women to acquire skills and confidence by supporting themselves. Most occasions of social change defy a simple account of life effects by giving rise to contradictory or varied consequences, depending on the individual's exposure to changes and adaptations in the new situation.

This research explores the longterm consequences of one type of social change for the life experiences of women who lived through that change; we trace the influences of the economic collapse of the 1930s on the life course development of a small number of women who were born at the turn of the century (from about 1890 to 1910). A common theme running through the Depression years and the later years of life for these women is the prevalence of loss. This study investigates the hypothesis that their degree of wellbeing in old age is partly a function of how they dealt with the problems of human and material loss during the 1930s, some 40 years earlier. Adaptations to loss are contingent on both the severity of the deprivation and the resources brought to the situation. From both perspectives, women in the middle class appear to have clear advantages over women in lower-status families. Indeed, few relationships in social science have been more widely documented than the inverse association between impaired health and socioeconomic position (Kohn, 1972, 1977; Langner & Michael, 1963; Srole, 1978). Among plausible accounts of this outcome, one theme stands out: *health is a product of the interaction between stressor and resources.*

Women in this study started their families during the prosperous 1920s and experienced the bust and boom of the 1930s and 1940s as wives, mothers, and often earners. All are members of the well-known Berkeley Study (Macfarlane, 1938), a longitudinal investigation of normal development in a sample of 211 middle and working-class children and their families. The children were systematically selected from a list of Berkeley births in 1928–29. Approximately 81 of their mothers were interviewed during the 1930s and then again in 1969–70 (mean age = 70). As might be expected from class differences in mortality and social participation, high-status and well-educated women were more likely than other women to be contacted in old age (Maas & Kuypers, 1974). These differences remain even with the deceased (about half of those lost in sample attrition) excluded from the comparison. Even so, the 1969–70 participants resemble other women of the original sample with regard to the incidence and severity of economic loss during the 1930s.

We view loss and adaptation as a conceptual bridge between hard times during early adulthood and later life some 40 years after the stock market crash. Losses after midlife generally represent a more expectable, culturally patterned sequence of experiences than the seemingly arbitrary deprivations of the 1930s. Nonetheless, the experience of having coped with such hardships in early adulthood is a potential resource among aging women who face social, material, and physical losses. On the other hand, a prolonged sequence of Depression misfortunes might have precisely the opposite effect through diminished inner resources and greater health risk when the inevitable losses and separations of old age occur. For middle-class families, the Great Depression often created a temporary economic setback lasting several years, while working-class adults were more likely to experience the economic losses of the 1930s as more of the same economic misfor-

tunes that already characterized their lives (Elder, 1974). We begin the study with an examination of class differences in the social and economic resources Berkeley women brought to the 1930s and then employ measurement and causal models (Jöreskog & Sörbom, 1979) to assess their psychological health in old age. Some preliminary issues are worth noting as background to the research.

A life course perspective on aging assumes that individuals assess and react to new situations in the light of their personal biographies. The ups and downs of a lifetime furnish lessons, liabilities, and resources that influence the ways in which men and women age and meet the realities of later life (Butler, 1975). The wisdom to make sound choices stemming from life experiences, positive and negative, may ensure a legacy of good health, adaptive skills, and material security in old age.

The course of individual development prompts a number of questions. What are the life course antecedents of successful aging (Neugarten, 1970)? How are life events distributed across the life span (Pearlin & Johnson, 1977)? Why do similar misfortunes during the early years appear to lead one person to become bitter (Bowlby, 1980) and another grateful? How can we account for the large number of lower-status people who manage adversity so well in their lives (Mechanic, 1972)? How do people in crisis or deprivational conditions manage without longstanding injury or impairments to self or others? Can we account for this difference between successful copers and the people who become ill or disabled?

For American women born around 1900, answers to these questions involve recognition of differential exposure to historical change, such as the economic collapse of the 1930s, as well as the differential resources families brought to the situation. Some families were exposed to severe economic hardship; others managed to avoid misfortune altogether. We shall use economic variation as a starting point in assessing the long-term effects of the Depression experience among the Berkeley women. The strategy entails systematic comparisons of the psychological health and coping resources of women who suffered economic hardships in the 1930s with those of women who managed to avoid such deprivations.

Four conditions bear upon the long-term effects of economic deprivation: (1) the degree or severity of the loss; (2) adaptive resources and options brought to this new situation (education, problem-solving skills, sense of efficacy); (3) definitions and assessments of the situation (causal attribution, cognitive appraisal, etc.); and (4) action or responses, such as job seeking or taking in boarders. The first two conditions influence definitions and responses which can produce such varying outcomes as enhanced efficacy and sense of control, on the one hand, and social withdrawal and disorganization, on the other. These outcomes, in turn, affect the likelihood of subsequent difficulties and the development of effective coping strategies, perpetuating cycles of advantage and disadvantage (Bandura, 1977; Duncan & Morgan, 1980; Peterson, 1980).

As the Berkeley women entered the 1930s, class position tells us something important about their Depression experience (severity of loss, adaptive resources, modes of response) and later life in the 1960s. According to the Oakland study (Elder, 1974, chap. 3), loss of status was especially painful to middle-class women, but they had more resources than lower-status women for dealing effectively with family hardship. Their educational, economic, and status advantages were expressed in stronger feelings of personal worth and more developed skills in problem solving. In contrast, working-class women were more vulnerable to the very real economic hardships that often seemed unmanageable. For them, family hardships reinforced feelings of inadequacy and helplessness. These issues are consistent with a "class interaction" hypothesis (see Kohn's [1972] interaction model): low socioeconomic status among women before the 1930s increased chances that hardship would impair their life

prospects in old age (economic, health). Beneficial effects from Depression losses are found mainly among women who entered the 1930s as members of the middle class.

The analysis is organized in three phases. We begin with women's resources when entering the early 1930s as young mothers. Do we find differences in social support and problem-solving skill between women from high and low-status families or between the economically deprived and the nondeprived? The most general issue here is whether social class and economic loss produced different pathways for women and their life outcomes. The second part of the analysis puts the "class interaction" hypothesis to a direct test by comparing the effects of the Depression on the mental health of elderly women from the middle and working classes. The analytic technique, LISREL (see Jöreskog & Sörbom, 1978), enables a comparative assessment of these effects in the middle and working classes while taking measurement error into account. The estimated models include pre-Depression psychological states so that analyses examine change in relative functioning as an outcome of differential exposure to Depression hardship (Bohrnstedt, 1969). Finally, we examine the long-term effects of economic loss on certain attitudes and behaviors that are related to an efficacious lifestyle for women in the later years.

Women's Resources From Childbearing to Old Age

In general, higher-status women had more in reserve cognitively and emotionally when they entered the 1930s, a decade that magnified many times over the life stresses that ordinarily pile up during the childbearing years. Hence, even before the Depression, working-class women were especially vulnerable to setbacks, barriers, and criticism, factors that soon became commonplace.

Economic loss did shape the lives of these women in at least two ways. First, women in the deprived middle-class group were much more likely than their nondeprived counterparts to go to work in the 1930s and to continue into the postwar years. Indeed, in the late 1930s (1936–39), 41% of the high-status women in deprived homes spent some time on a job, while only 10% of the nondeprived middle-class women did so. This difference was much less pronounced in the working class, where women in both the nondeprived and deprived groups commonly entered the labor market. In the late 1930s, 49% of the deprived and 43% of the nondeprived working-class women spent time in the paid labor force. Hence, any developmental value of working is likely to be confined to middle-class women who generally had the luxury of staying home if their families were sheltered from Depression hardship.

Second, deprived middle-class women were much more likely than the nondeprived to be widowed in 1969. Among the deprived high-status women, only one-fourth of the 1929 marriages survived to 1969. This figure, well below the 71% survival rate for middle-class marriages in families that were spared major setbacks in the 1930s, may reflect the pathogenic effects of job and income loss on men (see Brenner, 1973, p. 973; Cohn, 1978). In any case, the high rate of widowhood among women from the deprived middle class is manifested in their relative disadvantage with regard to financial status. Widows generally rank below married women in economic status.

Considering the available data on economic welfare and social networks in old age, there is little evidence of markedly different objective pathways from the Depression into the later years. Possibly, postwar affluence eliminated many of the economic disadvantages of the Depression (Elder & Rockwell, 1978). Hence, any long-term effects of the Depression are likely to operate through psychological resources and adaptive capacities. Resources brought to the 1930s lead to the expectation that economic deprivation will have a negative effect on well-being in old age among the working class and a possibly benign effect among the middle class. Limited resources and acute survival pressures in the deprived working class increased the risk of helplessness among these women. Feelings of efficacy had a better chance of evolving through the adaptational and problem solving efforts of women in the deprived middle class. Having managed on very little during the 1930s, these women could at least view the adversity of their later years with a belief that they had been there before and survived. Are such variations in health part of the Depression's legacy for women from the middle and working class?

Early Hardship and Subsequent Well-Being in Old Age

Overall, Depression loss added to the psychological disadvantage of working-class women—to their low self-esteem, feelings of insecurity, and dissatisfaction with life—but posed no such handicap for the middle class. Two groups of middle-class women, the privileged nondeprived and the economically deprived, entered the 1930s with similar inner resources. After the economic decline of the Depression, financial pressures, husband disability, and employment on a paid job were all more common in the latter group. Despite conditions of this sort, middle-class women who lived through Depression hardships occupy a position of relative advantage on psychological well-being in their later years. They claim less in the way of material goods than women from the nondeprived middle class but show greater acceptance of what they have. Gratitude and satisfaction are more common in their lives. For them, less is truly more.

Consistent with the interaction hypothesis, hardship experience during the 1930s is linked with assertiveness and mastery feelings among elderly women from the middle class, whereas passivity and helplessness stand out as more typical outcomes of early deprivation among lower-status women. Depression hardship increased the risk of widowhood and economic pressure for working-class women and both factors, as well as the direct effect of economic loss, favored a relatively passive, dependent adaptation in old age.

Resourcefulness and confidence in old age represent the more common legacy of Depression adversity among middle-class women. Neither hard times in the thirties nor economic misfortune and loss of spouse during the later years managed to turn these women toward a dysphoric outlook or helplessness. Even serious health problems became just another problem to some. "I get in a little difficulty," a Berkeley woman observed (Maas & Kuypers, 1974, p. 136); "I've had eight surgeries trying to correct it, but now I've just given up. I do the best I can and most of the time I get along very well." It is the middle-class women from the privileged, nondeprived sector and not the economically deprived who display a more victimized outlook during the later years of their life. The effects of Depression hardship varied across class strata as expected and the class difference is statistically reliable.

Economic Change and Health in the Life Course: A Concluding Note

These contrasting outcomes of Depression experience in the lives of middle and working-class women are partly anticipated in the empirical literature on socioeconomic factors in health. This research links the risk of impaired health to lower socioeconomic status and especially to economic setbacks in the lower strata. The direction of influence between economics and health has been questioned by analysts and the temporal span of longitudinal studies has been too short to permit estimates of the duration or persistence of economic effects. Also, research to date has viewed the economic factor largely in terms of men and their unemployment (Kasl, 1979) rather than as an influence in the lives of women. With its focus on hard times in the lives of women, this longitudinal study traces conditions of economic deprivation to psychological health in old age. Over a span of 40 years, we see diverse imprints of the Great Depression on patterns of aging.

From the evidence at hand, different processes seem to be at work in the life trajectories of middle and working-class women. Depression hardship increased the emotional resources, vitality, and self-efficacy of women from the deprived middle class as compared with the privileged nondeprived. For working-class women in the later years, exposure to Depression hardship generally entailed a set of disadvantages, including diminished mental skills and self-confidence, lower morale, and a sense of helplessness. The consistency of this class reversal is perhaps more impressive than its size. In the working class, the modest size of the negative effect leaves open for investigation the important question of how some women from deprived circumstances managed to rise above the limitations of their world. A larger sample and more complete life records are needed to specify elements in the causal process of change and continuity and in life patterns that break with customary schedules. Social support, as a moderator of economic pressures, should be examined across the life course of marriage, parent-child relations, distant kin, and friends.

Our theoretical rationale for linking the Depression and aging experiences of the Berkeley women centers on their common ground in losses and related adaptations. We argue that women who experienced particular losses and learned to deal with them are better equipped to manage subsequent events of this type. The particular coping skills acquired in periods of hard times are not activated by tranquil stages of the life course. It is only during trying periods of decremental change, such as the later years, that coping resources are brought forth and distinguish the prepared woman from the sheltered or untested one. From this perspective, there is reason to expect the health effects of Depression hardship in the late 1930s to be weaker than those observed in old age.

Despite the daily pressures on hard-pressed families, the relative health of the Berkeley women in the late 1930s shows no reliable differences between the deprived and nondeprived in either the middle or the working class. Two types of measures were used in the analysis: (1) a simple index of behavioral impairment in performing social roles (some evidence [1936–39] or no evidence) and (2) a five-point interviewer rating on "worrisome behavior" (1936–38) identical to the worrisome ratings (1930 and 1969) used in the causal models. Of the Berkeley women, 86% were judged as showing no evidence of behavioral impairment by the end of the thirties, and the likelihood of some impairment did not vary by hard times in either social class, although it was more prevalent in the working class. A similar picture emerges from the ratings on worrisome behavior. Average scores for the nondeprived and deprived were virtually identical in the two social classes. Though much additional work is needed on Depression influences during the 1930s, and their precise timing and form, these empirical observations generally support a situational thesis on loss and life-course development: that differential experiences with problems of loss are most visibly expressed in subsequent life situations that are typified by such events, as during old age.

To a remarkable degree, the contrasting effects of Depression hardship reported in this analysis parallel the life experience of a younger group of women who were born in 1920–21 and grew up in Oakland, California, during the 1930s. These women were young adolescents in the Depression era, and economic loss often forced them to take on adult work and domestic roles that normally would have been their parents' responsibilities. At the age of 40, when they generally had families of their own, these women were found to have long-term effects of their Depression experiences that differed by social class origin (Elder, 1974, p. 242). The assumption that "smooth sailing" in a protected childhood may not develop adaptive skills was borne out in the lives of women who had grown up in nondeprived homes in the middle class. They ranked lower on psychological health and resourcefulness at the age of 40 than middle-class women who as adolescents had encountered the emotional trauma and pressure of hard times at first hand. As in the Berkeley study, the health of the Oakland women from the deprived working class was impaired relative to that of women from the nondeprived working class. Neither a privileged life nor one of unrelenting deprivation ensures the inner resources for successful aging.

Social change and the normative order bring many contradictions to the life course. Some old people encounter losses without the prior experience that enables them to cope effectively with such events. The wisdom to make appropriate decisions may arrive too late, at a time when the most important choices have been made. In the words of a Berkeley woman: "It's only when you have lived through experiences and digested them that you come to acquire enough sense to know how to deal with them." According to both this personal perspective and scientific knowledge of behavioral adaptation, effective coping with personal loss through the middle years represents valuable preparation for the inevitable losses of old age.

References

Bandura, A. (1977). Self-efficacy: Toward a unifying theory of behavioral change. *Psychological Review, 84*, 191-215.

Bohrnstedt, G. W. (1969). Observations on the measurement of change. In E. F. Borgatta (Ed.), *Sociological methodology*. San Francisco: Jossey-Bass.

Bowlby, J. (1980). *Loss: Sadness and depression* (Vol. 3). New York: Basic Books.

Brenner, M. H. (1973). *Mental illness and the economy*. Cambridge, MA: Harvard University Press.

Butler, R. N. (1975). *Why survive? Being old in America.* New York: Harper & Row.

Cohn, R. M. (1978). The effect of employment status change on self-attitudes. *Social Psychology Quarterly, 41,* 81-93.

Duncan, G., & Morgan, J. (1980). The incidence and some consequences of major life events. In G. Duncan & J. Morgan (Eds.), *Five thousand American families* (Vol. 8, pp. 183-240). Ann Arbor: Institute for Social Research, University of Michigan.

Elder, G. H., Jr. (1974). *Children of the great depression.* Chicago: University of Chicago Press.

Elder, G. H., Jr., & Rockwell, R. C. (1978). Economic depression and postwar opportunity: A study of life patterns and health. In R. A. Simmons (Ed.), *Research in community and mental health* (pp. 249-303). Greenwich, CT: JAI.

Jöreskog, K. G., & Sörbom, D. (1978). *LISREL IV: Analysis of linear structural relationships by the method of maximum likelihood.* Chicago: International Educational Services.

Jöreskog, K. G., & Sörbom, D. (Eds.). (1979). *Advances in factor analysis and structural equation models.* Cambridge, MA: Abt.

Kasl, S. V. (1979). Changes in mental health status associated with job loss and retirement. In J. E. Barrett et al. (Eds.), *Stress and mental disorder* (pp. 179-200). New York: Raven.

Kohn, M. L. (1972). Class, family and schizophrenia: A reformulation. *Social Forces, 50,* 295-304.

Kohn, M. L. (1977). *Class and conformity.* Chicago: University of Chicago Press.

Langner, T. S., & Michael, S. T. (1963). *Life stress and mental health.* New York: Free Press.

Maas, H. S., & Kuypers, J. A. (1974). *From thirty to seventy: A forty-year longitudinal study of adult life styles and personality.* San Francisco: Jossey-Bass.

Macfarlane, J. W. (1938). Studies in child guidance: 1. Methodology of data collection and organization. *Monographs of the Society for Research in Child Development, 3,* 154.

Mechanic, D. (1972). Social class and schizophrenia: Some requirements for a plausible theory of social influence. *Social Forces, 50,* 305-309.

Neugarten, B. L. (1970). Dynamics of transition of middle age to old age: Adaptation and the life cycle. *Journal of Geriatric Psychiatry, 4,* 7187.

Pearlin, L. I., & Johnson, J. S. (1977). Marital status, lifestrains, and depression. *American Sociological Review, 42,* 704-715.

Peterson, C. (1980, October 5-6). *The sense of control over one's life: A review of recent literature.* Paper prepared for the Social Science Research Council Meeting, "Self and Personal Control Over the Life Span," New York.

Srole, L. (1978). *Mental health in the metropolis: The midtown Manhattan study* (rev. and enl. ed.). New York: New York University Press.

2

Arrival at Manzanar

Jeanne Wakatsuki Houston
James D. Houston

In December of 1941 Papa's disappearance didn't bother me nearly so much as the world I soon found myself in.

He had been a jack-of-all-trades. When I was born he was farming near Inglewood. Later, when he started fishing, we moved to Ocean Park, near Santa Monica, and until they picked him up, that's where we lived, in a big frame house with a brick fireplace, a block back from the beach. We were the only Japanese family in the neighborhood. Papa liked it that way. He didn't want to be labeled or grouped by anyone. But with him gone and no way of knowing what to expect, my mother moved all of us down to Terminal Island. Woody already lived there, and one of my older sisters had married a Terminal Island boy. Mama's first concern now was to keep the family together; and once the war began, she felt safer there than isolated racially in Ocean Park. But for me, at age seven, the island was a country as foreign as India or Arabia would have been. It was the first time I had lived among other Japanese, or gone to school with them, and I was terrified all the time.

This was partly Papa's fault. One of his threats to keep us younger kids in line was "I'm going to sell you to the Chinaman." When I had entered kindergarten two years earlier, I was the only Oriental in the class. They sat me next to a Caucasian girl who happened to have very slanted eyes. I looked at her and began to scream, certain Papa had sold me out at last. My fear of her ran so deep I could not speak of it, even to Mama, couldn't explain why I was screaming. For two weeks I had nightmares about this girl, until the teachers finally moved me to the other side of the room. And it was still with me, this fear of Oriental faces, when we moved to Terminal Island.

In those days it was a company town, a ghetto owned and controlled by the canneries. The men went after fish, and whenever the boats came back—day or night—the women would be called to process the catch while it was fresh. One in the afternoon or four in the morning, it made no difference. My mother had to go to work right after we moved there. I can still hear the whistle—two toots for French's, three for Van Camps—and she and Chizu[1] would be out of bed in the middle of the night, heading for the cannery.

The house we lived in was nothing more than a shack, a barracks with single plank walls and rough wooden floors, like the cheapest kind of migrant workers' housing. The people around us were hard-working, boisterous, a little proud of their nickname, *yo-go-re*, which meant literally *uncouth one*, or roughneck, or dead-end kid. They not only spoke Japanese exclusively, they spoke a dialect peculiar to Kyushu, where their families had come from in Japan, a rough, fisherman's language, full of oaths and insults. Instead of saying *ba-ka-ta-re*, a common insult meaning *stupid*, Terminal Islanders would say *ba-ka-ya-*

ro, a coarser and exclusively masculine use of the word, which implies gross stupidity. They would swagger and pick on outsiders and persecute anyone who didn't speak as they did. That is what made my own time there so hateful. I had never spoken anything but English, and the other kids in the second grade despised me for it. They were tough and mean, like ghetto kids anywhere. Each day after school I dreaded their ambush. My brother Kiyo, three years older, would wait for me at the door, where we would decide whether to run straight home together, or split up, or try a new and unexpected route.

None of these kids ever actually attacked. It was the threat that frightened us, their fearful looks, and the noises they would make, like miniature Samurai,[2] in a language we couldn't understand.

At the time it seemed we had been living under this reign of fear for years. In fact, we lived there about two months. Late in February the navy decided to clear Terminal Island completely. Even though most of us were American-born, it was dangerous having that many Orientals so close to the Long Beach Naval Station, on the opposite end of the island. We had known something like this was coming. But, like Papa's arrest, not much could be done ahead of time. There were four of us kids still young enough to be living with Mama, plus Granny, her mother, sixty-five then, speaking no English, and nearly blind. Mama didn't know where else she could get work, and we had nowhere else to move *to*. On February 25 the choice was made for us. We were given forty-eight hours to clear out.

The secondhand dealers had been prowling around for weeks, like wolves, offering humiliating prices for goods and furniture they knew many of us would have to sell sooner or later. Mama had left all but her most valuable possessions in Ocean Park, simply because she had nowhere to put them. She had brought along her pottery, her silver, heirlooms like the kimonos Granny had brought from Japan, tea sets, lacquered tables, and one fine old set of china, blue and white porcelain, almost translucent. On the day we were leaving, Woody's car was so crammed with boxes and luggage and kids we had just run out of room. Mama had to sell this china.

One of the dealers offered her fifteen dollars for it. She said it was a full setting for twelve and worth at least two hundred. He said fifteen was his top price. Mama started to quiver. Her eyes blazed up at him. She had been packing all night and trying to calm down Granny, who didn't understand why we were moving again and what all the rush was about. Mama's nerves were shot, and now navy jeeps were patrolling the streets. She didn't say another word. She just glared at this man, all the rage and frustration channeled at him through her eyes.

He watched her for a moment and said he was sure he couldn't pay more than seventeen fifty for that china. She reached into the red velvet case, took out a dinner plate and hurled it at the floor right in front of his feet.

The man leaped back shouting, "Hey! Hey, don't do that! Those are valuable dishes!"

Mama took out another dinner plate and hurled it at the floor, then another and another, never moving, never opening her mouth, just quivering and glaring at the retreating dealer, with tears streaming down her cheeks. He finally turned and scuttled out the door, heading for the next house. When he was gone she stood there smashing cups and bowls and platters until the whole set lay in scattered blue and white fragments across the wooden floor.

The name Manzanar meant nothing to us when we left Boyle Heights. We didn't know where it was or what it was. We went because the government ordered us to. And, in the case of my older brothers and sisters, we went with a certain amount of relief. They had all heard stories of Japanese homes being attacked, of beatings in the streets of California towns. They were as frightened of the Caucasians as Caucasians were of us. Moving, under what appeared to be government protection, to an area less directly threatened by the war seemed not such a bad idea at all. For some it actually sounded like a fine adventure.

Our pickup point was a Buddhist church in Los Angeles. It was very early, and misty, when we got there with our luggage. Mama had bought heavy coats for all of us. She grew up in eastern Washington and knew that anywhere inland in early April would be cold. I was proud of my new coat, and I remember sitting on a duffel bag trying to be friendly with the Greyhound driver. I smiled at him. He didn't smile back. He was befriending no one. Someone tied a numbered tag to my collar and to the duffel bag (each family was given a number, and that became our official designation until the camps were closed), someone else passed out box lunches for the trip, and we climbed aboard.

I had never been outside Los Angeles County, never traveled more than ten miles from the coast, had never even ridden on a bus. I was full of excitement, the way any kid would be, and wanted to look out the window. But for the first few hours the shades were drawn. Around me other people played cards, read magazines, dozed, waiting. I settled back, waiting too, and finally fell asleep. The bus felt very secure to me. Almost half its passengers were immediate relatives. Mama and my older brothers had succeeded in keeping most of us together, on the same bus, headed for the same camp. I didn't realize until much later what a job that was. The strategy had been, first, to have everyone living in the same district when the evacuation began, and then to get all of us included under the same family number, even though names had been changed by marriage. Many families weren't as lucky as ours and suffered months of anguish while trying to arrange transfers from one camp to another.

We rode all day. By the time we reached our destination, the shades were up. It was late afternoon. The first thing I saw was a yellow swirl across a blurred, reddish setting sun. The bus was being pelted by what sounded like splattering rain. It wasn't rain.

This was my first look at something I would soon know very well, a billowing flurry of dust and sand churned up by the wind through Owens Valley.

We drove past a barbed-wire fence, through a gate, and into an open space where trunks and sacks and packages had been dumped from the baggage trucks that drove out ahead of us. I could see a few tents set up, the first rows of black barracks, and beyond them, blurred by sand, rows of barracks that seemed to spread for miles across this plain. People were sitting on cartons or milling around, with their backs to the wind, waiting to see which friends or relatives might be on this bus. As we approached, they turned or stood up, and some moved toward us expectantly. But inside the bus no one stirred. No one waved or spoke. They just stared out the windows, ominously silent. I didn't understand this. Hadn't we finally arrived, our whole family intact? I opened a window, leaned out, and yelled happily "Hey! This whole bus is full of Wakatsukis!"

Outside, the greeters smiled. Inside there was an explosion of laughter, hysterical, tension-breaking laughter that left my brothers choking and whacking each other across the shoulders.

We had pulled up just in time for dinner. The mess halls weren't completed yet. An outdoor chow line snaked around a half-finished building that broke a good part of the wind. They issued us army mess kits, the round metal kind that fold over, and plopped in scoops of canned Vienna sausage, canned string beans, steamed rice that had been cooked too long, and on top of the rice a serving of canned apricots. The Caucasian servers were thinking the fruit poured over rice would make a good dessert. Among the Japanese, of course, rice is never eaten with sweet foods, only with salty or savory foods. Few of us could eat such a mixture. But at this point no one dared protest. It would have been impolite. I was horrified when I saw the apricot syrup seeping through my little mound of rice. I opened my mouth to complain. My mother jabbed me in the back to keep quiet. We moved on through the line and joined the others squatting in the lee of half-raised walls, dabbing courteously at what was, for almost everyone there, an inedible concoction.

After dinner we were taken to Block 16, a cluster of fifteen barracks that had just been finished a day or so earlier—although finished was hardly the word for it. The shacks were built of one thickness of pine planking covered with tarpaper. They sat on concrete footings, with about two feet of open space between the floorboards and the ground. Gaps showed between the planks, and as the weeks passed and the green wood dried out, the gaps widened. Knotholes gaped in the uncovered floor.

Each barracks was divided into six units, sixteen by twenty feet, about the size of a living room, with one bare bulb hanging from the ceiling and an oil stove for heat. We were assigned two of these for the twelve people in our family group; and our official family "number" was enlarged by three digits—16 plus the number of this barracks. We were issued steel army cots, two brown army blankets each, and some mattress covers, which my brothers stuffed with straw.

The first task was to divide up what space we had for sleeping. Bill and Woody contributed a blanket each and partitioned off the first room: one side for Bill and Tomi, one side for Woody and Chizu and their baby girl. Woody also got the stove, for heating formulas.

The people who had it hardest during the first few months were young couples like these, many of whom had married just before the evacuation began, in order not to be separated and sent to different camps. Our two rooms were crowded, but at least it was all in the family. My oldest sister and her husband were shoved into one of those sixteen-by-twenty-foot compartments with six people they had never seen before—two other couples, one recently married like themselves, the other with two teenage boys. Partitioning off a room like that wasn't easy. It was bitter cold when we arrived, and the wind did not abate. All they had to use for room dividers were those army blankets, two of which were barely enough to keep one person warm. They argued over whose blanket should be sacrificed and later argued about noise at night—the parents wanted their boys asleep by 9:00 PM—and they continued arguing over matters like that for six months, until my sister and her husband left to harvest sugar beets in Idaho. It was grueling work up there, and wages were pitiful, but when the call came through camp for workers to alleviate the wartime labor shortage, it sounded better than their life at Manzanar. They knew they'd have, if nothing else, a room, perhaps a cabin of their own.

Notes

1. Woody's wife; the author's sister-in-law.

2. Japanese warrior class from the twelfth to the end of the nineteenth century.

3

Puerto Rican Paradise

Piri Thomas

Poppa didn't talk to me the next day. Soon he didn't talk much to anyone. He lost his night job—I forget why, and probably it was worth forgetting—and went back on home relief. It was 1941, and the Great Hunger called Depression was still down on Harlem.

But there was still the good old WPA. If a man was poor enough, he could dig a ditch for the government. Now Poppa was poor enough again.

The weather turned cold one more time, and so did our apartment. In the summer the cooped-up apartments in Harlem seem to catch all the heat and improve on it. It's the same in the winter. The cold, plastered walls embrace that cold from outside and make it a part of the apartment, till you don't know whether it's better to freeze out in the snow or by the stove, where four jets, wide open, spout futile, blue-yellow flames. It's hard on the rats, too.

Snow was falling. "My *Cristo*," Momma said, "*qué frío*. Doesn't that landlord have any *corazón?*[1] Why don't he give more heat?" I wondered how Pops was making out working a pick and shovel in that falling snow.

Momma picked up a hammer and began to beat the beat-up radiator that's copped a plea from so many beatings. Poor steam radiator, how could it give out heat when it was freezing itself? The hollow sounds Momma beat out of it brought echoes from other freezing people in the building. Everybody picked up the beat and it seemed a crazy, good idea. If everybody took turns beating on the radia-tors, everybody could keep warm from the exercise.

We drank hot cocoa and talked about summertime. Momma talked about Puerto Rico and how great it was, and how she'd like to go back one day, and how it was warm all the time there and no matter how poor you were over there, you could always live on green bananas, *bacalao*,[2] and rice and beans. "*Dios mío*," she said, "I don't think I'll ever see my island again."

"Sure you will, Mommie," said Miriam, my kid sister. She was eleven. "Tell us, tell us all about Porto Rico."

"It's not P*o*rto Rico, it's P*ue*rto Rico," said Momma.

"Tell us, Moms," said nine-year-old James, "about P*ue*rto Rico."

"Yeah, Mommie," said six-year-old José.

Even the baby, Paulie, smiled.

Moms copped that wet-eyed look and began to dream-talk about her *isla verde*,[3] Moses' land of milk and honey.

"When I was a little girl," she said, "I remember the getting up in the morning and getting the water from the river and getting the wood for the fire and the quiet of the greenlands and the golden color of the morning sky, the grass wet from the *lluvia*[4] . . . *Ai, Dios*, the *coquís*[5] and the *pajaritos*[6] making all the *música* . . ."

"Mommie, were you poor?" asked Miriam.

"*Sí, muy pobre*, but very happy. I remember the hard work and the very little bit we had, but it was a good little bit. It counted very much. Sometimes when you have too much, the good gets lost within and you have to look very hard. But when you have a little, then the good does not have to be looked for so hard."

"Moms," I asked, "did everybody love each other—I mean, like if everybody was worth something, not like if some weren't important because they were poor—you know what I mean?"

"*Bueno hijo,* you have people everywhere, who, because they have more, don't remember those who have very little. But in Puerto Rico those around you share *la pobreza*[7] with you and they love you, because only poor people can understand poor people. I like *los Estados Unidos,* but it's sometimes a cold place to live—not because of the winter and the landlord not giving heat but because of the snow in the hearts of the people."

"Moms, didn't our people have any money or land?" I leaned forward, hoping to hear that my ancestors were noble princes born in Spain.

"Your grandmother and grandfather had a lot of land, but they lost that."

"How come, Moms?"

"Well, in those days there was nothing of what you call *contratos,*[8] and when you bought or sold something, it was on your word and a handshake, and that's the way your *abuelos*[9] bought their land and then lost it."

"Is that why we ain't got nuttin' now?" James asked pointedly.

"Oh, it—"

The door opened and put an end to the kitchen yak. It was Poppa coming home from work. He came into the kitchen and brought all the cold with him. Poor Poppa, he looked so lost in the clothes he had on. A jacket and coat, sweaters on top of sweaters, two pairs of long johns, two pairs of pants, two pairs of socks, and a woolen cap. And under all that he was cold. His eyes were cold; his ears were red with pain. He took off his gloves and his fingers were stiff with cold.

"*Cómo está?*"[10] said Momma. "I will make you coffee."

Poppa said nothing. His eyes were running hot frozen tears. He worked his fingers and rubbed his ears, and the pain made him make faces. "Get me some snow, Piri," he said finally.

I ran to the window, opened it, and scraped all the snow on the sill into one big snowball and brought it to him. We all watched in frozen wonder as Poppa took that snow and rubbed it on his ears and hands.

"Gee, Pops, don't it hurt?" I asked.

"Sí, but it's good for it. It hurts a little first, but it's good for the frozen parts."

I wondered why.

"How was it today?" Momma asked.

"Cold. My God, ice cold."

Gee, I thought, *I'm sorry for you, Pops. You gotta suffer like this.*

"It was not always like this," my father said to the cold walls. "It's all the fault of the damn depression."

"Don't say 'damn,' " Momma said.

"Lola, I say 'damn' because that's what it is—*damn.*"

And Momma kept quiet. She knew it was "damn."

My father kept talking to the walls. Some of the words came out loud, others stayed inside. I caught the inside ones—the damn WPA, the damn depression, the damn home relief, the damn poorness, the damn cold, the damn crummy apartments, the damn look on his damn kids, living so damn damned and his not being able to do a damn thing about it.

And Momma looked at Poppa and at us and thought about her Puerto Rico and maybe being there where you didn't have to wear a lot of extra clothes and feel so full of damns, and how when she was a little girl all the green was wet from the *lluvias.*

And Poppa looking at Momma and us, thinking how did he get trapped and why did he love us so much that he dug in damn snow to give us a piece of chance? And why couldn't he make it from home, maybe, and keep running?

And Miriam, James, José, Paulie, and me just looking and thinking about snowballs and Puerto Rico and summertime in the street and whether we were gonna live like this forever and not know enough to be sorry for ourselves.

The kitchen all of a sudden felt warmer to me, like being all together made it like we wanted it to be. Poppa made it into the toilet and we could hear everything he did, and when he finished, the horsey gurgling of the flushed toilet told us he'd soon be out. I looked at the clock and it was time for "Jack Armstrong, the All-American Boy."

José, James, and I got some blankets and, like Indians, huddled around the radio digging the All-American Jack and his adventures, while Poppa ate dinner quietly. Poppa was funny about eating—like when he ate, nobody better bother him. When Poppa finished, he came into the living room and stood there looking at us. We smiled at him, and he stood there looking at us.

All of a sudden he yelled, "How many wanna play 'Major Bowes' Amateur Hour'?"

"Hoo-ray! Yeah, we wanna play," said José.

"Okay, first I'll make some taffy outta molasses, and the one who wins first prize gets first choice at the biggest piece, okay?"

"Yeah, hoo-ray, *chevere*."

Gee, Pops, you're great, I thought, *you're the swellest, the bestest Pops in the whole world, even though you don't understand us too good.*

When the candy was all ready, everybody went into the living room. Poppa came in with a broom and put an empty can over the stick. It became a microphone, just like on the radio.

"Pops, can I be Major Bowes?" I asked.

"Sure, Piri," and the floor was mine.

"Ladies and gentlemen," I announced, "tonight we present 'Major Bowes' Amateur Hour,' and for our first number—"

"Wait a minute, son, let me get my ukulele," said Poppa. "We need music."

Everybody clapped their hands and Pops came back with his ukulele.

"The first con-tes-tant we got is Miss Miriam Thomas."

"Oh no, not me first, somebody else goes first," said Miriam, and she hid behind Momma.

"Let me! Let me!" said José.

Everybody clapped.

"What are you gonna sing, sir?" I asked.

"Tell the people his name," said Poppa.

"Oh yeah. Presenting Mr. José Thomas. And what are you gonna sing, sir?"

I handed José the broom with the can on top and sat back. He sang well and everybody clapped.

Everyone took a turn, and we all agreed that two-year-old Paulie's "gurgle, gurgle" was the best song, and Paulie got first choice at the candy. Everybody got candy and eats and thought how good it was to be together, and Moms thought that it was wonderful to have such a good time even if she wasn't in Puerto Rico where the grass was wet with *lluvia*. Poppa thought about how cold it was gonna be tomorrow, but then he remembered tomorrow was Sunday and he wouldn't have to work, and he said so and Momma said "*Sí*," and the talk got around to Christmas and how maybe things would get better.

The next day the Japanese bombed Pearl Harbor.

"My God," said Poppa. "We're at war."

"*Dios mío*," said Momma.

I turned to James. "Can you beat that," I said.

"Yeah," he nodded. "What's it mean?"

"What's it mean?" I said. "You gotta ask, dopey? It means a rumble is on, and a big one, too."

I wondered if the war was gonna make things worse than they were for us. But it didn't. A few weeks later Poppa got a job in an airplane factory. "How about that?" he said happily. "Things are looking up for us."

Things *were* looking up for us, but it had taken a damn war to do it. A lousy rumble had to get called so we could start to live better. I thought, *How do you figure this crap out?*

I couldn't figure it out, and after a while I stopped thinking about it. Life in the streets didn't change much. The bitter cold was followed by the sticky heat; I played stickball, marbles, and Johnny-on-the-Pony, copped girls' drawers and blew pot. War or peace— what difference did it really make?

Notes

1. heart
2. codfish
3. green island
4. rain
5. small treetoads
6. little birds
7. poverty
8. contracts
9. grandparents
10. How are you?

4

In Search of Our Mothers' Gardens

Alice Walker

I described her own nature and temperament. Told how they needed a larger life for their expression. . . . I pointed out that in lieu of proper channels, her emotions had overflowed into paths that dissipated them. I talked, beautifully I thought, about an art that would be born, an art that would open the way for women the likes of her. I asked her to hope, and build up an inner life against the coming of that day. . . . I sang, with a strange quiver in my voice, a promise song.

> Jean Toomer, "Avey"
> CANE

The poet speaking to a prostitute who falls asleep while he's talking—

When the poet Jean Toomer walked through the South in the early twenties, he discovered a curious thing: black women whose spirituality was so intense, so deep, so *unconscious*, that they were themselves unaware of the richness they held. They stumbled blindly through their lives: creatures so abused and mutilated in body, so dimmed and confused by pain, that they considered themselves unworthy even of hope. In the selfless abstractions their bodies became to the men who used them, they became more than "sexual objects," more even than mere women: they became "Saints." Instead of being perceived as whole persons, their bodies became shrines: what was thought to be their minds became temples suitable for worship. These crazy Saints stared out at the world, wildly, like lunatics—or quietly, like suicides; and the "God" that was in their gaze was as mute as a great stone.

Who were these Saints? These crazy, loony, pitiful women?

Some of them, without a doubt, were our mothers and grandmothers.

In the still heat of the post-Reconstruction South, this is how they seemed to Jean Toomer: exquisite butterflies trapped in an evil honey, toiling away their lives in an era, a century, that did not acknowledge them, except as "the *mule* of the world." They dreamed dreams that no one knew—not even themselves in any coherent fashion—and saw visions no one could understand. They wandered or sat about the countryside crooning lullabies to ghosts, and drawing the mother of Christ in charcoal on courthouse walls.

They forced their minds to desert their bodies and their striving spirits sought to rise, like frail whirlwinds from the hard red clay. And when those frail whirlwinds fell, in scattered particles, upon the ground, no one mourned. Instead, men lit candles to celebrate the emptiness that remained, as people do who enter a beautiful but vacant space to resurrect a God.

Our mothers and grandmothers, some of them: moving to music not yet written. And they waited.

They waited for a day when the unknown thing that was in them would be made known; but guessed, somehow in their darkness, that on the day of their revelation they would be long dead. Therefore to Toomer they walked, and even ran, in slow motion. For they were going nowhere immediate, and the future was not yet within their grasp. And men took our mothers and grandmothers, "but got no pleasure from it." So complex was their passion and their calm.

To Toomer, they lay vacant and fallow as autumn fields, with harvest time never in sight: and he saw them enter loveless marriages, without joy; and become prostitutes, without resistance; and become mothers of children, without fulfillment.

For these grandmothers and mothers of ours were not Saints, but Artists; driven to a numb and bleeding madness by the springs of creativity in them for which there was no release. They were Creators, who lived lives of spiritual waste, because they were so rich in spirituality—which is the basis of Art—that the strain of enduring their unused and unwanted talent drove them insane. Throwing away this spirituality was their pathetic attempt to lighten the soul to a weight their work-worn, sexually abused bodies could bear.

What did it mean for a black woman to be an artist in our grandmothers' time? In our great-grandmothers' day? It is a question with an answer cruel enough to stop the blood.

Did you have a genius of a great-great-grandmother who died under some ignorant and depraved white overseer's lash? Or was she required to bake biscuits for a lazy backwater tramp, when she cried out in her soul to paint watercolors of sunsets, or the rain falling on the green and peaceful pasturelands? Or was her body broken and forced to bear children (who were more often than not sold away from her)—eight, ten, fifteen, twenty children—when her one joy was the thought of modeling heroic figures of rebellion, in stone or clay?

How was the creativity of the black woman kept alive, year after year and century after century, when for most of the years black people have been in America, it was a punishable crime for a black person to read or write? And the freedom to paint, to sculpt, to expand the mind with action did not exist. Consider, if you can bear to imagine it, what might have been the result if singing, too, had been forbidden by law. Listen to the voices of Bessie Smith, Billie Holiday, Nina Simone, Roberta Flack, and Aretha Franklin, among others, and imagine those voices muzzled for life. Then you may begin to comprehend the lives of our "crazy," "Sainted" mothers and grandmothers. The agony of the lives of women who might have been Poets, Novelists, Essayists, and Short-Story Writers (over a period of centuries), who died with their real gifts stifled within them.

And, if this were the end of the story, we would have cause to cry out in my paraphrase of Okot p'Bitek's great poem:

O, my clanswomen
Let us all cry together!
Come,
Let us mourn the death of our mother,
The death of a Queen
The ash that was produced
By a great fire!
O, this homestead is utterly dead
Close the gates
With *lacari* thorns,
For our mother
The creator of the Stool is lost!
And all the young women
Have perished in the wilderness!

But this is not the end of the story, for all the young women—our mothers and grandmothers, *ourselves*—have not perished in the wilderness. And if we ask ourselves why, and search for and find the answer, we will know beyond all efforts to erase it from our minds, just exactly who, and of what, we black American women are.

One example, perhaps the most pathetic, most misunderstood one, can provide a backdrop for our mothers' work: Phillis Wheatley, a slave in the 1700s.

Virginia Woolf, in her book *A Room of One's Own*, wrote that in order for a woman to write fiction she must have two things, certainly: a room of her own (with key and lock) and enough money to support herself.

What then are we to make of Phillis Wheatley, a slave, who owned not even herself? This sickly, frail black girl who required a servant of her own at times—her health was so precarious—and who, had she been white, would have been easily considered the intellectual superior of all the women and most of the men in the society of her day.

Virginia Woolf wrote further, speaking of course not of our Phillis, that "any woman born with a great gift in the sixteenth century [insert "eighteenth century," insert "black woman," insert "born or made a slave"] would certainly have gone crazed, shot herself, or ended her days in some lonely cottage outside the village, half witch, half wizard [insert "Saint"], feared and mocked at. For it needs little skill and psychology to be sure that a highly gifted girl who had tried to use her gift for poetry would have been so thwarted and hindered by contrary instincts [add "chains, guns, the lash, the ownership of one's body by someone else, submission to an alien religion"], that she must have lost her health and sanity to a certainty."

The key words, as they relate to Phillis, are "contrary instincts." For when we read the poetry of Phillis Wheatley—as when we read the novels of Nella Larsen or the oddly false-sounding autobiography of that freest of all black women writers, Zora Hurston—evidence of "contrary instincts" is everywhere. Her loyalties were completely divided, as was, without question, her mind.

But how could this be otherwise? Captured at seven, a slave of wealthy, doting whites who instilled in her the "savagery" of the Africa they "rescued" her from . . . one wonders if she was even able to remember her homeland as she had known it, or as it really was.

Yet, because she did try to use her gift for poetry in a world that made her a slave, she was "so thwarted and hindered by . . . contrary instincts, that she . . . lost her health. . . ." In the last years of her brief life, burdened not only with the need to express her gift but also with a penniless, friendless "freedom" and several small children for whom she was forced to do strenuous work to feed, she lost her health, certainly. Suffering from malnutrition and neglect and who knows what mental agonies, Phillis Wheatley died.

So torn by "contrary instincts" was black, kidnapped, enslaved Phillis that her description of "the Goddess"—as she poetically called the Liberty she did not have—is ironically, cruelly humorous. And, in fact, has held Phillis up to ridicule for more than a century. It is usually read prior to hanging Phillis's memory as that of a fool. She wrote:

The Goddess comes, she moves divinely
fair, Olive and laurel binds her golden hair.
Wherever shines this native of the skies,
Unnumber'd charms and recent graces rise.
[My italics]

It is obvious that Phillis, the slave, combed the "Goddess's" hair every morning; prior, perhaps, to bringing in the milk, or fixing her mistress's lunch. She took her imagery from the one thing she saw elevated above all others.

With the benefit of hindsight we ask, "How could she?"

But at last, Phillis, we understand. No more snickering when your stiff, struggling, ambivalent lines are forced on us. We know now that you were not an idiot or a traitor; only a sickly little black girl, snatched from your home and country and made a slave; a woman who still struggled to sing the song that was your gift, although in a land of barbarians who praised you for your bewildered tongue. It is not so much what you sang, as that you kept alive, in so many of our ancestors, *the notion of song.*

Black women are called, in the folklore that so aptly identifies one's status in society, "the *mule* of the world," because we have been handed the burdens that everyone else— *everyone* else—refused to carry. We have also been called "Matriarchs," "Superwomen," and "Mean and Evil Bitches." Not to mention "Castraters" and "Sapphire's Mama." When we have pleaded for understanding, our character has been distorted; when we have asked for simple caring, we have been handed empty inspirational appellations, then stuck in the farthest corner. When we have asked for love, we have been given children. In short, even our plainer gifts, our labors of fidelity and love, have been knocked down our throats. To be an artist and a black woman, even today, lowers our status in many respects, rather than raises it: and yet, artists we will be.

Therefore we must fearlessly pull out of ourselves and look at and identify with our lives the living creativity some of our great-grandmothers were not allowed to know. I stress *some* of them because it is well known that the majority of our great-grandmothers knew, even without "knowing" it, the reality of their spirituality, even if they didn't recognize it beyond what happened in the singing at church—and they never had any intention of giving it up.

How they did it—those millions of black women who were not Phillis Wheatley, or Lucy Terry or Frances Harper or Zora Hurston or Nella Larsen or Bessie Smith; or Elizabeth Catlett, or Katherine Dunham, either— brings me to the title of this essay, "In Search of Our Mothers' Gardens," which is a personal account that is yet shared, in its theme and its meaning, by all of us. I found, while thinking about the far-reaching world of the creative black woman, that often the truest answer to a question that really matters can be found very close.

In the late 1920s my mother ran away from home to marry my father. Marriage, if not running away, was expected of seventeen-year-old girls. By the time she was twenty, she had two children and was pregnant with a third. Five children later, I was born. And this is how I came to know my mother: she seemed a large, soft, loving-eyed woman who was rarely impatient in our home. Her quick,

violent temper was on view only a few times a year, when she battled with the white landlord who had the misfortune to suggest to her that her children did not need to go to school.

She made all the clothes we wore, even my brothers' overalls. She made all the towels and sheets we used. She spent the summers canning vegetables and fruits. She spent the winter evenings making quilts enough to cover all our beds.

During the "working" day, she labored beside—not behind—my father in the fields. Her day began before sunup, and did not end until late at night. There was never a moment for her to sit down, undisturbed, to unravel her own private thoughts; never a time free from interruption—by work or the noisy inquiries of her many children. And yet, it is to my mother—and all our mothers who were not famous—that I went in search of the secret of what has fed that muzzled and often mutilated, but vibrant, creative spirit that the black woman has inherited, and that pops out in wild and unlikely places to this day.

But when, you will ask, did my overworked mother have time to know or care about feeding the creative spirit?

The answer is so simple that many of us have spent years discovering it. We have constantly looked high, when we should have looked high—and low.

For example: in the Smithsonian Institution in Washington, D.C., there hangs a quilt unlike any other in the world. In fanciful, inspired, and yet simple and identifiable figures, it portrays the story of the Crucifixion. It is considered rare, beyond price. Though it follows no known pattern of quilt-making, and though it is made of bits and pieces of worthless rags, it is obviously the work of a person of powerful imagination and deep spiritual feeling. Below this quilt I saw a note that says it was made by "an anonymous Black woman in Alabama, a hundred years ago."

If we could locate this "anonymous" black woman from Alabama, she would turn out to be one of our grandmothers—an artist who left her mark in the only materials she could afford, and in the only medium her position in society allowed her to use.

As Virginia Woolf wrote further, in *A Room of One's Own:*

Yet genius of a sort must have existed among women as it must have existed among the working class. [Change this to "slaves" and "the wives and daughters of sharecroppers."] Now and again an Emily Brontë or a Robert Burns [change this to "a Zora Hurston or a Richard Wright"] blazes out and proves its presence. But certainly it never got itself onto paper. When, however, one reads of a witch being ducked, of a woman possessed by devils [or "Sainthood"], of a wise woman selling herbs [our root workers], or even a very remarkable man who had a mother, then I think we are on the track of a lost novelist, a suppressed poet, of some mute and inglorious Jane Austen. . . . Indeed, I would venture to guess that Anon, who wrote so many poems without signing them, was often a woman. . . .

And so our mothers and grandmothers have, more often than not anonymously, handed on the creative spark, the seed of the flower they themselves never hoped to see: or like a sealed letter they could not plainly read.

And so it is, certainly, with my own mother. Unlike "Ma" Rainey's songs, which retained their creator's name even while blasting forth from Bessie Smith's mouth, no song or poem will bear my mother's name. Yet so many of the stories that I write, that we all write, are my mother's stories. Only recently did I fully realize this: that through years of listening to my mother's stories of her life, I have absorbed not only the stories themselves, but something of the manner in which she spoke, something of the urgency that involves the knowledge that her stories—like her life—must be recorded. It is probably for this reason that so much of what I have written is about characters whose counterparts in real life are so much older than I am.

But the telling of these stories, which came from my mother's lips as naturally as breathing, was not the only way my mother showed herself as an artist. For stories, too, were subject to being distracted, to dying without conclusion. Dinners must be started, and cotton must be gathered before the big rains. The artist that was and is my mother showed itself to me only after many years. This is what I finally noticed:

Like Mem, a character in *The Third Life of Grange Copeland,* my mother adorned with flowers whatever shabby house we were forced to live in. And not just your typical straggly country stand of zinnias, either. She planted ambitious gardens—and still does—with over fifty different varieties of plants that bloom profusely from early March until late November. Before she left home for the fields, she watered her flowers, chopped up the grass, and laid out new beds. When she returned from the fields she might divide clumps of bulbs, dig a cold pit, uproot and replant roses, or prime branches from her taller bushes or trees—until night came and it was too dark to see.

Whatever she planted grew as if by magic, and her fame as a grower of flowers spread over three counties. Because of her creativity with her flowers, even my memories of poverty are seen through a screen of blooms—sunflowers, petunias, roses, dahlias, forsythia, spirea, delphiniums, verbena . . . and on and on.

And I remember people coming to my mother's yard to be given cuttings from her flowers; I hear again the praise showered on her because whatever rocky soil she landed on, she turned into a garden. A garden so brilliant with colors, so original in its design, so magnificent with life and creativity, that to this day people drive by our house in Georgia—perfect strangers and imperfect strangers—and ask to stand or walk among my mother's art.

I notice that it is only when my mother is working in her flowers that she is radiant, almost to the point of being invisible—except as Creator: hand and eye. She is involved in work her soul must have. Ordering the universe in the image of her personal conception of Beauty.

Her face, as she prepares the Art that is her gift, is a legacy of respect she leaves to me, for all that illuminates and cherishes life. She has handed down respect for the possibilities— and the will to grasp them.

For her, so hindered and intruded upon in so many ways, being an artist has still been a daily part of her life. This ability to hold on, even in very simple ways, is work black women have done for a very long time.

This poem is not enough, but it is something, for the woman who literally covered the holes in our walls with sunflowers:

They were women then
My mama's generation
Husky of voice—Stout of
Step
With—fists as well as
Hands
How they battered down
Doors
And ironed
Starched white
Shirts
How they led
Armies
Headragged Generals
Across mined
Fields
Booby-trapped
Kitchens
To discover books
Desks
A place for us
How they knew what we
Must know
Without knowing a page
Of it
Themselves

Guided by my heritage of a love of beauty and a respect for strength—in search of my mother's garden, I found my own.

And perhaps in Africa over two hundred years ago, there was just such a mother; perhaps she painted vivid and daring decorations in oranges and yellows and greens on the walls of her hut; perhaps she sang—in a voice like Roberta Flack's—*sweetly* over the compounds of her village; perhaps she wove the most stunning mats or told the most ingenious stories of all the village storytellers. Perhaps she was herself a poet—though only her daughter's name is signed to the poems that we know.

Perhaps Phillis Wheatley's mother was also an artist.

Perhaps in more than Phillis Wheatley's biological life is her mother's signature made clear.

5

Lame Deer: Seeker of Visions

Lame Deer (John Fire)
Richard Erdoes

I was born a full-blood Indian in a twelve-by-twelve log cabin between Pine Ridge and Rosebud. *Maka tanhan wicasa wan*—I am a man of the earth, as we say. Our people don't call themselves Sioux or Dakota. That's white man talk. We call ourselves Ikce Wicasa—the natural humans, the free, wild, common people. I am pleased to be called that.

As with most Indian children, much of my upbringing was done by my grandparents—Good Fox and his wife, Pte-Sa-Ota-Win, Plenty White Buffalo. Among our people the relationship to one's grandparents is as strong as to one's own father and mother. We lived in that little hut way out on the prairie, in the back country, and for the first few years of my life I had no contact with the outside world. Of course we had a few white man's things—coffee, iron pots, a shotgun, an old buckboard. But I never thought much of where these things came from or who had made them.

When I was about five years old my grandma took me to visit some neighbors. As always, my little black pup came along. We were walking on the dirt road when I saw a rider come up. He looked so strange to me that I hid myself behind Grandma and my pup hid behind me. I already knew enough about riding to see that he didn't know how to handle a horse. His feet were hanging down to the ground. He had some tiny, windmill-like things coming out of his heels, making a tinkling sound. As he came closer I

started to size him up. I had never seen so much hair on a man. It covered all of his face and grew way down to his chest, maybe lower, but he didn't have hair where it counted, on top of his head. The hair was of a light-brown color and it made him look like a mattress come to life. He had eyes like a dead owl, of a washed-out blue-green hue. He was chewing on something that looked like a smoking Baby Ruth candy bar. Later I found out that this was a cigar. This man sure went in for double enjoyment, because he was also chomping on a wad of chewing tobacco, and now and then he took the smoking candy bar from his mouth to spit out a long stream of brown juice. I wondered why he kept eating something which tasted so bad that he couldn't keep it down.

This strange human being also wore a funny headgear—a cross between a skillet and a stovepipe. He had a big chunk of leather piled on top of his poor horse, hanging down also on both sides. In front of his crotch the leather was shaped like a horn. I thought maybe he kept his man-thing inside to protect it. This was the first saddle I had seen. His pitiful horse also had strings of leather on its head and a piece of iron in its mouth. Every time the horse stuck out its tongue I could hear some kind of roller or gear grinding inside it. This funny human being wore leather pants and had two strange-looking hammers tied to his hips. I later found out these were .45 Colts.

The man started to make weird sounds. He was talking, but we couldn't understand him because it was English. He pointed at my grandmother's pretty beaded moccasins and he took some square green frog hides from his pocket and wanted to trade. I guess those were dollar bills. But Grandma refused to swap, because she had four big gold coins in her moccasins. That man must have smelled them. This was the first white man I met.

When I got home I had a new surprise waiting for me. My grandpa was butchering something that I had never seen before, an animal with hoofs like a horse and the body of a dog. Maybe somebody had mated a dog with a horse and this funny creature was the result. Looking at its pink, hairless body, I was reminded of scary old tales about humans coupling with animals and begetting terrifying monsters. Grandpa was chopping away, taking the white meat and throwing the insides out. My little puppy was sure enjoying this, his first pig. So was I, but the pig smelled terrible. My grandpa said to save the fat for axle grease.

Most of my childhood days weren't very exciting, and that was all right with me. We had a good, simple life. One day passed like another. Only in one way was I different from other Indian kids. I was never hungry, because my dad had so many horses and cattle. Grandma always got up early in the morning before everybody else, taking down the big tin container with the Government-issue coffee. First I would hear her roasting the beans in a frying pan, then I would hear her grind them. She always made a huge pot holding two gallons of water, put in two big handfuls of coffee and boiled it. She would add some sweetener—molasses or maple syrup; we didn't like sugar. We used no milk or cream in our *pejuta sapa*—our black medicine.

Before anything else Grandma poured out a big soup spoon of coffee as an offering to the spirits, and then she kept the pot going all day. If she saw people anywhere near the house she called out to them, regardless of who they were, "Come in, have some coffee!"

When the black medicine gave out, she added water and a lot more coffee and boiled the whole again. That stuff got stronger and stronger, thicker and thicker. In the end you could almost stick the spoon in there and it would keep standing up-right. "Now the coffee is real good," Grandma would say.

To go with the coffee Grandma got her baking powder each morning and made soda bread and squaw bread. That squaw bread filled the stomach. It seemed to grow bigger and bigger inside. Every spring, as the weather got warmer, the men would fix up Grandma's "squaw-cooler." This was a brush shelter made of four upright tree trunks with horizontal lodge poles tied to the top. The whole was then covered with branches from pine trees. They rigged up an old wood burner for Grandma to cook on, a rough table and some logs to sit on. In the summer, much of our life was spent in the squaw-cooler, where you could always feel a breeze. These squaw-coolers are still very popular on the reservation.

Grandma liked to smoke a little pipe. She loved her *kinnickinnick*—the red willow-bark tobacco. One time she accidentally dropped some glowing embers into an old visitor's lap. This guy still wore a breech cloth. Suddenly we smelled something burning. That breech cloth had caught fire and we had to yank it off and beat the flames out. He almost got his child-maker burned up. He was so old it wouldn't have made a lot of difference, but he still could jump.

One of my uncles used to keep a moon-counting stick, our own kind of calendar and a good one. He had a special staff and every night he cut a notch in it until the moon "died"—that is, disappeared. On the other side of his staff he made a notch for every month. He started a new stick every year in the spring. That way we always knew when it was the right day for one of our ceremonies.

Every so often my grandparents would take me to a little celebration down the creek. Grandpa always rode his old red horse, which was well known in all the tribes. We always brought plenty of food for everybody, squaw bread, beef, the kind of dried meat we called *papa*, and *wasna*, or pemmican, which was meat pounded together with berries and kidney fat. We also brought a kettle of coffee, wild mint tea, soup or stuff like that. Grandfather was always the leader of the *owanka osnato*—the rehearsal ground. He prepared the place carefully. Only the real warriors were allowed to dance there—men like Red Fish or Thin Elk, who had fought in the Custer battle. With the years the dancers grew older and older and fewer and fewer. Grandfather danced too. Everybody could see the scars all over his arm where he had been wounded by the white soldiers.

Some women had scars, too. Grandpa's brother, White Crane Walking, had three wives. They were not jealous of one another. They were like sisters. They loved one another and they loved their husband. This old man was really taking it easy; the women did all the work. He just lay around the whole day long, doing nothing. Once in a while some men called him lazy, but he just laughed and told them, "Why don't you get a second wife?" He knew their wives were jealous and didn't want them to get a second one. When this old man finally passed away, the two wives who survived him buried him in the side of a hill. They took their skinning knives and made many deep gashes in their arms and legs to show their grief. They might have cut off their little fingers too, but somebody told them that this was no longer allowed, that the Government would punish them for this. So they cut off their hair instead. They keened and cried for four days and nights; they loved their husband that much.

I was the *takoja*—the pampered grandson—and like all Indian children I was spoiled. I was never scolded, never heard a harsh word. "*Ajustan*—leave it alone"—that was the worst. I was never beaten; we don't treat children that way. Indian kids are so used to being handled gently, to get away with things, that they often don't pay much attention to what the grownups tell them. I'm

a grandfather now myself and sometimes I feel like yelling at one of those brash kids, "Hey, you little son of a bitch, listen to me!" That would make him listen all right, but I can't do it.

When I didn't want to go to sleep my grandma would try to scare me with the *ciciye*—a kind of bogeyman. "*Takoja, istima ye*—Go to sleep, sonny," she would say, "or the *ciciye* will come after you." Nobody knew what the *ciciye* was like, but he must have been something terrible. When the *ciciye* wouldn't work anymore, I was threatened with the *siyoko*—another kind of monster. Nobody knew what the *siyoko* was like, either, but he was ten times more terrible than the *ciciye*. Grandma did not have much luck. Neither the *ciciye* nor the *siyoko* cared me for long. But when I was real bad, Grandma would say, "*Wasicun anigni kte*—the white man will come and take you to his home," and that scared me all right. *Wasicun* were for real.

It was said that I didn't take after my grandpa Good Fox, whom I loved, but after my other grandfather, Crazy Heart, whom I never knew. They said I picked up where he left off, because I was so daring and full of the devil. I was told that Crazy Heart had been like that. He did not care what happened to other people, or to himself, once he was on his way. He was hot-tempered, always feuding and on the warpath. At the same time he saved lots of people, gave wise counsel, urged the people to do right. He was a good speech-maker. Everybody who listened to him said that he was a very encouraging man. He always advised patience, except when it came to himself. Then his temper got in the way.

I was like that. Things I was told not to do—I did them. I liked to play rough. We played shinny ball, a kind of hockey game. We made the ball and sticks ourselves. We played the hoop game, shot with a bow and arrow. We had foot races, horse races and water races. We liked to play *mato kiciyapi*, the bear game, throwing sharp, stiff grass stems at each other. These could really hurt you and draw blood if they hit the bare skin. And we were always at the *isto kicicastakapi,* the pit-slinging game. You chewed the fruit from the rosebush or wild cherries, spit a fistful of pits into your hand and flung them into the other fellow's face. And of course I liked the Grab-Them-by-the-Hair-and-Kick-Them game, which we played with two teams.

I liked to ride horseback behind my older sister, holding onto her. As I got a little bigger she would hold onto me. By the time I was nine years old I had my own horse to ride. It was a beautiful gray pony my father had given me together with a fine saddle and a very colorful Mexican saddle blanket. That gray was my favorite companion and I was proud to ride him. But he was not mine for long. I lost him through my own fault.

Nonge Pahloka—the Piercing of Her Ears—is a big event in a little girl's life. By this ceremony her parents, and especially her grandmother, want to show how much they love and honor her. They ask a man who is respected for his bravery or wisdom to pierce the ears of their daughter. The grandmother puts on a big feed. The little girl is placed on a blanket surrounded by the many gifts her family will give away in her name. The man who does the piercing is much admired and gets the most valuable gift. Afterward they get down to the really important part—the eating.

Well, one day I watched somebody pierce a girl's ears. I saw the fuss they made over it, the presents he got and all that. I thought I should do this to my little sister. She was about four years old at the time and I was nine. I don't know anymore what made me want to do this. Maybe I wanted to feel big and important like the man whom I had watched perform the ceremony. Maybe I wanted to get a big present. Maybe I wanted to make my sister cry. I don't remember what was in my little boy's mind then. I found some wire and made a pair of "ear rings" out of it. Then I asked my sister, "Would you like me to put these on you?" She smiled. "*Ohan*— yes." I didn't have the sharp bone one uses

for the ear-piercing, and I didn't know the prayer that goes with it. I just had an old awl but thought would do fine. Oh, how my sister yelled. I had to hold her down, but I got that awl through her earlobes and managed to put the "ear rings" in. I was proud of the neat job I had done.

When my mother came home and saw those wire loops in my sister's ears she gasped. But she recovered soon enough to go and tell my father. That was one of the few occasions he talked to me. He said, "I should punish you and whip you, but I won't. That's not my way. You'll get your punishment later." Well, some time passed and I forgot all about it. One morning my father announced that we were going to a powwow. He had hitched up the wagon and it was heaped high with boxes and bundles. At that powwow my father let it be known that he was doing a big *otuhan*—a give-away. He put my sister on a rug, a pretty Navajo blanket, and laid out things to give away—quilts, food, blankets, a fine shotgun, his own new pair of cowboy boots, a sheepskin coat, enough to fit out a whole family. Dad was telling the people, "I want to honor my daughter for her ear-piercing. This should have been done openly, but my son did it at home. I guess he's too small. He didn't know any better." This was a long speech for Dad. He motioned me to come closer. I was sitting on my pretty gray horse. I thought we were both cutting a very fine figure. Well, before I knew it, Dad had given my horse away, together with its beautiful saddle and blanket. I had to ride home in the wagon and I cried all the way. The old man said, "You have your punishment now, but you will feel better later on. All her life your sister will tell about how you pierced her ears. She'll brag about you. I bet you are the only small boy who ever did this big ceremony."

That was no consolation to me. My beautiful gray was gone. I was heart-broken for three days. On the fourth morning I looked out the door and there stood a little white stallion with a new saddle and a silver-plated bit. "It's yours," my father told me. "Get on it." I was happy again.

After I was six years old it was very hard to make me behave. The only way one could get me to sit still was to tell me a story. I loved to listen to my grandparents' old tales, and they were good at relating the ancient legends of my people. They told me of the great gods Wi and Hanwi, the sun and the moon, who were married to each other. They told me about the old man god Waziya, whom the priests have made into Santa Claus. Waziya had a wife who was a big witch. These two had a daughter called Ite—the face—the most beautiful woman in the universe. Ite was married to Tate, the wind.

The trouble with this pairing was that Ite got it into her mind that the sun, Wi, was more handsome than her own husband, the wind. Wi, on his part, thought that Ite was much more beautiful than his own wife, the moon. Wi was having a love affair with Ite, and whenever the moon saw them misbehaving she hid her face in shame. "That's why on some nights we don't see the moon," Grandma told me.

The Great Spirit did not like these goings-on, and he punished Ite. She still remained the most beautiful creature in the world, but only if one looked at her from one side. The other half of her face had become so hideous and ugly that there were no words to describe it. From that time on she was known as Anunk-Ite, or Double-Face. When it comes to love the women always have the worst of it.

Many of these legends were about animals. Grandma told me about the bat who hid himself on top of the eagle's back, screaming, "I can fly higher than any other bird." That was true enough; even the eagle couldn't fly higher than somebody who was sitting on top of him. As a punishment the other birds grounded the bat and put him in a mouse hole. There he fell in love with a lady mouse. That's why bats now are half mouse and half bird.

Grandpa Good Fox told me about the young hunters who killed a buffalo with a big rattle for a tail. After eating of its meat these young men were changed into giant rattle-snakes with human heads and human voices. They lived in a cave beneath the earth and ruled the underworld.

The stories I liked best had to do with Iktome, the evil spiderman, a smart-ass who played tricks on everybody. One day this spider was walking by a lake where he saw many ducks swimming around. This sight gave him a sudden appetite for roast duck. He stuffed his rawhide bag full of grass and then he showed himself. When the ducks saw him they started to holler, "Where are you going, Iktome?"

"I am going to a big powwow."

"What have you got in your bag, Iktome?"

"It's full of songs which I am taking to the powwow, good songs to dance to."

"How about singing some songs for us?" begged the ducks.

The tricky spider made a big show of not wanting to do it. He told the ducks he had no time for them, but in the end he pretended to give in, because they were such nice birds. "I'll sing for you," he told the ducks, "but you must help me."

"We'll do what you want. Tell us the rules."

"Well, you must form three rows. In the front row, all you fat ones, get in there. In the second row go all those who are neither fat nor thin—the in-betweens. The poor scrawny ones go in the third row, way down there. And you have to act out the song, do what the words tell you. Now the words to my first song are 'Close your eyes and dance!' "

The ducks all lined up with their eyes shut, flapping their wings, the fat ones up front. Iktome took a big club from underneath his coat. "Sing along as loud as you can," he ordered, "and keep your eyes shut. Whoever peeks will get blind." He told them to sing so that their voices would drown out the "thump, thump" of his club when he hit them over the head. He knocked them down one by one and was already half done when one of those low-down, skinny ducks in the back row opened its eyes and saw what Iktome was up to.

"Hey, wake up!" it hollered. "That Iktome is killing us all!"

The ducks that were left opened their eyes and took off. Iktome didn't mind. He already had more fat ducks than he could eat.

Iktome is like some of those bull-shipping politicians who make us close our eyes and sing and dance for them while they knock us on the head. Democratic ducks, Republican ducks, it makes no difference. The fat, stupid ones are the first in the pot. It's always the skinny, no-account, low-class duck in the back that doesn't hold still. That's a good Indian who keeps his eyes open. Iktome is an evil schemer, Grandpa told me, but luckily he's so greedy that most of the time he outsmarts himself.

It's hard to make our grandchildren listen to these stories nowadays. Some don't understand our language anymore. At the same time there is the TV going full blast—and the radio and the phonograph. These are the things our children listen to. They don't care to hear an old-fashioned Indian story.

I was happy living with my grandparents in a world of our own, but it was a happiness that could not last. "Shh, *wasicun anigni kte*—be quiet or the white man will take you away." How often had I heard these words when I had been up to some mischief, but I never thought that this threat could become true, just as I never believed that the monsters *ciciye* and *siyoko* would come and get me.

But one day the monster came—a white man from the Bureau of Indian Affairs. I guess he had my name on a list. He told my family, "This kid has to go to school. If your kids don't come by themselves the Indian police will pick them up and give them a rough ride." I hid behind Grandma. My father was like a big god to me and Grandpa had been a warrior at the Custer fight, but they could not protect me now.

In those days the Indian schools were like jails and run along military lines, with roll calls four times a day. We had to stand at attention, or march in step. The B.I.A. thought that the best way to teach us was to stop us from being Indians. We were forbidden to talk our language or to sing our songs. If we disobeyed we had to stand in the corner or flat against the wall, our noses and knees touching the plaster. Some teachers hit us on the hands with a ruler. A few of these rulers were covered with brass studs. They didn't have much luck redoing me though. They could make me dress up like a white man, but they couldn't change what was inside the shirt and pants.

My first teacher was a man and he was facing a lot of fearful kids. I noticed that all the children had the same expression on their faces—no expression at all. They looked frozen, deadpan, wooden. I knew that I, too, looked that way. I didn't know a word of the white man's language and very little about his ways. I thought that everybody had money free. The teacher didn't speak a word of Lakota. He motioned me to my seat. I was scared stiff.

The teacher said, "Stand," "Sit down!" He said it again and again until we caught on. "Sit, stand, sit, stand. Go and stop. Yes and no." All without spelling, just by sound.

We also had a lady teacher. She used the same method. She'd hold up one stick and say, "One." Then she'd hold up two sticks and say, "Two," over and over again. For many weeks she showed us pictures of animals and said "dog" or "cat." It took me three years to learn to say, "I want this."

My first day in school was also the first time I had beans, and with them came some white stuff, I guessed it was pork fat. That night, when I came home, my grandparents had to open the windows. They said my air was no good. Up to then I had eaten nothing but dry meat, *wasna*, *papa*, dry corn mixed with berries. I didn't know cheese and eggs, butter or cream. Only seldom had I tasted sugar or candy. So I had little appetite at school. For days on end they fed us cheese sandwiches, which made Grandma sniff at me, saying, "Grandson, have you been near some goats?"

After a while I lost some of my fear and recovered my daring. I called the white man teacher all the bad names in my language, smiling at him at the same time. He beamed and patted me on the head, because he thought I was complimenting him. Once I found a big picture of a monkey in the classroom, a strange animal with stiff, white side whiskers. I thought this must be the Great White Father, I really did.

I went to the day school on the Rosebud Reservation, twelve miles south of Norris, South Dakota. The Government teachers were all third-grade teachers. They taught up to this grade and that was the highest. I stayed in that goddam third grade for six years. There wasn't any other. The Indian people of my generation will tell you that it was the same at the other schools all over the reservations. Year after year the same grade over again. If we ran away the police would bring us back. It didn't matter anyway. In all those years at the day school they never taught me to speak English or to write and read. I learned these things only many years later, in saloons, in the Army or in jail.

When I was fourteen years old I was told that I had to go to boarding school. It is hard for a non-Indian to understand how some of our kids feel about boarding schools. In their own homes Indian children are surrounded with relatives as with a warm blanket. Parents, grandparents, uncles, aunts, older brothers and cousins are always fussing over them, playing with them or listening to what they have to say. Indian kids call their aunt "Mother," not just as a polite figure of speech but because that aunt acts like a mother. Indian children are never alone. If the grown-ups go someplace, the little ones are taken along. Children have their rights just as the adults. They are rarely forced to do something they don't like, even if it is good for them. The parents will say, "He hates it so much, we don't have the heart to make him do it."

To the Indian kid the white boarding school comes as a terrific shock. He is taken from his warm womb to a strange, cold place. It is like being pushed out of a cozy kitchen into a howling blizzard. The schools are better now than they were in my time. They look good from the outside—modern and expensive. The teachers understand the kids a little

better, use more psychology and less stick. But in these fine new buildings Indian children still commit suicide, because they are lonely among all that noise and activity. I know of a ten-year-old who hanged herself. These schools are just boxes filled with homesick children. The schools leave a scar. We enter them confused and bewildered and we leave them the same way. When we enter the school we at least know that we are Indians. We come out half red and half white, not knowing what we are.

When I was a kid those schools were really bad. Ask the oldtimers. I envied my father, who never had to go through this. I felt so lonesome I cried, but I wouldn't cooperate in the remaking of myself. I played the dumb Indian. They couldn't make me into an apple—red outside and white inside. From their point of view I was a complete failure. I took the rap for all the troubles in the school. If anything happened the first question always was "Did you see John do it?" They used the strap on us, but more on me than on anybody else.

My teacher was a mean old lady. I once threw a live chicken at her like a snowball. In return she hit my palms with a ruler. I fixed an inkpot in such a way that it went up in her face. The black ink was all over her. I was the first to smile and she knew who had done it right away. They used a harness thong on my back that time and locked me up in the basement. We full-bloods spent much time down there. I picked up some good fox songs in that basement.

I was a good athlete. I busted a kitchen window once playing stickball. After that I never hit so good again. They tried to make me play a slide trombone. I tore it apart and twisted it into a pretzel. That mean old teacher had a mouth like a pike and eyes to match. We counted many coups upon each other and I still don't know who won. Once, when they were after me again for something I didn't do, I ran off. I got home and on my horse. I knew the Indian police would come after me. I made it to Nebraska, where I sold my horse and saddle and bought a ticket to Rapid City. I still had twelve dollars in my pocket. I could live two days on one dollar, but the police caught me and brought me back. I think in the end I got the better of that school. I was more of an Indian when I left than when I went in. My back had been tougher than the many straps they had worn out on it.

Some doctors say that Indians must be healthier than white people because they have less heart disease. Others say that this comes from our being hungrier, having less to eat, which makes our bodies lean and healthy. But this is wrong. The reason Indians suffer less from heart disease is that we don't live long enough to have heart trouble. That's an old folks' sickness. The way we have to live now, we are lucky if we make it to age forty. The full-bloods are dying fast. One day I talk to one, the next day he is dead. In a way the Government is still "vanishing" the Indian, doing Custer's work. The strange-looking pills and capsules they give us to live on at the Public Health Service hospitals don't do us much good. At my school the dentist came once a year in his horse and buggy with a big pair of pliers to yank our teeth, while the strongest, biggest man they could find kept our arms pinned to our sides. That was the anesthesia.

There were twelve of us, but they are all dead now, except one sister. Most of them didn't even grow up. My big brother, Tom, and his wife were killed by the flu in 1917. I lost my own little boy thirty-five years ago. I was a hundred miles away, caught in a blizzard. A doctor couldn't be found for him soon enough. I was told it was the measles. Last year I lost another baby boy, a foster child. This time they told me it was due to some intestinal trouble. So in a lifetime we haven't made much progress. We medicine men try to doctor our sick, but we suffer from many new white man's diseases, which come from the white man's food and white man's living, and we have no herbs for that.

My big sister was the oldest of us all. When she died in 1914 my folks took it so hard that our life was changed. In honor of her memory they gave away most of their possessions, even beds and mattresses, even the things without which the family would find it hard to go on. My mother died of tuberculosis in 1920, when I was seventeen years old, and that was our family's "last stand." On her last day I felt that her body was already gone; only her soul was still there. I was holding her hand and she was looking at me. Her eyes were big and sad, as if she knew that I was in for a hard time. She said, "Onsika, onsika—pitiful, pitiful." These were her last words. She wasn't sorry for herself; she was sorry for me. I went up on a hill by myself and cried.

When grandfather Crazy Heart died they killed his two ponies, heads toward the east and tails to the west. They had told each horse, "Grandson, your owner loved you. He has need of you where he's going now." Grandfather knew for sure where he was going, and so did the people who buried him according to our old custom, up on a scaffold where the wind and the air, the sun, the rain and the snow could take good care of him. I think that eventually they took the box with his body down from the scaffold and buried it in a cemetery, but that happened years later and by then he and his ponies had long gone to wherever they wanted to be.

But in 1920 they wouldn't even allow us to be dead in our own way. We had to be buried in the Christian fashion. It was as if they wanted to take my mother to a white boarding school way up there. For four days I felt my mother's *nagi*, her presence, her soul, near me. I felt that some of her goodness was staying with me. The priest talked about eternity. I told him we Indians did not believe in a forever and forever. We say that only the rocks and the mountains last, but even they will disappear. There's a new day coming, but no forever, I told him. "When my time comes, I want to go where my ancestors have gone." The priest said, "That may be hell." I told him that I'd rather be frying with a Sioux grandmother or uncle than sit on a cloud playing harp with a pale-faced stranger. I told him, "That Christian name, John, don't call me that when I'm gone. Call me Tahca Ushte— Lame Deer."

6

The World of Our Grandmothers

Connie Young Wu

Our grandmothers are our historical links. As a fourth-generation Chinese American on my mother's side, and a third-generation on my father's, I grew up hearing stories about ancestors coming from China and going back and returning again. Both of my grandmothers, like so many others, spent a lot of time waiting in China.

My father's parents lived with us when I was growing up, and through them I absorbed a village culture and the heritage of my pioneer Chinese family. In the kitchen my grandmother told repeated stories of coming to America after waiting for her husband to send for her. (It took sixteen years before Grandfather could attain the status of merchant and only then arrange for her passage to this country.) She also told stories from the village about bandits, festivals, and incidents showing the tyranny of tradition. For example, Grandma was forbidden by her mother-in-law to return to her own village to visit her mother: A married woman belonged solely within the boundaries of her husband's world.

Sometimes I was too young to understand or didn't listen, so my mother—who knew all the stories by heart—told me those stories again later. We heard over and over how lucky Grandpa was to have come to America when he was eleven—just one year before the gate was shut by the exclusion law banning Chinese laborers. Grandpa told of his many jobs washing dishes, making bricks, and working on a strawberry farm. Once, while walking outside Chinatown, he was stoned by a group of whites and ran so fast he lost

his cap. Grandma had this story to tell of her anger and frustration: "While I was waiting in the immigration shed, Grandpa sent in a box of *dim sum*. I was still waiting to be released. I would have jumped in the ocean if they decided to deport me." A woman in her position was quite helpless, but she still had her pride and was not easily pacified. "I threw the box of *dim sum* out the window."

Such was the kind of history I absorbed. I regret deeply that I was too young to have asked the questions about the past that I now want answered; all my grandparents are now gone. But I have another chance to recover some history from my mother's side. Family papers, photographs, old trunks that have traveled across the ocean several times filled with clothes, letters, and mementos provide a documentary on our immigration. My mother—and some of my grandmother's younger contemporaries—fill in the narrative.

A year before the Joint Special Committee of Congress to investigate Chinese immigration met in San Francisco in 1876, my great-grandmother, Chin Shee, arrived to join her husband, Lee Wong Sang, who had come to America a decade earlier to work on the transcontinental railroad. Chin Shee arrived with two brides who had never seen their husbands. Like her own, their marriages had been arranged by their families. The voyage on the clipper ship was rough and long. Seasick for weeks, rolling back and forth as she lay in the bunk, Chin Shee lost most of her hair. The two other women laughed, "Some newlywed you'll make!" But the joke was on them as they mistakenly set off with the wrong husbands, the situation realized only when one man looked at his bride's normal-sized feet and exclaimed, "But the letter described my bride as having bound feet!" Chin Shee did not have her feet bound because she came from a peasant family. But her husband did not seem to care about that nor that the back of her head was practically bald. He felt himself fortunate just to be able to bring his wife to Gum San.

Chin Shee bore six children in San Francisco, where her husband assisted in the deliveries. They all lived in the rear of their grocery store, which also exported dried shrimp and seaweed to China. Great-Grandma seldom left home; she could count the number of times she went out. She and other Chinese wives did not appear in the streets even for holidays, lest they be looked upon as prostitutes. She took care of the children, made special cakes to sell on feast days, and helped with her husband's work. A photograph of her shows a middle-aged woman with a kindly, but careworn face, wearing a very regal brocade gown and a long, beaded necklace. As a respectable, well-to-do Chinese wife in America, married to a successful Chinatown merchant, with children who were by birthright American citizens, she was a rarity in her day. (In contrast, in 1884 Mrs. Jew Lim, the wife of a laborer, sued in federal court to be allowed to join her husband, but was denied and deported.)

In 1890 there were only 3,868 Chinese women among 103,620 Chinese males in America. Men such as Lee Yoke Suey, my mother's father, went to China to marry. He was one of Chin Shee's sons born in the rear of the grocery store, and he grew up learning the import and export trade. As a Gum San merchant, he had money and status and was able to build a fine house in Toishan. Not only did he acquire a wife but also two concubines. When his wife became very ill after giving birth to an infant who soon died, Yoke Suey was warned by his father that she was too weak to return to America with him. Reminding Yoke Suey of the harsh life in Gum San, he advised his son to get a new wife.

In the town of Foshan, not far from my grandfather's village, lived a girl who was recommended to him by his father's friend. Extremely capable, bright, and with some education, she was from a once prosperous family that had fallen on hard times. A plague had killed her two older brothers, and her heartbroken mother died soon afterwards. She was an excellent cook and took good care of her father, an herb doctor. Her name was Jeong Hing Tong, and she was pretty, with bound feet only three and a half inches long. Her father rejected the offer of the Lee family at first; he did not want his daughter to be a concubine, even to a wealthy Gum San merchant. But the elder Lee assured him this girl would be the wife, the one who would go to America with her husband.

So my maternal grandmother, bride of sixteen, went with my grandfather, then twenty-six, to live in America. Once in San Francisco, Grandmother lived a life of confinement, as did her mother-in-law before her. When she went out, even in Chinatown, she was ridiculed for her bound feet. People called out mockingly to her, "Jhat!" meaning bound. She tried to unbind her feet by soaking them every night and putting a heavy weight on each foot. But she was already a grown woman, and her feet were permanently stunted, the arches bent and the toes crippled. It was hard for her to stand for long periods of time, and she frequently had to sit on the floor to do her chores. My mother comments: "Tradition makes life so hard. My father traveled all over the world. There were stamps all over his passport—London, Paris—and stickers all over his suitcases, but his wife could not go into the street by herself."

Their first child was a girl, and on the morning of her month-old "red eggs and ginger party" the earth shook 8.3 on the Richter scale. Everyone in San Francisco, even Chinese women, poured out into the streets. My grandmother, babe in arms, managed to get a ride to Golden Gate Park on a horse-drawn wagon. Two other Chinese women who survived the earthquake recall the shock of suddenly being out in the street milling with thousands of people. The elderly goldsmith in a dimly lit Chinatown store had a twinkle in his eye when I asked him about the scene after the quake. "We all stared at the women because we so seldom saw them in the streets." The city was soon in flames. "We could feel the fire on our faces," recalls Lily Sung, who was seven at the time, "but my sister and I couldn't walk very fast because we had to escort this lady, our neighbor, who had bound feet." The poor woman kept stumbling and falling on the rubble and debris during their long walk to the Oakland-bound ferry.

That devastating natural disaster forced some modernity on the San Francisco Chinese community. Women had to adjust to the emergency and makeshift living conditions and had to work right alongside the men. Life in America, my grandmother found, was indeed rugged and unpredictable.

As the city began to rebuild itself, she proceeded to raise a large family, bearing four more children. The only school in San Francisco admitting Chinese was the Oriental school in Chinatown. But her husband felt, as did most men of his class, that the only way his children could get a good education was for the family to return to China. So they lived in China and my grandfather traveled back and forth to the United States for his trade business. Then suddenly, at the age of forty-three, he died of an illness on board a ship returning to China. After a long and painful mourning, Grandmother decided to return to America with her brood of now seven children. That decision eventually affected immigration history.

At the Angel Island immigration station in San Francisco Bay, Grandmother went through a physical examination so thorough that even her teeth were checked to determine whether she was the age stated on her passport. The health inspector said she had filariasis, liver fluke, a common ailment of Asian immigrants which caused their deportation by countless numbers. The authorities thereby ordered Grandmother to be deported as well.

While her distraught children had to fend for themselves in San Francisco (my mother,

then fifteen, and her older sister had found work in a sewing factory), a lawyer was hired to fight for Grandmother's release from the detention barracks. A letter addressed to her on Angel Island from her attorney, C. M. Fickert, dated 24 March 1924, reads: "Everything I can legitimately do will be done on your behalf. As you say, it seems most inhuman for you to be separated from your children who need your care. I am sorry that the immigration officers will not look at the human side of your case."

Times were tough for Chinese immigrants in 1924 . Two years before, the federal government had passed the Cable Act, which provided that any woman born in the United States who married a man "ineligible for citizenship" (including the Chinese, whose naturalization rights had been eliminated by the Chinese Exclusion Act) would lose her own citizenship. So, for example, when American-born Lily Sung, whom I also interviewed, married a Chinese citizen she forfeited her birthright. When she and her four daughters tried to re-enter the United States after a stay in China, they were denied permission. The immigration inspector accused her of "smuggling little girls to sell." The Cable Act was not repealed until 1930.

The year my grandmother was detained on Angel Island, a law had just taken effect that forbade all aliens ineligible for citizenship from landing in America. This constituted a virtual ban on the immigration of all Chinese, including Chinese wives of U.S. citizens.

Waiting month after month in the bleak barracks, Grandmother heard many heart-rending stories from women awaiting deportation. They spoke of the suicides of several despondent women who hanged themselves in the shower stalls. Grandmother could see the calligraphy carved on the walls by other detained immigrants, eloquent poems expressing homesickness, sorrow, and a sense of injustice.

Meanwhile, Fickert was sending telegrams to Washington (a total of ten the bill stated) and building up a case for the circuit court.

Mrs. Lee, after all, was the wife of a citizen who was a respected San Francisco merchant, and her children were American citizens. He also consulted a medical authority to see about a cure for liver fluke.

My mother took the ferry from San Francisco twice a week to visit Grandmother and take her Chinese dishes such as salted eggs and steamed pork because Grandmother could not eat the beef stew served in the mess hall. Mother and daughter could not help crying frequently during their short visits in the administration building. They were under close watch of both a guard and an interpreter.

After fifteen months the case was finally won. Grandmother was easily cured of filariasis and was allowed—with nine months probation—to join her children in San Francisco. The legal fees amounted to $782.50, a fortune in those days.

In 1927 Dr. Frederick Lam in Hawaii, moved by the plight of Chinese families deported from the islands because of the liver fluke disease, worked to convince federal health officials that the disease was noncommunicable. He used the case of Mrs. Lee Yoke Suey, my grandmother, as a precedent for allowing an immigrant to land with such an ailment and thus succeeded in breaking down a major barrier to Asian immigration.

My most vivid memory of Grandmother Lee is when she was in her seventies and studying for her citizenship. She had asked me to test her on the three branches of government and how to pronounce them correctly. I was a sophomore in high school and had entered the "What American Democracy Means To Me" speech contest of the Chinese American Citizens Alliance. When I said the words "judicial, executive, and legislative," I looked directly at my grandmother in the audience. She didn't smile, and afterwards, didn't comment much on my patriotic words. She had never told me about being on Angel Island or about her friends losing their citizenship. It wasn't in my textbooks either. I may have thought she wanted to be a citizen because her sons and sons-in-law had fought for this country, and we lived in a land of freedom and opportunity, but my guess now is that she wanted to avoid any possible confrontation—even at her age—with immigration authorities. The bad laws had been repealed, but she wasn't taking any chances.

I think a lot about my grandmother now and can understand why, despite her quiet, elegant dignity, an aura of sadness always surrounded her. She suffered from racism in the new country, as well as from traditional cruelties in the old. We, her grandchildren, remember walking very slowly with her, escorting her to a family banquet in Chinatown, hating the stares of tourists at her tiny feet. Did she, I wonder, ever feel like the victim of a terrible hoax, told as a small weeping girl that if she tried to untie the bandages tightly binding her feet she would grow up ugly, unwanted, and without the comforts and privileges of the wife of a wealthy man?

We seemed so huge and clumsy around her—a small, slim figure always dressed in black. She exclaimed once that the size of my growing feet were "like boats." But she lived to see some of her granddaughters graduate from college and pursue careers and feel that the world she once knew with its feudal customs had begun to crumble. I wonder what she would have said of my own daughter who is now attending a university on an athletic scholarship. Feet like boats travel far?

I keep looking at the artifacts of the past: the photograph of my grandmother when she was an innocent young bride and the sad face in the news photo taken on Angel Island. I visit the immigration barracks from time to time, a weather-beaten wooden building with its walls marked by calligraphy bespeaking the struggles of our history. I see the view of sky and water from the window out of which my grandmother gazed. My mother told me how, after visiting hours, she would walk to the ferry and turn back to see her mother waving to her from this window. This image has been passed on to me like an heirloom of pain and of love. When I leave the building, emerging from the darkness into the glaring sunlight of the island, I too turn back to look at my grandmother's window.

7

Dear Tía

Carolina Hospital

I do not write.
The years have frightened me away.
My life in a land so familiarly foreign,
a denial of your presence.
Your name is mine.
One black and white photograph of your youth,
all I hold on to.
One story of your past.

The pain comes not from nostalgia.
I do not miss your voice urging me in play,
your smile,
or your pride when others called you my mother.
I cannot close my eyes and feel your soft skin;
listen to your laughter;
smell the sweetness of your bath.
I write because I cannot remember at all.

1   The readings in Part I all illustrate how particular historical times differently shape the opportunity structures of individuals who are disadvantaged by systems of inequality. In what ways were the opportunities of people in the readings limited by the historical experience in which they lived?

2   A major theme of Part I has been that certain individuals in certain historical time periods are relegated to circumscribed roles that narrow their life chances, increase their negative life events, and influence their adaptive resources. How were the life chances of the women of Elder and Liker's study, the Wakatsuki family, the Thomas family, Lame Deer, and the mothers and grandmothers in Walker's essay circumscribed by the particular historical period? What adaptive resources were available to these people?

3   We have emphasized the fact that the same historical period can differently shape the experiences of individuals who belong to the same cohort but occupy different positions in systems of inequality. Demonstrate your understanding of this principle by comparing the impact of the Depression of the 1930s on the lower- and middle-class women in Elder and Liker's study and of World War II on the Wakatsuki and Thomas families.

4   People's experiences in old age are influenced by the ways in which they adapt to particular life events. Both their life events and adaptive resources are influenced by the historical time period in which they live and their positions in interlocking systems of inequality. Illustrate this life course approach to old age by comparing Elder and Liker's lower-class women with the mothers and grandmothers in Walker's essay and the Chinese American women in Wu's article. In what ways were the life courses of these women similar? In what ways were they different?

5   Talk to older relatives or friends about their memories of the Great Depression, World War II, and the Civil Rights movement. In what ways do you think these events affected their lives? How was the impact of these events influenced by their age cohort? By their gender, race or ethnicity, or social class?

6   The sociologists Howard Schuman and Jacqueline Scott (1989) studied the ways a generation can be marked by the political events and social changes of its era. They concluded that the events and changes we experience during adolescence and early adulthood have the greatest impact in creating what they call "generational memories." What events or changes do you think will have the greatest impact on your cohort? Can you predict the long-term effects of these events or changes on your life as you grow old?

7   Native Americans were not the only group within U.S. society to encounter the effects of government policies based on the "melting pot" model. This model was also applied to the wave of immigrants who came to the United States from southern and eastern Europe between 1880 and 1920. The children of these immigrants are among today's elderly Americans. Interview older relatives or family friends whose parents were part of this immigration. Do they have any memories of living between "two worlds": that of their immigrant parents and the Americanized world of their friends and school? How do they think these early experiences have affected their lives? What special strategies might be required in delivering services to these older individuals?

8   Political barriers precluded visits by Cuban Americans to their island homeland. How do you think open immigration and more frequent visits "back home" might have affected the aging experience among elderly Cuban Americans? How do the experiences of first-generation Cuban Americans compare with the experiences of other Latino immigrants to the United States? Of immigrants from various Asian countries?

SUGGESTIONS FOR FURTHER READING

1   Sone, M. (1953). *Nisei daughter.* Boston: Little, Brown.

This autobiography by the American-born daughter of Japanese immigrants includes an account of her family's experience during World War II. Born in 1919, the narrator was 23 years old at the time of the internment.

2   Terkel, S. (1995). *Coming of age: The story of our century by those who lived it.* New York: The New Press.

Pulitzer-Prize-winning author Studs Terkel provides a portrait of the lives of elderly Americans whose lives sliced through 20th-century America. This anthology introduces us to 70 very different people, whose interviews underscore the ways in which times and biographies have changed.

3   Wilson, E. H., & Mullalley, S. (Eds.). (1983). *Hope and dignity: Older black women of the South.* Philadelphia: Temple University Press.

An anthology of short biographies based on interviews with older African American women. Although all of the central characters are disadvantaged on two hierarchies (gender and race), they represent a range of social class backgrounds, including a successful stockbroker on Wall Street and the wife of a college president.

4   Angelou, M. (1969). *I know why the caged bird sings.* New York: Random House.

This first of several autobiographical novels by the author illustrates the impact of race and sociohistorical time on the early life of the African American poet Maya Angelou, now in her sixties. This book chronicles her experiences growing up in Arkansas during the 1930s and introduces readers to the racially segregated world before the Civil Rights movement and the adaptive strategies African Americans developed to survive both physically and emotionally.

5   Jen, G. (1991). *Typical American.* Boston: Houston Mifflin.

This novel traces the experiences of three young Chinese immigrants—two women and one man—who come to the United States to study in the early 1950s. This contemporary story of the immigrant experience describes the experiences of a cohort of Chinese Americans who are in their sixties today.

6   Shurkin, J. N. (1992). *Terman's kids: The groundbreaking study of how the gifted grow up.* Boston: Little, Brown.

This renowned study by Lewis Terman, begun in 1921, followed a group of gifted children throughout their lives. The survivors are now in their seventies and eighties. The stories of "Ancel," "Jess," "Shelley," and "Emily Tadashi" illustrate how hierarchies based on gender and social class produce varied lives—even among these gifted children who grew up and grew old in the same historical period.

7   CBS Fox Video. (1990). *Come see the paradise* [Film]. New York.

The Japanese internment during World War II is experienced through the eyes of a Japanese American family living in "Little Tokyo" in Los Angeles at the outbreak of the war. The film traces the family's experience through the war, including the realities of internment, and illustrates the way particular life events can both strengthen and weaken adaptive resources.

8   National Film Board of Canada. (1991). *Strangers in good company* [Film]. Burbank, CA: Buena Vista Home Video.

This film introduces us to a group of women who discover friendship and resourcefulness when their bus breaks down in the Quebec wilderness. The women confront old age and share their lives through reminiscences and old photographs. The women are not professional actresses, and the film lets each woman tell her story in her own way.

9   Dorris, M. (1987). *A yellow raft in blue water*. New York: Warner.

Beginning in the present and told backward in time, Dorris's novel tells the stories of three generations of Native American women. Hearing three versions of events in their lives illustrates dramatically the impact of historical time on three women who share similar positions on hierarchies based on gender, race or ethnicity, and social class but experience particular segments of historical time at different points in the life course.

10 Clausen, J. A. (1993). *American lives*. New York: Free Press.

Drawing on the groundbreaking Berkeley studies of human development, this book traces the lives of a sample of people born in the 1920s. Clausen demonstrates how adaptive strategies developed during an adolescence that coincided with the Great Depression continue to influence the lives of these individuals as they enter old age.

11 Silko, L. M. (1981). Lullaby. In *The storyteller*. New York: Seaver.

The limited lifetime options and powerlessness of a Native American couple weaken their adaptive resources in old age.

12 Uhlenberg, P., & Miner, S. (1996). Life course and aging: A cohort perspective. In R. Binstock & L. George (Eds.), *Handbook of aging and the social sciences* (4th ed., pp. 208-228).

An introduction to the life course perspective: In this chapter, the authors present the life course framework for studying the link between lives and history. They also emphasize the importance of differentiating among subcohorts to understand the impact of inequality on the lives of people of similar ages.

13 Guterson, D. (1995). *Snow falling on cedars.* New York: Random House.

Set on an island north of Puget Sound in 1954, this novel recounts the events surrounding the death of a local fisherman and subsequent trial of Kabuo Miyamoto, a Japanese American man charged with his murder. The mystery captures the legacy of World War II on relationships between Americans of Japanese and European heritage in this remote part of the Pacific Northwest.

PART II

Social and Psychological Contexts of Aging

Cultural Images of Old Age

Old age is accompanied by physical changes. Our immune systems are less able to fight off disease, and our capacity to mobilize physical energy declines. Our hearing and vision become less acute. Changes in appearance, such as gray hair and wrinkled skin, become more prevalent. In the absence of disease, these changes seldom interfere with the ability to pursue desired activities or fulfill social obligations (Atchley, 1997). Age-related physical changes, however, occur within a cultural context that assigns meanings to physical characteristics, and often the symbolic rather than the functional consequences of age-related changes have the most negative impact on older people. Here, we will explore the impact of cultural images about old age and the ways older people respond to them. Our discussion will emphasize the following points:

1. The images of old age reflected in our culture and the ways in which these images vary along hierarchies based on gender, race, and class

2. The consequences of these images for older people and the strategies older people use to maintain positive self-concepts in the face of negative images or of positive images they cannot attain

3. The importance of considering variation within groups in interpreting comparisons between groups

Contemporary U.S. culture reflects mixed images of older people. On the positive side, older people have been viewed as wise, kind, understanding, family oriented, generous, happy, knowledgeable, and patriotic. On the negative side, they have been depicted as sad, forgetful, lonely, dependent, demanding, ill-tempered, nosy, complaining, senile, selfish, bored, and inflexible (Hummert, Garstka, Shaner, & Strahm, 1995; Schmidt & Boland, 1986). Negative images of aging are more common among people younger than 65 than among elders themselves. For example, in a recent national survey, a majority of people younger than 65 believed that older people were lonely (64%), felt they were not needed (57%), and suffered from poor health (57%). In reality, only 6% of people over 65 said they were lonely, only 8% did not feel needed, and only 15% reported poor health (Speas & Obenshain, 1995).

Interest in ways to avoid the most negative aspects of aging has grown rapidly over the past several decades. Bookstores stock an expanding collection of titles advising older readers about fitness, nutrition, finances, and sexuality. Elderly Americans are advised to "keep their emotional balance," "stay active and involved," "pursue new interests," and "lead productive lives." Gerontologists focus our attention on the concept of *successful aging,* which the MacArthur Foundation Study of Successful Aging defines as a combination of physical health, high cognitive functioning, continued productivity, and active involvement in social relationships (Rowe & Kahn, 1997). Indeed, the book jacket of the MacArthur Foundation studies promises to "show you how the lifestyle choices you make now—more than heredity—determine your health and vitality." What was once described as a "roleless role" has been transformed into a prescription for activity and personal growth, for an awareness of expanded options and possibilities. Marilyn Zuckerman's poem, "After Sixty," one of the selections that follows, illustrates this redefinition of old age in the lives of older women.

Positive though these images of aging may be, they often depict a lifestyle predicated on class privilege. Recommendations to join an exercise class, learn ballroom dancing, or take up lap swimming imply sufficient discretionary income to purchase lessons or gain access to appropriate facilities. Retirement financial planning assumes assets to invest, and preventive health care recommendations require insurance or other financial resources to pay for physician visits and laboratory tests. Older people with meager incomes and poor health, as well as older people isolated in rural settings by lack of transportation or in inner cities by fear of crime, are hard pressed to fulfill these popular recommendations for so-called successful aging.

The images of successful aging reflected in popular guides are also more applicable to people in their 60s and 70s than to people in their 80s and 90s. Extreme old age is more often characterized by losses—loss of a future, of health and mobility, of cherished roles, of people one loves. Shortly before she died, Caroline Preston (as quoted in Thone, 1992) commented on the downside of these prescriptions for successful aging: "Such optimistic views of aging are as hard on us as our previous invisibility. We find ourselves yearning to be like people in these pictures and belabor ourselves for failing these role models" (p. 15). Norms for appropriate behavior in extreme old age are more nebulous. Ruth Raymond Thone (1992) suggests that emergent norms, at least for old women, can be captured in the phrase "aging gracefully," which she defines as being

> flexible, loving, a lady, positive, appreciative, accepting, tidy, active, open-minded, optimistic, proud of one's achievements, to have a zest for life, inner beauty, a sense of humor, to still learn and take risks, not to complain of one's aches and pains or other's faults, and not to worry about old age. (p. 13)

Not all elderly Americans define successful aging by positive adaptation and optimism. For many elders of color, aging is perceived "not as a series of adjustments, but rather as a process of survival" (Burton, Dilworth-Anderson, & Bengston, 1991). These contrasting images can be seen in the poem, "Mother to Son," by Langston

Hughes and the brief essay, "If I Had My Life to Live Over," by Nadine Stair. Reflecting on her life, Stair concludes that she was "too sensible," that she worried about and prepared too much for difficulties that never materialized. She learned from her life experiences that many anticipated troubles were "imaginary" and that her efforts to avoid problems were often unnecessary. The elderly mother in Hughes's poem has reached no such conclusion. The struggle for survival that characterized her younger years is still the dominant theme in old age. She reflects not on daisies and merry-go-rounds but on tacks and splinters. Rather than advising the reader to travel lighter and be sillier, she admonishes her son not to fall or sit down on the steps but to follow her example of "still climbin'."

As our development of the life course perspective reminded us, elderly Blacks have lived through a period of upheaval and change in the status of persons of color in the United States. Jim Crow patterns of segregation in public establishments have disappeared. Like Miss Jane Pittman, the title character in Ernest J. Gaines's (1971) novel, many can remember the first time they drank out of a public water fountain that had previously been restricted to Whites or sat at a previously segregated lunch counter. They remember "help wanted" advertisements in newspapers that searched for "a young White woman" or a "strong colored boy." For many elders of color, dreams that their children would achieve professional occupational status became realities. Yet public pronouncements regarding the declining significance of race clash with their everyday experiences and with official statistics regarding race and ethnic differences in levels of poverty, morbidity and mortality, and victimization by crime. Toni Morrison's (1975) essay, "A Slow Walk of Trees," illustrates this contrast between optimism based on progress achieved and pessimism based on goals yet unmet. "Most of us are plagued," she writes, "by a sense of being worn shell-thin by constant repression and hostility as well as the impression of being buoyed by visible testimony of tremendous strides."

Permutations in Images and Meanings of Old Age
Images Related to Gender

Satchell Paige, who would never reveal his age but was probably the oldest man ever to play professional baseball, recognized old age as a social construct when he asked, "How old would you be if you didn't know how old you was?" For women in our society, the answer might well be "older than a man my age." Women are viewed as old at least a decade sooner than are men, and old age brings greater loss of status for women than for men. These gender differences in the social construction of age can be attributed to the emphasis on youth within our culture and to the association between youth and sexuality, especially for women (Andersen, 1997):

A man's wrinkles will not define him as sexually undesirable until he reaches his late fifties. For him, sexual value is defined much more in terms of personality, intelligence, and earning power than physical appearance. Women, however, must rest their case largely on their bodies. (Bell, 1989, p. 236)

Given this double standard of aging, it is no wonder that many women are reluctant to reveal their ages, try to "pass" as younger than they are, and are complimented when told they don't "look their age" (Bell, 1989).

Although men also face negative stereotypes and loss of status as they get older, these experiences occur at a more advanced age. Compare, for example, the complexion of the female model who plans to fight aging "every step of the way" by using a popular moisturizer to that of the male model who touches up his graying hair. Negative consequences of aging for men focus more on occupational success than physical attractiveness (Andersen, 1997).

Negative though cultural images appear, older people do not internalize them uncritically. Older women retain an image of themselves grounded in the past, a sense of self that stays the same despite physical changes (Kaufman, 1986). A common device in comedy involving older women has the character exclaim, "Who's that?" after catching an unexpected glimpse of herself in a passing window. A 70-year-old woman interviewed by Kaufman (1986) explains the discrepancy between her chronological age and her subjective experience:

I don't feel 70. I feel about 30. . . . I just saw some slides of myself and was quite taken aback. That couldn't be me. That's a nice looking woman, but it couldn't possibly be me. Even though I look in the mirror all the time, I don't see myself as old. (p. 8)

Dean Rodeheaver and Joanne Stohs (1991) argue that such misperceptions are adaptive strategies that help older women overcome the effects of negative images of aging. Indeed, a survey by Ronald Goldsmith and Richard Heims (1992) found that 73% of people in their 60s, 83% of people in their 70s, and all of the respondents in their 80s thought they looked younger than their chronological age; no one in their 20s thought they looked younger than their chronological age.

Older people can diminish the impact of negative images by reinterpreting them from the standpoint of their own experiences. Jenny Joseph's poem, "Warning," illustrates this process by turning upside down the negative stereotype of the senile old woman wearing inappropriate clothes of clashing colors as she spends her money frivolously and violates rules of proper decorum. To Joseph, this behavior reflects greater freedom from social sanctions that constrain women "to set a good example." For today's older women, who were told that happiness came from fulfilling the needs of people they love, old age can be a time of autonomy, a time for "rediscovering and recreating themselves" (Thone, 1992, p. 63).

Images Related to Race/Ethnicity

Images of older people also vary by race and ethnicity. In some cases, these images reflect stereotypes based on the group in general, whereas in other cases, they apply primarily to old people.

Classic descriptions of old age in American Indian cultures emphasized the respect accorded elderly people. Councils of elders were the centers of political decision making, and elders were responsible for transmitting culture across generations. The anthropologist Joan Weibel-Orlando (1989) studied contemporary characteristics of successful aging by interviewing American Indian elders. She identified six criteria, all of which reflected an active engagement in ethnic life. American Indian elders who ranked high on successful aging were involved in charitable activities with a wide range of kin, friends, and other coethnics. They evidenced a high level of involvement in community roles (e.g., head dancers at powwows, song and prayer leaders at sun dances, medicine men and women, tribal council members, family heads, and caretaking grandparents), roles for which elderly American Indians are revered and that provide service to the ethnic community. Good health in late life was also associated with successful aging. As Weibel-Orlando explains,

> Good health in old age is not thought to be a given. Rather, it is a blessing. Long life is an indicator that a person may have been protected by powerful guardian spirits that kept him or her from harm's way when less well-endowed and protected age peers succumbed to diabetes, hypertension, alcoholism, and depression. (p. 63)

Older Blacks have confronted multiple negative images throughout their lives. Black women have been objectified as mammies, matriarchs, welfare recipients, and hot mommas (Collins, 1990), whereas Black men have been stereotyped as lazy workers, unstable husbands and fathers, and dangerous criminals. These controlling images are not the province of isolated individuals. Racist images have permeated political discourse. Public debates on Black families, for example, often use value-laden terms, such as "disorganization, maladjustment, and deterioration" (Andersen, 1997). The infamous Moynihan report, published in 1965, attributed the "deterioration of the fabric of Negro society" (p. 5) to the matriarchal structure of Black families. Moynihan attributed poverty, welfare dependency, crime, and out-of-wedlock births to the fact that over 20% of Black households were headed by women. Moynihan's description of the "tangle of pathology" characterizing female-headed households assumed that family arrangements were the cause rather than the consequence of discrimination. Citing evidence that Black women had surpassed Black men in educational achievement and entrance in professional and semiprofessional occupations, the report suggested that Black women "slow down, become less achievement-oriented, and give up their independence" (Giddings, 1984, p. 328). It also urged the government not to rest "until every able-bodied Negro man was working, even if this meant that some women's jobs had to be redesigned to enable men to fulfill them" (Rainwater & Yancey, 1967, p. 29). As the historian Paula Giddings (1984) observed, "Not *White men's* jobs, mind you—women's jobs. . . . The Moynihan report was not so much racist as it was sexist" (pp. 328-329).

Stereotypical images also emerge from the popularization of research results. Studies of older minority populations often involve statistical comparisons of people of color with Whites. Readers are shown, for example, that the average income of older Blacks is lower than the average income of older Whites, that the percentage of elderly Hispanic Americans living below the poverty level is higher than the percentage of elderly Whites, or that the probability of living in substandard housing is higher for American Indians than for older Whites. These statistical comparisons are accurate, and analyses of this type have been used successfully to justify allocating government dollars for public programs addressing the plight of low-income minority elders. Comparisons of group means, however, tell only part of the story. To fully comprehend the situation of any group of older people, we also need to consider differences within that group. From a statistical perspective, we need to consider dispersion or variation as well as central tendency (as introductory statistics students are often told, a person who doesn't swim can drown crossing a river that has an average depth of 3 feet). Statistical descriptions based on means can create an artificial picture of an "average" old person, such as the characterization of old Black women Jacqueline Jackson (1988) extracted from published reports:

> To illustrate with only slight exaggeration, the average old black woman lives in a blighted section of an inner-city or in an isolated rural area. Poor, poorly educated, and in poor health, she is economically dependent upon Social Security and other income transfer or in-kind programs (e.g., food stamps, subsidized housing, and Medicaid).
>
> This average old black woman is beset by problems, not the least of which are substandard housing in high crime areas, insufficient transportation, and inadequate access to mainstream health facilities, in part because she is stymied by and unable to cope successfully with bureaucratic institutions. If she is not gainfully employed, it is only because she is unemployed, involuntarily retired, or too ill or disabled to work. Old black women like to work because they gain dignity through working.
>
> A poor woman, she rarely uses community resources for the elderly, such as a center for senior citizens, most often because

she does not know about them nor of their eligibility requirements. . . . Extremely religious and often the matriarch of an extended family, [she] is surrounded by children, grandchildren, other relatives, or fictive kin, and by friends and neighbors who gleefully minister to her instrumental and emotional needs. "Granny" is also very happy when she is given the responsibility of rearing her grandchildren. (pp. 31-32)

Generalizing statistics based on aggregate data to predict the behavior or experiences of individuals is a type of error referred to as the *ecological fallacy*. Although some older Black women are surrounded by supportive children and extended kin, others are isolated or are themselves caring for grandchildren whose parents are struggling with drug addiction or economic survival. Many older Black women are destitute, but others enjoy considerable affluence. Although their risk of poverty is considerably higher than it is among either White women or Black men, many older Black women live above the poverty line. And although some older Black women lack the educational resources to negotiate medical and social welfare organizations, others pursue careers as nurses, social workers, lawyers, or physicians. The biographical selection, "Esse Quam Videri," in Part III, "Productive Activity," illustrates the ways in which a person can be advantaged on one hierarchy (social class) yet disadvantaged on others (race and gender). Mrs. Jones's life provides a sharp contrast to the image J. J. Jackson (1988) abstracted from accumulated averages.

Stereotypes need not always be negative in content to be detrimental in their consequences. The "model minority" myth applied to Asian Americans implies that unlike other people of color, Asians have "made it," that their diligence and hard work have been rewarded by economic success. This myth has several outcomes. First, like the composite of the "average Black woman," the image of the model minority ignores variation both among Asian American nationality groups in the United States and between generations within groups, thus obscuring the economic hardship and cultural isolation that many older Asian Americans experience. Studies reporting higher incomes among Asian American households often fail to adjust for the greater prevalence of multiple wage earners in Asian households and for the higher cost of living in geographic regions with high concentrations of Asian Americans (Woo, 1989). Second, they fail to report the situation of elderly households with low incomes, an omission that highlights again the importance of dispersion. The myth also overlooks the isolation experienced by recent elderly immigrants from Southeast Asia, who feel isolated not only by a different language and way of life but by the acculturation of their children and grandchildren. As we discuss in Part IV, "Family," first-generation Asian immigrants, who adhere more strongly to traditional views of old age and filial piety, are often confused and disappointed by the treatment they receive from their more Americanized children and grandchildren (Cheung, 1989). Last, the model minority myth reinforces the ideology of a meritocracy and creates divisions among racial and ethnic groups. Claims that Asian Americans have succeeded because of values stressing hard work in school and career imply that the stratification system in the United States is open and fair and that other groups could be equally successful if only they had appropriate values.

As we saw with negative images based on gender, older people do not incorporate ethnic stereotypes uncritically. The combination of controlling images and a system of racial oppression taught minority elders the necessity of reflecting dominant images in many contacts outside their own communities. Although this behavior may have reinforced dominant group stereotypes, it did not necessarily mean that people of color had internalized negative stereotypes. Public displays of compliance with expectations of the dominant group often coexist with alternative conceptions of self. Ella Surrey, an elderly Black respondent in John Gwaltney's (1980) *Drylongso: A Self-Portrait of Black America,* described this situation: "We have always been the best actors in the world. . . . We've always had to live two lives—one for them and one for ourselves" (pp. 238, 240). The older domestic workers interviewed by the sociologist Judith Rollins (1985) had maintained positive self-concepts despite "attempts to lure them into accepting their employers' definition of them as inferior" (p. 212). Among the most powerful weapons in this resistance was their familiarity with intimate details of their employers' lives:

> Raising their voices to little girl pitch, adding hand and facial gestures suggesting confusion and immaturity, my interviewees would act out scenes from their past experiences—typically scenes in which the employer was unable to cope with some problem and had to rely on the guidance and pragmatic efficiency of the domestic. It was interesting that these domestics, described historically and by some of the employers as childlike, perceived their employers as "flighty" and childlike. How *could* they buy into the evaluations of women they so perceived? (p. 215)

Resistance to controlling images and assertions of alternative definitions of self have been important themes in writings by Blacks. Patricia Hill Collins (1990) explains that these alternative definitions have "allowed Black women to cope with and, in most cases transcend the confines of race, class and gender oppression. . . . Most African American women simply don't define ourselves as Mammies, Matriarchs, welfare mothers, mules or sexually denigrated women" (p. 93). This process of reclaiming the power of self-definition is a major component in the struggle to maintain personal integrity in a climate of racism. Zora Neale Hurston's essay, "How It Feels to Be Colored Me," illustrates the ways in which race influenced her identity.

In Part I, "The Life Course Perspective," we described the struggles of Black women to teach their daughters to confront negative images and racial discrimination while maintaining the emotional strength needed to survive. Elizabeth ("Bessie") Delany, who, with her sister Sarah ("Sadie"), chronicled her "first 100 years" in the book, *Having Our Say* (Delany & Delany, 1993), describes her early encounters with racism:

> This race business does get under my skin. I have suffered a lot in my life because of it. If you asked me how I endured it, I would have to say it was because I had a good upbringing. My parents did not encourage me to be bitter. If they had, I'd have been so mean it would have killed my spirit a long, long time ago.
>
> As a child, every time I encountered prejudice—which was rubbed in your face, once segregation started under Jim Crow—I would feel it down to my core. I was not a crying child, except when it came to being treated badly because of my race, like when they wouldn't serve us at the drugstore counter. In those instances, I would go home and sit on my bed and weep and weep and weep, the tears streaming down my face.
>
> Now, Mama would come up and sit on the foot of my bed. She never said a word. She knew what I was feeling. She just did not want to encourage my rage. So my Mama would just sit and look at me while I cried, and it comforted me. I knew that she understood, and that was the most soothing salve. (p. 74)

As their collaborator Amy Heart explains, each sister developed her own strategies for coping with racism. Bessie, who was a dentist, espoused confrontation. For some of today's Blacks, struggles against racism included confrontation, coupled with efforts to change the fabric of U.S. society. Today's elders of color were among the leaders of the Civil Rights movement, which began in the 1950s. Although most civil rights leaders in history books are Black men, women also provided leadership. The writers Gloria Hull, Patricia Bell Scott, and Barbara Smith (1982) captured this omission in the title of their anthology, *All the Women Are White, All the Blacks Are Men, But Some of Us Are Brave.* For example, the organzing efforts of the Women's Political Council, an organization of middle-class Black women in Montgomery, Alabama, played a central role in organizing that city's bus boycott, which was sparked by the arrest of Rosa Parks. An activist with the National Association for the Advancement of Colored People (NAACP), Mrs. Parks was arrested when she refused to give up her seat to a White male passenger.

Confrontation is not the only strategy for coping with racism. Sadie Delany, who was a schoolteacher, manipulated the system by role-playing, a strategy of which her sister did not always approve. Bessie describes one incident:

Once, when we were new to the neighborhood, a White policeman came knocking on the door. We were a little afraid. What did he want from us? Well, we went upstairs and opened the window and called down to him. That's what we do when we aren't sure about opening the door for someone. Sadie said to me, "Let me handle him." She leaned out the window and said:

"Officer, can I help you?"

And he called up: "We're raising money for the auxiliary, and I'm selling tickets to a dance."

And she giggled and said, "Why officer, thank you very much, but I'm too old to go to a dance!" And she giggled some more and shut the window.

Now, I just hate it when Sadie plays dumb like that! I told her, "Sadie, that fella must think you're the dumbest nigger alive." And she said, "So what? I didn't make him angry, did I? And I've still got my money, don't I?" It annoys me, but I have to admit she was right. (Delany & Delany, 1993, p. 194)

The excerpt from Pardee Lowe's autobiographical story, "Father Cures a Presidential Fever," provides another illustration of childhood encounters with racism among people who are elderly today. Lowe's selection describes a young Chinese American boy's encounter with what Marie Hong (1993) describes as "the precarious position of Asian Americans during the 1910s and 1920s" (p. 175).

Images Related to Social Class

Images of older people have always been tied to social class, but our cultural images of poverty and affluence in old age have changed in recent years. Along with poor health, poverty is one of the most dreaded aspects of old age. Images of destitute old men subsisting in skid row hotels or of "shopping bag ladies" carrying their lifetime of accumulated possessions in grocery carts have replaced images of the county poor farm in popular representations of poverty in late life. People today are less likely to blame older people for low economic status than they were earlier in this century. Pre-Depression beliefs that poverty in old age resulted from laziness and failure to save for the future have been displaced by images of older people as the "deserving poor," images that provide political justifications for income transfers, such as social security and medicare. These changes are recent, however, and today's older people grew up with the pre-Depression stereotypes of the elderly poor, stereotypes that blamed the victim. Values emphasizing hard work, thrift, and self-reliance can still undermine self-esteem and discourage acceptance of programs viewed as "welfare" or "poverty" among some old people, particularly those in the oldest cohorts.

Older people today are less likely to be poor than were older people in the past, and the economic situation of the average older

American has improved dramatically over the past two decades, particularly in comparison to younger people (Quinn & Smeeding, 1993). In 1959, 35% of people aged 65 and older had incomes below the official poverty level. By 1997, this percentage had dropped to below 11% (from U.S. Bureau of the Census, available at http://www.census.gov/hhes/poverty/poverty97/pv97est1.html). At the other end of the income distribution, a small percentage of the elderly population has increased their accumulation of wealth. Consistent with the growing disparity between the rich and the poor in the general population, the most affluent 5% of Americans over age 70 own 27% of all the aggregate wealth of that age cohort (Villa, Wallace, & Markides, 1997).

The relative improvement in the economic status of the older population has given rise to a new class-related stereotype: the affluent older person who collects unearned and unneeded benefits at the expense of less affluent workers. Older people have also become scapegoats for the burgeoning budget deficit. According to this "intergenerational inequity" argument, elderly people receive too large a portion of public social expenditures, primarily through social security and medical care benefits. Advocates of this approach posited a causal connection between improvements in the economic status of elderly people and increasing poverty rates among children (Cornman & Kingson, 1996). The sociologist Jill Quadagno (1999) challenges this causal link between old-age entitlements and childhood poverty. She attributes increases in childhood poverty to a growth in the number of families headed by single women who are struggling to support their families on inadequate earnings in a gender-segregated labor force. Quadagno also (1999) challenges the alleged rate of increase in government spending on entitlements for the elderly population. Her analyses indicate that, once we adjust for inflation, entitlement programs for older Americans have not grown significantly since the 1970s. She argues that the percentage increases in spending for programs like social security are a product of cuts in other discretionary programs (e.g., government-sponsored research, small business programs) and reduced taxes on individuals and corporations. Quadagno concludes that the rhetoric of crisis surrounding social security is largely a social construction designed to rally political support for further reducing government programs.

This new stereotype of the affluent elderly population has also been reflected in advertising. Twenty years ago, old people were absent from advertisements, except those selling products such as laxatives and denture adhesives. Today, advertisements geared specifically to older consumers feature tennis rackets, luxury automobiles, and Caribbean cruises, as well as vitamins, health insurance, and (almost invisible) hearing aids. The models in these ads, although visibly gray (or, more likely, silver haired), are active, physically fit adults enthusiastically pursuing or sagely planning their retirement leisure.

These new marketing strategies provide a welcome contrast to the negative images of old age in past advertising, but they can also deflect attention from the needs of low-income elders and from the precarious economic positions of elders just below the poverty level. Although fewer than 9% of older Americans have incomes below the poverty level, the risk of poverty increases to 25% for elderly Blacks and to 23.5% for elderly Hispanics. Among elderly women living alone, these risks increase to 48% for Blacks and 49% of Hispanics, in comparison to 21% among European Americans (U.S. Bureau of the Census, 1996). Another category of vulnerable elders is comprised of the 40% of all elderly persons whose incomes fall between 100% and 200% of the poverty threshold. The economist Tim Smeeding (1990) calls this group "'Tweeners," because their incomes are too high to qualify for "safety net" programs designed for the poor yet too low to guarantee an adequate lifestyle and economic security. The gerontologist Meredith Minkler (1989) is concerned that these disadvantaged elderly people not be hidden behind what she describes as a misleadingly homogeneous picture of the affluent older consumer: "As low income elderly persons are rendered less visible, . . . governments may find increasing justification for cutbacks in the programs and services that are most needed by those elderly people who fail to fit the new, affluent stereotype" (p. 22). Social security has been a policy success story, lifting 15 million elderly Americans out of poverty and relieving adult children of the burden of supporting impoverished elderly parents. The Social Security Administration estimates that without social security, half of American retirees—and 60% of all women—would fall below the poverty threshold. For two thirds of elderly Americans, social security is their primary source of income. For 18%, it is their only source.

Key Issues

Here, we have discussed the following issues:

1. Positive and negative images of older people and popular prescriptions for "successful aging"
2. The double standard of aging and images related to gender
3. Strategies for confronting negative images based on race or ethnicity
4. Positive and negative consequences of changing images of poverty and affluence in old age

The Readings

Several of the readings that follow illustrate attempts to embrace positive definitions of aging. Marilyn Zuckerman's poem, "After Sixty," reflects an awareness of expanded options and possibilities for women as they enter old age. Rejecting the view of postmenopausal women as no longer useful or productive, Zuckerman declares old age as a time to invent a new story for her life. Rather than mourning lost roles, she redefines them as "distractions" that she will "not take with her" on the rest of life's journey. On the "other side of sixty," there is still time to invent a new story.

Carolyn Heilbrun (1997) reflects on life beyond 60 in her recent book, *The Last Gift of Time.* A writer who has chronicled changes in women's lives over the past decades, Heilbrun ponders the unforeseen pleasures in old age from the perspective of a successful, well-educated White woman. The excerpt reiterates the theme of continuity of one's inner self despite changes in outward appearance. Her view of successful aging highlights the importance of intergenerational relationships—ties that have value for the young as well as the old.

Several selections illustrate the range of meanings people attach to old age. We already introduced several of these readings: Langston Hughes's poem, "Mother to Son;" Nadine Stair's essay, "If I Had My Life to Live Over;" and Jenny Joseph's poem, "Warning."

This process of defining oneself is also illustrated in Zora Neale Hurston's selection, "How It Feels to Be Colored Me." Hurston's descriptions of the "day that I became colored" and of the times when "my color comes" illustrate race as a social construct rather than as a biological trait. As a child in an all-Black community, Zora noticed differences in skin color, but these differences were not a central principle in organizing her identity. "During this period," she writes, "White people differed from colored to me only in that they rode through town and never lived there." Only when she left her small Florida town to attend school in Jacksonville did she become "a little colored girl . . . in my heart as well as in the mirror."

Encountering racism, however, did not mean internalizing its imagery. In recognizing the constraints a segregated world attempted to impose on her, she transcended their psychic impact. "I am not tragically colored," she writes. Instead, she confronted her world of barriers and opportunities with "a sharpened oyster knife." Not all older Blacks grew up in racially homogeneous towns. Most, however, grew up in racially homogeneous families and in racially homogeneous neighborhoods. As Jackson, McCullough, Gurin, and Broman (1991) have demonstrated, these racially homogeneous environments served an important insulating function in developing identities independent of racist imagery.

Pardee Lowe's autobiographical account, "Father Cures a Presidential Fever," provides another account of a child's encounter with the constraints of racism and with the contradiction between values and reality that the Swedish economist Gunnar Myrdahl characterized as "the American Dilemma." Told by his elementary teacher that "every single one of you can be President of the United States someday," the young Lowe is unprepared for the blatant prejudice and discrimination that faced Chinese Americans in the early decades of the century. Unlike the Black mothers we have described, Lowe's father did not grow up in the United States, and

Lowe's story illustrates a cultural conflict between the Chinese father and the Chinese American son. The 1910s and 1920s were characterized by a "melting pot" ideology, which frequently produced a wedge between foreign-born parents and their "Americanizing" children. Mr. Lowe, who is in his 90s, received an MBA from Harvard University in 1932 and was the U.S. State Department officer in charge of UNESCO Affairs in Asia, Africa, and the Middle East.

The selection, "When a House Is Not a Home," explores the meaning of shelter among chronically homeless older men. Christopher Elias and Thomas Inui describe the situation of some of the elderly poor who can be overlooked by media images stressing newfound affluence among older people. In the world of these 35 elderly men, shelter meant more than a place to stay warm and dry. Losing their homes meant losing their routines of life, a supportive domestic environment, an address and phone number, and a place to invite friends and family. The experiences of these men illustrate several key points. First, not all older Americans are characterized by the improvements in economic status reflected in aggregate statistics. Once again, we learn the importance of considering variation as well as central tendency. Second, these men are not passive victims. Despite poor health, limited financial resources, and a treacherous environment, these men manage to survive. Last, the reading reminds us of interlocking hierarchies based on gender, race, and class. All of the respondents are men, and the majority (29 out of 35) are White, yet they are clearly disadvantaged by social class.

Systems of inequality generate privilege as well as disadvantage, and the autobiographical statement, "The Big Boys," by Jack Culberg provides a glimpse of aging from the perspective of an affluent White man. A retired CEO, Culberg contrasts his experience of old age with those of earlier cohorts. The accumulation of advantage across his work life has provided him with a comfortable life style and the resources for coping with the challenges of retirement. Although missing the excitement—and prestige—that the corporate world provided, he was able to ease the transition by consulting and continuing to amass financial resources. "I still have my hand in," he says with some pride.

After Sixty

Marilyn Zuckerman

The sixth decade is coming to an end
Doors have opened and shut
The great distractions are over—
    passion . . . children . . . the long
    indenture of marriage
I fold them into a chest
I will not take with me when I go

Everyone says the world is flat and finite
    on the other side of sixty
That I will fall clear off the edge
    into darkness
That no one will hear from me again
    or want to

But I am ready for the knife slicing
    into the future
    for the quiet that explodes inside
    to join forces with the strong old woman
    to throw everything away and begin
    again

Now there is time to tell the story
    —time to invent the new one
Time to chain myself to a fence outside the
    missile base
To throw my body before a truck loaded
    with phallic images
To write Thou Shalt Not Kill
    on the hull of a Trident submarine
To pour my own blood on the walls of the
    Pentagon
To walk a thousand miles with a begging
    bowl in my hand

There are places on this planet
    where women past the menopause
    put on the tribal robes
    smoke pipes of wisdom
    —fly

Listening to the Young(er)

Carolyn Heilbrun

Although the old, as we are daily warned, are growing in numbers while the population of the young yearly declines, it is the young who influence the world we live in. Everyone from actors to tennis players to writers is getting younger. Except in advertisements of dentifrices designed for the wearers of false teeth or laxatives to rescue the aging from their constipation, the young dominate the airwaves, television, the fashion ads, the Internet (and the technology to access it), and the movies. The aging, while nervous about HMOs, Medicare, and Social Security, do not seem to play a very large role in this country's affairs—aging women even less than men. If, therefore, we wish to keep up with at least some part of what is going in the world, it is the young to whom we must turn.

Without my children, my graduate students, and my friends ten years younger than I and counting, I would probably be living in a state of sad self-satisfaction, ignorant of much that is happening around me. Not about politics, which one can follow readily enough, or events, like O. J. Simpson's trial, screaming at us from every corner, but the feel of life, its beat as it sounds each day. Lionel Trilling, speaking of what he called "manners," put this so well that I must let him say it for me:

What I understand by manners is a culture's hum and buzz of implication. I mean the whole evanescent context in which its explicit statements are made. It is that part of a culture which is made up of half-uttered or unuttered or unutterable expressions of value. They are hinted at by small actions, sometimes . . . tone, gesture, emphasis, or rhythm, sometimes by the words that are used with a special frequency or a special meaning.

It is precisely this that we ought to pick up from the young. To try and stay sufficiently *au courant* to know it all ourselves is difficult, tedious, and affected. Our deepest feelings are, I think, in a different place. But to cut the hum and buzz completely from our consciousness, dismissing it with a tired or, worse, critical gesture, is to cut ourselves off from our culture and the delightful sense of, however superficially, learning something new while regarding it with that peaceful (but never complacent) distance age provides.

The lives of the young tend to be tumultuous and thus offer us, if we have young friends, vicarious experience of the best kind, the kind it would be painful in the extreme, not to say ludicrous, to have to undergo oneself. Friendships between those of sufficiently different generations, so that the variance in years counts for markedly distinct experiences, offer satisfying knowledge and vicarious experience to the old. In the history of their sex lives, if in no other way, the young and I, am delighted to discover, might have belonged to cultures many miles and many centuries apart. My day-to-day experiences are, on the whole, and barring disasters, predictable; without hearing from the young, I would feel only half alive.

Most of my young friends are smarter than I am. They sometimes argue with me about this, which is kind of them and I appreciate it, but the young being smarter—which is not to say wiser—is the whole point. One of the dangers inherent in friendships among the old is that they are no smarter now than they ever were; one usually knows them all too well, and vice versa. In Virginia Woolf's *To the Lighthouse,* Mr. Bankes, regretting what has become of his relationship to Mr. Ramsay, thinks: "What with one thing and another, the pulp had gone out of their friendship. Whose fault it was he could not say, only, after a time, repetition had taken the place of newness. It was to repeat that they met." With those who are younger, one is much less likely to repeat.

An older woman has told me a story about my lawyer son when he was in law school that nicely demonstrates how the young may serve those further along in life. This older woman entered law school when she was past fifty and when her youngest child was in college, becoming my son's classmate. The work did not faze her, but long-entrenched guilt toward her children did, as it does most mothers. At the end of the first term, her child in college called to say: "But who will make the Christmas cookies?" Since my son, who is large, had raised her, who is small, over his head in celebration of her winning the moot court competition, she went to him for consolation over this complaint. My son looked at her: "Fuck the Christmas cookies," he pronounced. She told me this years later, filling my reluctant maternal heart with feminist pride, as hers had, for a single moment, overflowed with relief.

So if those who are younger talk, and those who are older listen, and if, as I believe, the young like to talk to or anyway "at" those older, for the very same satisfaction the difference in generations offers each, isn't it pretty much a one-way street? Do we who are getting on serve only to listen to the young? Have we nothing to tell them that is worth their hearing, even if they may feel a little bored hearing it? I do not mean that we sit silent and judgmental, like doctrinaire Freudian analysts; we speak, we respond, we question.

But as I pondered this a good while I came only recently to understand that it is our very presence that is important to the young. They want us to be there: not in their homes, perhaps, not watching them with a baleful eye as they go about their daily work, but *there.* We reassure them that life continues, and if we listen, we assure them that it matters to us that it continues. If we do not tiresomely insist that the past was better, that the present is without morals or good habits or healthy living or (heaven help us) family values, whatever they are; if we do not insist on recounting ancient anecdotes as original as a tape recording and as easily rendered audible; if we do not recount adventures in the past, even if requested to do so, then the young will sometimes actually seek—they will not openly ask—for something we are equipped to give them. What to call it? It is the essence of having lived long, it is the unstated assurance that most disasters pass, it is the survival of deprivation and death and rejection that renders our sympathy of value.

I can remember graduating from college and assuring myself that never, never would I look like those old fragile beings staggering along in the academic procession. Perhaps the young can sense what I now know: that I may look like some of those ancient beings, but inside of me I can still partake of all the spontaneous joy of youth—to which is added the exquisite unlikelihood of its recurrence. Like lovers parting in wartime, who may never meet again or know each other if they do, we who grow old can taste the biting edge of passion's anticipated annulment, and savor it as the young cannot. But I believe the young perceive what we cannot tell them.

Mother to Son

Langston Hughes

Well, son, I'll tell you:
Life for me ain't been no crystal stair.
It's had tacks in it,
And splinters,
And boards torn up,
And places with no carpet on the floor—
Bare.
But all the time
I'se been a-climbin' on,
And reachin' landin's,
And turnin' corners,
And sometimes goin' in the dark
Where there ain't been no light.
So boy, don't you turn back.
Don't you set down on the steps
'Cause you finds it's kinder hard.
Don't you fall now—
For I'se still goin', honey,
I'se still climbin',
And life for me ain't been no crystal stair.

If I Had My Life to Live Over

Nadine Stair

I'd dare to make more mistakes next time. I'd relax, I would limber up. I would be sillier than I have been this trip. I would take fewer things seriously. I would take more chances. I would climb more mountains and swim more rivers. I would eat more ice cream and less beans. I would perhaps have more actual troubles, but I'd have fewer imaginary ones.

You see, I'm one of those people who live sensibly and sanely hour after hour, day after day. Oh, I've had my moments, and if I had it to do over again, I'd have more of them. In fact, I'd try to have nothing else. Just moments, one after another, instead of living so many years ahead of each day. I've been one of those persons who never goes anywhere without a thermometer, a hot water bottle, a raincoat and a parachute. If I had to do it again, I would travel lighter than I have.

If I had my life to live over, I would start barefoot earlier in the spring and stay that way later in the fall. I would go to more dances. I would ride more merry-go-rounds. I would pick more daisies.

Warning

Jenny Joseph

When I am an old woman I shall wear
    purple
With a red hat which doesn't go, and
    doesn't suit me.
And I shall spend my pension on brandy
    and summer gloves
And satin sandals, and say we've no money
    for butter.
I shall sit down on the pavement when I'm
    tired
And gobble up samples in shops and press
    alarm bells
And run my stick along the public railings
And make up for the sobriety of my youth.
I shall go out in my slippers in the rain
And pick the flowers in other people's
    gardens
And learn to spit.

You can wear terrible shirts and grow more
    fat
And eat three pounds of sausages at a go
Or only bread and pickle for a week
And hoard pens and pencils and beermats
    and things in boxes.

But now we must have clothes that keep us
    dry
And pay our rent and not swear in the street
And set a good example for the children.
We must have friends to dinner and read
    the papers.

But maybe I ought to practise a little now?
So people who know me are not too
    shocked and surprised
When suddenly I am old, and start to wear
    purple.

How It Feels to Be Colored Me

Zora Neale Hurston

I am colored but I offer nothing in the way of extenuating circumstances except the fact that I am the only Negro in the United States whose grandfather on the mother's side was not an Indian chief.

I remember the very day that I became colored. Up to my thirteenth year I lived in the little Negro town of Eatonville, Florida. It is exclusively a colored town. The only white people I knew passed through the town going to or coming from Orlando. The native whites rode dusty horses, the Northern tourists chugged down the sandy village road in automobiles. The town knew the Southerners and never stopped cane chewing when they passed. But the Northerners were something else again. They were peered at cautiously from behind curtains by the timid. The more venturesome would come out on the porch to watch them go past and got just as much pleasure out of the tourists as the tourists got out of the village.

The front porch might seem a daring place for the rest of the town, but it was a gallery seat for me. My favorite place was atop the gate-post. Proscenium box for a born first-nighter. Not only did I enjoy the show, but I didn't mind the actors knowing that I liked it. I usually spoke to them in passing. I'd wave at them and when they returned my salute, I would say something like this: "Howdy-do-well-I-thank-you-where-you-goin'?" Usually automobile or the horse paused at this, and after a queer exchange of compliments, I would probably "go a piece of the way" with them, as we say in farthest Florida. If one of

my family happened to come to the front in time to see me, of course negotiations would be rudely broken off. But even so, it is clear that I was the first "welcome-to-our-state" Floridian, and I hope the Miami Chamber of Commerce will please take notice.

During this period, white people differed from colored to me only in that they rode through town and never lived there. They liked to hear me "speak pieces" and sing and wanted to see me dance the parse-me-la, and gave me generously of their small silver for doing these things, which seemed strange to me for I wanted to do them so much that I needed bribing to stop. Only they didn't know it. The colored people gave no dimes. They deplored any joyful tendencies in me, but I was their Zora nevertheless. I belonged to them, to the nearby hotels, to the country—everybody's Zora.

But changes came in the family when I was thirteen, and I was sent to school in Jacksonville. I left Eatonville, the town of the oleanders, as Zora. When I disembarked from the riverboat at Jacksonville, she was no more. It seemed that I had suffered a sea change. I was not Zora of Orange County any more, I was now a little colored girl. I found it out in certain ways. In my heart as well as in the mirror, I became a fast brown—warranted not to rub nor run.

But I am not tragically colored. There is no great sorrow dammed up in my soul, nor lurking behind my eyes. I do not mind at all. I do not belong to the sobbing school of Negrohood who hold that nature somehow has given them a lowdown dirty deal and whose feelings are all hurt about it. Even in the helter-skelter skirmish that is my life, I have seen that the world is to the strong regardless of a little pigmentation more or less. No, I do not weep at the world—I am too busy sharpening my oyster knife.

Someone is always at my elbow reminding me that I am the granddaughter of slaves. It fails to register depression with me. Slavery is sixty years in the past. The operation was successful and the patient is doing well, thank you. The terrible struggle that made me an American out of a potential slave said "On the line!" The Reconstruction said "Get set!"; and the generation before said "Go!" I am off to a flying start and I must not halt in the stretch to look behind and weep. Slavery is the price I paid for civilization, and the choice was not with me. It is a bully adventure and worth all that I have paid through my ancestors for it. No one on earth ever had a greater chance for glory. The world to be won and nothing to be lost. It is thrilling to think—to know that for any act of mine, I shall get twice as much praise or twice as much blame. It is quite exciting to hold the center of the national stage, with the spectators not knowing whether to laugh or to weep.

The position of my white neighbor is much more difficult. No brown specter pulls up a chair beside me when I sit down to eat. No dark ghost thrusts its leg against mine in bed. The game of keeping what one has is never so exciting as the game of getting.

I do not always feel colored. Even now I often achieve the unconscious Zora of Eatonville before the Hegira.[1] I feel most colored when I am thrown against a sharp white background.

For instance at Barnard. "Beside the waters of the Hudson" I feel my race. Among the thousand white persons, I am a dark rock surged upon, and overswept, but through it all, I remain myself. When covered by the waters, I am; and the ebb but reveals me again.

Sometimes it is the other way around. A white person is set down in our midst, but the contrast is just as sharp for me. For instance, when I sit in the drafty basement that is The New World Cabaret with a white person, my color comes. We enter chatting about any little nothing that we have in common and are seated by the jazz waiters. In the abrupt way that jazz orchestras have, this one plunges into a number. It loses no time in circumlocutions, but gets right down to business. It constricts the thorax and splits the heart with its tempo and narcotic harmonies. This orchestra grows rambunctious, rears on its hind legs and attacks the tonal veil with primitive fury, rending it, clawing it until it breaks through to the jungle beyond. I follow those heathen—follow them exultingly. I dance wildly inside myself; I yell within, I whoop; I shake my assegai[2] above my head, I hurl it true to the mark *yeeeeoouw!* I am in the jungle and living in the jungle way. My face is painted red and yellow and my body is painted blue. My pulse is throbbing like a war drum. I want to slaughter something—give paid, give death to what, I do not know. But the piece ends. The men of the orchestra wipe their lips and rest their fingers. I creep back slowly to the veneer we call civilization with the last tone and find the white friend sitting motionless in his seat, smoking calmly.

"Good music they have here," he remarks, drumming the table with his fingertips.

Music. The great blobs of purple and red emotion have not touched him. He has only heard what I felt. He is far away and I see him but dimly across the ocean and the continent that have fallen between us. He is so pale with his whiteness then and I am so colored.

At certain times I have no race, I am *me*. When I set my hat at a certain angle and saunter down Seventh Avenue, Harlem City, feeling as snooty as the lions in front of the Forty Second Street Library, for instance. So far as my feelings are concerned, Peggy Hopkins Joyce on the Boule Mich with her gorgeous raiment, stately carriage, knees knocking together in a most aristocratic manner, has nothing on me. The cosmic Zora emerges. I belong to no race nor time. I am the eternal feminine with its string of beads.

I have no separate feeling about being an American citizen and colored. I am merely a fragment of the Great Soul that surges within the boundaries. My country, right or wrong.

Sometimes, I feel discriminated against, but it does not make me angry. It merely astonishes me. How can any deny themselves the pleasure of my company? It's beyond me.

But in the main, I feel like a brown bag of miscellany propped against a wall. Against a wall in company with other bags, white, red and yellow. Pour out the contents, and there is discovered a jumble of small things priceless and worthless. A first-water diamond, an empty spool, bits of broken glass, lengths of string, a key to a door long since crumbled away, a rusty knife-blade, old shoes saved for a road that never was and never will be, a nail bent under the weight of things too heavy for any nail, a dried flower or two still a little fragrant. In your hand is the brown bag. On the ground before you is the jumble it held—so much like the jumble in the bags, could they be emptied, that all might be dumped in a single heap and the bags refilled without altering the content of any greatly. A bit of colored glass more or less would not matter. Perhaps that is how the Great Stuffer of Bags filled them in the first place—who knows?

Notes

1. Refers to Mohammad's flight from Mecca in 622 and more generally means an escape from danger. [Eds.]

2. Hunting spear. [Eds.]

14

Father Cures a Presidential Fever

Pardee Lowe

How I came to be infected with Presidentitis even now I find somewhat difficult to explain. That it was not congenital was amply demonstrated by Father's matter-of-fact superiority over such divine foolishness. And Mother, bless her realistic Chinese soul, never affected awareness of such mundane matters until the political clubs of our neighborhood (we lived in the toughest one in East Belleville) celebrated under her very nose with torchlight parades, drunken sprees, black eyes, and cracked skulls the glorious victories of their Men of the People. Whenever this happened she would exclaim, "My, my, what queer people the Americans are!"

The first time Father discovered how long the firstborn man child of his household had been exposed to the ravages of this dread disease, he was horrified. "Unbelievable!" he stormed. But Mother, who had a strong will of her own, flew right back at him. And when she cried aloud, with Heaven as her witness that she did not know how I caught it or how she could have prevented it, Father recognized the justice of her remarks. She couldn't. Kwong Chong, our own neighborhood dry-goods store, household duties, and two new babies kept Mother so harassed that she had no time to chase us about the streets or down the back alleys. Later, to still her flow of tears, Father even grudgingly admitted his full responsibility. By moving our family to an American neighborhood, according to Mother, he had needlessly exposed us all to the malady.

That this was the source of the trouble, probably no one knew better than Father.

When the 1906 San Francisco earthquake and fire consumed all his worldly goods and forced him to flee Chinatown with his wife, two babies in arms, and a motley feudal retinue of kinsmen, relatives, and garment-sewing employees, he merely considered it more or less a blessing in disguise. From the ashes of this catastrophe, which represented for Mother the end of her Chinatownian world, Father's thoughts and plans for the future soared like a phoenix.

At long last the visions and dreams for his offspring, present and potential, would be realized. His family would rub shoulders with Americans. They would become good American citizens albeit remaining Chinese. They would inhabit a hyphenated world. By some formula, which he never was able to explain, they would select only the finest attributes of each contributory culture. They would reflect everlasting credit on him and on the name of Lowe.

(Even then, Father's faith passed all human understanding. He expected us somehow to muddle through. We did—but in a manner totally unexpected.)

From Father's point of view, we children were to be raised at home according to the old and strict Chinese ideal. But in that ever-widening circle of American neighborhood life beyond the narrow confines of our home, Father had no control. A daily commuter to his shop in San Francisco's Chinatown, an hour's ride away by steam train and ferry, he was never fully apprised of our actions until too late.

He was ignorant, for instance, of what transpired in the large wooden public school situated some three short blocks from our home. He was confident we were in good hands. If he had only known what was awaiting his son there, he might not have been so eager to have me acquire an American schooling.

When at the age of five I entered the portals of this mid-Victorian architectural firetrap, surrounded by its iron-spiked fence and tall trees, for the first time, I recognized it as an international institution in which I was free to indulge my own most un-Chinese inclinations—and, unintentionally to be sure, to undermine Father's high hopes.

I can still vividly remember the strange excitement of the first morning roll call, which was to be repeated daily for many years to come. Clumsily, the teacher pronounced our names. As we rose, she checked our nationality.

"Louisa Fleishhacker—*Austrian.*" She underlined the word *Austrian.* "Elsie Forsythe—*English.* Penelope Lincoln—*American Negro.* Yuri Matsuyama—*Japanese.* Nancy Mullins—*Irish.* Maria Pucinelli—*Italian.* Stella Saceanu—*Rumanian.* Anna Zorich—*Serbian.*" Finishing with the girls, she turned the page. "Michael Castro—*Portuguese.* Heinz Creyer—*German.* Thorvald Ericson—*Swedish.* Philippe Etienne—*French.* Nicholas Katanov—*Russian.* Pardee Lowe—*Chinese.* Robert MacPherson—*Scotch.* And Francisco Trujillo—*Mexican.*"

There we stood. In the company of fifteen other beginners no two in the entire group of the same nationality, I was embarking upon a new and glorious adventure, the educational melting pot, which was to make every one of us, beyond peradventure, an American.

It pleased Father no end to know that I liked to go to American school. He informed Mother proudly that it denoted a scholarly spirit well becoming a Chinese. If he had only glimpsed what lay back of my mind as I saw him gaily off on the morning seven-forty commuters' train he might have derived much less satisfaction.

No sooner was Father's back turned than I would dash madly to the streetcar line. On my way I would stop and pick a bunch of posies from our neighbors' back yards, praying fervently that I would be the only pupil waiting for Miss McIntyre, our teacher. Disappointment invariably awaited me, for I was not alone. Anna, Nancy, Penelope, and Robert, sharing exactly the same sentiments, always managed to get there ahead of me.

As soon as we spotted Miss McIntyre's tall figure alighting from the car, we sprang forward. With a warm smile of affection which enfolded us all, she allowed us to grab her hands, snatch her books from her arms and literally drag her from the rear step of the car to the front steps of the school, happily protesting every step of the way: "Now, children! . . . Now *children!*"

Coming mainly from immigrant homes where parents were too preoccupied with earning a living to devote much time to their children, we transferred our youthful affections to this one person who had both the time and the disposition to mother us. We showered upon our white-haired teacher the blind, wholehearted loyalty of the young. Our studies we readily absorbed, not because we particularly liked them so much as because it was "she" who taught us. Thus, with the three R's, games, stories, a weekly bath which she personally administered in the school's bathroom—two pupils at a time— and her love, she whom we staunchly enshrined in our hearts laid the rudimentary but firm foundation of our personal brand of American culture.

Then, one day it happened. Miss McIntyre, herself the daughter of an Irish immigrant who had come to California during the Gold Rush, read to us with deep emotion the life of George Washington. The virtues displayed by the Father of Our Country, particularly when confessing his act of chopping down the cherry tree, were, she led us to believe, the very ones which would, if faithfully practiced, win us equal fame. Concluding the narrative, she looked in turn at Anna, Penelope, and Robert. She was challenging us to higher things. As her eyes caught mine, she added with conviction, "And every single one of you can be President of the United States someday!"

I shall never forget that occasion. To be President in our minds was like being God, with the difference that everybody knew what the President looked like. His pictures were in every newspaper. Even in the funny sheets, I sometimes saw him. Big as life, with his grinning mouthful of teeth, eyeglasses gleaming, and his mustache bristling in the breeze of the political opposition—he looked the spitting image of Father. The only difference I could detect was that Father preferred the bamboo duster to the "Big Stick," and "*Jun Ho Ah!*" was as near as he ever came to "Bully!"

Everything I did from this moment on served only to strengthen the grandiose dream whose chief interlocking threads included myself, Father, and the Presidency. Much to the disgust of my more active playmates and the envy of my bookworm friends, I became a walking encyclopedia of American history. I could repeat the full names and dates of every President of these United States. And I knew the vivid, gory details, authentic and apocryphal, of every important military engagement in which Americans took part—and always victoriously.

I hounded the settlement librarian for books, and more books. Like one famished, I devoured all of James Fenimore Cooper's novels. Lodge and Roosevelt's *Hero Tales from American History* fascinated me. As I read Abbot's *The Story of Our Navy* and Johnston's *Famous Scouts, Including Trappers, Pioneers and Soldiers of the Frontier*, my sense of patriotism quickened. So stirred was I by Tomlinson's narrative that in my childish imagination I followed George Washington as a young scout, or marched resolutely forward to engage the Iroquois and Red Coats. Of all the books, however, Coffin's *Boys of '76* was my favorite. And many were the evenings in which I descended from the New Hampshire hills with sixteen-year-old Elijah Favor to fight at Lexington and Concord and finally to share the fruits of Revolutionary victory at Yorktown.

However, by the time I could recite with relish and gusto Scott's lines:—

Breathes there the man, with soul so dead,
Who never to himself hath said,
This is my own, my native land! . . .

the President's picture had changed. In the course of the years, he had become huge, the size of a bear, but he still wore a mustache. He was less like Father now. And while I found it difficult to imagine myself becoming as stout, I felt that even flabby avoirdupois, if associated with the Presidency, had its compensations. No matter what his shape, I told myself, everybody still loved and worshiped the President of the United States.

Of this deadly and insidious fever that racked my chubby frame, Father was totally ignorant. Nor would he have ever divined my secret if it had not been for our journey to the Mother Lode country.

It was our first long overnight trip away from home together. The train ride, needless to say, was nothing short of glorious. For two whole days I had all to myself a father whom I seldom saw, but to whom I was thoroughly devoted. Besides, a city boy, I had never seen mountains so tall or sights so strange and fleeting. But the most enjoyable part of all was to bounce on the redplush train seats and stop the vendor whenever he passed by with his hamper filled with peanuts, candies and soda pop.

After a full day's ride, we arrived at our destination, a small silver-mining town in the Sierra Nevada. At the station platform, Father and I were met by a roly-poly Westerner dressed in baggy clothes, riding boots, and a huge sombrero and mouthing ominously an equally formidable black cigar. After "How-de-doing" us, the stranger offered Father a cigar. A "cheroot" I think he called it. Then followed a ritual that filled me with amazement.

While Mr. Brown sized up Father skeptically, Father planted himself firmly on both feet, rolled the unlighted cigar in his hands, stroked it gently, and drew it slowly beneath his nose. With a deep sigh of satisfaction, he inhaled deeply.

"Havana Perfecto?" inquired Father, more as a statement of fact than a question.

"Splendid!" assented Mr. Brown with a vigorous nod. Smiling broadly for the first time, he slapped Father approvingly on the back and swept me up into his arms. As we drove majestically down the dusty street in his creaky cart, our now genial host vouchsafed that Father was one of the few "damned furriners" and certainly the first "Chinaman" to pass this unusual inspection.

By the way that Father puffed at his cigar and blew magnificent smoke rings, I could see that he was pleased with Mr. Brown's compliment. But never a word did he mention about his being the proprietor of Sun Loy, the largest tobacco shop in Chinatown. Since he didn't, neither did I.

Arriving at a large two-story hotel, resembling in size, shape, and color an old Southern mansion, Mr. Brown, whom we now knew to be the proprietor, roared from his sagging wagon seat: "Hi there, folks! I've picked up my Chinamen!"

Out trooped the few American residents of the hotel, glad to witness anything that would break the monotony of a long hot summer's day, followed by six white-clad Chinese domestics who greeted us with an explosion of the Fragrant Mountain dialect. "*Ah Kung Ah!*" (Respected Great-Uncle!) "We hope all is well with you!"

It gave me a great thrill to see everybody, even the Americans, so deferential to Father. There was something about him that commanded universal respect. Chinese in Western clothes, especially of the latest cut, were a decided rarity in those days. And Father in his first suit of tailor-mades from a nobby American clothier looked simply grand. Tall, well-built, and sporting a bushy mustache, he looked every inch a distinguished personage. I could well understand why his American business associates persisted in nicknaming him "The Duke."

Mr. Brown, having already been informed of the purpose of our visit, drew quietly aside. So did the Americans, no longer interested in a group of jabbering, gesticulating Orientals. This gave a few of my kinsmen an opportunity to converse with me in our dialect, which I understood, but, much to their chagrin, could not speak. Shocked that a Chinese boy should be ignorant of his own dialect, the eldest exclaimed, "*Chow Mah!*" (Positively disgraceful!) The way he said it made me more than a little ashamed of myself.

However, Father cut short my uncomfortable moment by introducing me to the object of our visit. "This—" indicating a short, slender chap who appeared exceedingly glum— "is your Fourth Paternal Uncle, Precious Fortune."

Fourth Uncle, despite his title, was only a distant kinsman and, from his point of view, had every reason for sulkiness. Just as he had conveniently forgotten about his grieving mother and childless wife in China for the pleasures of Chinatown's gambling tables, Father appeared—and Fourth Uncle didn't like it one bit. Father was the personification of outraged Chinese family conscience on the warpath. To him, in place of his own father, Fourth Uncle had to account for his glaring lapses in filial piety. He had to explain, for example, why he had not written them in three years; why he never sent them money; and, worst of all, why he persisted in leaving his aging mother grandchildless.

As the Clan's Senior Elder Uncle, Father took his Greater Family responsibilities very seriously. All through dinner, he informed Mr. Brown spiritedly that Fourth Uncle would have to leave. At first, Mr. Brown replied that he hated to part with an excellent cook, but when we came to dessert he finally agreed that in view of Fourth Uncle's wicked profligacy, it appeared the wisest course.

Having disposed of the fried chicken, apple pie, and Fourth Uncle so satisfactorily, Mr. Brown next turned to me. "Son," he inquired, "what are you studying to become? Would you like to stay with me and be my cook, taking your uncle's place?"

The last question passed me by completely; I answered the first one. "I want to be President," I said.

A sharp silence smote the mellow dining room. Now the secret was out. I was amazed at my own stupidity. Happily absorbed with my second helping of apple pie and fresh rich country milk, I had recklessly given vent to my Presidential aspirations. Now what would Father say?

Father, uncertain of the exact nature of the enchantment that had suddenly ensnared his son, looked at me queerly as though he doubted his ears. Mr. Brown laughed long and loud with a strange catch in his voice. "Sure, son, that's right," he added. "Study hard and you'll be President someday."

I wondered then why Mr. Brown's laughter sounded so odd, but I never associated this with pity until much, much later. By then, however, I had been thoroughly cured by Father.

Homeward bound Father said precious little. Not even to Fourth Uncle, still glum, whom we brought home with us to start life anew. Father's silence was disturbing and he attempted to cloak it, and his thoughts, with liberal benefactions. When we reached Belleville Junction I had no further use for the newspaper vendor and his basket of allurements—and Father no use for silence. In his own mind he had worked out a series of special therapeutic treatments to counteract my desperate malady, Presidentitis.

A few days after our return from the Sierra Nevada, Father said gently, "Glorious Descendant, how would you like to go to a private boarding school in China?"

I shuddered at the full significance of his suggestion. To be separated from America and from my family? And never to see them again for years and years? "No! no!" I wailed. "I don't want to go!" Rejecting the idea with all the vehemence at my command, I added, "I want to stay in America!"

Father dwelt patiently on all the advantages of such a schooling but to no avail. Nothing he said moved me. What about my future, inquired Father, didn't I care? Of course, I replied, but I didn't want to be a mandarin or a Chinese merchant prince at such a terrific sacrifice. Father's questions became more penetrating; they stripped the future of everything but realities. Could I, as

a Chinese, ever hope to find a good job in American society? At this, I laughed. Miss McIntyre, I told him, had plainly said that I could even be President.

In these sessions, I revealed to Father the seriousness of my infection. I opened the gates to that part of my youthful life he had never known. I told him in no uncertain terms that I loved America, particularly East Belleville, which I considered to be the grandest place in all the world. Besides, I continued, why would I wish to go to China? All the things I had heard from our kinsfolk about the old country were bad, with no redeeming features. After all, I added as my clinching argument, if this were not so, why should our kinsmen wish to come to the United States?

Our cousins and uncles, Father tried desperately to explain, really wanted to stay at home with their wives and children, but because times seemed so difficult in China they were compelled, by economic necessity, to come and work in the Golden Mountains. "Don't think you're the only one who loves his family and hates to leave it," concluded Father somewhat angrily.

The argument became endless. The more Father pleaded, the more determined I became. America, I swore, was God's own country. It abounded in free public schools, libraries, newspapers, bathtubs, toilets, vaudeville theaters, and railroad trains. On the other hand, I reminded him, China was a place where anything might happen: One might be kidnapped, caught in a revolution, die from the heat, perish from the cold, or even pick up ringworm diseases which left huge bald patches on one's scalp.

Finally Father was convinced. Since I did not personally regard his idea with favor, trying to send me to China was hopeless. This by no means exhausted Father's remedial efforts on my behalf. Plan number one having failed, Father put number two into operation. He decided that if I wouldn't go to China I was to spend an extra hour each day on my Chinese studies for Tutor Chun.

Now I knew leisure no longer. My American playmates, and endless trips to the settlement library, were given up—but not forgotten. And I discovered to my painful sorrow that I had only substituted one necessary evil for another. Every evening from five to eight I despondently memorized, recited, and copied endless columns of queer-shaped characters which bore not the slightest resemblance to English. As I went to this school on Saturday mornings and studied my lessons on Sunday, I envied Penelope, Heinz and Francisco, my poorest foreign playmates, their luxurious freedom. They did not have to learn Chinese.

Unlike my American education, my Chinese one was not crowned with success. It was not that I was entirely unwilling to learn, but simply that my brain was not ambidextrous. Whenever I stood with my back to the teacher, my lips attempted to recite correctly in poetical prose Chinese history, geography or ethics, while my inner spirit was wrestling victoriously with the details of the Battle of Bunker Hill, Custer's Last Stand, or the tussle between the *Monitor* and *Merrimac*.

When it became apparent to Tutor Chun that, in spite of my extra hour a day, I was unable to balance cultural waters on both shoulders, he mercifully desisted flailing me with the bamboo duster. No amount of chastising, he informed me bitterly, would ever unravel the cultural chop suey I was making of my studies. But, in the long run, even the gentle soul of the Chinese teacher could not tolerate my muddle-headedness. One day after a particularly heart-rending recitation on my part, he telephoned Mother in despair. "Madame," he exclaimed in mortal anguish, "never have I had a pupil the equal of your son. I strain all my efforts but, alas, I profoundly regret that I am unable to teach him anything!"

Father was appalled at this news, but since he was not the kind of man who gave up easily, his determination waxed all the stronger. Subtler methods, bribery, were tried. Perhaps, he reasoned, I might develop a taste for Chinese as well as English literature if it were only made financially worth my while. Each Sunday a shining quarter would be mine, he said, if I would present him with a daily ten-minute verbal Chinese translation of the latest newspaper reports on European war developments.

Lured by this largess, I made my translations. They were, to be sure, crude and swiftly drawn. But then, ten minutes was all too brief a period in which to circumnavigate the globe and report on its current events. I endowed the military movements of von Kluck's, Foch's and Haig's armies with the élan of Sheridan's sweep down the Shenandoah, unencumbered with the intricate mechanized paraphernalia of modern warfare. And long before Wilson, Clemenceau and Lloyd George assembled at Versailles, I had made and remade the map of Europe a dozen times.

Father's clever scheme not only worked, but it proved mutually beneficial. During the four years of the war, we kept it up. Thanks to the revolutionary *Young China*, and the *Christian Chinese Western Daily*, he was never entirely in the dark as to which armies won which campaign and who finally won the war. Naturally, Father learned a great deal about history that wasn't so, but he did not particularly mind. I was improving my Chinese.

During this period my youthful cup of patriotism was filled to overflowing. In the first place our Americanism had finally reached the ears of the White House. The christening of my twin brothers brought two important letters of congratulation from Washington, which Father proudly framed and hung conspicuously in his private office. As might be imagined, they exerted a profound influence on all our lives.

When I felt particularly in need of encouragement, I would go to the back wall of Father's office and read aloud Vice-President Marshall's letter to Father. It was a human one, glowing with warmth and inspiration. There was one sentence which stood out: "To be a good American citizen, in my judgment, is about the best thing on earth, and while I cannot endow your children with any worldly goods, I can bless them with the hope that they may grow up to be an honor to their parents and a credit to the commonwealth."

I recall this Vice-Presidential blessing so vividly because it was the crux of our family problem. It summed up our difficulties as well as our goal. For me, at least, it was difficult to be a filial Chinese son and a good American citizen at one and the same time. For many years I used to wonder why this was so, but I appreciate now it was because I was the eldest son in what was essentially a pioneering family. Father was pioneering with Americanism—and so was I. And more often than not, we blazed entirely different trails.

When America finally entered the War, even Father's sturdy common sense softened somewhat under the heat waves of patriotism that constantly beat down upon us. I was in paradise. My youthful fancies appreciated that only strife and turmoil made heroes. When I recalled that practically every great President—Washington, Jackson, Lincoln, Grant, and Roosevelt—had once been a soldier, I bitterly lamented the fact that I was not old enough. I'd show those "Huns" (by this time I had already imbibed freely at the fount of propaganda) a thing or two, I informed Father. But Father only snorted something about waiting until I could shoulder a gun, and studying Chinese.

The next summer, my thirteenth, I decided to go to work during vacation. I needed spending money badly for my first term in high school. Father applauded this show of independence until I informed him that I intended, if possible, to become an office boy in an American business firm. Then he was seized with profound misgivings. "Would they hire you?" Father inquired.

Why shouldn't they, I replied, with overweening self-confidence. "See!" I pointed to the Sunday editions of the *San Francisco Chronicle*. "I can hold any of these jobs."

Father looked at the classified advertisements I had checked. Whether he knew what all the abbreviations meant, I wasn't certain. I didn't, but that was totally immaterial. The world was new, I was young, and for $40 a month I was willing to learn the ins. or exp. bus., work for good opps., be ready to asst. on files, and, for good measure, do gen. off. wk. for perm. adv.

Father remarked that he wasn't so certain that the millennium had arrived, but he was open to conviction. He agreed to let me proceed on one condition: If I failed to find a job I was to return to Tutor Chun and study my Chinese lessons faithfully.

Blithely one sunny July morning I went forth job hunting, well-scrubbed, wearing my Sunday suit and totally unaware of the difficulties that confronted me. In my pocket were ten clipped newspaper advertisements, each one, I thought, with a job purposely made for me.

I took out the most promising one. It was for seven enterp. boys, between the ages of 12 and 16; and they were wanted at once for a bond house which offered good opps. as well as $50 per month. The address was on California Street.

Stopping in front of an imposing marble palace of San Francisco finance, I compared the address with the clipping. It checked. How simply grand it would be to work for such a firm, I thought, as the elevator majestically pulled us up to the ninth floor. I trembled with eager anticipation as I pushed open the glass door of Richards and Mathison, for it seemed as though a new world were swimming into view.

"Wad-a-ya-wunt?" barked the sharp voice of a young lady. I looked in her direction. There she sat behind a shiny, thin brass cage, just like a bank teller—or a monkey, for above her head hung a sign. It read INFORMATION.

"Please, ma'am," I asked, "can you tell me where I can find Mr. Royal?"

"Humph!" she snorted, as she looked me up and down as if to say I didn't have a chance. "He's busy, you'll have to wait."

After what seemed hours, the girl threw open the office gate and motioned me to enter. I followed her down a long aisle of desks, every one as large as a kitchen table. At each desk sat a man or a girl shuffling large cards or scribbling on long sheets of paper. As we passed, they stopped their work and looked at me queerly. I noticed several boys of my own age putting their heads together. I knew they were talking about me. And when they snickered, I wanted to punch their noses.

Opening a door marked PRIVATE, the girl announced: "Mr. Royal, here is another boy." He raised his head.

There it was. On Mr. Royal's lean, smooth-shaven face was the same look of incredulity that I had once noticed on Mr. Brown's. But only for a moment. For he suddenly reached for a cigarette, lit it and looked at me quizzically, while I hopped on one foot and then on the other.

"Young man," he said, "I understand you would like to work for us? Well then, you'd better tell us something of yourself."

"Why, of course," I said, "of course." And impulsively I told everything: all about my graduation from grammar school, my boy-scout training, and my desire to earn my own keep during the summer.

Mr. Royal seemed visibly impressed. When a faint smile replaced his frown, I stopped fidgeting. I fully expected him to ask me to come to work in the morning. Therefore, I was appalled when he told me that he was sorry, but all the jobs were taken. It never occurred to me that our interview would end like this.

My face fell. I hadn't expected such an answer. To soften the blow, Mr. Royal added that if I filled out an application he would call me if there were any openings.

I filled out the application under the unsympathetic eyes of the information girl, and stumbled miserably out of the office, vaguely sensible of the fact that there would never be any opening.

The feeling was intensified as I made the round of the other nine firms. Everywhere I was greeted with perturbation, amusement, pity or irritation—and always with identically the same answer. "Sorry," they invariably said, "the position has just been filled." My jaunty self-confidence soon wilted. I sensed that something was radically, fundamentally wrong. It just didn't seem possible that overnight all of the positions could have been occupied, particularly not when everybody spoke of a labor shortage. Suspicion began to dawn. What had Father said? "American firms do not customarily employ Chinese." To verify his statement, I looked again in the newspaper the next morning and for the week after and, sure enough, just as I expected, the same ten ads were still in the newspaper.

For another week, I tried my luck. By now I was thoroughly shellshocked. What had begun as a glorious adventure had turned into a hideous, long-drawn nightmare.

Father during this trying period wisely said nothing. Then, one morning, he dusted off my dog-eared paperbound Chinese textbooks. When I came to breakfast I found them on my desk, mute but eloquent reminders of my promise. I looked at them disconsolately. A bargain was a bargain.

When our clock struck nine, I picked up my bundle of books. Fortunately for me, Father had already commuted to work. Only Mother saw me off. Patting me sympathetically on the shoulder, she regarded me reflectively. It was an invitation for me to unburden my heart. But not even for her would I confess my full recovery from a nearly fatal disease. That moment was reserved for my long walk to language school.

I marched out of the house insouciant. When I wasn't whistling I was muttering to myself a Jewish slang phrase I had just picked up. It was "Ishkabibble" and it meant that I didn't care. And I didn't until I reached the park where all my most vivid daydreaming periods were spent. There, I broke down and wept. For the first time I admitted to myself the cruel truth—I didn't have a "Chinaman's chance" of becoming President of the United States. In this crash of the lofty hopes which Miss McIntyre had raised, it did not occur to me to reflect that the chances of Francisco Trujillo, Yuri Matsuyama, or Penelope Lincoln were actually no better than mine. But after a good cry I felt better—anyway, I could go to an American school again in the fall.

15

When a House Is Not a Home: Exploring the Meaning of Shelter Among Chronically Homeless Older Men

Christopher J. Elias
Thomas S. Inui

This study explored the world of 35 chronically homeless older men in downtown Seattle, with special attention to their experience of shelter and its effect on health-seeking behavior. We found that their experience of shelter is intertwined with their perceptions of self and use of alcohol. For many, the public shelter provides safety, support, community, and an opportunity to regain sobriety—attributes of shelter often unattainable in single-room occupancy hotels—but only temporarily.

Recently there has been growing concern about the problem of homelessness in America. The resurgence of this highly visible form of dispossession has challenged health and social policymakers (Rossi, 1990). Many health researchers have focused primarily on the difficult tasks of enumerating and characterizing homeless persons and identifying their special service needs (Rossi & Wright, 1987; Scharer, Berson, & Brickner, 1990). The result has been the development of a substantial body of demographic and descriptive epidemiologic information (Brickner et al., 1990; Institute of Medicine, 1988). But successful incorporation of these numerical data into assistance programs for homeless persons requires a complementary insight into their life experiences.

Historically, chronically homeless older men living on "Skid Row" have provided America's image of homelessness (Bogue, 1963; Hoch & Slayton, 1989; Wallace, 1965). Although the proportion of the homeless represented by these men is declining, the number of such men is actually rising. It is estimated that between 14.8% and 28% of the homeless are age 50 or older (Aging Health Policy Center, 1985). Most of the older homeless are men and between the ages of 50 and 65. Estimates reveal proportionately fewer men over age 65, a finding attributed to higher mortality, improved access to social entitlements with age, and sampling difficulties (Institute of Medicine, 1988).

The health problems of older homeless men are considerable. Age, high levels of alcohol addiction, and chronic exposure all interact to produce a precarious health situation (Gelberg, Linn, & Mayer-Oakes, 1990). Analysis of the clinic-based data collected from 16 of the 19 Johnson-Pew Health Care for the Homeless projects indicated that 19.7% of homeless persons presenting for care were over age 50 (Wright & Weber, 1987). The prevalence of both acute and chronic physical disorders was very high in this age cohort (Institute of Medicine, 1988). Community-based samples have corroborated this high level of physical illness among the older homeless. A study of Bowery men found they were in much poorer physical health than an age-matched sample of housed community men (Cohen, Teresi, & Holmes, 1988a). A related study revealed a high prevalence of mental illness, particularly depression, among these men (Cohen, Teresi, & Holmes, 1988b).

Despite the greater health care needs of chronically homeless older men, data suggest that, like other homeless persons, these men face considerable obstacles in accessing health services (Doolin, 1986). Lack of health insurance, facilities, and providers partly explain the late and often sporadic utilization of health services by these men. A complete understanding of their interactions with the health care system, however, requires an insight into their health-seeking behavior and decision making. Such health-related behavior is, in turn, related to broader patterns of social interaction and survival.

Cohen and colleagues have done extensive quantitative and qualitative research concerning the survival strategies of older homeless men living on the Bowery in lower Manhattan (Cohen et al., 1988; Cohen & Sokolovsky, 1983, 1989). Their analysis of social networks suggests that historical descriptions of these men as "kinless," transient, atomistic, and devoid of intimacy are inaccurate. Although the Bowery men do appear more isolated using certain sociometric instruments, among their peers the men "adhere to a strict norm of reciprocity" (Cohen & Sokolovsky, 1983). Cohen and colleagues conclude that the patterns of social interaction among these men primarily reflect adaptation to environmental factors (e.g., extreme poverty, violence, and crime) rather than the "ingrained personality features" previously suggested. In addition, work concerning the environmental perceptions and experience of "home" in later life suggests that aging itself can be expected to affect the lived experience of "homelessness" among older persons (Golant, 1984; Rowles, 1978; Sixsmith & Sixsmith, 1991).

This article describes an exploration of the life world of chronically homeless older men in Seattle, with special attention to their experience of shelter. Our objective was to develop an insight into the central issues shaping the daily experiences of these men. Comprehension of these experiences proved essential to understanding their interactions with health and other social services.

The majority of the interviews took place at a large public shelter exclusively serving older homeless men in Seattle. This shelter restricted admission to men over 50, allowed stays of indefinite duration, and operated at or close to its capacity of 210 men throughout the study. With the exception of a small number of "respite" beds requiring medical authorization, all men were required to leave the shelter during the daytime.

Results

The median age of participants was 55 (range: 50-68). Of the 35 men interviewed there were 29 Caucasians, 3 Native-Americans, 2 African-Americans, and 1 Pacific Islander.

The phenomenon of shelter experienced by the chronically homeless older men interviewed for this study was complex. Their need for shelter reflected needs for safety, privacy, locality, support, and community. In the past decade these attributes of shelter have become harder to find, necessitating a greater reliance on public shelter facilities and assistance. The result is an intricate relationship involving the men's experiences of shelter, self-perceptions, and the use of alcohol, which, in turn, greatly influence their interaction with health and social service systems.

The declining availability of affordable housing resulted in frequent displacement and fewer housing options for these men. They described increasing difficulty in finding work that paid a "livable wage." For many this was the result of physical disability. For others, aging impaired their ability to compete for work in the strenuous jobs that had once provided their livelihood (e.g., migrant farm work, construction, logging, and the longshore). Consequently, most men worked "spot jobs" for minimum wage through temporary employment centers. The men were generally well informed about rents and conditions in various housing facilities. Most men could afford housing only by spending well over half their income from spot jobs, assistance, disability payments, and/or pensions. In such a context the only housing potentially available was at the very lowest end of the market. Such facilities were often dangerous and chaotic:

Now they do have some places around here that I, as an individual, wouldn't want to live in. There are hotels around here, cheap seedy hotels around here, but because of the traffic that's going on, people would rather stay here [at the public shelter]. You got a lot of drugs, prostitution. I don't want to be caught up in that. I want to go somewhere where when I go into my house. I can be in peace, I don't have to worry about the police gonna go through and knock down the door. I'm not doing it but I might have to go because I'm in the building.

The high incidence of violence and crime in the lives of these men was particularly striking.

Violence . . . there's a lot more violence out there now than there was say 20 years ago. I'm not sure why that is. I guess different kinds of drugs . . . there are people out there who I call jack rollers, who are just targeting the older people—retired alcoholics who can no longer defend themselves. They know they're getting the checks monthly and they just kind of wait for them. That's their life-style. And there seems almost no way to protect them. Police can't help them until after the fact: Yeah, there's a lot of violence aimed right at older people.

Many men described a regular movement between the streets, the public shelter, and single-room occupancy hotels in the downtown area. These movements often reflected changes in their drinking behavior and the need for companionship:

This place [the public shelter], actually when you're in line down there, the guys who is drunk aggravate me, and when you're going through the line for chow they aggravate you . . . but when you have the guys that you have drank with before that's not drinking at this particular time, they'll sit out there at those tables all night long and talk.
And it's like, when you're in an apartment you watch TV so long, which is fine, it gets harder—you eat by yourself—you get all secluded by yourself at times— maybe a guy will drop by once in awhile . . . you just don't know what to do with yourself, you come down here [to the public shelter] and sit here at night . . . it helps a lot. Because you're talking to someone who is not drunk, but yet you can communicate with him.

The men commonly described binge drinking. Initiation of a binge was often attributed to loneliness or the claim that companionship was only available in a tavern. During the binge men typically lost employment and ultimately housing—either by exhausting funds or exhibiting disruptive behavior. Often the men fell victim to street violence during these binges. Exposure-related injuries were also common as many men "slept out" on the streets and avoided public shelters during a binge. The binges most often ended at "detox" (the city's acute alcohol detoxification unit), often following referral from emergency services or street outreach. After 1 to 3 days at detox, the men came to the public shelter. Although men were often actively drinking while residing at the public shelter, it also served as a place to attain and maintain sobriety, at least temporarily. In describing the characteristics of the public shelter that encouraged sobriety, the men focused on the sense of community, personal support, and companionship.

Down on that line tonight there will probably be 150 guys down there. I could probably get a drink from probably 10 people down there. But they are nice enough to where they know that I'm not drinking right now, so they will say, "Oh, you're not drinking right now, that's good, keep it up" . . . They're pretty good that way.

Staying here, I have found that I'm better off for it. It's easier to deal with it this way—to come off of booze. Even though I'm going to [a residential treatment center] this here is a kind of treatment too—'cause I'm having a chance to meet other people, having a chance to deal on a one-to-one basis with my life with people. I've met some wonderful people; so that's helped a whole lot.

The public shelter consequently meets a number of human needs generally fulfilled at "home," needs often unmet in the isolation of SRO housing.

Some of these guys, they've gotten so used to the fact that they can come in here, they know everybody here, or mostly. That this is their home. I wouldn't say they were "homeless." It's a crowded situation . . . but they're so damn lonely that if they do get an apartment, within a month or so they're right back here. So to a lot of guys, this is their home, this is their family . . . it's where they identify.

The experiences of these men suggest that shelter has important attributes beyond those of safety and affordability. Indeed, the support and community available in crowded public shelter facilities occasionally makes

them preferable to the minimal privacy and locality obtainable in poor-quality SRO hotels. This explicit, stated preference reflects the existential challenge of surviving in a chaotic, lonely, and violent environment, as well as the need for support in their struggle with alcohol addiction.

However, the public shelter provides only temporary sanctuary in this world of loneliness and addiction. As one man described, every morning there is "the great exodus from the mission":

Well, where are you gonna go? You catch the bus [from the shelter] at 6:00 in the morning; okay. You go up to the service center, you stay there 'til about 20 minutes to 8, and then you go up to the senior center; at 8:00 it opens; you have coffee at 9:00 and you either read or watch television or play pool. If you've got nothing to do and someone comes along and says "Hey, come on up to my apartment, I got a bottle up there." If there's nothing else to do, that's what you do, you go up there . . . and you drink, and you have a cup of coffee at lunch instead of eating, and you go and get another bottle and sit there until it's time to go down to the bus . . . it's an escape.

One respondent referred to this daily routine as being a "victim of the clock." The men described the monotonous cycle of moving from streets to shelter as one that focused their attention on immediate events and discouraged long-range planning or a consideration of future prospects. They described the difficulty of breaking this routine to deal with acute problems, such as illness.

I think some of us develop a trapped attitude. When we get here we get kind of on the merry-go-round. It's get up, you've got to be out of here by 7:30 in the morning . . . you've got to be back down there by 6:30 . . . you can rapidly let yourself go and develop a sense of no responsibility.

Losing a "sense of responsibility," "self-respect," and "self-esteem" was described as a common effect of staying in public shelter and following the daily routine. The threat of this loss became more imminent as the men perceived that, even if they could obtain employment, decent housing would still be out of reach.

When a man can't afford a place to stay, that's what breaks down a lot of people's spirit. You don't just go to work to go to work, you want to be able to get shit, the basic needs from working is to get food, clothing, and shelter. And you trying to manage a little money the best you can with what you have. And yet you still can't get within reach of it. That's the part that, if you're not careful, will really get to you.

The importance of self-perceptions was an underlying theme that affected a wide range of behaviors including health care seeking, drinking, use of social service programs, interactions with family, and the avoidance of physical harm. The mechanism of these effects can be understood partly as a breakdown of their capacity for self-care.

Some of these guys just said, "the hell with it" and gave up . . . maybe without realizing it we're ashamed of where we live, the shape we're in, our circumstances . . . the guys that come out here [to the shelter], first they're in the shower every night, then maybe it's one every other night, then finally they just say, "the hell with it." Until somebody makes them shower.

Inattention to personal hygiene, appearance, and dress were commonly cited as evidence of "giving up"—a process involving loss of self-respect and responsibility. Ultimately, "giving up" fostered the cycle of alcohol addiction among these men.

Alcohol addiction was clearly a dominant force in the lives of most of these men. When asked to estimate what percentage of shelter

residents had alcohol problems, responses ranged from 50% to 95%. Indeed, the men were much more likely to describe themselves as "alcoholics" than as "homeless people." It was impossible to elicit a consensus concerning alcohol use. Whereas most men agreed that "it's up to the individual," many contradictory statements were made about the dynamics of alcohol use and sobriety. These contradictions could often be found in the comments of the same respondent, leaving the impression of an ongoing struggle and lack of certainty.

An important subtlety in interpreting the experiences of these men is grasping the interactive association of alcohol use with self-perceptions and self-care. Once begun, excessive alcohol use contributes to the loss of responsibility and self-respect and results in a further deterioration of self-care. Eventually, it becomes part of the routine.

Around here they've given up. All they want is a place to sleep, they don't even want soap and water. Just wake me up before the 6:00 a.m. bus leaves so I can get downtown and get a chair and White Port. Sit down there at the bus stop and wait for the 6:30 p.m. bus to pick me up so I can come back and crash. Same thing every day.

Appreciating this complex phenomenology of shelter, self, and addiction has important implications for understanding the interactions of these men with health and social services. Self-perceptions had a strong impact on the utilization of services:

If you don't [have medical coupons], they still will take you down at [the clinic] . . . That's a good place; that's kinda homey down there; it's nice, it's relaxed—[But, I have medical coupons]; that gives you, you know, you feel better. Like, well, I don't really owe 'em; they're gonna get paid. You get a guilt complex or something when you don't have anything to offer . . . You feel guilty; I do. And you find most of these street people—they aren't very clean to start with—so they tend to shy away from any kind of help . . . figure maybe they look too disreputable to be going into a place like that. Afraid they'll either get thrown out the back door, or they just feel bad about being in there looking like they do, their circumstances.

As the capacity for self-care eroded, utilization of services declined, until eventually the men became primarily dependent on outreach and rescue efforts. This reflected a complex decision-making process in which the perceived benefit of services declined as the perceived costs of accessing services increased. The men reported a number of characteristics of the medical care system that discouraged their utilization of services, including long waits, "red tape," having to tolerate multiple providers, unsafe facilities, and the excessive use of physical restraints in busy emergency rooms. The men expressed widely different opinions about the same health facilities—a variation that largely reflected more central issues of self-perception, alcohol use, and shelter. This suggested that, while there were certainly structural aspects of the medical care system that presented barriers to access, the impact of those barriers was largely determined by experiences outside the medical realm.

This impression was corroborated by further exploration of the men's health decision making, which revealed a much greater concern with the quality of provider interactions than with traditional issues of access.

Respondent: I would not go to [hospital A], I would go to [hospital B].
Interviewer: And why is that?
Respondent: It was the way I was treated between the two hospitals. I was patronized by Dr. [X], though he was good, and he still is good. I was having other problems, the way I was living in the streets. He's a good doctor, but I also know the difference between being treated and be-

ing patronized. And that's why I won't go back to [hospital A].

The men were particularly sensitive to interactions where they were labeled or treated like a "bum" or "street person."

The minute you mention [the public shelter], forget it. They figure you're a drunk, a wino, a thief, a panhandler, a bum. It's bad news.

Respondent: . . . if I got a broken bone, I'll go in. But if it's something I figure minor or something, I pass it by.
Interviewer: And why do you think people are reluctant to go in?
Respondent: I guess they don't want to trouble anybody. You feel like if you're just on the streets, you're nothing. Why take up somebody else's time; they're gonna just give you the runaround anyway. That's the way you feel, or I feel; people I talk to feel that way.
Interviewer: Why do you think they feel that way?
Respondent: I don't know; they're just not particularly fond of street people. You know, put 'em out of sight, out of mind . . . they can make you feel pretty unwanted.

Ten of the men interviewed had an opportunity to obtain affordable housing at a facility specifically developed for chronically homeless older men. Focus groups with men at the public shelter were used during the design of this facility to identify their special needs. The facility provides private SRO units in a secure building located on the periphery of the downtown area with complete meal services. The men pay 60% of their income for room and board, and all residents are older men who were homeless for 1 or more years. The facility has several communal areas, including television rooms, a pool table, and a library. Hotel policy (for example, the designation of nonsmoking areas within the facility) is made at a biweekly resident's meeting.

In describing the benefits of this housing over the public shelter or downtown SROs, the men emphasized the importance of having privacy, safety, the ability to secure personal belongings, community with the other men, and the support of facility staff (which included health outreach and case management services). They also stressed the importance of having a stable address, phone number, and "home" to which they were proud to invite friends and relatives. In addition, being master of their own time encouraged "looking forward" and facilitated the acquisition of employment and social services.

The most dramatic impact of residence at this facility was on self-perceptions, an impact reflected in an improvement in hygiene and other aspects of self-care.

Like this morning the guys were complaining there's no hot water; they wanted to shave. Hot water thing blew up and caught fire, and it's not going to be fixed until this afternoon. But you notice that the guys noticed; at the shelter they wouldn't care.

Utilization of health services also improved, again associated with an improvement in self-perceptions:

You feel like you're entitled to courtesy and respect and things like that. On the other hand, if you're living as a street person you're psychologically less demanding— you don't have any clout or any strength . . . . your perception of yourself is just a nonentity that's obviously reinforced by being on the street.

References

Aging Health Policy Center. (1985). *The homeless mentally ill elderly.* Working paper. San Francisco: University of California.

Bogue, D. (1963). *Skid row in American cities.* Chicago: University of Chicago Press.

Brickner, P. W., Scharer, L. K., Conanan, B. A., Savarese, M., & Scanlan, B. C. (Eds.). (1990). *Under the safety net: The health and social-welfare of the homeless in the United States.* New York: Norton.

Cohen, C. I., & Sokolovsky, J. (1983). Toward a concept of homelessness among aged men. *Journal of Gerontology, 38,* 81-89.

Cohen, C. I., & Sokolovsky, J. (1989). *Old men of the Bowery: Strategies for survival among the homeless.* New York: Guilford.

Cohen, C. I., Teresi, J., & Holmes, D. (1988a). The physical well-being of old homeless men. *Journal of Gerontology: Social Sciences, 43,* S121-128.

Cohen, C. I., Teresi, J., & Holmes, D. (1988b). The mental health of old homeless men. *Journal of the American Geriatrics Society, 36,* 492-501.

Cohen, C. I., Teresi, J., Holmes, D., & Roth, E. (1988). Survival strategies of older homeless men. *The Gerontologist, 28,* 58-65.

Doolin, J. (1986). Planning for the special needs of the homeless elderly. *The Gerontologist, 26,* 229-231.

Gelberg, L., Linn, L. S., & Mayer-Oakes, S. A. (1990). Differences in health status between older and younger homeless adults. *Journal of the American Geriatrics Society, 38,* 1220-1229.

Golant, S. M. (1984). *A place to grow old: The meaning of environment in old age.* New York: Columbia University Press.

Hoch, C., & Slayton, R. A. (1989). *New homeless and old: Community and the skid row hotel.* Philadelphia: Temple University Press.

Institute of Medicine (U.S.), Committee on Health Care for Homeless People. (1988). *Homelessness, health, and human needs.* Washington, DC: National Academy Press.

Rossi, P. H. (1990). The old homeless and the new homeless in historical perspective. *American Psychologist, 45,* 954-959.

Rossi, P. H., & Wright, J. D. (1987). The determinants of homelessness. *Health Affairs, 6,* 19-32.

Rowles, G. D. (1978). *Prisoners of space? Exploring the geographical experience of older people.* Boulder, CO: Westview.

Scharer, L. K., Berson, A., & Brickner, P. W. (1990). Lack of housing and its impact on human health: A service perspective. *Bulletin of the New York Academy of Medicine, 66,* 515-525.

Sixsmith, A. J., & Sixsmith, J. A. (1991). Transitions in home experience in later life. *Journal of Architectural and Planning Research, 8*(3), 181-191.

Wallace, S. E. (1965). *Skid row as a way of life.* Totowa, NJ: Bedminster.

Wright, J. D., & Weber, E. (1987). *Homelessness and health.* New York: McGraw-Hill.

16

The Big Boys

Jack Culberg, 79
CHICAGO, ILLINOIS

Studs Terkel

The corporation is a jungle. It's exciting. You're thrown in on your own and you're constantly battling to survive. When you learn to survive, the game is to become the conqueror, the leader.
—Larry Ross (pseudonym for Jack Culberg), *Working*, 1970.

He is now a corporate consultant. Over the years, he has served as CEO of several conglomerates.

We're a new generation. When we grew up anybody fifty or sixty was considered old. I remember as a young boy, thirteen, fourteen, attending the twenty-fifth wedding anniversary of my mother and father. Everybody was dancing and singing and having a wonderful time. I remember saying to myself: "What are they so happy about? They're on the verge of dying." They were maybe fifty-five.

There's a new breed now. I'm going to be seventy-nine in July and I don't for a second consider myself old. I still play a good game of golf, and I exercise and swim and am active in business. There are many corporations out there that feel you're old and should be out of it, no matter how you look or feel. You have to quit at sixty-five or seventy. You can't be on the board. I don't feel that way at all. I'm still involved. I don't feel any older than them in any way. I feel I have more vitality than those who call me an old man. You turn around and want to know who the hell they're talking about.

What I said about the corporate jungle twenty-five years ago still goes. I've been in it ever since 1942. When you suddenly leave it, life is pretty empty. I was sixty-five, the age people are supposed to retire. I started to miss it quite a bit. The phone stops ringing. The king is dead. You start wanting to have lunch with old friends. At the beginning, they're nice to you, but then you realize that they're busy, they're working. They've got a job to do and just don't have the time to talk to anybody where it doesn't involve their business. I could be nasty and say, "Unless they can make a buck out of it"—but I won't. [*Chuckles*] You hesitate to call them.

You get involved in so-called charity work. I did a lot of consulting for not-for-profit organizations. It was encouraging for a while, but the people who run that world are a different breed. They're social workers who've become managers. The great curse of business is amateurs running things. They can't make it. It's amazing how much money is foolishly wasted in charitable organizations.

But Jobs for Youth is something else. It's a sensational group. It takes dropouts from high school, ages seventeen to twenty-one. We train them, get them a diploma, counseling, and jobs. We place eight hundred to nine hundred a year. I'm still on the board.

As for the corporate jungle, it's even worse today. The circle of power is becoming smaller and smaller with fewer and fewer dominant people in control. IBM can lay off fifty thousand, or General Motors. They're not talking about blue-collar workers necessarily. They're talking about middle management who aspire to become CEOs. Today lots more people are fired or forced to retire before they reach the 50 percent mark on the way to the top. The jungle has become worse. You can smell the insecurity and fear all over the place. And the people who lose those jobs have nowhere else to go.

Most big corporations suggest early retirement. It isn't as much pension as you'd get if you lived out the entire thing. You take it. A genteel form of being fired.

Of course, you're more afraid now than when we last met, twenty-five years ago. If you lost your job then, there were many more opportunities to find another. Today there are fewer companies. I'm talking about middle management and up. Let's say you're the manager of a company division and they're merged or bought out. They cut down on the bureaucrats and you're fired. Where do you go? A lot of them are taking lesser jobs.

Most of these people live on their investments or whatever they saved up. The interest rate is so low, they're having great difficulty. Let's say you have a million dollars saved. In the old days, it was an astronomical amount of money. If you're getting an interest of 3 percent, that's $30,000 a year. You can't live on that. So you have to go into the principal. It's very uneasy now. In the old days, it didn't mean a hell of a lot because nobody lived that long. The longer the life span, the more the insecurity—for the great majority.

I happen to be one of the lucky ones. When I retired at the age of sixty-five, I thought I had enough money to live comfortably. If things hadn't happened for me during my retirement, I'd have a rough time now. With retirement, I started doing some consulting. I wasn't satisfied just playing golf or spending winters in Florida. I was too involved in the business world because it was exciting. It had been my whole life.

So I started dabbling around. The LBO [leveraged buy-out] swing came in. One of the top men in the business is someone I've known for years. I found some businesses for him. For at least nine years, I've been involved with these companies. I'm still the chairman of one. In the last seven, eight years, I've made myself an awful lot of money—I was able to work three to four days a week and have a ball. Now I spend maybe two days a month. I still have a hand in. I have a fax machine at home and daily reports, but I'm not in active management.

Because you're a top businessman, you don't stop being a human being. Human frailties exist in the corporate world as they do outside. The top executive is the loneliest guy in the world because he can't talk confidentially to the board of directors. They expect him to be strong and know everything. They don't want a guy that's doubtful or weak. He can't talk to the people working for him because he's got a guy who'll say yes to anything he says and the other guy wants his job. So he doesn't have anybody to talk to. So he becomes insecure and makes the decisions covering his ass.

The board of directors will never take the blame. They're heads of big corporations and don't have time to spend on this particular one. It's more or less a social thing.

With fewer companies, the tension is at its greatest in fifty years. There's a joke that someday there will be one manufacturing and one retailing concern. The retailer will say to the manufacturer, "I don't like your line." And the business dies. There used to be a business saying: "Eighty-twenty." Eighty percent of your volume comes from 20 percent of your customers. Eighty percent of the work is done by 20 percent of the workers. Today I think it's changed to ninety-five–five. Today, Wal-Mart, K-Mart, Target, Service Merchandise. People aren't buying less. There are as many places to buy, but they're controlled by fewer people.

Youngsters are coming up now and want a crack at the big jobs. In the old days, to become president of a company, top man, you had to be in your fifties and sixties. Today, you've got CEOs that are thirty-seven years old, twenty-nine. When I started out in the jungle, you were considered a baby at forty-one.

Also, there's a new way of doing business. A lot of older people didn't keep up with the modern ways. It's difficult, too, because computers are running the world. Yet people are still vigorous at seventy, seventy-five.

Ageism is a tremendous problem today. Investment bankers will tell you they're uncomfortable with old people running anything. Business analysts don't give a good rating if a seventy-five-year-old guy is running the company. What the hell, he's going to die any minute, a change in management, an upset. It starts getting dangerous at sixty, sixty-five.

A guy was saying the other day, "You people on Medicare are making it awful tough. The costs are unbelievable." There is that feeling: taxes wouldn't be so high if it weren't for the old geezers.

As for me, if I didn't work, I'd deteriorate and die. My doctor tells me to keep active, keep your brain going, keep your body going. Some people my age have hobbies—painting, gardening. That keeps them alive. Unfortunately, I'm not one of these. I love golf, I love swimming, but that doesn't stimulate the mind. I need something else.

Power, age, greed. These are human qualities. They don't disappear when you become a CEO. Having the telephone constantly ring, all the perks, people catering to you, asking your opinions, asking you on boards. It's very flattering and ego-building. Many of the top executives start to believe their publicity and think they walk on water. Many of the business failures today are the result of top executives feeling that they walk with God.

People of my age are a lost generation. What's left for him to do if he's not creating? Every businessman feels he's doing something creative. What the hell are you alive for? It's nice being a great father and a great grandfather—but they're a different genera-tion, your kids, no matter how close you are to them. I don't know what's to be done.

We're living longer and we're cursed with such things as Alzheimer's, heart attacks, and strokes. That's the great fear with us. But if you're busy running a business, you don't sit around and think about your sicknesses. You have this big struggle not to deteriorate. When you create and contribute, you feel marvelous.

One of the nice things at this age is the luxurious morning. Before, you had to get up, get out, get going. Now, I can lay around, read the paper, *Wall Street Journal*, trade magazines, take my time with breakfast, go over the mail. Then I talk on the phone, spend time with my investment counselor. If it's a nice day, play golf or find someone to have lunch with. I'll take long walks, walk the treadmill, swim at about four o'clock, and then I'm ready for dinner. [*Pauses*] It sounds pretty dull.

Yeah, I get a little bored. The pain of being unneeded and unwanted is uncomfortable at every stage. There are some guys who are unneeded 100 percent of the day. That would drive me absolutely insane. There are some guys who play golf in the morning, play cards in the afternoon, go out for dinner at night, spend the summers here and winters in Florida or Palm Springs, do the same things there. I don't know how they live.

When you're CEO, people are always after you. [*Snaps his fingers.*] What are we gonna do here? What are we gonna do there? What do you think about this guy? That guy? Mr. Culberg, so-and-so called and wants to have lunch with you at two o'clock. You're being wanted always. That ties in with being needed. That's a massive human desire.

When you're a CEO, my goodness, you're at the office at eight o'clock. You have meetings going on, correspondence, phone, this guy calls you, that guy calls you, planning for a board meeting, people problems, manufacturing problems. And they need somebody for a final decision.

Your social circle has diminished by the deaths. Mostly what's left of your social world are the widows. [*Chuckles.*] You read the obituaries by habit now.

As for politics, I've become a cynical old man. I don't believe in miracles anymore. I don't believe anybody walks on water. It's kind of a hopeless feeling. There's a lot to be done, but I don't think it can ever be done because the people will never allow it. I don't think the human species has changed since it was created. The horrors of centuries ago are still happening today. What have we learned? The human failing. And the CEO is no different than the rest of us.

1   Imagine that you are a gerontologist from a distant planet sent to Earth to learn about the experience of aging in the contemporary United States. You decide to gather your information by reading magazines and watching television. What would you conclude about old age? How might your views of aging vary by gender, race, and class? How accurate and complete a picture would you likely bring back to your home planet?

2   What are the meanings of old age reflected in birthday cards? Are there any differences in cards designed for men and cards designed for women? Try your hand at designing a line of birthday greetings that avoid ageist messages.

3   A major theme of this book centers on the interlocking hierarchies based on gender, race, and social class. We argued in the Introduction that people can be privileged on some dimensions but disadvantaged on others. In what ways can this model help us understand the experiences of old men, of Pardee Lowe, and of the mother in Langston Hughes's poem?

4   Children who are members of disadvantaged racial or ethnic groups face the challenge of developing positive self-concepts in the face of racist imagery. How was this challenge handled by Sadie and Bessie Delany, by Pardee Lowe, and by Zora Neale Hurston?

5   Old age also forces us to confront changes in social roles and relationships as well as physical appearance. In the Introduction, we argued that the social context in which we experience these changes mediates their impact on how we feel about ourselves. How did the social worlds of Jack Culberg and Carolyn Heilbrun influence both the consequences of and their responses to the aging process?

SUGGESTIONS FOR FURTHER READING

1   Martz, S. H. (Ed.). (1987). *When I am an old woman I shall wear purple* and (1992), *If I had my life to live over, I would pick more daisies.* Watsonville, CA: Papier-Mache.

We selected the title pieces of these anthologies of writings about older women for this book; others of the stories, poems, and essays illustrate the ways in which women's choices, from childhood to old age, are influenced by their ethnic and cultural identity, social class and economic resources, age, and gender. The women write about the personal meanings of old age in a culture that celebrates youth.

2 Banner, L. (1983). *American beauty.* New York: Knopf.

Lois Banner chronicles the history of perceptions of feminine beauty in the United States. Changing definitions and standards of beauty are linked to other social and cultural events in different historical periods. Banner interprets beauty as both a source of power and a source of oppression for women.

3 Terkel, S. (1992). *Race: How blacks and whites think and feel about the American obsession.* New York: Doubleday.

More than 80 diverse voices speak about the experience of race in U.S. society and in their everyday lives. Terkel has captured the changing social and cultural landscape through interviews with a cross section of Americans over the past three decades.

4 Collins, P. H. (1990). *Black feminist thought: Knowledge, consciousness, and the politics of empowerment.* Boston: Unwin Hyman.

The selection "Mammies, Matriarchs, and Other Controlling Images" describes how negative images and standards of beauty of African American women operate as ideological justifications for oppression. The book, which won the C. Wright Mills Award, shares the voices of many African American women and demonstrates the new insights that emerge from seeing social reality from different standpoints.

5 Myerhoff, B. (1978). *Number our days.* New York: Simon & Schuster.

The anthropologist Barbara Myerhoff studied a group of elderly Jewish people attending a community center in Venice, California. While documenting daily problems of poverty, loneliness, and poor health, Myerhoff also demonstrates how the Jewish community provided a forum for constructing meaning in old age, for celebrating individual biography, and for sharing lessons of survival. Her work expands our understanding of the impact of World War II on today's elders by exploring the impact of the Holocaust.

6 Goings, K. W. (1993). Memorabilia that have perpetuated stereotypes about African Americans. In V. Cyrus (Ed.), *Experiencing race, class and gender in the United States* (pp. 165-167). Mountain View, CA: Mayfield.

Kenneth Goings analyzes racial and gender stereotypes in commonplace objects such as housewares, toys, and lawn ornaments produced over the past 100 years. Described by collectors as memorabilia, these items were part of the everyday environment in which today's cohorts of older Americans grew up. The pervasiveness of the negative images contribute to their most pernicious effects.

7 Gates, H. L., Jr. (1989, November 12). TV's black world turns— but stays unreal. *New York Times,* sec. II, pp. 1 ff.

Professor Gates analyzes images of African Americans on television over the past 40 years. His insightful analyses highlight the subtle ways in which popular television programming denies the reality of oppression and reinforces racial stereotypes. Gates provides us with a new lens through which to see both contemporary programs and reruns from decades past.

8 *The long walk home* [Film]. (1991). Van Nuys, CA: Live Home Video.

The Montgomery Bus Boycott is the setting for this film about a domestic worker and her employer who are caught up in the early years of the Civil Rights movement. The courage of the domestic worker in risking her job to honor the boycott forces her employer to confront the consequences of racism in her own life.

9 Campbell, B. M. (1992). *Your blues ain't like mine.* New York: G. P. Putnam.

Set in the American South of the 1950s, Campbell's novel illustrates the climate of racism and sexism and the harsh realities of class inequality in which current cohorts of elderly Americans experienced their early and middle adult years. The main characters illustrate the impact of varying positions along hierarchies of race, class, and gender on the social contexts that shaped their lives.

10 Delany, S., & Delany, E. (with A. H. Hearth). (1993). *Having our say: The Delany sisters' first 100 years.* New York: Kodansha America.

Sisters Sadie and Bessie Delany recall growing up in turn-of-the-century North Carolina. They recount their confrontations with Jim Crow and local segregation, the World War I era migration North, and their lives as professional women during the heyday of Harlem. The daughters of the nation's first elected African American Episcopal bishop, the sisters were disadvantaged by race and gender but advantaged by social class.

PART III

Productive Activity

Paid and Unpaid

Expanding the Definition of Productivity in Old Age

What are productive activities? By economic definition, they are behaviors that add to the stock and flow of valued goods and services. Traditionally, paid work has been the exclusive measure of productivity. Recent arguments, however, have favored expanding the definition to include unpaid activities. This would be useful for two reasons. First, many unpaid activities also fit the definition of productivity, because they produce valued goods or services. Second, using paid work as the only measure does not give a complete picture of productivity in certain disadvantaged groups in the population: the elderly, women, minorities, and individuals with handicapping lifetime paid work experiences. The contributions of these groups to society are underestimated when unpaid work is not included along with paid work in calculating their productivity.

Here, we develop an inclusive approach to the study of productive activity in late life that will more accurately assess the contributions to society of disadvantaged members of systems of inequality. This approach has three goals:

1. To view productivity as a continuum over the life span
2. To broaden the definition of productivity to include both paid and unpaid work
3. To expand definitions of productivity beyond experiences of the dominant group

Productivity Over the Life Course

Humans have engaged in productive activity from the beginning of time. Evidence from other cultures indicates that such activity was varied and endured across the life course. Probably the most common pattern connecting age and productive roles in preindustrial societies was for people to shift to less physically demanding tasks as they got older (Cowgill, 1986). For example, among the Inuit people in Alaska, older men who could no longer hunt or fish made and repaired tools and weapons used by younger men (Guemple, 1983). Advanced age had less impact on the productivity of older women, as they could "continue their normal domestic activities into very advanced stages of debility" (Cowgill, 1986, p. 120).

In some societies, such as that of the Bushmen of the Kalahari Desert in South Africa, everyone is encouraged to work as long as possible. Older men continue to hunt to the extent they are physically able and make decisions about moving to new hunting areas (Thomas, 1959). Older women share the knowledge they have accumulated during their lives about where to find berries and tubers. Elderly people are also responsible for distributing food. In other societies, people move through a series of increasingly important productive roles as they age. For example, among the Sidamo in Ethiopia, promotion to elderhood in middle age is eventually followed by elevation to *woma*, a status Cowgill (1986) defines as "one who personifies the highest ideals of the culture. Such a person embodies courage, truth, justice, and wisdom and is even believed to possess the power to foretell the future" (p. 113).

In contrast to these images of productivity in preindustrial societies, contemporary U.S. society has not viewed productivity as continuous. Instead, retirement is thought to mark the end of productive work and the beginning of leisure. Historical and anthropological evidence, survey research, and personal accounts, however, all belie this simplistic view. Production of valued goods and services continues well into old age. For example, Herzog, Kahn, Morgan, Jackson, and Antonucci (1989) examined both paid work and unpaid productive activities, including volunteer work in organizations, informal help to family and friends, maintenance and repair of home and possessions, and housework, among a national sample of people aged 25 and over. Although older people were less likely than younger people to participate in the labor force as paid workers, individuals 65 and over participated in unpaid productive activities at levels comparable to those of middle-aged and younger people.

The Impact of Ignoring Unpaid Work on Estimates of Productivity

A number of social trends are forcing gerontologists to rethink definitions of productivity in late life. As we move into the 21st century, more people will live to 100 and more people will need to combine the unpaid work of caring for the increasing number of very old family members with other types of paid and unpaid activities. The growing disparity between the rich and the poor that has characterized the American economy since the 1980s forecasts increasing disparity in the financial resources people bring to old age. Market analysts have already discovered the "gray market" of affluent elders (Minkler, 1989), and some gerontologists predict an increase in consumer products and services targeted to this privileged sector (Haug, 1995). At the same time, workers who lost economic ground during the final decades of the 20th century due to layoffs from job automation, downsizing, or corporation mergers may need to pursue paid work longer than they had anticipated, if restricted pension benefits and limited assets make retirement financially difficult. As the baby boom cohort moves into retirement age, the ratio of retirees to workers will increase dramatically unless the size of the labor force changes through manipulation of retirement incentives or increased immigration of younger people. Will this change in the old-age dependency ratio be offset by increased productivity of paid workers? Does it make sense for paid work to stop at age 60 or 65 when an individual can expect to live 35 more years? Is it fair to discount unpaid social care provided mainly by women in national assessments of productivity and in individual eligibility for retirement benefits? What are the consequences of defining work and retirement according to the labor market experiences of White middle-class men? These are some of the questions that beg a reevaluation of definitions of productivity and a reconsideration of the ways different activities contribute to society.

Treating paid work as the whole of productive activity underestimates the productivity of women, minorities, and people in low-level occupations. Estimates of productivity that only count paid work will conclude that these individuals are less productive than White men employed in highly paid occupations. However, when unpaid work is also considered, these individuals are no less productive than their more privileged counterparts. People who are disadvantaged along hierarchies based on gender, race, and social class also have different patterns of paid work over their life course than their more privileged counterparts. By ignoring the restrictions on their opportunities in the labor market, culturally defined responsibility for housework and care of family members, and the adaptive strategies many women develop to manage these restrictions, we overlook the ways in which they blend paid and unpaid productive work to survive and to provide for their families.

Patterns of Productivity Based on Gender

Researchers studying work and family have documented both differences in the paid work patterns of men and women and changes in the pattern of these differences over time. Furthermore, within particular cohorts, women's participation in the paid labor force has varied by social class and by race or ethnicity. These differences influence types of productive activity and the economic resources that men and women bring to old age.

First, women are less likely than men to maintain continuous labor force participation throughout their adult lives. Stone (1989) describes the checkered work histories that disadvantage women in paid work over a lifetime:

Many women who work for pay exhibit interrupted work patterns including mid-life career entry, intermittent employment throughout the work cycle, and frequent job changes. Erratic work history is most often the consequence of childbearing and childrearing, which cause many women to delay or interrupt their work careers. Thus, women have an in and out pattern of the worklife. (p. 207)

Women are also more likely than men to participate in a broad range of unpaid activities that produce valued goods and services yet are not included in national assessments of their productivity:

> The division of labor with regard to caregiving does not stop with childrearing but continues throughout the life cycle. Just as women are beginning to anticipate the empty nest, many are faced with the responsibility of caring for disabled husbands, parents, and other adult family members. A large proportion also must deal with the competing demands of employment and eldercare. (Stone, 1989, p. 207)

In addition to caring for the needs of family members, women are responsible for the majority of housework. The economist F. Thomas Juster (1965) studied the division of household labor in 1965, when today's cohorts of elderly people were middle-aged adults, and found that, among married couples, wives performed about 80% of the unpaid housework. The productive value of these goods and services becomes obvious when we consider replacing the unpaid work that women perform in their roles as wives, mothers, and housewives with goods produced in the market or with services performed by paid workers.

Nona Malbin-Glazer (1976) estimated the value of women's unpaid family work at $13,000 per year. Translating that figure into 1999 dollars results in an estimate of $37,241. Lack of recognition of this unpaid domestic labor has long-term consequences for women's access to pension and other resources in old age. Gerontologists stress the potentially large financial costs to women who leave the labor force or retire early to care for children, grandchildren, or frail elderly relatives, not only in lost wages but also in the ability to develop higher earnings profiles and subsequent retirement benefits (Fischer, 1984). Amy Horowitz (1985) reminds us that these long-term economic costs may ultimately be shared by the public in terms of losses of current tax contributions and future increased costs of public assistance to impoverished elderly women.

Gender differences in types of productive activity also continue into old age (Verbrugge, Gruber-Baldini, & Fozard, 1996). Elderly women spend more time on unpaid work, including housework, child care, and volunteer activities, than older men. They are also more active in religious and voluntary organizations. Elderly men are more likely to pursue paid employment and to spend more time doing yard work and household maintenance tasks. Estimates of productivity that count only paid work would conclude that older men are more productive than older women. However, when both paid work and unpaid work are considered, women's greater unpaid work balances out men's greater investment in paid work, leading Herzog et al. (1989) to conclude that the total productivity of men and women does not differ.

Discrepancies between work histories of men and women have lessened over the past 30 years, as successive cohorts of women have exhibited more continuous labor force attachment. Women's rate of labor force participation have risen gradually since 1950, with the steepest rise occurring since 1965. These increases have been most dramatic for White, middle-class, married women, because they were most likely to leave the labor force to care for young children. Poor women and women of color have always exhibited more continuous labor force participation. Today, the typical woman, like the typical man, is working full-time in the paid labor force (Renzetti & Curran, 1997). This means greater similarity in the paid work experience of future cohorts of elderly men and elderly women, although the continued wage gap between men and women will translate into a future gap in retirement benefits and accumulated assets, especially among elderly women who cannot pool resources with a second wage earner. Future cohorts of elderly women may also retain responsibility for the majority of unpaid domestic labor, if we can project the division of household labor in old age from patterns established earlier in life (Hochschild, 1989). Nevertheless, there is some evidence of greater sharing of house work and child care among younger cohorts (Bond, Galinsky, & Swanberg, 1997). Whether this trend will continue into old age remains an empirical question for future research.

Patterns of Productivity Based on Social Class

As with gender inequality, people who are disadvantaged by their social class also exhibit patterns of overall productivity that differ from those of their more privileged counterparts. People from affluent backgrounds experience more opportunities throughout their lives to accumulate various types of financial resources. Their paid employment experiences provide them with investment opportunities, sufficient discretionary income for savings, pension benefits, and insurance protection. In contrast, people from poor or working-class backgrounds have a lifetime of lower wages, less job security, fewer pension and other fringe benefits, and greater risk of occupational injury than more middle- and upper-class workers (Crystal & Shea, 1990). As a result, they are less able to afford to retire completely from paid work when they are older. Economists and sociologists define these different patterns of opportunities as *cumulative advantage* and *cumulative disadvantage*. People who begin life with more privileges are able to perpetuate their advantages and accumulate resources throughout their lives, whereas individuals who begin their lives in a disadvantaged position continue to lose ground across the life course (O'Rand, 1996). Toni Calasanti and A. Bonanno (1992) describe the situation of a retired working-class woman named Betty. Despite a lifetime of paid work, she was unable to accumulate enough resources to support herself in retirement. To supplement her limited income, she continues to produce valued goods and services, which she exchanges for the support she needs. Betty survives by providing domestic labor, with irregular pay, for her live-in brother-in-law. Both recognize that he could not otherwise afford the services she provides and that his financial contributions are vital to her survival:

> I worry about him. If I lost him, I'd lose a major part out of my life because not only does he help me financially for taking care of him, which he said he'd have to pay 3 or 4 times as much if he had to be put in a nursing home. You see, you look at both sides of the question. He helps me out and I help him. Now he doesn't actually pay me money but like if something comes up, why like if I have to have something done to my car, he'll help me pay for it. Or something goes wrong with the house, why he'll have to pay for it, see. We go grocery shopping and he mostly pays for the groceries . . . so that's money in a way. (p. 144)

Patterns of Productivity Based on Race

Minority workers also have checkered work lives that lead to underestimates of their total productivity and undermine their ability to accumulate financial resources to support their retirement. For example, between ages 45 and 64, Blacks, Hispanic Americans, and American Indians constitute larger proportions of the unemployed labor force than do White Americans. Furthermore, these simple comparisons of the percentage of Whites and so-called non-Whites who are employed are conservative estimates of disadvantage, because they obscure the greater tendency for minorities to be part-year, part-time, and seasonal workers or to be discouraged workers (i.e., people who want to work but have given up looking for jobs) who are not even counted in labor force statistics.

As with the work patterns of women, looking only at paid work fails to tell the whole story. Older minorities are engaged in many types of unpaid yet productive activities. James Jackson, Toni Antonucci, and Rose Gibson (1993) applied a typology of three types of economic exchange networks to illuminate the range of productive activities performed by older members of minority groups. In the regular economic network, exchanges of labor are made for pay and are regulated by government accounting and tax systems. Workers pay income taxes and social security contributions on the money that they earn. The government is aware of these activities, and they are counted in national estimates of productivity. Workers not only earn credit toward social security and other pensions, but they are protected through worker's compensation in the event of on-the-job injuries and unemployment compensation in the event of lay-offs.

In the irregular economic network, pay is also involved, but economic exchanges are informal and not subject to government regulations or taxation. Payment for services is often described as "under the table," and this exchange network is often referred to as the *underground* or *shadow* economy. The government is not likely to be aware of these activities, which include such things as cutting hair in your basement for pay or performing domestic labor or yard work when payment is in cash and the income is not reported to the government either through income tax or social security contributions. Furthermore, workers in the underground economy have no protection against arbitrary employers, downturns in the economy, or on-the-job injuries, and they have no opportunity to accumulate future retirement benefits such as social security and medicaid. In the social economic network, people do not receive direct cash payments for the work they do. Goods and services are reciprocally exchanged independent of money payment—favor for favor. For example, a person who owns a car may run errands or shop for an older neighbor who, in turn, will watch the younger woman's children after school.

Production of valued goods and services in the irregular and social economic networks by Blacks and other disadvantaged Americans are well documented. Carol Stack (1974) describes exchanges within these networks among residents of The Flats, the poorest section of a Black community in a midwestern city:

> Black families living in The Flats need a steady source of cooperative support to survive. They share with one another because of the urgency of their needs. Alliances between individuals are created around the clock as kin and friends exchange and give and obligate one another. They trade food stamps, rent money, a TV, hats, dice, a car, a nickel here, a cigarette there, food, milk, grits and children. (p. 32)

Stack concludes that it is this kin-based exchange network that protects residents of The Flats from going hungry.

Community organizations, particularly churches, provide another setting for informal exchanges of goods and services. Within Black communities, churches are a resource through which people can provide services to others and on which they can draw in times of need. Sister Minnie, the elderly member of the A.M.E. Church we met in the Introduction, relied on the church for support. As Cole (1986) explains, "When the social services she and her family needed were not provided by the city, state, or federal government, it was to her sisters and brothers in the church that she turned for help" (p. 310). Unlike social services provided by various levels of government, however, services contributed by church members are not counted in estimates of economic productivity. Neither are the child care activities of the "othermothers" we describe in Part IV on family. This kind of bartering with family, friends, church members, and neighbors in the irregular or social economic networks is facilitated by patterns of family interdependence, by the importance of religion and the church, and by values that emphasize group rather than individual achievement (Cantor, 1979; Stack, 1974).

Gibson, Jackson, and Antonucci (1993) estimated productivity levels for older Blacks, including unpaid or uncounted activities in the irregular and social economic networks. Although comparisons of time spent in paid labor often suggest that Blacks are less productive than White Americans, this more inclusive approach of counting activities in all three economic networks indicated that older Blacks are as productive as their White counterparts.

In summary, we suggest that the productivity of people who are disadvantaged in systems of inequality—women, minorities, and those of low socioeconomic status—is underestimated when paid work is the only criterion. For an inclusive approach to the study of productivity, on both individual and societal grounds, definitions of productivity need broadening to include unpaid behaviors that also produce valued goods or services. The Alzheimer patient's unpaid caretaker at home is no less productive than his or her paid caretaker in a nursing home setting. The volunteer typist in a church or hospital is no less productive than the typist sitting next to him or her who receives a salary. The person who cleans and cooks for pay in the homes of others is no more productive than the person who does the same work for his or her own household (Herzog et al., 1989). In all of these cases, the product is identical and the work equally productive.

Differences in the Availability of Productive Activity Roles

As the previous discussion suggests, people's positions within systems of inequality influence the way they allocate their time between paid and unpaid activities. Position along interlocking hierarchies based on gender, race, and social class also influences people's access to particular types of each category of productive activity. For example, although women typically perform more unpaid domestic labor than men, women's social class position determines how they execute this work. Whereas poor and working-class women generally do their own housework, more affluent women are able to delegate some of these responsibilities to paid workers. By hiring domestic help, they are "relieved of the drudgery of doing housework themselves. They become, instead, the managers of the drudgery of domestic work done by other women" (Cole, 1986, p. 8).

Social class determines access to volunteer roles. Susan Ostrander's (1984) book, *Women of the Upper Class,* describes the activities of upper-class volunteers. The upper-class women interviewed by Ostrander served on boards of directors of community organizations, setting policy and planning fund-raising campaigns. These leadership positions contrast with the more hands-on activities of middle- and working-class people, for whom volunteer work more often involves activities such as tutoring children in after-school programs, delivering flowers or mail to hospital patients, soliciting door-to-door contributions for a local charity, or staffing the entry desk at the museum. "Community Volunteer," one of the chapters in

Ostrander's book, focuses on the experiences of Mrs. Sharpe, the wife of a wealthy stockbroker, now in her 60s. Mrs. Sharpe's productive activities are unpaid and therefore not counted in conventional national accounting systems that focus on wages and salaries. Because of her upper-class status, she has access to volunteer roles that enable her to exercise power and to garner respect. In fact, several of Ostrander's subjects explained that volunteer work is more rewarding psychologically than would be the paid work roles available to women in her age cohort. For Mrs. Sharpe, receiving a salary for her productive activity was less important than the benefits she received from her unpaid volunteer work: a context for recognition and accomplishment and an opportunity to contribute to society while upholding and legitimating the dominance of the upper class.

People's positions on interlocking systems of inequality also influence access to different types of paid productive activity. Not all people have equal access to the most desirable occupations. Prevailing social structures limit the opportunities of people with certain sociodemographic characteristics to pursue particular jobs. Several of the selections that follow portray working conditions faced by some members of today's cohorts of older Americans during the historical period when they were entering the workforce. Tillie Olsen's poem, "I Want You Women Up North to Know," describes the working conditions of Hispanic garment workers in the Southwest; Victoria Byerly's selection tells the story of Southern mill worker Aliene Walser; and Studs Terkel's interview with Mike LeFevre describes work in the steel mills of Chicago.

As social structures change across historical times, so does the availability of certain occupations, and today's elderly members of minority groups have experienced changes in their occupational opportunities over their life course. Nevertheless, many elderly Blacks today entered the labor force at a time when their opportunities were severely constricted. We can illustrate this process by considering two types of paid productive activity traditionally available to Blacks: domestic worker and Pullman porter.

Before World War II, workers of color were locked into a narrow band of jobs at the bottom of the occupational hierarchy. Nearly all Black women workers were domestics. This was—and continues to be—an occupation with long hours, low wages, and poor working conditions. This excerpt from "Slave Markets Typify Exploitation of Domestics," written by Louise Mitchell in 1940, describes the exploitation of domestic workers in New York City:

> Every morning, rain or shine, groups of women with brown paper bags or cheap suitcases stand on street corners in the Bronx and Brooklyn waiting for a chance to get some work. Sometimes they are 15, sometimes 30, some are old, many are young and most of them are Negro women waiting for employers to come to the street corner auction blocks to bargain for their labor.

They come as early as 7 in the morning, wait as late as 4 in the afternoon with the hope that they will make enough to buy supper when they go home. Some have spent their last nickel to get to the corner and are in desperate need. When the hour grows late, they sit on boxes if any are around. In the afternoon their labor is worth only half as much as in the morning. If they are lucky, they get about 30 cents an hour scrubbing, cleaning, laundering, washing windows, waxing floors and woodwork all day long; in the afternoon, when most have already been employed, they are only worth the degrading sum of 20 cents an hour.

Once hired on the 'slave market,' the women often find after a day's backbreaking toil, that they worked longer than was arranged, got less than was promised, were forced to accept clothing instead of cash and were exploited beyond human endurance. Only the urgent need for money makes them submit to this routine daily. . . . They have no social security, no workmen's compensation, no old age security. (pp. 275-281)

As late as 1935, Black women did housework and laundry for $3 a week and Black washerwomen did a week's wash for 75 cents. The historian Elsa Barkley Brown describes her mother's search for employment after graduating from college with a degree in mathematics in 1938:

It took some time but finally she did find a job, with an employer who was suitably impressed with all this young Black girl had accomplished; yes, it would be so refreshing to have an intelligent maid for a change. (p. 80)

Domestic work continues to be demanding and underpaid. The sociologist Judith Rollins (1985) documented the hard working conditions and physical ailments (e.g., leg and lower back problems, varicose veins) experienced by domestic workers even today. Women work long hours with few breaks, often using outdated or dilapidated equipment. They complain of monotony, repetitiveness, and isolation with minimal job security and few benefits. Rollins also described deference requirements and paternalistic behavior of employers, who called domestic workers by their first names, described them to others as "my girl," spoke to others in their presence as if they were invisible, and expected gratitude for gifts of old clothes and discarded household goods.

Employment of Black men as Pullman porters is another example of how people with specific sociodemographic characteristics are channeled into certain productive activities in particular historical times. The Pullman porter was to railroad travel what the skycap and flight attendant are to airplane travel. Many Black Pullman porters of the 1920s and 1930s were college and university graduates. Among them were physicians, attorneys, pharmacists, and PhDs. Because they completed college and sought employment in an era of legalized racial discrimination, they were relegated to jobs near the bottom of the occupational hierarchy. The Black Pullman porter is yet another example of how prevailing social structures impose limits on the types of paid productive activities available for certain individuals. The concentration of many educated Black men in this occupation also illustrates how being advantaged along two hierarchies (gender and class) but disadvantaged along another (race) still limited available employment opportunities.

The employment experiences of many elders of color, particularly members of younger cohorts, improved over their lifetimes. In June 1941, President Franklin D. Roosevelt issued Executive Order 8802 banning discrimination in defense industries and in government because of race, creed, color, or national origin. This governmental intervention plus increased labor shortages brought more minority workers into the labor force and began to improve their status. One of the more significant shifts in the occupational structure was the movement of Black women from domestic work into the steel foundries, munitions and aircraft plants, the army, canneries, and hospitals (Baxandall, Gordon, & Reverby, 1976). In earlier years, the majority of Black women were private household workers, but by 1960, the proportion had dropped to 34%. By 1977, only 8% were employed in domestic work. The Civil Rights movement, passage of the Civil Rights Act of 1964, and affirmative action programs have reduced but not eliminated employment barriers for Americans of color. Future cohorts of minority elders will include a growing number of people who enter old age with pensions and other financial assets accumulated over a lifetime of employment in middle-class and upper-middle-class occupations. But for many Blacks, earnings have dropped in recent years as factory jobs have moved to low-income nations where wages are lower. The growing disparity between the rich and the poor characterized minority populations as well. Despite widely publicized gains, median income of Black families in 1995 represented only 61% of the median income of White families, and households headed by Blacks were 3 times as likely to be poor as households headed by Whites (U.S. Bureau of the Census, 1996). This level of income inequality provides little reason to believe that racial differentials in income will diminish among future cohorts of elderly Americans.

The Impact of Productive Activity Across the Life Course on Economic Well-Being in Old Age

The financial resources available to people in old age reflect patterns of productive activity over the life course. For example, the "in-and-out" labor force experiences of many women decrease their opportunities to become vested in pension plans and limit their ability to establish earnings profiles that translate into higher pensions and social security benefits when they retire. Stone (1989) sums up the ways in which paid and unpaid productive activities of women shape their life course and financial well-being in old age:

> In order to understand why women are more likely than men to be poor in old age, it is important to recognize that the economic status of elderly persons depends on their lifelong marital and family obligations and their employment history. Paternalistic customs and laws that encouraged female dependency, the division of labor between genders with women as primary caregivers, and labor market discrimination are important determinants of gender differences in poverty among the elderly. (p. 27)

People with continuous labor force attachment generally have more resources than people who have intermittent employment patterns. But the sector of the economy in which one has been employed also influences a person's opportunity to accumulate resources. People seeking jobs face a dual labor market. Workers employed in the primary labor market enjoy higher wages, greater opportunities for advancement, greater job stability, better working conditions, and better pension and health insurance benefits. The secondary labor market, where women workers and workers of color have been disproportionately concentrated, offers poorer working conditions, lower wages, limited fringe benefits, and unstable employment. Even if they work continuously during their adult lives, workers employed in the secondary labor market enter old age with fewer resources. Because their wages were low, their social security benefits will be low, and they are less likely to have accumulated assets such as stocks or bonds. They are also less likely to have private pensions or private health insurance. Workers whose paid productive activity has been concentrated in the irregular economic network may not even be eligible for social security and medicare because much of their income was never reported to the government.

In contrast, White men from affluent backgrounds are disproportionately concentrated in professional and managerial positions in which their continuous labor force attachment is rewarded with salary increases, promotion opportunities, job security, challenging and interesting work, pension benefits, and opportunities to shelter income in individualized retirement accounts (Crystal, Shea, & Krishnaswami, 1992). Stephen Crystal and Dennis Shea (1990) have argued that the effects of early advantages accumulate across the life course, producing large differences in economic resources in old age:

> Over the life course, the structure of retirement income programs interacts with the workings of the labor market and with patterns of consumer behavior, such as savings and investment, in producing the distribution of economic outcomes. . . .

Respondents with more education had access to higher status jobs; were able to continue work longer; and were more likely to be self-employed, all tending to increase adjusted income. . . .

Tax-advantaged private pension systems provide benefits predominantly to those who held the "better" jobs in the economy and had stable employment patterns; IRA, Keogh, and other industrial savings systems benefiting from tax deferral similarly benefit higher-income individuals disproportionately. . . .

These findings suggest that stratification established early in the life course continues at least as sharply in the later years. (Crystal et al., 1992, p. S220)

Differences in the Meaning of Retirement and Productive Activity in Old Age

Common wisdom suggests that older people retire from paid employment and shift from productive activity to leisure pursuits. The more inclusive definition of productivity we develop here indicates that retirement from paid work often means reallocation of time to various types of paid and unpaid productive activity. Choices regarding paid and unpaid activities and the meanings people attach to these choices vary according to their positions along hierarchies based on gender, race, and class.

Affluent elderly people enjoy the greatest discretion in choosing among productive and leisure activities in late life. Although they may retire from occupations they found personally rewarding, they can often continue to exert leadership roles through volunteer positions in the community. They have the financial resources to pursue leisure activities. Given the association between socioeconomic status and health (see Part V), they encounter fewer restrictions in mobility than their less affluent counterparts.

Not all older people can afford to retire completely. For some working-class elderly people, retirement income falls short of meeting their basic needs or maintaining their former lifestyles. Some of these individuals need to supplement their economic resources with part-time work. Toni Calasanti and Alessandro Bonanno (1992) introduce us to two workers facing this situation:

After retiring from a low-pay job, Lorraine continued to work part-time another eight years in low-wage positions—cleaning in a nursing home and tending a laundromat counter. Mindful of her reliance on this income, her feeling is that retirement is "wonderful, if I can work." (p. 144)

Poor health forced Marie to retire from a monopoly firm in her fifties. Although she worked since very young, she was always a marginal worker. She held seasonal jobs, usually in a tobacco factory, waited tables, and worked for various firms as a sewing machine operator. Finally, monopoly firm work stabilized her employment, but at low pay. After 20 years, her job yields less than $100 a month in pension. Her total monthly income of about $400 must cover a house payment and all other expenses, including prescription medications. To supplement, she makes things at home to sell. She sews such things as ducks and pillows, and makes quilts until her fingers hurt from being pricked. Then she switches to crocheting things such as Easter egg covers. One of her prouder accomplishments is a yarn poodle she can now finish "in just 5 days." She sells these days of labor for $25. These activities are crucial to her survival; as she puts it, "if it's the end of the month and I can sell a duck for $5, it helps me pay my medicine." (p. 143)

Even with these financial pressures, retirement is still viewed positively by many working-class and low-income elders. Compared with more advantaged workers, disadvantaged workers are more likely to have experienced chronic unemployment, work disability, or part-time, part-year, seasonal, and joyless work. For these older people, the paid worker role may be less satisfying than for more privileged workers who were rewarded not only with high incomes but with prestige, deference, and challenging opportunities. Retirement can also have a special meaning for older people with a lifetime of sporadic work: For the first time in their lives, a check—social security or supplemental security income payments—comes every month!

Not all older people consider themselves retired. For both older Blacks and older Mexican Americans, checkered work lives often continue into old age. Economic need requires many to continue their lifelong pattern of sporadic work in low-paying jobs. The continuation of the in-and-out employment pattern seems to blur the line between work and nonwork to the extent that these minority elders do not always think of themselves as retired, despite the fact they are not consistently working. The availability of disability pay provides both an alternative identity and an alternative source of income for older people who are also work disabled. Defining themselves as disabled often has greater economic benefits than calling themselves retired, because disability benefits are often higher than retirement benefits based on a lifetime of low-wage work (Gibson, 1987; Zsembik & Singer, 1990).

Rose Gibson (1987) also demonstrates the ways in which productive activity roles earlier in life shape both economic well-being in old age and the meanings of work and retirement roles. The Blacks she studied had worked in "low status jobs characterized by sporadic work patterns and low earnings." These lifetime work patterns produced a precarious financial situation such that "work in old age, in the same low status jobs, becomes a necessity for many." Her article also illustrates the ways in which concepts based on the experiences of the dominant group can mask diversity in the experience of retirement. Many studies consider individuals retired if they are not working full-time, if they define themselves as retired, and if they receive retirement income (e.g., social security or other pension benefits). Defining retirement according to work patterns of White middle-class men causes researchers to overlook the experiences of poor Black workers who maximize their economic resources in late life by labeling themselves disabled rather than retired. By this definition, poor, disabled elderly people who choose disability benefits over less lucrative social security or pension benefits would not be considered retired. Neither would a retired person who at the time a study was conducted had taken a temporary position to supplement inadequate retirement income. Neither would a widow who had spent most of her life caring for her children, her elderly parents, and her terminally ill husband. As Gibson warns, developing more inclusive definitions of retirement is a prerequisite to designing research and policy to "enhance the lives of all elderly individuals in American society."

Gerontologists have not yet given sufficient attention to the ways in which gender or minority status influence satisfaction with retirement among people who do leave the labor force. Retirement satisfaction is strongly influenced by health and financial status and with the degree of choice surrounding the decision to retire (Hardy & Quadagno, 1995), and available evidence suggests that these findings generalize across systems of inequality (Calasanti, 1996). Continuity theorists emphasize the importance of preserving relationships and activities that preserve a person's self-concept. People whose identities are overly invested in their paid work roles can find the transition to retirement more challenging than people who have maintained a broader repertoire of meaningful activities. Like the retired farmer in the song by Kitty Farmer, adjusting to life in a Florida retirement community can be difficult if "his heart is still planting wheat fields back home."

Key Issues

The availability and meaning of both paid and unpaid productive activities, the ways in which these activities influence the life course, and the linkages between early-life and late-life productive activities are different for people who occupy different positions in systems of inequality. Our discussion and the following readings emphasize several points:

1. Productive activity continues over the life course.
2. Using traditional definitions of productivity inaccurately assesses the productivity of people who are disadvantaged in systems of inequality.
3. Differences due to membership in various systems of inequality arise in

a. the availability of productive activity roles,
b. the way productive activity roles affect the life course,
c. the meanings attached to productive activity roles, and
d. role transitions and the links between early- and late-life roles.

The Readings

Several of the readings that follow provide insight into the paid work experiences of today's cohorts of elderly Americans. The quotation from Louise Mitchell's essay, "Slave Markets in New York City," and the selection by Gwendolyn Brooks are vivid portrayals of the consequences of limited job opportunities for Black women prior to and just after World War II. The labor market for Black women during this period was almost exclusively limited to domestic work. The women in "Slave Markets in New York City" bargained for wages of 20 to 30 cents an hour (or, converted into 1995 figures, $2.14 to $3.21 per hour, considerably below minimum wage). The quotation and the article illustrate the constraints experienced by individuals who are disadvantaged on three systems of inequality: gender, race, and class.

The selection, "I Didn't Have No Family Before I Was Married," from Victoria Byerly's collection, *Hard Times Cotton Mill Girls*, recounts the experiences of a White female mill worker, Aliene Walser, during the 1940s. Her history of paid work dramatically illustrates the way social class disadvantage constrains opportunity structures even among workers who are advantaged by their race. Orphaned at 6 years old, Walser quit school and began working as a domestic at age 14. The same year, she married and found employment in a textile mill. Within the mill, both jobs and the meager economic benefits available were structured according to gender:

> There were men all around me doing jobs that were easier than what I was doing and they were making more money. . . . When Christmas-time came around, the men got a big bonus and we women might get a little one.

In addition to her work in the mill, she also shouldered the unpaid domestic work typically assigned to women. Caught in a web of limited opportunities, she still hopes for a better future for her own children.

Tillie Olsen's poem, "I Want You Women Up North to Know," is based on a letter written by Felipe Ibarro published in 1934 in *New Masses*, a radical newspaper. The poem describes the paid productive activity of poor Hispanic women shortly after the Great Depression, offering another example of the relegation of poor women of color, who are disadvantaged on three hierarchies, to a narrow band of productive activities at the bottom of the occupational hierarchy. It dramatically illustrates the ways in which productive activities can severely circumscribe people's life chances. Last, it makes visible the ways in which lives of privilege are built on systems of oppression.

Olsen pleads with the affluent women who purchase "dainty children's dresses" with "exquisite work, madame, exquisite pleats" to remember the suffering of the women who work "for three dollars a week from dawn to midnight." Olsen's argument parallels Cole's analysis of domestic work: Affluent women can be relieved of the drudgery of housework by becoming managers of the work performed by less privileged women.

Several of the other readings also illustrate the consequences of occupying privileged positions along some hierarchies and disadvantaged positions on others. The interview that Studs Terkel conducted with Chicago steelworker Mike LeFevre illustrates the work experiences of a White working-class man. Despite being advantaged by race and gender, LeFevre feels "dehumanized" by his work. He describes himself as "a dying breed. A laborer. Strictly muscle work." His position within the hierarchy based on social class constrains his options. He sees few opportunities for improving his own situation, but he, like the mill worker Aliene Walser, is determined to provide a better future for his child.

The reading "From Homemaker to Housing Advocate: An Interview With Mrs. Chang Jok Lee" focuses on the productive activities of a Chinese American woman, now in her early 70s. Mrs. Lee does volunteer work, thus her productive activities are unpaid and therefore not counted in conventional national accounting systems that focus on wages and salaries. The article underscores the point that Mrs. Lee's productivity started early in life and lasted well into older age—taking different forms as she aged. The essay also is an example of how being a member of a minority group (Mrs. Lee's family was Chinese in Japan during the Sino-Japanese war) shapes the type and duration of productive activity roles over the life course. Like Mrs. Sharpe in Ostrander's book (described earlier), Mrs. Lee finds volunteer work has psychological, if not monetary, payoffs: "Being active keeps me alive. I don't play mah-jongg or go to Reno, so I take care of my granddaughter, and I go to meetings." Unlike Mrs. Sharpe, however, Mrs. Lee is not of the upper class.

"Esse Quam Videri" is an essay about the life of a Black woman of the middle class, a college president's wife. Susie Jones is an example of how privilege in one hierarchy— class—and disadvantage in two others—gender and race—interlock to shape opportunities for productive activity. The impact of these interlocking hierarchies is evident in comparing the experiences of Mrs. Jones, Mrs. Chang Jok Lee, the women looking for work in the Brooklyn slave market, and the Black woman in Gwendolyn Brooks's story. How very different were the productive activities of the women in the slave market and those of Susie Jones, although both were disadvantaged on race and gender. Mrs. Jones and Mrs. Sharpe were both affluent women, but the social construct of race structured their lives in different ways.

The excerpt from the article, "Women's Work and Caregiving Roles: A Life Course Approach," by Phyllis Moen, Julie Robison, and Vivian Fields, illustrates that role involvement varies by location in the social structure. They suggest that two productive activity roles, caregiving and employment, combine differently for men and women and differently for women of lower and higher class. They document 30 years of transitions between caregiving and work roles to show that productive activity continues over women's adult life course. The essay also indicates that (a) using only paid work definitions of productivity inaccurately assesses the total productivity of women, and (b) differences in role transitions and the way productive activity roles affect the life course are due in part to gender and class.

Harvest Moon Eyes's short story, "The Day the Crows Stopped Talking" (from Clifford Trafzer's anthology *Earth Song, Sky Spirit: Short Stories of the Contemporary American Indian Experience*, 1992), illustrates two key issues in this section. First, the availability of productive activity roles depends on positions in systems of inequality. Second, the meanings attached to productive activity roles differ not only by positions in systems of inequality but by birth cohort as well. This reading, about life on a reservation, shows how older and younger generations of the same minority group are in conflict about the meaning of productive activity—traditional views of productive activity versus the new phenomenon on reservations, gambling casinos. The story illustrates how changes in economic activities can undermine the traditional authority of the council of elders and how positions of privilege can be used to restrict access to productive activity among people disadvantaged on systems of inequality. This is a story of generation versus generation and the powerful versus the powerless.

In the selection, "On the Edge of the Barrio," from Ernesto Galarza's autobiography, *Barrio Boy*, two key issues presented in this section are illustrated. First, solely using traditional definitions of productivity—paid work in the regular labor force—inaccurately assesses the productivity of the disadvantaged in systems of inequality. Second, certain productive activity roles are closed to these disadvantaged individuals. Ernesto Galarza was a Mexican American migrant worker who experienced a string of other menial jobs before going on to become a labor organizer, sociologist, and teacher. The article demonstrates how control is exerted over the productive activities of those at lower levels of the inequality hierarchy by those at the top.

"At the Burns-Coopers', " from Gwendolyn Brooks's novel, *Maud Martha* (1953), was published more than 30 years ago and reflects the state of Black women's work roles in those times. Before World War II, and a few years thereafter, the majority of Black women were domestic workers—one of the few work roles open to them. The selection illustrates two key issues of this section: Differences due to membership in various systems of inequality are found in the availability of productive activity roles and the meanings attached to those roles. In this selection, a Black woman reveals her thoughts about the often demeaning and humiliating experience of domestic work.

Paid domestic workers are still primarily poor women of color. In states with large immigrant populations (e.g., California, New York, and Texas), domestic work is most often performed by immigrant women from Latin America and the Caribbean (Hondagneu-Sotelo, 1996). The selection, "Like One of the Family," by Alice Childress provides a contemporary story of a domestic worker responding to patronizing employer behavior of the type described by Judith Rollins (1985).

The sociologists Mark Hayward, Samantha Friedman, and Hsinmu Chen demonstrate the cumulative disadvantage over the life course of restricted opportunities for Black men. Furthermore, the race gap in occupational opportunities is exacerbated by a race gap in health. They argue that studies of race differences in occupational attainment "have ignored the constraints that poor health may place on achievement over the career cycle." Consistent with Gibson's findings, the authors of this reading highlight race differences in the retirement life cycles of elderly Blacks and Whites.

17

I Didn't Have No Family Before I Was Married

Aliene Walser, as told to Victoria Byerly

I didn't have no family before I was married. My mother died when I was five, my father died when I was six, and I was switched here and yonder and everywhere. My mother's sister was mainly responsible for raising me. There were thirteen children in her family—three girls and ten boys. She kept me from the time I was five years old until I was ten. Then she said she couldn't keep me no more. Well, they brought me over here to the Baptist orphanage and tried to put me in that orphanage home. But they said my mother and father had died of tuberculosis, so they wouldn't take me. We had to have x-rays every six months, me and my two brothers. Honey, I can't tell you what a bad experience that was, living with my aunt. I would wake up crying for my mother and daddy at night and she'd turn the cover back and whip me. She'd whip me and shut me in the closet. Now I'm scared of getting into somewhere I can't get out of. That's the way I was treated. Then my aunt said she didn't want me no more, that they couldn't keep me no longer. So I went to stay with my grandmother and I stayed there about a year before she said that she couldn't keep me.

My brother was five years older than me and he didn't have nowhere to go. He used to sleep on porches. He'd come to my aunt's house where I was staying and sit down to eat dinner and she'd run him away from the table. I never will forget that. He would get up crying and leave. Finally, when my brother got married, I came to live with them in Thomasville. His wife and him separated when I was fourteen years old, so I quit school and went to housekeeping for this family who had four children. Two dollars a week for cooking and scrubbing. That's when I met my husband Anderson. When me and him was dating, before we was married, we had to take the children with us, so we've been with children before we were married and ever since.

Then one day I decided to go back home. So they got me back down there below Denton, and I stayed one night with my uncle—I knew I couldn't live there and then I hired my uncle to bring me back, and me and Anderson went to Virginia to get married. Got one of my friends to go with me. He was seventeen and I was fourteen, but Anderson told them in Virginia that he was twenty and that I was eighteen. I had on my first pair of high-heel shoes. I never will forget trying to walk up them courthouse steps. And honey, I could stand under your arm, I didn't weigh but seventy-four pounds. Well, the magistrate looked at us and he said, "You younguns go home." So we come back home. See, I didn't have no one to sign for me. So his mother and one of his aunts and us went to the courthouse in Lexington and got our license. They signed for us and we came back to Thomasville. Preacher James out here on Fisher Ferry Street married us. That night, I'd say we got married about one-thirty in the afternoon, at four o'clock he went in to work at the mill. The girl who lived across the street came over there and she liked to pick and joke, and oh, she had me scared to death that she was going to crawl under my bed and going to do this and going to do that. She embarrassed me to death.

Then we lived with his parents in a mill house over there on Concord Street right behind the mill. It had six rooms. We had two rooms, a kitchen and a bedroom. His parents lived in the other rooms. That was all right, Anderson's mother was like a mother to me. We lived there until my first baby was born. When I was pregnant for the first time, I was sitting there sewing with my mother-in-law one night and I said, "I wouldn't mind having this baby if I didn't have to have my stomach cut open." She looked at me and said, "Honey, you mean that you don't know no better than that and fixin' to have a baby?" I said, "What do you mean?" And when she told me I said, "Ain't no way I'm going to go through that." That like to have scared me to death. See, I didn't understand anything about my body. If I had, I wouldn't have had so many children.

The first time I ever started my period I was going to the spring to get a bucket of water. I was living with my brother and his wife then. All at once I looked and blood was going down my leg and it scared me to death. I didn't know what to do. I ran in the house and told my brother's wife and she told me what to do. She said for me to go in there and get something to put on. I was ashamed to tell my grandfather. And that was all that was ever said to me about it. That's all I ever knowed. She told me that it would happen again. I said, "What for?" She never did explain nothing like that to me. Didn't nobody.

I had my first two babies at home. His mother was there and she fixed my bed and told me to get in it. She helped me put on my gown and she would always have pads just about this wide, about four feet across, and she would put a lot of cotton padding in it to use under me. That way they could be thrown away afterwards. Then she called the doctor. And I laid there in pain until he got there. They didn't give you anything for the pain, you know. I remember that doctor sitting there and me hurting so bad. He was sitting there beside my bed and he went off to sleep! So I kicked him. Then after my first baby was

born I told him I never was having another one, this was my last. And then, when my second one came along, he looked at me and said, "I thought you weren't going to have another one."

I was fifteen when I had my first baby and thirty-two when I had my eighth. I raised seven of them. No, I didn't know how not to have babies. If I had known, I don't think I would have had eight. No, I never heard tell of birth control pills. Lordy mercy, honey, them things come out since I quit having kids. I wish I had had them back then. Maybe I wouldn't have been so tired.

I went to work in the cotton mill in 1940. I remember I was scared to death. I knowed I was doing everything wrong. I was scared the boss man would say something to me. I was actually scared to death! I didn't do anything wrong but I thought I was doing everything wrong. I was running a winder and it was called a spool winder. It had wooden tubes on it that were long and the thread went around it. When you first start them off that metal makes an awful racket. Well, I didn't know that. First time I had ever run them. Well, when I started that thing up and it started making this horrible noise, I run out of the alley and started crying like a baby. The boss man come up and said, "What's the matter?" And I said, "I've torn that thing up." Finally some women that worked around me got me calmed down and told me that it always does that. I got used to that noise finally, but I never did like to run that machine.

I stayed at the mill until World War II. Then my husband went into the service and my brother moved in with me because the children were small and I was pregnant again. I had my baby on the ninth and my husband left to go into the service that day. After he took his training, they sent him overseas. He didn't even get to come home to see the youngest until she was two years old. I waited until my baby was about four months old and then my brother's wife took care of the children so I went to work at the Erlanger Mill in Lexington. My sister-in-law taught me to wind over there. Then my husband came home and we moved down close to Charlotte. I went to work in a mill down there in the winding room. We stayed down there six years and then we came back to Thomasville. I went back to work in the Amazon Cotton Mill as a winder and I worked I don't know how many years winding. Then I was switched from that to running twisters. I don't know if you know what twisters are, but it twists yarn together, nylon and wool. I worked on that job for about four years. Then they put me to keeping the time sheets and stamping yarn and keeping what pounds the people would get off. You know, they got paid by the pound. I'd been there so long, I knew it all by heart.

There were better jobs, yeah. Some of them were happy doing the same old job day in and day out but I wasn't. I wanted more money. There were men all around me doing jobs that were easier than what I was doing and they were making more money. That bothered me. My husband was a boss man out there for a good long while, but I don't care if he was, when Christmas-time came around, the men got a big bonus and we women might get a little one. I just didn't think that was fair. We had to work as hard as the men. Harder! They were sitting on their rears writing down numbers. They said it was brain work. And I said, "What brain?" Yeah, I know I was working hard. Some of them were afraid to say anything though. See, they were scared they would lose their jobs, I reckon. And they probably would have. Mill people take a lot. But you'll find one or two that's not like that. They put me working with this man one time and he'd come in of a morning and maybe he'd be a little grouchy. I'd say, "Now listen here, I feel bad too, so get your butt off your shoulders." That's what I'd tell him and he'd start laughing at me.

Before I was married, I remember hearing that mill people wasn't nothing but slum people, that there wasn't nothing to them. I've heard it said that mill people are a lower class of people. A lot of them that worked at the furniture factory thought that they was better than mill workers. I got about seven or eight uncles that worked there and I know. They

thought they was better than mill people and still do. I didn't know whether that was true or not until I went to work in the mill and learned the truth. There's a lot of good people working in there. I've got friends that work in the mill and they have been good to me. Those that think we're a lower class of people ought to go in the mill and find out for themselves, if they got sense enough to do the work. People were moving in and out all the time on mill hill. Different types that drank, fuss and fight, and goings on. But now there was some real good people on the mill hill. You could have real good neighbors. They would do anything in the world for you, they could.

We wanted to own our own home, but we had seven children to put through high school. I cooked three meals a day, forty biscuits for each meal. I got to where I knew how to make that bread so that it would be forty biscuits every time. And they would eat it up. We ate a lot of beans and potatoes and had meat about three times a week. On Sundays always. I tried to raise my girls differently than how I had been raised. I tried to tell them when they first started wanting to date that I didn't want them to start dating early, which they didn't. They said, "But Mama, you did." And I'd say, "Yes, but I don't want you to do what I done." I said, "I got married when I was just a child. You need to get a little more out of life than just getting married, having children, and working in that mill." I explained to my girls about going with boys and things like that, and having babies and things like that. We just talked about it like there wasn't nothing to it. There was some of my boys that I even talked to. My youngest one I did, about going with girls. I said, "You might think that if something happened to a girl you was going with, it wouldn't be on you," but I said it would. "You've got to be careful with girls. Anything like that you need to have marriage first before you think about it, because," I said, "anything could happen and you might have to get married. And them kind of marriages sometimes just don't work out." Yeah, I tried to bring them up in the church which I think I have, most of them. My youngest son used to have a temper like nobody's business, but now he goes to Liberty Baptist. He got saved and now he's changed.

I didn't want my girls to have to work in the mill. I know people out there who have been hurt real bad on the job. I was working on the first shift and this woman was working on the second. She had long beautiful blonde hair and she bent over some way and her hair got caught in the machine. When it did, it just pulled her scalp off. They said blood was just pouring down her. Her boss man like to have passed out. They took her on to the hospital and sent somebody to go over there and get her scalp out of that thing and see if they could, you know, but nothing they could do. She stayed in the hospital for a long time. That happened about seven or eight years ago. Last thing I knew she was still going to the doctor's because she started having severe headaches. The insurance company fought it because they didn't want to pay off. So they took her to court. She didn't like for anyone to see her without her wig but they made her pull it off in court and they said she was crying. It was so pitiful.

I was working on second or third shift until the last job I had was on the first shift. My husband worked on one shift and I worked on the other. At the mill we had an understanding, he'd leave in time to get home so that I could get there in time to start work. Well, when I worked on the second shift, I'd sleep, say, about five hours a night. I have worked on third when I wouldn't get but three hours sleep. I worked on third one time and I wouldn't get no sleep at all because I would come in from work of a morning and I'd have to cook my breakfast and get the kids off to school. My husband was working on second. Then I'd do my wash or whatever I had to do and lay down maybe about ten thirty or eleven o'clock. I got my nerves so bad that time that my boss man told me I was going to have to go on another shift. I had gotten down to seventy-some pounds.

Then I worked on that shift until I was seven months pregnant with my last child. My boss man came and told me I was going to have to quit because they didn't want nobody in there after they were six months pregnant. They were scared something would happen and it would be on their hands. So I got a leave of absence for six months, but I didn't go back for six years. I just couldn't go back.

18

I Want You Women Up North to Know

Tillie Olsen

I want you women up north to know
how those dainty children's dresses you buy
   at macy's, wannamakers, gimbels,
marshall fields,
are dyed in blood, are stitched in wasting
   flesh,
down in San Antonio, "where sunshine
   spends the winter."
I want you women up north to see
the obsequious smile, the salesladies trill
   "exquisite work, madame, exquisite
   pleats"
vanish into a bloated face, ordering more
   dresses,
   gouging the wages down,
dissolve into maria, ambrosa, catalina,
   stitching these dresses from dawn to
   night,
   In blood, in wasting flesh.

Catalina Rodriguez, 24,
   body shrivelled to a child's at twelve,
catalina rodriguez, last stages of
   consumption,
   works for three dollars a week from
   dawn to midnight.
A fog of pain thickens over her skull, the
   parching heat
   breaks over her body,

and the bright red blood embroiders the
   floor of her room.
   White rain stitching the night, the

bourgeois poet would say.
   white gulls of hands, darting, veering,
   white lightning, threading the clouds,
this is the exquisite dance of her hands over
   the cloth,
and her cough, gay, quick, staccato,
   like skeleton's bones clattering,
is appropriate accompaniment for the
   esthetic dance
   of her fingers,
and the tremolo, tremolo when the hands
   tremble with pain.
Three dollars a week,
two fifty-five,
seventy cents a week,
no wonder two thousand eight hundred
   ladies of joy
are spending the winter with the sun after
   he goes down—
for five cents (who said this was a rich
   man's world?) you can
   get all the lovin you want
"clap and syph aint much worse than sore
   fingers, blind eyes, and
   t.b."

Maria Vasquez, spinster,
   for fifteen cents a dozen stitches
   garments for children she
   has never had.

Catalina Torres, mother of four,
   to keep the starved body starving,
   embroiders from dawn
   to night.

Mother of four, what does she think of,
    as the needle pocked fingers shift over
    the silk—
    of the stubble-coarse rags that stretch on
    her own brood,
    and jut with the bony ridge that marks
    hunger's landscape
    of fat little prairie-roll bodies that will
    bulge in the
    silk she needles?
(Be not envious, Catalina Torres, look!
    on your own children's clothing,
    embroidery,
    more intricate than any a thousand
    hands could fashion,
    there where the cloth is ravelled, or
    darned,
    designs, multitudinous, complex and
    handmade by Poverty
    herself.)
Ambrosa Espinoza trusts in god,
    "Todos es de dios, everything is from
    god,"
    through the dwindling night, the
    waxing day, she bolsters
    herself up with it—
but the pennies to keep god incarnate, from
    ambrosa,
and the pennies to keep the priest in wine,
    from ambrosa,
ambrosa clothes god and priest with
    hand-made children's dresses.

Her brother lies on an iron cot, all day and
    watches,
on a mattress of rags he lies.
For twenty-five years he worked for the
    railroad, then they laid
    him off.
(racked days, searching for work;
    rebuffs; suspicious eyes of
    policemen.
goodbye ambrosa, mebbe in dallas I find
    work; desperate
    swing for a freight,
    surprised hands, clutching air, and the
    wheel goes over a
    leg,

the railroad cuts it off,
as it cut off
twenty-five years of his
life.)
She says that he prays and dreams of
    another world, as he lies
    there, a heaven (which he does not
    know was brought to
    earth in 1917 in Russia, by workers like
    him).

Women up north, I want you to know
when you finger the exquisite hand-made
    dresses
what it means, this working from dawn to
    midnight,
on what strange feet the feverish dawn
    must come
    to maria, catalina, ambrosa,
how the malignant fingers twitching over
    the pallid faces jerk
them to work,
and the sun and the fever mount with the
    day—
    long plodding hours, the eyes burn like
    coals, heat jellies
    the flying fingers,
down comes the night like blindness.
    long hours more with the dim eye of the
    lamp, the breaking back,
    weariness crawls in the flesh like
    worms, gigantic like earth's
    in winter.
And for Catalina Rodriguez comes the
    night sweat and the blood
    embroidering the darkness.
    for Catalina Torres the pinched faces of
    four huddled
    children,
    the naked bodies of four bony children,
    the chant of their chorale of hunger.
And for twenty eight hundred ladies of joy
    the grotesque act gone
    over—the wink—the grimace—the
    "feeling like it baby?"
And for Maria Vasquez, spinster,
    emptiness, emptiness,

flaming with dresses for children she
    can never fondle.
And for Ambrosa Espinoza—the skeleton
    body of her brother on
his mattress of rags, boring twin holes in
    the dark with his eyes
to the image of christ, remembering a leg,
    and twenty five years

cut off from his life
    by the railroad.

Women up north, I want you to know,
I tell you this can't last forever.

I swear it won't.

19

Mike LeFevre

Studs Terkel

It is a two-flat dwelling, somewhere in Cicero, on the outskirts of Chicago. He is thirty-seven. He works in a steel mill. On occasion, his wife Carol works as a waitress in a neighborhood restaurant; otherwise, she is at home, caring for their two small children, a girl and a boy.

At the time of my first visit, a sculpted statu-ette of Mother and Child was on the floor, head severed from body. He laughed softly as he indi-cated his three-year-old daughter: "She Doctor Spock'd it."[1]

I'm a dying breed. A laborer. Strictly mus-cle work . . . pick it up, put it down, pick it up, put it down. We handle between forty and fifty thousand pounds of steel a day. (Laughs.) I know this is hard to believe—from four hun-dred pounds to three- and four-pound pieces. It's dying.

You can't take pride any more. You remem-ber when a guy could point to a house he built, how many logs he stacked. He built it and he was proud of it. I don't really think I could be proud if a contractor built a home for me. I would be tempted to get in there and kick the carpenter in the ass (laughs), and take the saw away from him. 'Cause I would have to be part of it, you know.

It's hard to take pride in a bridge you're never gonna cross, in a door you're never gonna open. You're mass-producing things and you never see the end result of it. (Muses.) I worked for a trucker one time. And I got this tiny satisfaction when I loaded a truck. At least I could see the truck depart loaded. In a steel mill, forget it. You don't see where nothing goes.

I got chewed out by my foreman once. He said, "Mike, you're a good worker but you have a bad attitude." My attitude is that I don't get excited about my job. I do my work but I don't say whoopee-doo. The day I get excited about my job is the day I go to a head shrinker. How are you gonna get excited about pullin' steel? How are you gonna get excited when you're tired and want to sit down?

It's not just the work. Somebody built the pyramids. Somebody's going to build some-thing. Pyramids, Empire State Building— these things just don't happen. There's hard work behind it. I would like to see a building, say, the Empire State, I would like to see on one side of it a foot-wide strip from top to bottom with the name of every bricklayer, the name of every electrician, with all the names. So when a guy walked by, he could take his son and say, "See, that's me over there on the forty-fifth floor. I put the steel beam in." Picasso can point to a painting. What can I point to? A writer can point to a book. Every-body should have something to point to.

It's the not-recognition by other people. To say a woman is *just* a housewife is degrad-ing, right? Okay. *Just* a housewife. It's also degrading to say *just* a laborer. The difference is that a man goes out and maybe gets smashed.

When I was single, I could quit, just split. I wandered all over the country. You worked just enough to get a poke, money in your pocket. Now I'm married and I got two kids . . . (trails off). I worked on a truck dock one time and I was single. The foreman came over and he grabbed my shoulder, kind of gave me a shove. I punched him and knocked him off the dock. I said, "Leave me alone. I'm doing my work, just stay away from me, just don't give me the with-the-hands business."

Hell, if you whip a damn mule he might kick you. Stay out of my way, that's all. Working is bad enough, don't bug me. I would rather work my ass off for eight hours a day with nobody watching me than five minutes with a guy watching me. Who you gonna sock? You can't sock General Motors, you can't sock anybody in Washington, you can't sock a system.

A mule, an old mule, that's the way I feel. Oh yeah. See. (Shows black and blue marks on arms and legs, burns.) You know what I heard from more than one guy at work? "If my kid wants to work in a factory, I am going to kick the hell out of him." I want my kid to be an effete snob. Yeah, mm-hmm. (Laughs.) I want him to be able to quote Walt Whitman,[2] to be proud of it.

If you can't improve yourself, you improve your posterity. Otherwise life isn't worth nothing. You might as well go back to the cave and stay there. I'm sure the first caveman who went over the hill to see what was on the other side—I don't think he went there wholly out of curiosity. He went there because he wanted to get his son out of the cave. Just the same way I want to send my kid to college.

I work so damn hard and want to come home and sit down and lay around. *But I gotta get it out.* I want to be able to turn around to somebody and say, "Hey, fuck you." You know? (Laughs.) The guy sitting next to me on the bus too. 'Cause all day I wanted to tell my foreman to go fuck himself, but I can't.

So I find a guy in a tavern. To tell him that. And he tells me too. I've been in brawls. He's punching me and I'm punching him, because we actually want to punch somebody else. The most that'll happen is the bartender will bar us from the tavern. But at work, you lose your job.

This one foreman I've got, he's a kid. He's a college graduate. He thinks he's better than

everybody else. He was chewing me out and I was saying, "Yeah, yeah, yeah." He said, "What do you mean, yeah, yeah, yeah. Yes, *sir.*" I told him, "Who the hell are you, Hitler? What is this *'Yes, sir'* bullshit? I came here to work, I didn't come here to crawl. There's a fuckin' difference." One word led to another and I lost.

I got broke down to a lower grade and lost twenty-five cents an hour, which is a hell of a lot. It amounts to about ten dollars a week. He came over—after breaking me down. The guy comes over and smiles at me. I blew up. He didn't know it, but he was about two seconds and two feet away from a hospital. I said, "Stay the fuck away from me." He was just about to say something and was pointing his finger. I just reached my hand up and just grabbed his finger and I just put it back in his pocket. He walked away. I grabbed his finger because I'm married. If I'd a been single, I'd a grabbed his head. That's the difference.

You're doing this manual labor and you know that technology can do it. (Laughs.) Let's face it, a machine can do the work of a man; otherwise they wouldn't have space probes. Why can we send a rocket ship that's unmanned and yet send a man in a steel mill to do a mule's work?

Automation? Depends how it's applied. It frightens me if it puts me out on the street. It doesn't frighten me if it shortens my work week. You read that little thing: What are you going to do when this computer replaces you? Blow up computers. (Laughs.) Really. Blow up computers. I'll be goddamned if a computer is gonna eat before I do! I want milk for my kids and beer for me. Machines can either liberate man or enslave 'im, because they're pretty neutral. It's a man who has the bias to put the thing one place or another.

If I had a twenty-hour workweek, I'd get to know my kids better, my wife better. Some kid invited me to go on a college campus. On a Saturday. It was summertime. Hell, if I had a choice of taking my wife and kids to a picnic or going to a college campus, it's gonna be the picnic. But if I worked a twenty-hour week, I could go do both. Don't you think with that extra twenty hours people could really expand? Who's to say? There are some people in factories just by force of circumstance. I'm just like the colored people. Potential Einsteins don't have to be white. They could be in cotton fields, they could be in factories.

The twenty-hour week is a possibility today. The intellectuals, they always say there are potential Lord Byrons, Walt Whitmans, Roosevelts, Picassos working in construction or steel mills or factories. But I don't think they believe it. I think what they're afraid of is the potential Hitlers and Stalins that are there too. The people in power fear the leisure man. Not just the United States. Russia's the same way.

What do you think would happen in this country if, for one year, they experimented and gave everybody a twenty-hour week? How do they know that the guy who digs Wallace[3] today doesn't try to resurrect Hitler tomorrow? Or the guy who is mildly disturbed at pollution doesn't decide to go to General Motors and shit on the guy's desk? You can become a fanatic if you had the time. The whole thing is time. That is, I think, one reason rich kids tend to be fanatic about politics: They have time. Time, that's the important thing.

It isn't that the average working guy is dumb. He's tired, that's all. I picked up a book on chess one time. That thing laid in the drawer for two or three weeks, you're too tired. During the weekends you want to take your kids out. You don't want to sit there and the kid comes up: "Daddy, can I go to the park?" You got your nose in a book? Forget it.

I know a guy fifty-seven years old. Know what he tells me? "Mike, I'm old and tired all the time." The first thing happens at work: When the arms start moving, the brain stops. I punch in about ten minutes to seven in the morning. I say hello to a couple of guys I like, I kid around with them. One guy says good morning to you and you say good morning. To another guy you say fuck you. The guy you say fuck you to is your friend.

I put on my hard hat, change into my safety shoes, put on my safety glasses, go to the bonderizer. It's the thing I work on. They rake the metal, they wash it, they dip it in a paint solution, and we take it off. Put it on, take it off, put it on, take it off, put it on, take it off . . .

I say hello to everybody but my boss. At seven it starts. My arms get tired about the first half-hour. After that, they don't get tired any more until maybe the last half-hour at the end of the day. I work from seven to three thirty. My arms are tired at seven thirty and they're tired at three o'clock. I hope to God I never get broke in, because I always want my arms to be tired at seven thirty and three o'clock. (Laughs.) 'Cause that's when I know that there's a beginning and there's an end. That I'm not brainwashed. In between, I don't even try to think.

If I were to put you in front of a dock and I pulled up a skid in front of you with fifty hundred-pound sacks of potatoes and there are fifty more skids just like it, and this is what you're gonna do all day, what would you think about—potatoes? Unless a guy's a nut, he never thinks about work or talks about it. Maybe about baseball or about getting drunk the other night or he got laid or he didn't get laid. I'd say one out of a hundred will actually get excited about work.

Why is it that the communists always say they're for the workingman, and as soon as they set up a country, you got guys singing to tractors? They're singing about how they love the factory. That's where I couldn't buy communism. It's the intellectuals' utopia, not mine. I cannot picture myself singing to a tractor, I just can't. (Laughs.) Or singing to steel. (Singsongs.) Oh, whoop-dee-doo, I'm at the bonderizer, oh how I love this heavy steel. No thanks. Never happen.

Oh yeah, I daydream. I fantasize about a sexy blonde in Miami who's got my union dues. (Laughs.) I think of the head of the union the way I think of the head of my company. Living it up. I think of February in Miami. Warm weather, a place to lay in. When I hear a college kid say, "I'm oppressed," I don't believe him. You know what I'd like to do for one year? Live like a college kid. Just for one year. I'd love to. Wow! (Whispers.) Wow! Sports car! Marijuana! (Laughs.) Wild, sexy broads. I'd love that, hell yes, I would.

Somebody has to do this work. If my kid ever goes to college, I just want him to have a little respect, to realize that his dad is one of those somebodies. This is why even on— (muses) yeah, I guess, sure—on the black thing . . . (Sighs heavily.) I can't really hate the colored fella that's working with me all day. The black intellectual I got no respect for. The white intellectual I got no use for. I got no use for the black militant who's gonna scream three hundred years of slavery to me while I'm busting my ass. You know what I mean? (Laughs.) I have one answer for that guy: Go see Rockefeller. See Harriman.[4] Don't bother me. We're in the same cotton field. So just don't bug me. (Laughs.)

After work I usually stop off at a tavern. Cold beer. Cold beer right away. When I was single, I used to go into hillbilly bars, get in a lot of brawls. Just to explode. I got a thing on my arm here (indicates scar). I got slapped with a bicycle chain. Oh, wow! (Softly.) Mmm. I'm getting older. (Laughs.) I don't explode as much. You might say I'm broken in. (Quickly.) No, I'll never be broken in. (Sighs.) When you get a little older, you exchange the words. When you're younger, you exchange the blows.

When I get home, I argue with my wife a little bit. Turn on TV, get mad at the news. (Laughs.) I don't even watch the news that much. I watch Jackie Gleason. I look for any alternative to the ten o'clock news. I don't want to go to bed angry. Don't hit a man with anything heavy at five o'clock. He just can't be bothered. This is his time to relax. The heaviest thing he wants is what his wife has to tell him.

When I come home, know what I do for the first twenty minutes? Fake it. I put on a smile. I got a kid three years old. Sometimes she says, "Daddy, where've you been?" I say, "Work." I could have told her I'd been in Disneyland. What's work to a three-year-old kid? If I feel bad, I can't take it out on the kids. Kids are born innocent of everything but birth. You can't take it out on your wife either. This is why you go to a tavern. You want to release it there rather than do it at home. What does an actor do when he's got a bad movie? I got a bad movie every day.

I don't even need the alarm clock to get up in the morning. I can go out drinking all night, fall asleep at four, and bam! I'm up at six—no matter what I do. (Laughs.) It's a pseudo-death, more or less.

Notes

1. *Doctor Spock:* Dr. Benjamin Spock, prominent U.S. child-care expert (b. 1903).

2. *Walt Whitman:* influential U.S. poet (1819–1892); best known for *Leaves of Grass* (1855).

3. *Wallace:* George C. Wallace (b. 1919), governor of Alabama in three separate terms spanning three decades. Wallace was a key opponent of school desegregation in 1963, but recanted and won significant black support in the 1982 election.

4. *Harriman:* Edward Harriman, railroad tycoon (1848–1909) and father of New York governor W. Averell Harriman. Like Rockefeller, a rich, powerful man.

20

From Homemaker to Housing Advocate: An Interview With Mrs. Chang Jok Lee

Nancy Diao

I first met Mrs. Lee in 1976 at a rally in front of the International Hotel and then again in 1985 in the midst of a financial crisis in the San Francisco Housing Authority. The agency was more than $9 million in debt, and its executive director Carl Williams had been asked to resign by Mayor Diane Feinstein. During this time, the Ping Yuen Residents Improvement Association (PYRIA) remained the best organized and most effective tenant association in the city. Much of its strength was due to the consistent participation of Mrs. Lee. She had been the backbone of a monumental effort to protect the rights of low-income tenants in San Francisco's China-town. This is an unusual role for an immigrant woman whose Chinese tradition frowns upon women activists.

What struck me was Mrs. Lee's dedication to working for social change, an unusual choice for a woman her age. Instead of playing mah-jongg with her contemporaries, she prefers to attend community meetings, testify at city hearings, and help fellow tenants settle disputes. Mrs. Lee is in her late fifties, but looks much younger. With glasses and short black hair, permed and fashionably kept, she is always well groomed and impeccably dressed. For a Chinese woman, she is rather big-framed, but looks sturdy and confident. She speaks her mind freely, from telling stories about her favorite granddaughter to tales about growth pains with the tenant association or gossip in the Chinese commu-

nity. Though she speaks a combination of Chinese dialects, with a mixture of some English words, she looks you straight in the eye when she talks. You can't help but notice her sincerity and passion.

Growing Up in Japan

In a 1985 interview, Mrs. Lee told of how poverty and discrimination have plagued her since her childhood in Japan. Born in 1927, in Kobe, she was the third of eight children, and the second girl. Her family suffered the hard life of Chinese immigrants in Japan, and she remembers growing up poor, segregated from the Japanese.

My family was very poor when I was born. We didn't even have money to buy soy sauce. When I was two years old, my father got a job as a chef in the Egyptian Embassy, so our entire family lived in the servants' quarters of the embassy. My mother helped out with the housecleaning and ironing.

We didn't have much contact with the Japanese except when we went shopping. In Kobe, the Chinese operated pastry, coffee, tailoring, and other shops and had two Chinese schools. I went to the Mandarin school until the sixth grade, but we didn't have enough money for me to continue; my sister went only to night school.

The heavy responsibilities she assumed as a girl helped to groom her for her later leadership role in the Chinatown tenants' group. When her family returned to the Zhongshan district in southeastern China during the Sino-Japanese War, and while her father and older brother remained in Japan, Mrs. Lee had to bear the bulk of caring for the family though she was only eleven years old. This responsibility continued even after the family reunited in Japan one year later. More aggressive and verbal than her older, frail sister, Mrs. Lee represented the family at air raid exercises and in food ration lines. After the sixth grade, she worked in a Taiwanese-owned shoe factory and then in a candy factory to help with the family income.

Along with other Chinese in Japan, she and her family were subjected to many forms of discrimination because Japan and China were on opposite sides of a war.

Some pharmacies would use slogans like "Can even kill the Nanking Bloodsuckers" as advertisements for the effectiveness of pesticides. In many Japanese shops we would have to wait until the Japanese customers were served first. We were also discriminated against in employment and were only able to get lower class jobs regardless of our education, skills, and abilities. This situation forced many of us to start our own small businesses such as cafe/restaurants, tailor shops, and painting stores.

When the United States began bombing Kobe in 1944, life became even harsher for Mrs. Lee's family.

Whole families died in air raid shelters, smothered by smoke. When the planes came, everyone in my family went into caves or shelters; only my older brother and I stayed behind to watch our house. One time our house was firebombed, and I tried to put out the fire by stomping, but in vain. My brother went looking for me all over the place, but the fire and smoke had spread so fast that he couldn't see anything. Fortu-

nately I had escaped, and he did thereafter. We lost our house, and our family split up. I was sent to live with a family friend who came from the Fukien province.

Romance Leads to America

While living with the Fukienese family and working for them to earn her keep, Mrs. Lee met her future husband, George, through her first boyfriend. George was a Chinese American GI who was stationed in Yokohama after the surrender of the Japanese government at the end of World War II. When asked how she met George, Mrs. Lee giggled. Her face lit up and she blushed. Then her eyes softened with a watery glow. Compared to her first boyfriend, who treated her like a "good little workhorse," George was considerate and romantic, though they didn't talk much in those days.

George always treated me with kindness and respect, very different from my first boyfriend. He always saved me a seat on the bus and gave me little gifts, whereas my boyfriend never showed any appreciation. [For instance], when my boyfriend's family's house was bombed, and he lost all of his belongings, I stayed up all night to knit him a sweater. He never even said "thank you."

Mrs. Lee and George married in 1946, and their first son was born one year later. When the son was just six months old, George returned to the United States while Mrs. Lee remained in Japan with her parents till her husband came back to get her. They arrived in San Francisco in 1950, and in two years moved into one of the Ping Yuen public housing apartments in Chinatown. She remembers her life being full, but also one of poverty.

We were so poor that most of the time we didn't even have a penny in the house, but I wasn't scared or worried. We raised eight children, four boys and four girls, and from them I learned some English.

When the children were small, Mrs. Lee spent all of her time raising them; but as they grew older, she found more time to think about her own needs and interests. She began to become more active in the community, beginning first with just singing and socializing, and then onto more serious work.

When the children were all grown up, I started learning Mandarin and singing songs at the Asian Community Center. Since I went to a Mandarin school in Japan, I wanted to keep it up. While I was learning Mandarin, I had the opportunity to read a lot of newspapers and books, and went to May Day celebrations with George. Ever since George got disabled from a car accident in 1972, he has had a lot of free time to get involved in community issues.

Confrontation With Housing Issues

The Asian Community Center was a commercial tenant of the International Hotel block, which soon became the focal point of the early conflict of interests between low-income tenants and land developers. Mrs. Lee's association with the center eventually led to her involvement with community housing issues.

In 1977, when my youngest daughters, Sylvia, Patricia, and Teresa, were twenty-one, nineteen, and ten, I became involved in the International Hotel struggle. I would take my youngest daughter, Teresa, to meetings and classes with me. Because I knew some of the tenants who lived in the International Hotel, I got upset when I saw leaflets about the possibility of them being evicted; I did not want to see them homeless. The young people at the Asian Community Center encouraged me to go to meetings on the third floor of the I-Hotel. It took me a while to get used to meetings

and rallies, but eventually I even spoke with bullhorns at demonstrations.

On August 3, 1977, the night of the eviction, George, Teresa, Patricia, and I were there. It was a warm night; there were four hundred policemen on horses, in addition to the tactical squad. The I-Hotel was surrounded by thousands of people—Asian, white, black, young and old, including many from Reverend Jim Jones's church who came in busloads. It seemed that we all stood on the sidewalk for hours. Suddenly the horses charged. I screamed, and everywhere there was yelling, screaming, and crying. We wanted the horses to stop charging, but the tactical squad used their billy clubs to hold us back on the sidewalk. As the horses rushed and trampled, the human chain around the hotel broke. People fell down. Tears poured out of my eyes as I heard Hongisto (then chief of police) breaking down the door to the I-Hotel. We stayed in front of the I-Hotel until three in the morning—watching every tenant being either dragged out or carried out of the hotel; then we went to Portsmouth Square.

Even as Mrs. Lee's support of the I-Hotel continued, she transferred more energy toward improving living conditions in Ping Yuen. In 1977 all the pipes in Ping Yuen were rotting, but in spite of repeated calls to the San Francisco Housing Authority, nothing was being done to fix the problem. Eventually George and some members of the tenant association initiated a massive petition drive to get the plumbing repaired. At the end of 1977, the housing authority finally repaired all of the pipes and painted the exterior walls of half of the buildings. And George was elected president of the association.

A year later, when the housing authority proved unresponsive in meeting the tenants' demands for better security, Mrs. Lee participated in the Ping Yuen tenants' first rent strike. The action was instigated by the brutal rape and murder of tenant Judy Wong. It was an intense period for Mrs. Lee.

I remember passing out leaflets door to door, talking to the tenants, attending lots of meetings, and collecting rent for fifteen days of each month at the association office on Pacific Avenue. The strike lasted for four months, with numerous press conferences and tedious negotiations with the housing authority, at the end of which we got our security guards.

The second strike followed at the end of 1979, when housing authority groundskeepers and office workers struck for higher pay. The city-wide Public Housing Tenants Association (PHTA) wanted to strike in support, but only the Ping Yuen tenants actually did. When the city employees went back to work, the Public Housing Tenants Association withdrew their support. But the Ping Yuen group continued the strike for maintenance issues, such as fixing apartment interiors and elevators, repairing floors, and painting. It was a long and drawn-out fight, but the tenants' persistence brought them victory.

We started with eighty households, but some tenants discontinued their strike support for fear of eviction. We held many meetings and visited people door to door. We also had membership drives and sponsored activities to keep the striking tenants together. Since I was the treasurer, I collected the rent, put it in escrow, and kept the books. After two years, we finally got our demands met.

At the end of the strike, most of the tenants chose to donate 50 percent of the escrow interest, about ten thousand dollars, to PYRIA for a color television in the community room and a banquet at Asia Garden. At the banquet the tenants surprised Mrs. Lee and George with two round-trip tickets to Japan to show their appreciation for the couple's efforts in the strike.

During her husband's term as president of the improvement association, from 1979 to 1981, Mrs. Lee worked on two major projects that brought additional benefits to the Ping Yuen tenants. In 1979, at the request of the tenant population, Mrs. Lee went door to door at least two hours a day to sign up enough tenants to pressure Cablevision to install cable television services. Second, Mrs. Lee took over the coordination of the vegetable garden and established new rules: each member had an opportunity to have a garden and the size of all the lots was made equal. She thereby abolished all favoritism in the distribution of garden plots.

Reactions to Activism

Though Mrs. Lee can now act fearlessly, this was not so when she first became active in the community.

At first I was scared, or rather, kind of embarrassed. I didn't speak English and was not used to speaking in front of people. But after a while, I got used to it. As long as I am fighting for a just cause, then I am not scared.

Since Mrs. Lee's own family has remained in Japan, and George is also alone in the United States, neither has had to face pressure and criticism from relatives, who traditionally might have frowned on women's activism. She and her husband have, however, had some run-ins with the more conservative element of the community.

I didn't really get much reaction from getting involved in I-Hotel, but when I became active in the business of the association, I started getting a lot of harassment. The wall near our apartment was often spray painted with the word "commies!" with a black arrow pointing to our apartment. Everytime we challenged the previous PYRIA administration's way of doing things, we were called "commies." There were also flyers and posters attacking us.

Neither have her relationships with other tenants always been smooth. Some have criticized her for "doing too much." Take, for example, the laundromat project.

One of the officers of the association says that I am stupid to sweep the floors of the laundryroom. But when the laundryroom is dirty, I just can't stand it. It took so much out of us to get this project done; I feel like it's my own. So, when people don't clean up after themselves and youths abuse the furniture and write on walls, it really hurts me. But what hurts me more is when other officers nag at me for "doing too much." If they do some and if everybody does something, then I wouldn't have to do so much. Sometimes I squeeze in the sweeping when the baby is taking a nap.

After a recent officers' meeting, Mrs. Lee went home crying. The stress brought her a few sleepless nights and some additional white hair. At times like these, she wonders about whether her efforts are worth all the headaches and talks about quitting, but she stays. She remains undaunted about making Ping Yuen a better place to live and confident about the tenants' overall good feelings towards her.

Deep down, I know a lot of tenants really like me. They respect me and support George. The maintenance worker, Mr. Wong, complains about the youths not listening to him, but I don't have any problems with them. I just tell them to get out [of the laundryrooms] and they do. Most of the tenants listen to me, and whenever there is something bothering them, they always either ask me questions or ask me to help them.

Sometimes even her children scold her for "wasting her time." Yet other times they have helped out by protecting her at demonstrations or doing errands.

Some of my children get down on me for doing so much volunteer work. They say that I am crazy for spending so much time on the association when I don't get paid. They don't really understand me. I am happier when I am active, though there is nothing material to gain. It keeps me young. I don't have much white hair or wrinkles [*she points to her head*], do I?

Sylvia doesn't get down on me for doing so much. She just doesn't want me and George to be taken advantage of; she helps me out a lot. She is the one who taught me how to do books, how to do a membership drive, and keep a membership list. Her husband took off work a couple of times to take care of their daughter whom I watch [five days a week], so that I could be freed up to go to the public hearings on the Orangeland Project at the City Planning Commission.

Teresa . . . knows that I am happier when I am active. She doesn't complain when I am not home to cook dinner, and sometimes she even translates for me.

Conclusion: Balancing Life's Demands

When asked if it has been hard to balance all the demands in her life—being a wife, mother of eight, grandmother of eleven now (eight when she was interviewed), and a housing activist—she laughed:

From these activities, I learned that there is nothing to fear. I feel alive when I come out to do things. But I do take a lot of abuse from people—gripes, complaints, blames, and a lot of headaches. Even George and I have differences sometimes, and he is very stubborn. But basically we are alike, so things don't get too bad at home. At least he doesn't bug me about housework or cooking; sometimes we just go out to eat. . . .

In the past a lot of the community leaders courted George and me. They always invited us to events and asked us to help. Now no one comes. I guess they realize that they can't just use us anymore. I try to keep up with the issues. Sometimes I get upset about association business, and I can't sleep at night. But most of the time, being active keeps me alive. I don't play mahjongg or go to Reno, so I take care of my granddaughter, and I go to meetings.

On 10 July 1985, Mrs. Chang Jok Lee was honored for her dedication and hard work with the Ping Yuen Residents Improvement Association at the eighth anniversary celebration of the Chinatown Neighborhood Improvement Resources Center, which has spearheaded much of the effort to retain housing in San Francisco's Chinatown. In front of 550 people, she said in Chinese, "I don't really deserve this, but I know that if we all work together, anything can be done." Then, the fifty-eight-year-old grandmother smiled and curtsied.

21

Esse Quam Videri:
Susie Williams Jones

Emily Herring Wilson
Susan Mullalley

Susie Jones invites visitors to come in, open-ing the door of her comfortable white clap-board home, which served as the President's residence on the Bennett College campus in Greensboro. Mrs. Jones extends her hand, and, if there is a certain formality in the ges-ture, it is relieved by her smile.

The house is muted in shadows across drapery and chairs, across the ridges of many books, falling on the keys of the piano. Over the mantel there is a large abstract painting; beneath, logs are laid for use in the fireplace. Carved ivory statues rest on shelves and ta-bles. Everywhere there are books of poetry, art, and history. There is music, but not from the piano; it comes from Mrs. Jones's high, flute-like voice. She comes to her guests with freshly made orange juice on a china plate, with a linen napkin. She turns the conversa-tion to ask about our families. The hour passes until the room seems to be filled, with sunlight.

Here is the home to which Bennett girls came for breakfast with her husband, David D. Jones, who served the school from 1926 until his death in 1956. Here there were teas, parties, and dinners presided over by a woman who is widely regarded as one of the most gracious hostesses in Greensboro. Here there were the activities of their four children, en-couraged to participate in the life of Bennett College. Here there was good sense, good manners, and good will.

Susie Jones, now in her ninetieth year, is one of the best-known and best loved women in North Carolina. Her years of service with her husband during his presidency of Bennett College and with the YWCA, the Methodist Church, and the United Council of Church Women have given her unique opportunities to advance humanitarian concerns and the progress of what she, in an old-fashioned way, refers to as "our group." By this she means, of course, all black Americans. Born into a family where education was more ex-tensive than that of many Southerners and where attitudes were broadly democratic, she grew up with an informed understanding of human rights. From this kind of environ-ment, she developed a deep resourcefulness which sustains her now.

Her lifetime of involvement in schools and organizations, her travels, and her con-tacts with people of national importance have not separated her from other lives unlike her own. Whether her concern is for the black

AUTHORS' NOTE: Acknowledgement is made to the Black Women Oral History Project, sponsored by the Arthur and Elizabeth Schlesinger Library on the History of Women in America of Radcliffe College, for permission to quote from an interview conducted with Mrs. Jones by Dr. Merze Tate.

children who were thrust into integrated schools or the first black contestants in the Miss America pageant, or the numbers of blacks in jails, she is especially sensitive to the lives of members of her own race, particularly those who have had a less protected environment than her own. Although she is comfortable in the college home on the Bennett campus, Susie Jones will never be satisfied until her own comforts are shared by a larger number of black Americans. Thus, she lives both with the serenity which a long life of family success has brought her and with the quiet insistence that other black families come to experience a better day.

To begin her story, we go back from Greensboro, the center for the first civil rights sit-ins which changed the nation, to Kentucky, where her family was perhaps already preparing for a new America.

"I was born in Danville, Kentucky, April 30, 1892. This was my grandmother's home. It was our custom every year, as soon as school was dismissed, to go to Danville and spend the summer. We always went on the train from Cincinnati, Ohio, because my mother insisted that we were interstate travelers, and this meant we did not have to use the segregated coaches. I did not understand this at that time, but I can remember that she would often have arguments with the conductor as to where we would sit. We all looked forward to going to visit Grandmother, because my mother was a very practical woman, and she had many interests in the community as well as the responsibilities of her home. We lived a very simple life; we had a very simple upbringing. But Grandmother did not feel that way about it. She felt that all of our underskirts should have lace sewed on them and that it was important for children to have a party every summer. She brought lots of glamour into our lives. I think I have heard my sisters say, and I know I have said often to myself, 'I do hope I can grow old gracefully as Grandmother did.' I have my grandmother's cups and saucers. They are old Haviland, and during our summers in Danville, one of the things Grandmother did al-

ways was to entertain her club of friends. And for this club, my uncle, my mother's brother who was a very sought-after caterer, would send her either pastries or strawberries from Cincinnati. He would send them by porters on the train, and we would go down and pick them up. He and his wife added a great deal to our lives. They thought it was important for us to have kid gloves and simple jewelry that every girl appreciates. He had great love for his family and was mindful of them. My grandmother was also a very good seamstress, and she did beautiful handiwork. Every year during the winter months, she would make her mother a cap to wear, a cap made of lace and fine material. One of our jobs when we came in the summer was to 'go out to the hill,' as we called it, where my great-grandmother lived, to carry her this cap.

"My grandmother had great influence on my life and on the lives of my sisters and brother. She was the slave of a Presbyterian minister, and it was his custom to read to his wife every evening. He always insisted on my grandmother sitting there, listening to him, and so she learned to read and was a great reader all her life. When my two oldest children were about three and four, I took them to see her, and she recited for us, sitting in her rocking chair on the front porch, all of Byron's *Prisoner of Chillon*. She had a great love for English and Irish literature. I think you can understand why she felt it was important for her daughter to go to college. My mother started her college work at Allegheny, where she had an uncle living, and then transferred to Berea, and there she met my father. She had been the favorite in her own home and family. Her college education was rare for a woman at that time. She made a brilliant record, and she would stand no interference with her plans. It was she who decided that my sister, Frances, must go to Mt. Holyoke College. They had not enrolled a colored student at Holyoke for years, and when she applied for admission for Frances, they wrote her that Frances would probably be happier in an environment where she was more at home, and she answered, 'Frances's happiness is none of your business; that's my business. I want to know if you will admit her.' And they did. When my youngest son went to Andover, his teacher said to him, 'You are the best prepared Latin student that I have had in years. Where did you study your Latin?' His reply was, 'My grandmother.' He had studied with his grandmother while in high school. She was on the advisory committee for the national YWCA before Negroes were on the board. At seventy, she resigned all the clubs she belonged to and became a member of the recently organized League of Women Voters. At her death we found that she had adopted a child under CARE.

"My mother and father graduated from Berea College, receiving their bachelor's degrees. My first experience in race [discrimination] was when the Negro students, because of the Day Law that was passed by the legislature in Kentucky, were put out of Berea.[1] Lincoln Institute was established for them. Some of the Negro graduates of Berea protested this. My father was leader of the group that protested, so my first racial experience was hearing very heated discussions on this matter. The president at that time was Dr. Foust. He came to our house several times to meet with this group to try to work out a satisfactory arrangement, but this never was realized. Although in these later years, under Dr. Hutchins, Berea opened again her doors to Negro students, my mother never forgave them, and so she never made a contribution to the college. My father did give, but she did not. Because, you would probably remember, Berea was founded for Negroes and mountain whites, and she felt that they had in such a large way betrayed their heritage.

"My father was a great teacher. As I was growing up, he was a teacher in Louisville, Kentucky. Later, he became principal of the high school in Covington, Kentucky. This was a very significant event in our lives, because he immediately enrolled in the University of Cincinnati for advanced work. He was the only Negro principal of a high school in St. Louis for years. We saw him take demotions and new assignments. He had made Sumner

High School one of the first high schools in the country, and he was moved to a downtown high school that had a very bad image, the Vashon High School. It was located in the inner city, and the majority of the students came from deprived homes. One of the first things he did, which to me was fascinating, he sat on a stool in the hall, and as the children came into the building, he would say, 'Good morning' to each of them. He believed clearly in certain principles. One of the marked ones of these was thrift, and he thought our group would never make the kind of progress they should make until they were adequate economically. And so one of his first activities in the St. Louis community was to organize the New Age Building and Loan Association. Another thing he deplored was the housing of Negroes in St. Louis. Those of you who know St. Louis know that there were many very large houses there, and St. Louis was something like Brooklyn in that these houses were grouped around. As people moved to the west, and Negroes went into these large houses, the only way they could sustain themselves was to sublet. And so there was a feeling in St. Louis that property would go down when Negroes moved into the area. And my father was greatly concerned about this. We had all at this time graduated from college, and out of his earnings, he had saved enough money to build an apartment building for Negroes. This building was built by one of the leading construction firms of St. Louis, and the building was very adequate, very impressive looking outside. And so there happened one of these strange phenomena of how people that you're trying to help turn on you, and my father faced a severe school fight. Interestingly enough, a friend, who came by one day as he sat on his porch, said to him, since there was his own home, the apartment next door, and a housing unit next, 'Mr. Williams, this is your trouble. You are looking too prosperous.' But he did live to see all the leaders in the school fight come to him for some favor. I can well remember one time being there when a teacher came to him with his monthly check, and I said to my father, 'What does this mean?' He said, naming the teacher, 'He does not seem to be able to handle his finances, and the Board of Education is continuing his employment if he will come to me every month with his check, and we will sit down and make a budget, and he will keep out of the hand of vendors and people accusing him of not paying his bills.' "

A grandmother who recited poetry, a mother who read Latin, a father who was a community leader—these were the earliest influences in the life of Susie Williams Jones. Her future looked bright, indeed. She entered kindergarten when she was three years old and continued through elementary and high schools in Kentucky. After graduation, she took an additional year at Woodward High School in Cincinnati, the alma mater of William Howard Taft, to qualify for entrance to the University of Cincinnati. "At Woodward High School," she remembers, "there was quite a tradition not only for a certain type of education, but for relationships of students and faculty. I remember our Latin teacher, a Mr. Peabody from Boston Latin School, had been teacher there for years. The days at Woodward, you can understand, had certain adjustments that had to be made because I was entering the senior class. Most of the students had been with each other through all of their high school experiences. But I was reasonably happy. I did not feel that I had any particular problems. I think our parents had been successful in bringing us up with an acceptance of people as people, and this was the important thing. We had certain normal situations with people of the white race, but I never was particularly impressed with what color they were, or whether they were Negroes or whites. In the yearbook, the comment under my picture read: Susie believes in our class motto, *Esse quam videri*, To be rather than to seem. Our parents were very anxious, as far as their means allowed, to give us experiences of enrichment that were wider in scope than life in this small Kentucky town. One of our Christmas presents was always a season ticket to lectures given in Cincinnati on Sunday afternoons during the fall and winter. We heard prominent leaders in the country. Through this kind of an experience and attending political meetings in Cincinnati involving national politics, we had a feeling of world outreach.

"The matter of race did not really hit me until I went to college. Although there were just a very few Negroes who attended the University of Cincinnati at that time, it was largely a municipal college. It had no dormitories, and so the students came from the Cincinnati area, and if not immediately from Cincinnati, from some of the smaller Kentucky towns. One of the most outstanding irritations that I suffered was that an English teacher, who was from the North, left a vacant seat on both sides of me. I went to the head of the department and complained about this. After our initial conversation he sent for me to come back. Dr. Miller did not want me to transfer; he wanted me to stay in the class. This was a very difficult experience for me, but not difficult enough to deter me in any way. When it was necessary to use the same material, or if I wanted to see somebody else's notebook, or they wanted to see mine, we would just move in the seats of our own accord, and so it did not deter me, but it really was my most unpleasant experience in college. When I graduated, I had persuaded my father, who was not easy to persuade, to let me go to the University of Chicago for a summer session, so that I could graduate early. He granted this request. There, too, I found discrimination of a different kind, people not willing to even answer simple questions. I later found out that there were a great many Southerners who came for the summer session, and I am sure unfriendliness was more or less common because there were a great many Negroes attending the summer sessions. So my racial experiences came along at the time of life that I was mature. I must have taken them in stride as most Negroes do, and worked with them when I could. I always had enough pleasant experiences to outbalance those that were difficult. I never felt persecuted, and I really never felt that I couldn't do anything I wanted to do because of race. Those of us who grew up in a more or less protected environment, where we did not have to use public transportation, where we did not have to—now, I can remember my mother on this, you just never bought anything at a store where the clerks were in any way rude to you. You go to another store because there were plenty of stores where they were kind and gracious to you. And my grandmother's home, although it was right in the heart of the bluegrass, she had a horse and buggy and so you know you weren't up against a lot of things that some people had to contend with. I think that—I don't quite know how to say this—but I think that as I grew older and began to understand more of the system and what was happening in the world, I began to feel that I must do whatever I could to work on this matter. I was able to work in the Methodist Church and in the United Council of Church Women, where there are both white and Negro women working together for solutions. This was a most exciting experience. I also was here for the first sit-ins and marched and participated in all of the activities that were a part of this movement in Greensboro, North Carolina.

"Just as race was not emphasized in my family, neither was the matter of sex. My father had both men and women as faculty members, and so I never felt there was any question about my identity as a woman. I never grew up feeling that there should be preferences. Just as I acquired a deeper knowledge of the race issue as I grew older, so I became conscious of the problem of women. In my married life, I was always interested in the YWCA, and I inherited this from my mother. But the women's movements, except the League of Women Voters, were not as clearly defined in focus or in activities as they are today. And so I have a mixed feeling about the women's movement, not that I am specifically against it, but I feel that there are some strategies that are questionable. I feel strongly that the struggle for racial equality and the struggle for women's rights have been two parallel struggles in American life. I feel that it is important, since women are moving out into the mainstream of life, and our home responsibilities have become less, I do think it is important that they be supported by non-discrimination of all kinds. In many ways I am very grateful for the movement, but at the same time as I have seen some of it from the sideline, which is quite different from being responsible for things, I have felt that there were certain things in our struggle for rights that we did not want to lose out on. Just as Mr. Hooks, present director of the NAACP, was saying in his 'Face the Nation' interview, that he was dedicated, he wanted liberty for everybody, but he was committed to seeking it out for people who had been deprived. I think that what we do in these movements is so dependent upon the kinds of people that we are, and I don't think that I have been over-aggressive in the area of race because that's just not my nature. I can remember a man came in my house one day; I can't remember just why he was there, but he had his hat on, and I asked him to take off his hat, please, and so I dropped my voice and he took it off. Then I can remember when we lived in Atlanta, I volunteered to take nursery school children to the clinic at Grady Hospital. Registration cards had to be made out for each child, and the woman who was head of this part of the work asked me one day, what was my name, and I said, 'My name is Mrs. Jones.' She replied, 'We do not call Negroes by titles.' I suggested that she not use my name because I would be uncomfortable if she attempted to use my first name. Her reply was, 'I will call you what you wish. I can't let you be more polite than I.'"

After marriage to David Jones in 1915, when she was twenty-three, Mrs. Jones settled down to a life in which the family and home were of primary importance. When Mr. Jones, a graduate of Wesleyan College and the University of Chicago, was interviewed by Edward R. Murrow for *This I Believe*, he said, "From the outset my wife and I have had the feeling that no matter what else we did in life, we had to devote our best thinking and our best living to our children." After Mr. Jones became president of Bennett College in 1926, Susie Jones and their four young children became part of the campus family. The children were included in receptions and dinners in the home which were given for distinguished visitors. And "there were chores to be done, the grass was to be weeded, and the trips to the post office and banks were made daily. This was a priceless heritage. The children learned to work, and they knew when work was well done. There was a far greater blessing that came to them and came to me as their mother. We were starting a new enterprise and there were people who were willing to help; and so in and out of the home there were visitors who greatly enriched all of our lives. I can remember one Sunday evening, the youngest boy was with us as we were taking Mrs. Mary McLeod Bethune to the station. And he said in the car going down, 'Daddy, you know this is the first time I ever heard a speech where I understood all the speaker said.' And Mrs. Bethune laughed in her characteristic way and said, 'Well, Dave, I really put the cookies on the lower shelf today, didn't I?'

"I would like to say a deep word of gratitude for the opportunities that were ours on the college campus. Mr. Jones's illness in the 1950s stopped all of my outside activities. At his death, the trustees were kind enough to elect me vice-president of the college. I felt that I should not accept this. I wanted to be sure not to presume on the college in any way, and whatever I did, I wanted people to understand that it would be something that was important for the on-going of the college. And so I asked that instead of being elected vice-president, I should be elected registrar, work which I had done voluntarily in the early days of the college and an office where I had started the college records. And so I worked in this office until I was seventy-two years of age."

The four children of Susie and David Jones attended public schools in Greensboro, the boys finishing their secondary training in northern preparatory schools. Later, they studied at some of the most distinguished colleges and universities in America—Wesleyan, Harvard, Boston University. Their daughter, now on the staff of Harvard University Medical School, is still proud of the training she received at Bennett College.

"I hope as I have talked," Mrs. Jones concludes, "I have not made it seem that life was without struggle, because my life has been filled with ups and down. [One of the tragedies of her life was the death of her oldest son in 1976.] My father was wont to say that the good life does not necessarily mean that you do not have trouble, but it does mean that you get the breaks. My husband used to say to the Bennett girls, 'The next most certain thing to death is that effort counts.' "

For Susie Jones the "good life" has meant a legacy of education, manners, and opportunity received from her parents, which she, in turn, has passed on to her children and grandchildren.

Note

1. The Kentucky Day Law 71904 prohibited co-racial education in the state.

22

Women's Work and Caregiving Roles:
A Life Course Approach

Phyllis Moen
Julie Robison
Vivian Fields

This study drew on a life course approach and a sample of 293 women from four birth cohorts in upstate New York to examine the relationship over time between women's paid work and their informal caregiving of aging or infirm relatives. We find that such caregiving is an increasingly likely role for women, both as they age and across birth cohorts. One in four (24%) women became caregivers at some time between ages 35–44, and over one in three (36%) of these same women became caregivers between ages 55–64. Only 45 percent of the oldest cohort (born 1905–1917) were ever caregivers, compared to 64 percent of the most recent cohort (born 1927–1934), an increase of almost 20 percent. Clearly changes in the labor force participation of more recent cohorts of women do not appear to alter their caregiving responsibilities. In fact, women in this sample were equally likely to become caregivers, regardless of whether or not they were employed.

Adulthood and aging can be depicted as a series of role changes, and while role loss may be concomitant with aging, role gain may also occur (Moen, Dempster-McClain, and Williams, 1992; Riley and Riley, 1989).

Women have always been the family caregivers (Coward and Dwyer, 1990; Lee, 1992; Stoller, 1983; Stone, Cafferata, and Sangl, 1987), but an aging population and the ongoing revolution in women's roles is placing this previously taken-for-granted responsibility in the spotlight.

One concern is the extent to which women's paid employment may be disrupted by caregiving responsibilities for ailing or dependent adult kin (Breslau, Salkever, and Staruch, 1982; Brody et al., 1987; Steuve and O'Donnell, 1989). As women move into the labor force in unprecedented numbers (Moen, 1992), traditional role obligations, such as caregiving for infirm relatives, become increasingly problematic. Do prolonged caregiving spells preclude women's on-going involvement in a paid job in the same way that caring for preschoolers has? Do adult caregiving demands hinder women's entry or reentry into the labor force?

While caregiving may well curtail employment, so too may employment serve as a possible deterrent to women becoming caregivers.

Propositions. We hypothesize that role entrances and exits, whether to or from caregiving or employment, are in fact contingent on women's current role occupancy. Specifically, we anticipate that: (a) women currently in the labor force are less likely than full-time homemakers to take on caregiving, and are unlikely to leave their jobs in the face of new or ongoing caregiving responsibilities; and (b) women who are already caregivers are unlikely to take on the additional role of paid worker.

A life course approach suggests that the relationships between employment and caregiving will vary depending on women's age. For example, as women grow older we expect caregiving to become more, and paid work less, salient. But this may also be affected by social class, with college-educated women more invested in the worker role, and correspondingly, less apt to take on caregiving than those with only a high school education (Stone and Short, 1990).

A life course approach also presumes that the linkages between work and caregiving may well have changed historically, with women born into different historical circumstances having vastly different experiences with these two roles. We hypothesize that more recent birth cohorts of women will be more likely than women born earlier in the century to be involved in both roles. With increases in longevity, we in the United States are facing a situation where there will be more people requiring informal family care (Berg and Cassells, 1990; Coward, Horne, and Dwyer, 1992). At the same time, due to demographic shifts in family size, families have fewer siblings to share caregiving obligations. This trend was temporarily reversed for the cohorts born during the post World War II baby boom; however, the secular trend since the turn of the century has been one of reduced fertility. The women in the sample analyzed here were born before the baby boom. Therefore, despite their increasing commitment to employment, the more recent cohorts of women in our analyses are more likely to have both aging relatives requiring care and fewer siblings among whom to distribute caregiving tasks (e.g., Seccombe, 1992; Stoller, 1983; Treas, 1977).

Sample

We draw on life history data from the Women's Role Survey, a study of 313 wives and mothers from a mid-sized community in upstate New York.

(For a more detailed description of the sample, see Moen, Dempster-McClain, and Williams, 1989, 1992.)

Measures and Procedures

To assess the patterning of paid work and caregiving roles over the prime adult years (ages 18–55), we analyzed our data for the sample as a whole, by birth cohort, by age categories, and by educational level. The four cohorts in our sample consist of women who were born between 1905–1917 ($n = 87$), 1918–1922 ($n = 88$), 1923–1926 ($n = 52$), and 1927–1934 ($n = 66$). We divided the sample into four birth cohorts in order to test for differences due to changes in the historical and social climate in which the respondents lived. The cohorts were constructed according to when these women became adults and in relation to the timing of historical events in their lives. The older of these women (born 1905 to 1917) came to adulthood during the years of the Great Depression when women's employment was often economically critical for families and when caregiving was a taken-for-granted aspect of women's lives. They turned 65 in the 1970s, the decade of the women's movement. The second cohort (born 1918 to 1922) reached adulthood during the second World War, when employment of women was portrayed as a patriotic duty. They reached retirement age in the 1980s. The third cohort (born 1923 to 1926) became adults during the early postwar period, a time of transition from a wartime to peacetime economy, and are just now moving into their mid-sixties. The youngest cohort (born 1927 to 1934) began their adulthood in the 1950s, when women's lives were expected to be family and home oriented. They will reach their 60s during the decade of the 1990s. Each of these cohorts has experienced major historical, demographic, and social changes affecting gender role expectations and, possibly, their expectations about caregiving.

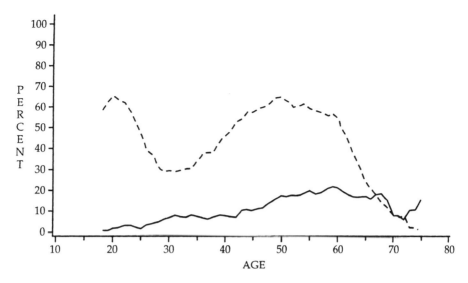

Figure 1. Percent of women working and caregiving, by age (*n* = 293). Solid line, caregiving; dashed line, working.

To examine the possible effects of social change on women's role choices, we looked for differences among these cohorts in involvement in work and caregiving. We also describe the incidence of caregiving and paid work up until age 75 (for those respondents who were 75 or older at the time of the second interview).

We created spells (episodes) of work and caregiving, where each spell represents a particular combination of paid work and caregiving roles. For each spell there is a specific start and end date, with a change in either working or caregiving status marking the beginning of a new spell. We calculated: (1) the percent of women engaged in caregiving and or paid work for various age groups and by birth cohort; (2) the duration of time spent in various work/caregiving role combinations; (3) the probability of making a transition from one work/caregiving role combination to any other; and (4) the relationship between educational level, paid work, and caregiving. The transitions are contingent upon: (a) the particular originating role combination and (b) the existence of a move (i.e., censored spells are eliminated). In addition, we examined various age categories to note age-related changes in roles across the course of women's lives. Because employment in particular is a function of age, when looking at both roles together we analyze the probability of paid work and caregiving from ages 18 to 55. All tests of significance were conducted with F-tests, unless otherwise noted.

Results

Figure 1 depicts the distribution of involvement in paid work and caregiving over the course of women's lives. While employment in this sample of women born before 1935 follows the traditional "M" shape (with women leaving the labor force while their children are young), the incidence of caregiving increases slowly but steadily over their life course.

The caregiving curve is quite flat compared to the employment curve. The percentage of women caregiving at any one point in time from age 46 through age 69 varies by at most 10 percent, from a low of 11 percent at age 46 to a high of 21 percent at age 59. This pattern suggests that caregiving may be less sensitive to other life course transitions, such as childbearing, than is employment. Neither

TABLE 1 Transition Rates and Mean Durations Prior to Transition, in Years

	Number of Spells	Transition Rates	Mean Duration (in years)	Standard Deviation of Duration
1. From Working and Caregiving to:				
a. Caregiving only	20	.15	2.6	3.1
b. Working only	110	.83	1.6	2.5
c. Neither	2	.02	0.25	0.00
2. From Caregiving Only to:				
d. Caregiving and working	30	.23	1.7	2.4
e. Working only	1	.01	2.0	
f. Neither	101	.77	1.9	2.8
3. From Working Only to:				
g. Caregiving and working	119	.15	5.6	5.9
h. Caregiving only	9	.01	7.2	5.5
i. Neither	658	.85	3.5	4.1
4. From Neither Working nor Caregiving to:				
j. Working and caregiving	4	.00	8.9	8.4
k. Caregiving only	121	.15	8.3	8.9
l. Working only	707	.84	4.5	6.0
Total number of spells	1882			

does caregiving appear to be as normatively prescribed by age constraints as is employment. In other words, women apparently do not "retire" from the caregiving role at particular ages.

We analyzed data for each woman from the time she was 18 to her 55th birthday and calculated the rates of transition to four possible work and caregiving role combinations: working and caregiving, caregiving only, working only, and neither working nor caregiving (see Transition Rates column in Table 1). These transitions are conditional upon starting in a given state. For any given starting state there are three possible changes. What is important to note is that women were as likely to move from working only to caregiving and working (row g), as they were to move from neither working nor caregiving to caregiving only (row k).

For example, one woman had been working full time as a real estate agent at the time of her husband's diagnosis of Alzheimer's disease in May 1985 when she was 68. She started working part time late in 1986 and was continuing in both roles at the time of her interview. Another woman worked as a secretary for an aircraft manufacturing company from 1963 to 1981, during ages 46 to 64. She also cared for her elderly aunt who lived with her from 1967 until the aunt's death in 1977. Thus, contrary to our hypothesis, being employed does not seem to preclude becoming a caregiver. In fact, women were both workers and caregivers at the same time during as many spells (132—see row 1) as they were caregivers alone (132—see row 2). The number of years from age 18 to age 55 spent working and caregiving versus caregiving alone are almost identical (see column 3, rows 1 and 2).

Women who were both working and caregiving (row 1) were more likely to stop caregiving (row b) than to stop working (row a). Examples of women undergoing such transitions include a grade school teacher who cared for her father-in-law in her home for seven years beginning in 1954, when she was 43, until he moved into a nursing home; and a woman who ran a riveting machine from 1953 to 1957 (and was continuously employed in various occupations until 1980, when she was 56), who started caring for her

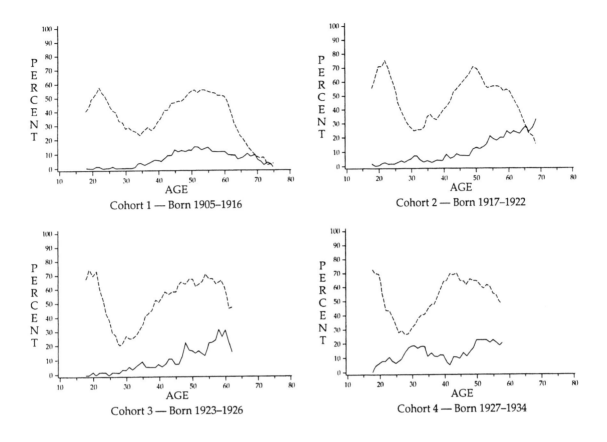

Figure 2. Percent of women working and caregiving, at each age (*n* = 293). Solid line, caregiving; dashed line, working.

mother in 1955 but stopped after two months and did not care for her again up to the mother's death in 1972. A significant proportion of women who were caregiving only (row 2) moved into employment (.23, see row d), although most stopped caregiving without taking on employment (.77, see row f). One woman, age 31, who had stopped working to have children, was caring for her infant daughter with cerebral palsy in 1955, but went back to work as a full-time private nurse when her daughter was 3 years old. Another woman, who had not worked outside the home since her marriage, cared for her husband who had cancer from 1975, when she was 56, until his death in 1978, after which she remained out of the labor force.

Cohort differences in women's paid work and caregiving. When we divide the sample into four birth cohorts we find that the earliest cohort (born 1905–1917) was the least involved in caregiving, regardless of age or stage of the life course (see Figure 2). At no age does the percentage of women in cohort 1 who were caregiving exceed 15 percent. By contrast, the caregiving curve for women in cohort 2 (born 1918–1922) rises rather steadily with age to a high of 32 percent at age 68. Women in cohort 3 (born 1923–1926) show a similar level of caregiving to those in cohort 2. Among women in cohort 3, however, caregiving activity peaks at 33 percent, 10 years earlier than for those in cohort 2. The caregiving curve for the most recent cohort (born

1927–1934) is more erratic than those of the earlier cohorts. It is flatter than those for cohorts 2 and 3. Except for a dip in activity during their early 40s, caregiving levels stay between 10 and 23 percent from age 28 to age 55 (the age of this cohort when interviewed). Since this cohort is right censored at age 55, it is quite likely that the percentage of caregiving might rise even higher as this cohort ages.

As can be seen in Table 2, women in the two most recent cohorts (born 1923–1934) tend to be more active in both work and caregiving roles than women in the two earlier cohorts (born 1905–1922). Sixty-four percent of women in cohort 4 (1927–1934) had some experience with caregiving during ages 18–55, while only 45 percent of the earliest cohort (born 1905–1917) did. We find a statistically significant ($p = .01$) difference in the likelihood of taking on the caregiving role between the two oldest and the two youngest cohorts, with the more recent cohorts more likely to have been caregivers than those born earlier, despite the fact that the most recent cohort is younger. Even more of these younger women may yet become caregivers as they move into later adulthood.

We also examined the patterns of transitions between the various combinations of working and caregiving roles across cohorts (as described for the whole sample in Table 1). We found that women in the most recent cohort (born 1927 to 1934) were significantly ($p = .0001$) more likely to make a transition from neither working nor caregiving to caregiving only than were women in the other three cohorts (data not shown).

Differences in women's paid work and caregiving as they age. In order to examine variations in work and caregiving patterns over time, we divided each woman's life into 10-year segments, starting with ages 35–44 and ending with ages 65–74. The age categories themselves were arbitrary, but provide convenient markers of moving through the adult years. We find relatively little involvement in caregiving prior to age 35, but the 35 to 44 decade sees a fourth of women experiencing caregiv-

ing. Over the next 20 years the proportion of these women becoming caregivers increases to 35 percent. Most women were also paid workers during this same period, from ages 45–64. This finding points to the importance of caregiving in women's lives in late midlife, and the potential for role strain and overload as significant numbers of women in their forties and fifties combine employment with caregiving.

As shown in Table 3, the drop-off in involvement in caregiving as women reach age 65 is less sharp than that for employment, since a smaller proportion of women are engaged in caregiving in the first place, and since caregiving remains a significant role in the later years. Note that fully one fourth of women aged 65–74 were caregiving at some time during these years, more than were in the paid labor force. However, the proportion of years spent caregiving during these older years (65–74) is about half the time these women spent caregiving during their previous decade (ages 55–65).

Women combine caregiving and working or are caregivers exclusively for only a small percentage of time during their prime adult years from age 18 to 55. However, over the life course we see relatively more time spent caregiving exclusively and less time spent working exclusively (see Table 3).

When we test for significant differences in transition rates of change to a given work/caregiving status between age categories, we find that women ages 45 to 54 are significantly ($p = .0002$) more likely to add caregiving responsibilities to work than they are at other ages. In other words, they are significantly more likely to move from working only to working and caregiving (row g, Table 1) in their late 40s and early 50s. When women reach their late 50s and early 60s (ages 55–64), they are significantly ($p = .004$) more likely to make the transition from both working and caregiving to caregiving only than they were as younger women (row a, Table 1). This could well reflect the decision to retire in the face of caregiving responsibilities, or it may simply mark the societal trend toward

TABLE 2 Women's Paid Work and Caregiving Experiences (Ages 18 to 55) by Cohort

	Cohort 1 (n = 87) b. 1905–1917	Cohort 2 (n = 88) b. 1918–1922	Cohort 3 (n = 52) b. 1923–1926	Cohort 4 (n = 66) b. 1927–1934	Total Sample
Paid work experience					
Ever worked in paid job	94.25[a]	95.45[a]	98.08[a]	100.00[a]	96.59
Never worked in paid job	5.75	4.55	1.92	0	3.41
Median duration (of those employed)	16.89	17.52	19.58	18.35	17.75
Percentage of 18–55 years employed	45.65	47.35	52.94	49.65	42.28
Median age first job (if by age 55)	19.28	18.61	18.08	18.00	18.29
Caregiving experience					
Ever gave care	44.83[a]	45.45[a]	53.85[a]	63.64[a]	50.9
Never gave care	55.17	54.55	46.45	36.36	49.1
Median duration (of those who gave care)	1.64	1.71	2.35	2.99	2.00
Percentage of 18–55 years caregiving	4.43	4.62	6.34	8.08	5.42
Median age first gave care (if by age 55)	43.60	43.61	43.86	37.60[b]	42.01
Joint paid work and caregiving experiences: Duration in years					
Working and caregiving					
Mean (SD)	1.2 (3.3)	.67 (1.8)	1.1 (2.5)	1.5 (3.2)[b]	1.1 (2.8)
Median	0.0	0.0	0.0	0.0	0.0
Caregiving exclusively					
Mean (SD)	1.1 (3.1)	.73 (1.9)	.8 (2)	1.5 (3.7) $p = .01$[b]	1.1 (2.8)
Median	0.0	0.0	0.0	0.0	0.0
Working exclusively					
Mean (SD)	14.1 (9.8)	15.6 (9.2)	15.7 (10)	16.3 (8.5)	15.3 (9.8)
Median	15.6	16.5	14.6	16.7	15.6
Neither caregiving nor working					
Mean (SD)	20.6 (9.8)	20.0 (9.3)	19.4 (10)	17.2 (9.1) $p = .03$[b]	19.5 (9.6)
Median	19.9	19.2	17.2	17.7	18.6

a. According to t-tests, women in earlier cohorts (1 and 2) are significantly less likely to have given care ($p = .02$) or worked ($p = .05$) than women in later cohorts (3 and 4).

b. According to t-tests, woment in the latest cohort differ significantly ($p = .05$) from women in all other cohorts combined, with respect to these variables.

171

TABLE 3 Women's Paid Work and Caregiving Over Their Life Course

	Ages 35–44 [a] n = 293	Ages 45–54 n = 289	Ages 55–64 n = 159	Ages 65–74 n = 32	F-value	Ages 35–74 [b] n = 293
Paid work experience						
Perecentage who ever worked during given ages	66.21	73.70	65.41	21.86	41.5**	84.30
Proportion of given years employed (of those who were employed)	72.10	95.80	74.84	40.84	63.92**	56.62
Caregiving experience						
Percentage who ever gave care during given ages	23.55	34.95	35.85	25.00	5.15**	62.80
Percentage of given years spent caregiving (for those who did caregiving)	10.65	24.12	39.13	19.60	6.69**	11.21
Joint paid work and caregiving experiences: Duration in years						
Working and caregiving						
Mean (SD)	.27 (1.1)	.63 (1.8)	.47 (1.5)	.0 (0)	7.27**	1.4 (3.2)
Caregiving only						
Mean (SD)	.30 (1.3)	.53 (1.7)	.95 (2.3)	.98 (2.5)	3.30*	1.8 (4.0)
Working only						
Mean (SD)	3.9 (4.0)	5.2 (4.1)	4.2 (3.8)	.73 (1.9)	55.9**	12.7 (9.3)
Neither caregiving nor working						
Mean (SD)	5.5 (4.2)	3.7 (4.0)	4.4 (3.9)	8.3 (2.9)	89.92**	14.8 (10.5)

a. Age categories include only those women who had reached the oldest age by the time of the interview, since younger women's work and caregiving experiences are not necessarily complete for the given age category.

b. This may be an undercount since at the time of the interview some women were not yet age 74. Younger women may work or caregive in the future. The figure for proportion of given years spent working or caregiving calculates the proportion of possible years spent in the given activity.

*p < .05; **p < .01.

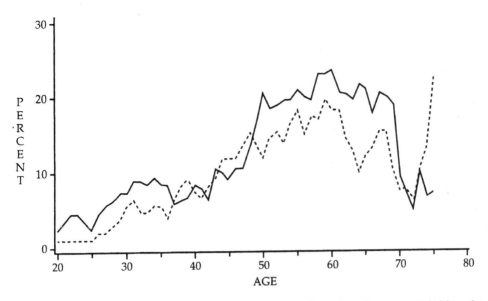

Figure 3. Percent of women caregiving over the course of their lives, by education. Solid line, high school education or less; dashed line, more than high school education.

earlier retirement (U.S. Bureau of the Census, 1989). Another possible explanation for this finding is that older women do not earn enough to pay for formal caregivers to replace them, and find it easier to stop working than to find substitutes for their own caregiving.

Differences in women's paid work and caregiving by education level. Thus far we have considered similarities and differences in women's employment and caregiving by age and by birth cohort, but women's role involvements may also vary by their location in the social structure.

Do the pathways to caregiving in fact differ for women with different educational backgrounds?

When we examine working and caregiving in light of educational level (high school or less vs. as least some college), we find, not surprisingly, that women with college training are more likely to be working at paid jobs later in life (from age 44 to their late 60s) than are less educated women (see Figure 3). However, the opposite pattern appears with respect to caregiving. That is, between ages 57

and 71, less educated women are more likely to be caregivers than are those with more education (see Figure 3). College-educated women are likely to spend more postretirement years (65–74) neither caregiving nor working than are those with only a high school education. (Note in Figure 3 that the proportion of college-educated women in the role of caregiver increases at age 71, but the very small sample size at this age level makes it unclear whether this is a true trend.)

Summary of the Findings

Caregiving is an increasingly common role for women in the United States.

Caregiving is usually a short-term, intermittent role, and one frequently combined with employment.

While caregiving may be a major interruption in one's anticipated life experiences, we found that it does not necessarily interrupt women's labor force participation.

Our findings suggest that women are as likely to be combining working and caregiving as they are to be caregivers exclusively, and in one in five cases home-makers who are caregivers take on employment in addition to caregiving. When women who are employed take on caregiving tasks, they are unlikely to leave the labor force as a result, despite any possible strains they may experience.

Neither does employment appear to preclude women's subsequent caregiving responsibilities. Again contrary to our hypothesis, women are equally likely to become caregivers, whether or not they are employed. In the case of women who are both workers and caregivers, they are more likely to stop caregiving than to leave their jobs.

Caregiving appears to be increasingly a role that is more, not less, characteristic of women's lives, as seen by the rising incidence of caregiving across succeeding birth cohorts. We found that more recent cohorts of American women are more likely than those born earlier in the century to take on the caregiving role, despite their increased involvement in the paid labor force and the societal revolution in gender expectations.

Thus, it does not appear that as women become more involved in the paid labor force the prevalence of their caregiving declines. Women seem to be adding to their role repertoire rather than experiencing shifts in roles.

The apparent disparity by cohort, evidenced by the fact that caregiving is increasing across cohorts, suggests that changes in family structure and in longevity are indeed increasing the demand for informal family care (Coward, Horne, and Dwyer, 1992; Dwyer and Coward, 1992).

Position in the social structure, as operationalized by level of education, also affects the likelihood of working and caregiving. During the later years of adulthood, more educated women are more apt to be in the work force than are women with less education, but the pattern is reversed for caregiving. Women with only a high school education (or less) may lack the resources to purchase care for ailing relatives; they may also be less in a position to have alternative claims—such as a professional career—on their time.

Policy Implication

It is also of crucial importance that policy makers take into consideration the fact that caregiving is frequently concomitant with employment (e.g., Neal et al., 1993; Seccombe, 1992), since the odds are that combining these two roles will become more common for future cohorts. We have seen, from the findings of this study, that working women are as likely to become caregivers as are those out of the labor force. Both flexibility at work and community-based programs to aid family caregivers may help women (and men) to better manage their work and caregiving obligations. Caregiving responsibilities throughout the life course may also affect women's socioeconomic status in later life (Arendell and Estes, 1991). The development of care-providing institutional alternatives as well as job flexibility will shape family caregiving in future decades, even as advances in longevity increase its likelihood.

Acknowledgments

This research was supported by grant no. RO1 AG05450 from the National Institute on Aging, Phyllis Moen and Robin M. Williams, Jr., principal investigators, Donna Dempster-McClain, project director; by Hatch grant 3217420, Phyllis Moen, principal investigator; and by grant 1P50 AG11711-01 from the National Institute on Aging, Karl Pillemer and Phyllis Moen, principal investigators. The authors appreciate the considerable efforts of Donna Dempster-McClain in producing the data archive.

Address correspondence to Dr. Phyllis Moen, Life Course Institute, MVR Hall, Cornell University, Ithaca, NY 14853.

References

Arendell, Terry and Carroll L. Estes. 1991. "Older Women in the Post-Reagan Era." *International Journal of Health Services* 21:59-73.

Berg, Robert R. and Joseph S. Cassells (Eds.). 1990. *The Second Fifty Years: Promoting Health and Preventing Disability.* Washington, DC: National Academy Press.

Breslau, Naomi, David Salkever, and Kathleen S. Staruch. 1982. "Women's Labor Force Participation and Responsibilities for Disabled Dependents: A Study of Families with Disabled Children." *Journal of Health and Social Behavior* 23:169-183.

Brody, Elaine M. 1990. *Women in the Middle: Their Parent-Care Years.* New York: Springer.

Brody, Elaine M., Morton H. Kleban, Pauline T. Johnson, Christine Hoffman, and Claire B. Schoonover. 1987. "Work Status and Parent Care: A Comparison of Four Groups of Women." *The Gerontologist* 27:201-208.

Coward, Raymond T. and Jeffrey W. Dwyer. 1990. "The Association of Gender, Sibling Network Composition, and Patterns of Parent Care by Adult Children." *Research on Aging* 12:158-181.

Coward, Raymond T., Claydell Horne, and Jeffrey W. Dwyer. 1992. "Demographic Perspectives on Gender and Family Caregiving." In Jeffrey W. Dwyer and Raymond T. Coward (Eds.), *Gender, Families, and Elder Care.* Newbury Park, CA: Sage.

Dwyer, Jeffrey W. and Raymond T. Coward (Eds.). 1992. *Gender, Families, and Elder Care.* Newbury Park, CA: Sage.

Lee, Gary R. 1992. "Gender Differences in Family Caregiving: A Fact in Search of a Theory." In Jeffrey W. Dwyer and Raymond T. Coward (Eds.), *Gender, Families, and Elder Care.* Newbury Park, CA: Sage.

Moen, Phyllis. 1992. *Women's Two Roles: A Contemporary Dilemma.* New York: Auburn House.

Moen, Phyllis, Donna Dempster-McClain, and Robin M. Williams, Jr. 1989. "Social Integration and Longevity: An Event History Analysis of Women's Roles and Resilience." *American Sociological Review* 54:635-647.

Moen, Phyllis, Donna Dempster-McClain, and Robin M. Williams, Jr. 1992. "Successful Aging: A Life Course Perspective on Women's Multiple Roles and Health." *American Journal of Sociology* 97:1612-1638.

Neal, Margaret B., Nancy J. Chapman, Berit Ingersoll-Dayton, and Arthur C. Emlen. 1993. *Balancing Work and Caregiving for Children, Adults, and Elders.* Newbury Park, CA: Sage.

Riley, Matilda W. and John W. Riley, Jr. 1989. "The Lives of Old People and Changing Social Roles." *The Annals of the American Academy of Political and Social Science* 503:14-28.

Seccombe, Karen. 1992. "Employment, the Family, and Employer Based Policies." In Jeffrey W. Dwyer and Raymond T. Coward (Eds.), *Gender, Families, and Elder Care.* Newbury Park, CA: Sage.

Steuve, Ann and Lydia O'Donnell. 1989. "Interactions Between Women and Their Elderly Parents: Constraints of Daughters' Employment." *Research on Aging* 11:331-353.

Stoller, Eleanor Palo. 1983. "Parental Caregiving by Adult Children." *Journal of Marriage and the Family* 45:851-858.

Stone, Robyn I., Gail Lee Cafferata, and Judith Sangl. 1987. "Caregivers of the Frail Elderly: A National Profile." *The Gerontologist* 27:616-626.

Stone, Robyn I. and Pamela F. Short. 1990. "The Competing Demands of Employment and Informal Caregiving to Disabled Elders." *Medical Care* 28:513-526.

Treas, Judith. 1977. "Family Support Systems for the Aged: Some Social and Demographic Considerations." *The Gerontologist* 17:486-491.

U.S. Bureau of the Census. 1989. "Projections of the Population of the United States, by Age, Sex, and Race: 1988 to 2080." *Current Population Reports series 25, no. 1018.* Washington, DC: U.S. Government Printing Office.

23

The Day the Crows Stopped Talking

Harvest Moon Eyes

I remember the day they found Sky dead. I was thirty-eight and I had already lived a lifetime. It was Smitty and Gray Buck that found her over by the tribal hall. Shrouded in a protective fence of oak trees, her neck had been broken and she lay crumpled. Like the oak trees, she'd never been able to bend with the wind.

Many big, black crows live in those oak trees. They talk throughout the day. Sometimes they gossip about us with visiting crows from other reservations. It is wise never to talk under the oak trees. One never knows to whom they tell our secrets. The crows cannot be trusted.

When they're not gossiping, they warn us of approaching visitors. As annoying as they can be with their constant chatter, we know that when the crows stop talking, something is very, very wrong here. The day they found Sky dead, the crows stopped talking.

* * *

Sky slowly made her way across the pasture toward the oak trees that were clustered around the tribal hall. Her long black hair was clasped tightly in a bun at the nape of her neck. Haunted by memories of too many nights in too many different beds, dark circles had become a permanent fixture under her intense blue eyes. But last night's dream had been different.

"For once it's nice to dream about someone other than myself," Sky mused as she made her way carefully around the cow dung scattered throughout the pasture. Earlier in the day, Sky had met with her friend Maggie under the oak trees to tell her about the dream. It was Maggie who had told her to go see Aunt Lil, the reservation's resident dream interpreter. Her conversation with Aunt Lil had left her tired and confused; and now she was making her way to the hill that overlooked the reservation. For years, everyone on the reservation had watched Sky make her way to the top of that hill every time she had a problem.

Sky didn't belong to this reservation. Actually, Sky didn't belong anywhere. She was an unenrolled mixed-blood, an outsider, who years ago roamed onto the reservation in a cloud of drugs and alcohol. She ended up staying. No one seemed to mind. She was harmless and she was pretty; so she always seemed to have a bed for the night and a free meal. Everyone on the reservation knew Sky; and though she was liked, she always knew she was an outsider. Some things were just never talked about in front of her, but she didn't mind. Sky was used to it. Her entire life she had felt like an outsider—not really white, but not really Indian; and like a stray bullet looking for a place to land, she had often become wedged into places and things where she did not belong.

Standing on the hill at the lookout point above Aunt Lil's place, Sky could see the wind weaving its way throughout the reservation. Miniature dust balls of grit and loose ends of reservation life merged with the wind. Choking on the fragments, the wind split the dust across the valley. Settling down among the cacti, Sky's eyes rested on Aunt Lil and Maggie far below. While Lil and Maggie chattered on Lil's porch, dusk stealthily slid its way across them creating two shadows cackling in the dark.

Sky's thoughts darted back and forth like flickering shadows; dancing separately and together, they whirled around and pressed themselves against each other.

Tired from the day, Sky pulled her knees tight to her chest, wrapped her arms around her legs, and rested her chin between her knees. While she braced herself against the oncoming night, her conversation with Lil and Maggie was temporarily abandoned.

"I wonder what dusk and day do in the dark," mused Sky. Her left hand removed a strand of hair the wind had wedged between her pressed lips. She reached her hands back to the nape of her neck and checked the clasp that held her bun.

The wind reached down and slowly, steadily began to pull and tug at the roots of Sky's hairline. The wind pulled in one direction while her clasp braced itself against the onslaught.

Sky's hands moved to the nape of her neck again. Gnarled hands, hands too old for the rest of her body, held onto her bun in an attempt to keep her thoughts from escaping. But the wind would have its own way.

Sky watched her thoughts escape and she was afraid. She was afraid that her thoughts might break loose from the wind's grasp and settle in someone's mind below. Her thoughts would no longer be her own. Sky knew that the wind could sprinkle her thoughts like dust particles throughout the reservation. People would begin to talk. Secrets would come out. Sky knew she would be the one to blame.

A woman is a powerful thing, thought Sky as she tucked some loose strands of hair back into the clasp. Her eyes wandered down the length of her blue jeans, across the tips of her worn boots, and onto the particles of sand that reached out toward the horizon and the reservation far below. In the daytime, the reservation seemed so peaceful and serene. Children played among the abandoned junk cars

and cows grazed lazily in the pastures. But with the night, despair whored its way throughout the reservation—seldom resting until dawn. Sun brings temporary relief and rest from the nightmares of reality. But then comes the night again, and the circle remains unbroken.

After reaching for a handful of sand, Sky watched it trickle through her fingers. The sand faded from view and in its place she saw her dream from the night before. Rising up from the faded sand, the apparition appeared cloudlike, haunting, until it came into clarity.

Sky saw silver hair braided with alternating pieces of silver and feathers. Then she saw long, dark hair moving like fingers scaling a piano. Lightly the dark hair entwined itself with the silver hair. Tears fell through the clouds to the valley below.

Maggie's spirit stood by Lil on the porch. She no longer wore peach lipstick. Her eyes no longer beckoned to the men on the reservation. She watched as Lil moved through emotional quicksand across the shadowed porch.

Lil moved toward the picture hanging crooked on the wall. The picture that captured Lil and Maggie before they both became old was placed softly across the quilt. The binoculars, Lil's eyes for so many years, hung loosely from around Lil's neck. Maggie spoke to Lil, but Lil could not hear her. Maggie was not there for Lil.

As Lil bent to lift the rocking chair into her arms, her eyes rested on the small airplanes lined up on the airfield below. The runway stretched itself tightly over the land that was once occupied by tribal buildings like tights across a whore's thighs.

The houses that once dotted the hillside had been moved. Loose dirt, dirt darker than the dirt that surrounded the empty lots, was all that remained to mark what was once reservation life.

Lil's house was still there. Her house was the last house to be moved, the last life to be uprooted. Only one slice of the past stood untouched. The lookout point with its cacti garden remained. Beyond the hill, where once there were empty valleys, estates sprawled, border to border, electric fence to electric fence, touching each other yet separate from each other. Sky wondered if something was being locked in or if something was being locked out. Maybe both.

The oak trees were gone along with the crows. Unable to compete with the airplanes, the crows moved to somewhere unknown. The crows' chatter was replaced by the high-pitched whine of dirt bikes racing along the hillside. Cows that once wandered lazily across the dirt roads were replaced by fast cars whizzing to and from the small airfield.

Sky trembled from the chill left by the dream. Stretching her bare arms forward, she pushed the dream away; and hearing a noise behind her, she turned and stood up. Struggling against the darkness that grasped her, she crumpled against its force.

It was the next morning that Smitty and Gray Buck found Sky among the oak trees next to the tribal hall.

The reservation was the only real family that Sky had, so most of the people showed up for the burning the following evening. There wasn't much to burn: a pair of blue jeans, an old flannel shirt, and a worn Bible were all that marked the passing of her life. The wake that followed was quiet: There were only a few tears, but a lot of eating; and by morning, Sky was quietly buried on top of the hill that she loved so much.

No one ever notified Les McCann, the sheriff out of Smateren Creek, about the murder. It was just one of those many tacit agreements found in reservation life. Death had long ago become an everyday matter on the reservation; and after all, why involve an outsider about someone's death if the person wasn't going to be missed? Besides, Sky's death was of little importance compared to the larger issue that was being debated down at the tribal hall.

Tom Crow sat with his back to the open windows that faced the oak trees. Wiping sweat from his forehead, he tried again to adjust the electric fan so that the cross breeze would cool him down without blowing his papers all over the tribal council chambers. It

had proven to be hotter than usual during the meeting he'd had with Aunt Lil and her Council of Elders, the Gray Panthers of the reservation.

Through years of negotiations as tribal chairman, Tom Crow had learned to affect an easygoing manner. Wearing Western clothes, chomping on a toothpick, he'd lean back in his black swivel chair, his arms and legs open for any discussion. But these theatrics had, as usual, no effect on Aunt Lil and the Council of Elders.

"They've become a collective thorn in my ass," Tom grumbled as he spit out what was left of his chewed-up toothpick. After reaching for the phone, he dialed George Brent's number. Wiping a trickle of sweat from the back of his neck, he cradled the receiver while he tried to adjust the fan again.

"Hello, George? Tom Crow here. Listen, we've got a little problem out here. We need to talk before the vote tonight. Got a few minutes?

"Yeah, George, I know I told you everything looked good for the land purchase, but some of the elders have doubts. They're capable of influencing a vote either way," said Tom as he tapped the end of his pencil on his empty coffee cup.

"Well, what they're concerned about is selling part of our land. It seems they've changed their minds; and now all they want the tribe to do is lease the land to your people on a hundred-year lease," Tom continued. "Yeah, I know I told you we were all for selling part of our land, but ever since a white girl died out here, the elders have been acting strange.

"It seems this girl told a couple of the elders about some dream she'd had, and now the elders think they're going to lose the reservation," Tom said nervously.

"You don't understand, George—wait, hold on a second," said Tom as he froze in midsentence.

"Sorry, I thought I heard something—anyway, as I was saying, there's still a lot of superstition out here. People put a lot of weight into Lil Pachuca's dream interpretations. No, I'm not saying I believe or I don't believe her, it's just that I've never known her to be wrong, that's all," Tom said as he adjusted the fan again.

"Listen, all I'm trying to say is that I can't openly go against the elders. It would show disrespect and I could just kiss my career good-bye as tribal chairman. But I've got an idea—hold on again, George." After putting down the phone, Tom quietly crossed over to the open windows. Looking out, he saw some cows grazing near the oak trees.

"Sorry about the interruptions, George, but I thought I heard someone outside my window.

"Okay, George, I'll see you out here in about an hour and we'll go over things before the vote tonight.

"Worried—no, I think we can work something out. Yeah, see ya later," said Tom. Hanging up the phone, he turned toward the open windows and watched a shadow pass out of sight among the oak trees.

Sitting in a rocking chair on her porch with an old red-and-white patchwork quilt thrown across her lap, Aunt Lil waved as Indian Joe flew by in his jeep. Long silver hair waved back at her.

Joe is still a good-lookin' man after all these years. It's too bad that his emotions are as reckless as his driving, thought Lil as she reached for the binoculars that were hidden beneath her rocking chair.

Scanning the reservation with her binoculars, she focused in on the Mercedes Benz parked outside the tribal hall. Other than George Brent's car, things seemed pretty much as usual: The tribal hall looked stark against the backdrop of grazing cattle and junk cars. But it wasn't always this empty. Anyone could rent the tribal hall for fifty dollars a night. Lil had heard whispered that the tribal council, like a high-class call girl, went for even higher stakes than the hall. But no one had ever proven any of the talk was true.

Lil lowered the binoculars and thought about the meeting that had occurred earlier in the day between the elders and Tom Crow.

When Lil, acting as spokesperson for the Council of Elders, told Tom about Sky's dream, he had seemed genuinely interested in hearing her interpretation. This had surprised Lil and some of the other elders. Ever since Tom had graduated from college, he had seemed more white than Indian: He seldom showed up at any of the pow-wows; and he rarely consulted with the elders about tribal affairs. Although he seemed interested in what Lil had to say, when she told him the dream meant that they were going to lose their land to outsiders, Tom had patiently reminded her that Sky was white, and not one of their people. How could she have a dream about their future? This, she was at a loss to explain. But until she could adequately explain away Sky's dream, she and the other elders had vowed to Tom Crow that they would vote against the selling of the land to George Brent for the building of his casino.

But, as it turned out, Lil and the other elders lost the fight that ensued later at the tribal meeting. They were outvoted by the younger ones; and so George Brent was allowed to purchase land for his casino. In return for the vote of support, George agreed to hire only Indians to work the casino. The reservation's guaranteed 40 percent profit margin would be divided into equal shares among the heads of each family on the reservation. Everyone was happy. Everyone except the elders.

Lil never knew for sure why the elders lost the fight, but she did know that within two months of the casino's completion, some people on the reservation were driving new cars and wearing new clothes. At first she, and some of the elders, thought that Tom Crow had sold the reservation out, but his lifestyle never changed, and so once again he was voted in for another term as tribal chairman.

It's hard to believe it's been two years now since Sky was killed and the casino was built. I'm forty now, and lately I've been feeling more like fifty.

No one ever found out who killed Sky or why. It was too bad about Sky, but that silly dream of hers caused a lot of unnecessary trouble and nearly disrupted plans for a casino.

The reservation still hasn't seen its 40 percent profit, but my money's safe in a Keogh plan and my oldest boy is at Stanford. I really didn't want to kill Sky, but she never could keep her mouth shut about anything. I had to do it. I'd feel better about it, though, if the crows would start talking again.

Swiveling in his chair, Tom Crow turned his back to the open windows and the oak trees beyond.

On the Edge of the Barrio

Ernesto Galarza

I had been reading stories in the *Sacramento Bee* of the Spanish influenza. At first it was far off, like the war, in places such as New York and Texas. Then the stories told of people dying in California towns we knew, and finally the *Bee* began reporting the spread of the flu in our city.

One Sunday morning we saw Uncle Gustavo coming down the street with a suitcase in his hand, walking slowly. I ran out to meet him. By the front gate he dropped the suitcase, leaned on the fence, and fainted. He had been working as a sandhog on the American River, and had come home weak from fever.

Gustavo was put to bed in one of the front rooms. Uncle José set out to look for a doctor, who came the next day, weary and nearly sick himself. He ordered Gustavo to the hospital. Three days later I answered the telephone call from the hospital telling us he was dead. Only José went to Gustavo's funeral. The rest of us, except my stepfather, were sick in bed with the fever.

In the dining room, near the windows where the sunlight would warm her, my mother lay on a cot, a kerosene stove at her feet. The day Gustavo died she was delirious. José bicycled all over the city, looking for oranges, which the doctor said were the best medicine we could give her. I sweated out the fever, nursed by José, who brought me glasses of steaming lemonade and told me my mother was getting better. The children were quarantined in another room, lightly touched by the fever, more restless than sick.

Late one afternoon José came into my room, wrapped me in blankets, pulled a cap over my ears, and carried me to my mother's bedside. My stepfather was holding a hand mirror to her lips. It didn't fog. She had stopped breathing. In the next room my sister was singing to the other children, "A birdie with a yellow bill/hopped upon my window-sill,/cocked a shiny eye, and said,/'Shame on you, you sleepyhead.'"

The day we buried my mother, Mrs. Dodson took the oldest sister home with her. The younger children were sent to a neighbor. That night José went to the barrio, got drunk, borrowed a pistol, and was arrested for shooting up Second Street.

A month later I made a bundle of the family keepsakes my stepfather allowed me to have, including the butterfly sarape, my books, and some family pictures. With the bundle tied to the bars of my bicycle, I pedaled to the basement room José had rented for the two of us on O Street near the corner of Fifth, on the edge of the barrio.

José was now working the riverboats and, in the slack season, following the round of odd jobs about the city. In our basement room, with a kitchen closet, bathroom, and laundry tub on the back porch and a woodshed for storage, I kept house. We bought two cots, one for me and the other for José when he was home.

Our landlords lived upstairs, a middle-aged brother and sister who worked and rented rooms. They were friends of doña Tránsito, the grandmother of a Mexican family that lived in a weather-beaten cottage on the corner. Doña Tránsito was in her sixties, round as a barrel, and she wore her gray hair in braids and smoked hand-rolled cigarettes on her rickety front porch. Living only three houses from doña Tránsito, saying my saludos to her every time I passed the corner, I lived inside a circle of security when José was away.

José had chosen our new home because it was close to the Hearkness Junior High School, to which I transferred from Bret Harte. As the jefe de familia[1] he explained that I could help earn our living but that I was to study for a high school diploma. That being settled, my routine was clearly divided into school time and work time, the second depending on when I was free from the first.

Few Mexicans of my age from the barrio were enrolled at the junior high school when I went there. At least, there were no other Mexican boys or girls in Mr. Everett's class in civics, or Miss Crowley's English composition, or Mrs. Stevenson's Spanish course. Mrs. Stevenson assigned me to read to the class and to recite poems by Amado Nervo, because the poet was from Tepic and I was, too. Miss Crowley accepted my compositions about Jalcocotán and the buried treasure of Acaponeta while the others in the class were writing about Sir Patrick Spence and the Beautiful Lady Without Mercy, whom they had never met. For Mr. Everett's class, the last of the day, I clipped pieces from the *Sacramento Bee* about important events in Sacramento. From him I learned to use the ring binder in which I kept clippings to prepare oral reports. Occasionally he kept me after school to talk. He sat on his desk, one leg dangling over a corner, behind him the frame of a large window and the arching elms of the school yard, telling me he thought I could easily make the debating team at the high school next year, that Stanford University might be the place to go after graduation, and making other by-the-way comments that began to shape themselves into my future.

Afternoons, Saturdays, and summers allowed me many hours of work time I did not need for study. José explained how things now stood. There were two funerals to pay for. He would pay the rent and buy the food. My clothes, books, and school expenses would be up to me.

On my vacations and when he was not on the riverboats, he found me a job as water boy on a track gang. We chopped wood together near Woodland and stacked empty lug boxes in a cannery yard. Cleaning vacant houses and chopping weeds were jobs we could do as a team when better ones were not to be had. As the apprentice, I learned from him how to brace myself for a heavy lift, to lock my knee under a loaded hand-truck, to dance rather than lift a ladder, and to find the weakest grain in a log. Like him I spit into my palms to get the feel of the ax handle and grunted as the blade bit into the wood. Imitating him, I circled a tree several times, sizing it up, tanteando, as he said, before pruning or felling it.

Part of one summer my uncle worked on the river while I hired out as a farmhand on a small ranch south of Sacramento. My senior on the place was Roy, a husky Oklahoman who was a part-time taxi driver and a full-time drinker of hard whiskey. He was heavy-chested, heavy-lipped, and jowly, a grumbler rather than a talker and a man of great ingenuity with tools and automobile engines. Under him I learned to drive the Fordson tractor on the place, man the gasoline pump, feed the calves, check an irrigation ditch, make lug boxes for grapes, and many other tasks on a small farm.

Roy and I sat under the willow tree in front of the ranch house after work, I on the grass, he on a creaky wicker chair, a hulking, sour man glad for the company of a boy. He counseled me on how to avoid the indulgences he was so fond of, beginning his sentences with a phrase he repeated over and over, "as the feller says." "Don't aim to tell you your business," he explained, "but as the feller says, get yourself a good woman, don't be no farmhand for a livin', be a lawyer or a doctor, and don't get to drinkin' nohow. And there's another thing, Ernie. If nobody won't listen to you, go on and talk to yourself and hear what a smart man has to say."

And Roy knew how to handle boys, which he showed in an episode that could have cost me my life or my self-confidence. He had taught me to drive the tractor, walking alongside during the lessons as I maneuvered it, shifting gears, stopping and starting, turning and backing, raising a cloud of dust wherever we went. Between drives Roy told me about the different working parts of the machine, giving me instructions on oiling and greasing and filling the radiator. "She needs to be took care of, Ernie," he admonished me, "like a horse. And another thing, she's like to buck. She can turn clear over on you if you let 'er. If she starts to lift from the front even a mite, you turn her off. You hear?"

"Yes, sir," I said, meaning to keep his confidence in me as a good tractor man.

It was a few days after my first solo drive that it happened. I was rounding a telephone pole on the slightly sloping bank of the irrigation ditch. I swung around too fast for one of the rear tracks to keep its footing. It spun and the front began to lift. Forgetting Roy's emphatic instructions, I gunned the engine, trying to right us to the level ground above the ditch. The tractor's nose kept climbing in front of me. We slipped against the pole, the tractor bucking, as Roy said it would.

Roy's warning broke through to me in my panic, and I reached up to turn off the ignition. My bronco's engine sputtered out and it settled on the ground with a thump.

I sat for a moment in my sweat. Roy was coming down the ditch in a hurry. He walked up to me and with a quick look saw that neither I nor the tractor was damaged.

"Git off," he said.

I did, feeling that I was about to be demoted, stripped of my rank, bawled out, and fired.

Roy mounted the machine, started it, and worked it off the slope to flat ground. Leaving the engine running, he said: "Git on."

I did.

"Now finish the disking," he said. Above the clatter of the machine he said: "Like I said, she can buck. If she does, cut 'er. You hear?" And he waved me off to my work.

Except for food and a place to live, with which José provided me, I was on my own. Between farm jobs I worked in town, adding to my experience as well as to my income. As a clerk in a drugstore on Second and J, in the heart of the lower part of town, I waited on Chicanos who spoke no English and who came in search of remedies with no prescription other than a recital of their pains. I dispensed capsules, pills, liniments, and emulsions as instructed by the pharmacist, who glanced at our customers from the back of the shop and diagnosed their ills as I translated them. When I went on my shift, I placed a card in the window that said "Se habla español." So far as my Chicano patients were concerned, it might as well have said "Dr. Ernesto Galarza."

From drugs I moved to office supplies and stationery sundries, working as delivery boy for Wahl's, several blocks uptown from skid row. Between deliveries I had no time to idle. I helped the stock clerk, took inventory, polished desks, and hopped when a clerk bawled an order down the basement steps. Mr. Wahl, our boss, a stocky man with a slight paunch, strutted a little as he constantly checked on the smallest details of his establishment, including myself. He was always pleasant and courteous, a man in whose footsteps I might possibly walk into the business world of Sacramento.

But like my uncles, I was looking for a better chanza, which I thought I found with Western Union, as a messenger, where I could earn tips as well as wages. Since I knew the lower part of town thoroughly, whenever the telegrams were addressed to that quarter the dispatcher gave them to me. Deliveries to the suites on the second floor of saloons paid especially well, with tips of a quarter from the ladies who worked there. My most generous customer was tall and beautiful Miss Irene, who always asked how I was doing in school. It was she who gave me an English dictionary, the first I ever possessed, a black bound volume with remarkable little scallops on the pages that made it easy to find words. Half smiling, half commanding, Miss Irene said to me more than once: "Don't you stop school without letting me know." I meant to take her advice as earnestly as I took her twenty-five-cent tip.

It was in the lower town also that I nearly became a performing artist. My instructor on the violin had stopped giving me lessons after we moved to Oak Park. When we were back on O Street he sent word through José that I could work as second fiddler on Saturday nights in the dance hall where he played with a mariachi. Besides, I could resume my lessons with him. A dollar a night for two hours as a substitute was the best wages I had ever made. Coached by my teacher, I second-fiddled for sporting Chicanos who swung their ladies on the dance floor and sang to our music. Unfortunately I mentioned my new calling to Miss Crowley when I proposed it to her as a subject for a composition. She kept me after school and persuaded me to give it up, on the ground that I could earn more decorating Christmas cards during the vacation than at the dance hall. She gave me the first order for fifty cards and got subscriptions for me from the other teachers. I spent my Christmas vacation as an illustrator, with enough money saved to quit playing in the saloon.

It was during the summer vacation that school did not interfere with making a living—the time of the year when I went with other barrio people to the ranches to look for work. Still too young to shape up with the day-haul gangs, I loitered on skid row, picking up conversation and reading the chalk signs about work that was being offered. For a few days of picking fruit or pulling hops I bicycled to Folsom, Lodi, Woodland, Freeport, Walnut Grove, Marysville, Slough House, Florin, and places that had no name. Looking for work, I pedaled through a countryside blocked off, mile after mile, into orchards, vineyards, and vegetable farms. Along the ditch banks, where the grass, the morning glory, and the wild oats made a soft mattress, I unrolled my bindle and slept.

In the labor camps I shared the summertime of the lives of the barrio people. They gathered from barrios of faraway places like Imperial Valley, Los Angeles, Phoenix, and San Antonio. Each family traveling on its own, they came in trucks piled with household goods or packed in their secondhand fotingos[2] and chevees. The trucks and cars were ancient models, fresh out of a used-car lot, with license tags of many states. It was into these jalopies that much of the care and a good part of the family's earnings went. In camp they were constantly being fixed, so close to scrap that when we needed a part for repairs, we first went to the nearest junkyard.

It was a world different in so many ways from the lower part of Sacramento and the residences surrounded by trim lawns and cool canopies of elms to which I had delivered packages for Wahl's. Our main street was usually an irrigation ditch, the water supply for cooking, drinking, laundering, and bathing. In the better camps there was a faucet or a hydrant, from which water was carried in buckets, pails, and washtubs. If the camp belonged to a contractor and it was used from year to year, there were permanent buildings—a shack for his office, the privies, weatherworn and sagging, and a few cabins made of secondhand lumber, patched and unpainted.

If the farmer provided housing himself, it was in tents pitched on the bare baked earth or on the rough ground of newly plowed land on the edge of a field. Those who arrived late for the work season camped under trees or raised lean-tos along a creek, roofing their trucks with canvas to make bedrooms. Such camps were always well away from the house of the ranchero, screened from the main road by an orchard or a grove of eucalyptus. I helped to pitch and take down such camps, on some spot that seemed lonely when we arrived, desolate when we left.

If they could help it, the workers with families avoided the more permanent camps, where the seasonal hired hands from skid row were more likely to be found. I lived a few days in such a camp and found out why families avoided them. On Saturday nights when the crews had a week's wages in their pockets, strangers appeared, men and women, carrying suitcases with liquor and other contraband. The police were called by the contractor only when the carousing threatened to break into fighting. Otherwise, the weekly bouts were a part of the regular business of the camp.

Like all the others, I often went to work without knowing how much I was going to be paid. I was never hired by a rancher, but by a contractor or a straw boss who picked up crews in town and handled the payroll. The important questions that were in my mind—the wages per hour or per lug box, whether the beds would have mattresses and blankets, the price of meals, how often we would be paid—were never discussed, much less answered, beforehand. Once we were in camp, owing the employer for the ride to the job, having no means to get back to town except by walking and no money for the next meal, arguments over working conditions were settled in favor of the boss. I learned firsthand the chiseling techniques of the contractors and their pushers—how they knocked off two or three lugs of grapes from the daily record for each member of the crew, or the way they had of turning the face of the scales away from you when you weighed your work in.

There was never any doubt about the contractor and his power over us. He could fire a man and his family on the spot and make them wait days for their wages. A man could be forced to quit by assigning him regularly to the thinnest pickings in the field. The worst thing one could do was to ask for fresh water on the job, regardless of the heat of the day; instead of iced water, given freely, the crews were expected to buy sodas at twice the price in town, sold by the contractor himself. He usually had a pistol—to protect the payroll, so it was said. Through the ranchers for whom he worked, we were certain that he had connections with the Autoridades, for they never showed up in camp to settle wage disputes or listen to our complaints or to go for a doctor when one was needed. Lord of a

ragtag labor camp of Mexicans, the contractor, a Mexican himself, knew that few men would let their anger blow, even when he stung them with curses.

As a single worker, I usually ate with some household, paying for my board. I did more work than a child but less than a man—neither the head nor the tail of a family. Unless the camp was a large one, I became acquainted with most of the families. Those who could not write asked me to chalk their payroll numbers on the boxes they picked. I counted matches for a man who transferred them from the right pocket of his pants to the left as he tallied the lugs he filled throughout the day. It was his only check on the record the contractor kept of his work. As we worked the rows or the tree blocks during the day, or talked in the evenings where the men gathered in small groups to smoke and rest, I heard about barrios I had never seen but that must have been much like ours in Sacramento.

The only way to complain or protest was to leave, but now and then a camp would stand instead of run, and for a few hours or a few days work would slow down or stop. I saw it happen in a pear orchard in Yolo when pay rates were cut without notice to the crew. The contractor said the market for pears had dropped and the rancher could not afford to pay more. The fruit stayed on the trees while we, a committee drafted by the camp, argued with the contractor first and then with the rancher. The talks gave them time to round up other pickers. A carload of police in plain clothes drove into the camp. We were lined up for our pay, taking whatever the contractor said was on his books. That afternoon we were ordered off the ranch.

In a camp near Folsom, during hop picking, it was not wages but death that pulled the people together. Several children in the camp were sick with diarrhea; one had been taken to the hospital in town and the word came back that he had died. It was the women who guessed that the cause of the epidemic was the water. For cooking and drinking and washing it came from a ditch that went by the ranch stables upstream.

I was appointed by a camp committee to go to Sacramento to find some Autoridad who would send an inspector. Pedaling my bicycle, mulling over where to go and what to say, I remembered some clippings from the *Sacramento Bee* that Mr. Everett had discussed in class, and I decided the man to look for was Mr. Simon Lubin, who was in some way a state Autoridad.

He received me in his office at Weinstock and Lubin's. He sat, square-shouldered and natty, behind a desk with a glass top. He was half-bald, with a strong nose and a dimple in the center of his chin. To his right was a box with small levers into which Mr. Lubin talked and out of which came voices.

He heard me out, asked me questions, and made notes on a pad. He promised that an inspector would come to the camp. I thanked him and thought the business of my visit was over; but Mr. Lubin did not break the handshake until he had said to tell the people in the camp to organize. "Only by organizing," he told me, "will they ever have decent places to live."

I reported the interview with Mr. Lubin to the camp. That part about the inspector they understood and it was voted not to go back to work until he came. The part about organizing was received in silence, and I made my first organizing speech.

The inspector came and a water tank pulled by mules was parked by the irrigation ditch. At the same time the contractor began to fire some of the pickers. I was one of them.

I finished that summer nailing boxes on a grape ranch near Florin.

When my job ended, I pedaled back to Sacramento, detouring over country lanes I knew well. Here and there I walked the bicycle over dirt roads rutted by wagons. The pastures were sunburned and the grain fields had been cut to stubble. Riding by a thicket of reeds where an irrigation ditch swamped, I stopped and looked at the red-winged blackbirds riding gracefully on the tips of the canes. Now and then they streaked out of the green clump, spraying the pale sky with crimson dots in all directions.

Crossing the Y Street levee by Southside Park, I rode through the barrio to doña Tránsito's, leaving my bike hooked on the picket fence by the handlebar.

I knocked on the screen door that always hung tired, like the sagging porch coming unnailed. No one was at home.

It was two hours before time to cook supper. From the stoop I looked up and down the cross streets. The barrio seemed empty.

I unhooked the bicycle, mounted it, and headed for the main high school, twenty blocks away, where I would be going in a week. Pumping slowly, I wondered about the debating team and the other things Mr. Everett had mentioned.

Notes

1. *jefe de familia:* head of the household (literally, "head of the family")
2. *fotingos:* old cars (often travel-worn Fords)

25

At the Burns-Coopers'

Gwendolyn Brooks

It was a little red and white and black woman who appeared in the doorway of the beautiful house in Winnetka.

About, thought Maud Martha, thirty-four. "I'm Mrs. Burns-Cooper," said the woman, "and after this, well, it's all right this time, because it's your first time, but after this time always use the back entrance."

There is a pear in my icebox, and one end of rye bread. Except for three Irish potatoes and a cup of flour and the empty Christmas boxes, there is absolutely nothing on my shelf. My husband is laid off. There is newspaper on my kitchen table instead of oilcloth. I can't find a filing job in a hurry. I'll smile at Mrs. Burns-Cooper and hate her just some.

"First, you have the beds to make," said Mrs. Burns-Cooper. "You either change the sheets or air the old ones for ten minutes. I'll tell you about the changing when the time comes. It isn't any special day. You are to pull my sheets, and pat and pat and pull till all's tight and smooth. Then shake the pillows into the slips, carefully. Then punch them in the middle.

"Next, there is the washing of the midnight snack dishes. Next, there is the scrubbing. Now, I know that your other ladies have probably wanted their floors scrubbed after dinner. I'm different. I like to enjoy a bright clean floor all the day. You can just freshen it up a little before you leave in the evening, if it needs a few more touches. Another thing, I disapprove of mops. You can do a better job on your knees.

"Next is dusting. Next is vacuuming—that's for Tuesdays and Fridays. On Wednesdays, ironing and silver cleaning.

"Now about cooking. You're very fortunate in that here you have only the evening meal to prepare. Neither of us has breakfast, and I always step out for lunch. Isn't that lucky?"

"It's quite a kitchen, isn't it?" Maud Martha observed. "I mean, big."

Mrs. Burns-Cooper's brows raced up in amazement.

"Really? I hadn't thought so. I'll bet"—she twinkled indulgently—"you're comparing it to your *own* little kitchen." And why do that, her light eyes laughed. Why talk of beautiful mountains and grains of alley sand in the same breath?

"Once," mused Mrs. Burns-Cooper, "I had a girl who botched up the kitchen. Made a botch out of it. But all I had to do was just sort of cock my head and say, 'Now, now, Albertine!' Her name was Albertine. Then she'd giggle and scrub and scrub and she was *so* sorry about trying to take advantage."

It was while Maud Martha was peeling potatoes for dinner that Mrs. Burns-Cooper laid herself out to prove that she was not a snob. Then it was that Mrs. Burns-Cooper came out to the kitchen and, sitting, talked and talked at Maud Martha. In my college days. At the time of my debut. The imported lace on my lingerie. My brother's rich wife's Stradivarius. When I was in Madrid. The charm of the Nile. Cost fifty dollars. Cost one hundred dollars. Cost one thousand dollars. Shall I mention, considered Maud Martha, my own social triumphs, my own education, my travels to Gary and Milwaukee and Columbus, Ohio? Shall I mention my collection of fancy pink satin bras? She decided against it. She went on listening, in silence, to the confidences until the arrival of the lady's mother-in-law (large-eyed, strong, with hair of a mighty white, and with an eloquent, angry bosom). Then the junior Burns-Cooper was very much the mistress, was still, cool, authoritative.

There was no introduction, but the elder Burns-Cooper boomed, "Those potato parings are entirely too thick!"

The two of them, richly dressed, and each with that health in the face that bespeaks, or seems to bespeak, much milk drinking from earliest childhood, looked at Maud Martha. There was no remonstrance; no firing! They just looked. But for the first time, she understood what Paul endured daily. For so—she could gather from a Paul-word here, a Paul-curse there—his Boss! when, squared, upright, terribly upright, superior to the President, commander of the world, he wished to underline Paul's lacks, to indicate soft shock, controlled incredulity. As his boss looked at Paul, so these people looked at her. As though she were a child, a ridiculous one, and one that ought to be given a little shaking, except that shaking was—not quite the thing, would not quite do. One held up one's finger (if one did anything), cocked one's head, was arch. As in the old song, one hinted, "Tut tut! now now! come come!" Metal rose, all built, in one's eye.

I'll never come back, Maud Martha assured herself, when she hung up her apron at eight in the evening. She knew Mrs. Burns-Cooper would be puzzled. The wages were very good. Indeed, what could be said in explanation? Perhaps that the hours were long. I couldn't explain *my* explanation, she thought.

One walked out from that almost perfect wall, spitting at the firing squad. What difference did it make whether the firing squad understood or did not understand the manner of one's retaliation or why one had to retaliate?

Why, one was a human being. One wore clean nightgowns. One loved one's baby. One drank cocoa by the fire—or the gas range—come the evening, in the wintertime.

26

Like One of the Family

Alice Childress

Hi, Marge! I have had me one hectic day. . . . Well, I had to take out my crystal ball and give Mrs. C . . . a thorough reading. She's the woman that I took over from Naomi after Naomi get married. . . . Well, she's a pretty nice woman as they go and I have never had too much trouble with her, but from time to time she really gripes me with her ways.

When she has company, for example, she'll holler out to me from the living room to the kitchen. "Mildred dear! Be sure and eat *both* of those lamb chops for your lunch!" Now you know she wasn't doing a thing but tryin' to prove to the company how "good" and "kind" she was to the servant, because she had told me *already* to eat those chops.

Today she had a girl friend of hers over to lunch and I was real busy afterwards clearing the things away and she called me over and introduced me to the woman. . . . Oh no, Marge! I didn't object to that at all. I greeted the lady and then went back to my work. . . . And then it started! I could hear her talkin' just as loud . . . and she says to her friend, "We *just* love her! She's *like* one of the family and she *just adores* our little Carol! We don't know *what* we'd do without her! We don't think of her as a servant!" And on and on she went . . . and every time I came in to move a plate off the table both of them would grin at me like chessy cats.

After I couldn't stand it any more, I went in and took the platter off the table and gave 'em both a look that would have frizzled a egg. . . . Well, you might have heard a pin

drop and then they started talkin' about something else.

When the guest leaves, I go in the living room and says, "Mrs. C . . ., I want to have a talk with you."

"By all means," she says.

I drew up a chair and read her thusly: "Mrs. C . . ., you are a pretty nice person to work for, but I wish you would please stop talkin' about me like I was a *cocker spaniel* or a *poll parrot* or a *kitten*. . . . Now you just sit there and hear me out.

"In the first place, you do not *love* me; you may be fond of me, but that is all. . . . In the second place, I am *not* just like one of the family at all! The family eats in the dining room and I eat in the kitchen. Your mama borrows your lace tablecloth for her company and your son entertains his friends in your parlor, your daughter takes her afternoon nap on the living room couch and the puppy sleeps on your satin spread . . . and whenever your husband gets tired of something you are talkin' about he says, 'Oh, for Pete's sake, forget it. . . .' So you can see I am not *just* like one of the family.

"Now for another thing, I do not *just* adore your little Carol. I think she is a likable child, but she is also fresh and sassy. I know you call it 'uninhibited' and that is the way you want your child to be, but *luckily* my mother taught me some inhibitions or else I would smack little Carol once in a while when she's talkin' to you like you're a dog, but as it is I just laugh it off the way you do because she is *your* child and I am *not* like one of the family.

"Now when you say, 'We don't know *what* we'd do without her' this is a polite lie . . . because I know that if I dropped dead or had a stroke, you would get somebody to replace me.

"You think it is a compliment when you say, 'We don't think of her as a servant. . . .' but after I have worked myself into a sweat cleaning the bathroom and the kitchen . . . making the beds . . . cooking the lunch . . . washing the dishes and ironing Carol's pinafores . . . I do not feel like no weekend house guest. I feel like a servant, and in the face of that I have been meaning to ask you for a slight raise which will make me feel much better toward everyone here and make me know my work is appreciated.

"Now I hope you will stop talkin' about me in my presence and that we will get along like a good employer and employee should."

Marge! She was almost speechless but she *apologized* and said she'd talk to her husband about the raise. . . . I knew things were progressing because this evening Carol came in the kitchen and she did not say, "I want some bread and jam!" but she did say, "*Please,* Mildred, will you fix me a slice of bread and jam."

I'm going upstairs, Marge. Just look . . . you done messed up that buttonhole!

27

Race Inequities in Men's Retirement

Mark D. Hayward
Samantha Friedman
Hsinmu Chen

A multistate life table model is used to identify how labor force experiences and mortality determine the labor force participation rates (LFPRs) and the qualities of the retirement life cycle of Black and White older men. LFPRs and the life cycle measures are compared to assess inequities of retirement access for the racial groups. The results show that Blacks' lower LFPRs are a function of disability. Despite lower LFPRs than Whites, however, Blacks spend a greater portion of their lives both working and disabled, reducing the retirement period. Race differences in the retirement life cycle also are highly sensitive to mortality. Reducing Black mortality to that of Whites would substantially narrow the life cycle differences. The combination of higher disability and mortality rates among Blacks suggests that health is a key determinant of retirement inequity.

Much of what is currently known about differences in the work-to-retirement transition is based on labor force participation rates (LFPRs). Older Black men are less likely to participate in the labor force than similarly aged White men (e.g., Parsons, 1980), and among persons out of the labor force, Blacks are more likely to report that they are disabled compared to Whites (Bound, Schoenbaum, & Waidmann, in press; Siegel, 1993). A variety of explanations have been offered to account for these differences. Older Blacks'

LFPRs have been attributed, for example, to Social Security disability benefits relative to wage levels (e.g., Parsons, 1980), permanent labor force withdrawal at younger ages carried forward to retirement ages (Welch, 1990), declining job-market opportunities for Blacks (Wilson, 1987), and the economic and psychological benefits among older Blacks of adopting the disabled worker role (Gibson, 1991). In addition, the health of Black middle-aged men is generally worse than the health of White men (Bound et. al., in press; Gibson, 1994; Manton, Patrick, and Johnson, 1987). Black men, for example, are more likely to report having difficulties performing various physical activities (Bound et al., in press), and declines in functional abilities are more rapid for Blacks compared to Whites between the ages of 45 and 64 (Gibson, 1994).

Each of these explanations of the race gap in labor force participation hinges on some particular type of labor force behavior. Parson's and Gibson's explanations, although somewhat different theoretically, both suggest that the race gap in labor force participation is due to differences in leaving the labor force because of disability. The confluence of health data also supports this view. And, while Parson's and Gibson's work does not explicitly focus on race differences in the duration of disability, the health data suggest that Blacks suffer from longer spells of disability than Whites, leading to a greater proportion of Blacks being disabled. Welch (1990) suggests that the race gap in older men's labor force participation is less a consequence of behavior at older ages compared to younger ages. Specifically, Welch posits a selection process where younger Black men are more likely to remove themselves permanently from the labor force compared to White men, and this gap in labor force participation moves forward with age. Wilson's argument implies that older Blacks may be more likely to exit the labor force due to the lack of job opportunities and less likely to return should they leave. Whether Blacks are more likely to adopt the disabled status, according to Wilson, is not clear.

While it is impossible to adjudicate fully between these alternative theoretical perspectives, this study provides evidence showing which race differences in labor force behavior determine the race gap in labor force participation. In this manner, we provide some insights into the consistency between the various theoretical perspectives and the behavioral record. A working life table model of labor force participation is developed, showing how the retirement life cycle experiences of Black and White men govern differences in the labor force participation and work disability rates. This model allows us to juxtapose and evaluate a variety of experiences for Blacks and Whites as men approach and enter the retirement years. Do Blacks and Whites differ in their propensity to exit the labor force for non-health reasons? Are Blacks disadvantaged relative to Whites in terms of their ability to return to the labor force? To what extent do race differences in LFPRs depend on difference in the onset and duration of work disability? Are younger Blacks lower labor supply levels carried forward into the retirement years? What role might differential mortality selection play? These questions signify the types of retirement life cycle experiences potentially accounting for race differences in LFPRs. Moreover, they allow us to examine how qualities of the retirement life cycle itself (e.g., the number of years persons can expect to spend working, retired, or dis-

abled; the expected number of lifetime retirement and disability events; and chances of post-retirement labor force participation) align with the LFPRs of Blacks and Whites.

The qualities of the retirement life cycle provide an alternative and potentially very different benchmark of race inequity (Clogg, 1979). As noted above, labor force participation rates are the standard means to gauge inequity. Equity would be achieved by equalizing the current labor force attachment of Black and White men—that is, equalizing the proportions of Black and White men in the labor force. Achieving equity in terms of the retirement life cycle implies closing the gap in the experiences of Blacks and Whites over some period of their lives. For example, equity might imply similar years of work, disability, and retirement for Blacks and Whites. Given race differences in mortality, it also might imply similar proportions of life spent in these labor force statuses. As we will show in this analysis, the inequities implied by the race gap in labor force participation are very different from those implied by measures of the retirement life cycle of Black and White men.

Although race differences in the work-to-retirement transition have clear implications for the quality of life of retirement-aged persons, their demand for social services, and the consumption of public pension benefits, current evidence on the retirement life cycle of Blacks and Whites is surprisingly sparse beyond that provided by the general age profiles of labor force participation rates. Smith (1986) provides some preliminary evidence on race differences in the retirement process using data from the 1979 Current Population Survey (CPS). She calculated, for example, that White men aged 55 had a two-year advantage over same-aged Black men in working life expectancy (8 vs. 6 years) and their LFPR exceeded that of Blacks by 7.5 percent (82.7 vs. 75.1%). White men of this age also exhibited lower rates of movement into and out of the labor force. By age 60, Smith's estimates showed a narrowing of the race gap in working life expectancy (4.5 years for Whites vs. 3.3 years for Blacks), although the gap in

LFPRs grew (64% for Whites and 50% for Blacks). The race differences in exiting and entry rates also held.

This study extends Smith's foray into this topic in several ways. First, we take advantage of data from a prospective cohort study, the National Longitudinal Survey of Older Men, rather than relying on synthetic cohort data. This allows us to identify how a cohort's mobility experiences determine both the structure of labor force attachment and the qualities of the retirement life cycle. Second, we differentiate nonparticipation in the labor fore according to disability to show how self-reported, health-motivated labor force exits as compared to non-health-related exits contribute to labor force attachment and the retirement life cycle. Third, we use a multivariate hazard modeling approach to derive race-specific schedules of transition rates—the input to calculate the working life tables for Blacks and Whites. Analytically, this approach allows us to test whether race has a statistically significant effect on specific types of labor force exit and entry experiences. Finally, we use the life table results to show how race differences in the transition rates determine the gap in labor force participation rates as well as differences in the qualities of the overall retirement life cycle for the two race groups. We then compare the inequities of retirement access implied by the labor force participation rates and measures of the retirement life cycle.

Results

• To what extent does race influence specific transitions out of and into the labor force? The hazard results show for most transitions that race is not a statistically significant determinant of older men's labor force behavior. The exception is the race effect for disability; as expected, Blacks have a significantly greater chance of becoming disabled. However, Blacks are no more or less likely to retire, or to return to the labor force from disability or retirement. Blacks have elevated

mortality risks among both labor force incumbents and retirees, and the race effect is relatively similar across these two labor force status groups. Blacks' life chances, however, are *not* lower than Whites once disabled. Once health has declined to a level precluding working, race no longer carries any advantages or disadvantages for future life chances.

• Race differences in LFPR attachment are due to two factors: higher disability rates at older ages among Blacks and higher disability rates at younger ages carried forward. What do these factors portend for Blacks' and Whites' retirement life cycle experiences? Further, although mortality differences have little effect on LFPRs, what consequences might they have for the retirement life cycle?

• Immediately apparent are the number of years both groups spend in "post-retirement" jobs, although Whites aged 45 years can expect to spend about one year more in these jobs than Blacks. Note that Blacks' post-retirement work opportunities are curtailed by substantially fewer retirements and greater chances of disability and death. Race is a clear marker of retirement access inequity.

• Erasing the labor force disadvantages incurred at younger ages, for example, has very little effect on Blacks' total working life expectancy at age 45, but it does increase retirement expectancy slightly while lowering disability expectancy. Improving mortality substantially increases Blacks' working and retirement life expectancies, with little effect on disability life expectancy. Finally, lowering disability rates not only would lower Blacks' disability life expectancy, but it also would have a positive effect on retirement life expectancy. The factor having the greatest impact on extending Blacks' retirement life expectancy is mortality improvement—a variable not generally thought to be policy manipulable—at least in the short term.

Discussion

It is a social fact in American society that fewer opportunities for achievement exist for

Black men compared to White men. This is reflected in Blacks' lower educational attainment, lower wages, concentration in physically demanding and intrinsically unrewarding jobs, higher unemployment rates, higher rates of alcoholism and drug use, and higher mortality rates. An extensive literature has documented these problems, especially for Black youth, describing a turbulent transition to adulthood and what is often a truncated life course.

This study shows that Blacks' unequal footing in the labor market persists into the retirement years. Although a variety of explanations have been advanced to account for the race gap in older men's labor force attachment, the pattern of results is most consistent with the argument that race differences in health are the proximal determinant of the gap after age 45 (Bound et al., in press). Blacks' higher rates of disability at both older ages and the disability rates of younger Blacks carried into middle age account for almost all of the race difference in labor force participation rates. Once disabled, Blacks are not more or less likely to die than Whites, suggesting that the adoption of the disability status among Blacks is not simply a socially desirable response to constrained economic opportunities. Moreover, the lack of any significant race difference in labor force reentry among disabled persons suggests that once the disabled status is adopted, it is an equally permanent status, for both race groups. The same holds for persons adopting the retired status. Differential economic opportunities for Blacks and Whites do not appear to be a factor stratifying post-retirement work experiences, once disability status is controlled. Our conclusion parallels that of Bound and colleagues in their analysis of race differences in older men's labor force attachment using a variety of nationally representative data sets. Black men's poorer health status is a dominant and proximal factor accounting for their lower labor force attachment.

This does not negate Parsons' (1980) arguments regarding the importance of Social Security disability programs for race differences in older men's labor force attachment. Such programs define a social context which allows individualistic factors such as health status to come into play in determining labor force attachment. Were such programs drastically curtailed, the necessity of working might well increase Blacks' levels of attachment (while simultaneously lowering the overall health of older Black workers). Our analysis also does not contradict Gibson's (1991) argument that Blacks have a greater preference for the disabled worker role due to life-long marginal labor force attachment. What our work suggests is that the poorer health status of older Black men (and the adoption of the disabled worker role) is a reflection of the confluence of social class factors such as life-long poverty or near poverty, and the overrepresentation in physically demanding and unrewarding jobs. Blacks' preferences for the disabled worker role thus are an outgrowth of greater rates of chronic health problems, which, in turn, devolve from social class disadvantages. Such preferences are reinforced at older ages by the continued absence of economic opportunities.

More generally, our analysis points to the importance of considering health status as a proximal determinant of the race gap in labor force participation throughout a significant portion of the career cycle. By extension, a portion of the race gap in career achievement may be a reflection of race differences in health status. In general, social stratification research on race differences in attainment has ignored the constraints that poor health may place on achievement over the career cycle. The results shown here suggest that at least some of the race gap in career attainment is affected by Blacks' lower likelihood of participating in the labor force due to poorer health (differential selection) as well as race differences in the health "stock" of labor force participants.

LFPRs are attractive measures of labor force inequity because of measurement ease, simplicity of interpretation, and their historical longevity as part of federal and local population statistics. Our analysis suggests caution in using these measures, however, when formulating policies to resolve race inequities. That is, LFPRs mask significant differences in Blacks' and Whites' retirement life cycle experiences, experiences which are the crux of manpower and pension policies. For example, viewing labor force inequity through the lens of LFPRs, a logical solution to resolve the race gap in older men's attachment would be to develop policies to increase Blacks' attachment through a reduction in disability. Older Blacks' lower LFPRs foster the perception that middle-aged and older Blacks spend less of their lives in the labor force compared to Whites, an idea reinforced by the fact that significant numbers of younger Black men do not and probably will not participate in the civilian labor force.

The retirement life cycle of Blacks, however, is more complex than the image conveyed by LFPRs. When status life expectancies are compared relative to total life expectancy, Blacks actually spend more—not less—of their lives in the labor force compared to Whites. Moreover, Blacks spend a greater portion of their lives disabled. That portion of older age traditionally described in economic terms as "leisure" is highly circumscribed for Blacks relative to that for Whites. Retirement is more a White experience than a Black experience, while the reverse is true with regard to disability. In contrast to the sorts of policies implied by the LFPRs, the life table analysis shows that erasing race differences in the retirement life cycle and improving retirement access among Blacks could be accomplished by reducing Black mortality. Policy targets might be the eradication of persistent poverty, higher rates of educational attainment, and job and wage inequality; these factors are the basis for social class differences in health. Note that mortality reduction as long-term policy goal is not typically addressed by policy makers concerned with equity of retirement access. More common policy tools include pension policies, job training programs, preretirement training programs, and the enforcement of antidiscrimination policies. Although our analysis does not rule out the importance of such tools, our findings do suggest that equity of retirement access is partly a public health issue and almost certainly a function of life-long poverty and its associated health consequences.

Our results also point to the importance of investigating how health and work are intertwined for Blacks and Whites to better understand race differences in the work-to-retirement transition. Do Blacks and Whites differentially define health conditions as problematic for continued work? What type of physical health conditions arise for the two race groups (including timing, duration, and severity), and how are these physical conditions related to functional limitations? To what extent are the health problems of Black men manifestations of adverse occupational circumstances and lower socioeconomic status? Are Blacks and Whites differentially able to accommodate their health problems due to occupational position or alternative career opportunities? Answers to these questions will enhance understanding of health's role as a key source of the apparent inequity of retirement access for Black and White men.

Acknowledgments

We would like to dedicate this article to our colleague, Clifford Clogg, whose work provided much of the intellectual foundation for the analytic approach used. His classic book, *Measuring Underemployment*, introduced the idea of using life table models rather than prevalence rates to assess life cycle inequity across population subgroups. We also would like to thank Daniel T. Lichter and John Bound for their comments on an earlier draft.

Partial support for this research was provided by grants from the National Institute on Aging (AG-11758 and AG-09338).

References

Bound, J., M. Schoenbaum, and T. Waidman. In press, "Race and Education Differences in

Disability Status and Labor Force Attachment." *Journal of Human Resources.*

Clogg, C. C. 1979. *Measuring Underemployment.* New York: Academic Press.

Gibson, R. C. 1991. "The Subjective Retirement of Black Americans." *Journal of Gerontology: Social Sciences* 46:S204-S209.

Gibson, R. C. 1994. "The Age-by-Race Gap in Health and Mortality in the Older Population: A Social Science Research Agenda." *The Gerontologist* 34:454-462.

Manton, K. G., C. H. Patrick, and K. W. Johnson. 1987. "Health Differentials Between Blacks and Whites: Recent Trends in Mortality and Morbidity." *Milbank Quarterly* 65(Supp. 1): 129-199.

Parsons, D. O. 1980. "Racial Trends in Male Labor Force Participation." *American Economic Review* 70:911-920.

Siegel, J. 1993. *A Generation of Change, A Profile of America's Older Population.* New York: Russell Sage Foundation.

Smith, S. J. 1986. "Worklife Estimates: Effects of Race and Education." Bulletin 2254, Bureau of Labor Statistics. Washington, DC: USGPO.

Welch, F. 1990. "The Employment of Black Men." *Journal of Labor Economics* 8:S26-S74.

Wilson, W. J. 1987. "The Obligation to Work and the Availability of Jobs: A Dialogue between Lawrence M. Mead and William Julius Wilson." *Focus* (Summer 1987).

1   Aliene Walser, Mike LeFevre, and Mrs. Sharpe were all white and therefore privileged in one system of inequality: race. But there were differences among these three people in the availability of productive activity roles and of the economic rewards associated with these roles. What were these differences? What factors account for the differences?

2   The women in the New York City slave market, the workers in Olsen's poem, Mrs. Lee, Sky, and Mrs. Susie Jones were all women of color. Thus they were disadvantaged in two systems of inequality: race and gender. Yet there were differences in the effects of their productive activities on their lives. What were these differences? What accounts for the differences?

3   Gender structures opportunities for paid productive activity and responsibilities for unpaid productive activity. The readings introduced you to a number of women: Aliene Walser, Mrs. Jones, Mrs. Lee, the women in the New York City slave market, the African American woman at the Burns-Coopers', and the garment workers in Olsen's poem. What similarities and what differences do you see in the meanings they attached to their productive activities and in their disillusionments and satisfactions with their work? Can you explain the patterns you observe?

4   Mrs. Jones and Mrs. Sharpe were both privileged on class and disadvantaged on gender, yet there were some differences in their attitudes toward the availability and meaning of productive activity roles. What were they? Why do you think these differences existed? To what degree do their lives illustrate an "accumulation of advantage"?

5   What types of productive activity (both paid and unpaid) do you anticipate pursuing over the next 50 years? How do you think your position on hierarchies based on gender, race, and class will influence the availability of various productive roles? Place yourself about 50 years hence. How will your lifetime of productive activity influence the resources you have available in old age?

6   Tillie Olsen's poem about Hispanic garment workers is written in the form of a letter to the "women up North" who buy the clothes in local department stores. Draft a letter in response to Olsen's poem as it might have been written by Mrs. Sharpe or by other women sharing her position of privilege.

7   Moen, Robison, and Fields's discussion of ways in which women's employment and caregiving combine over the life course illustrates how gender and class structure productive activities. How might pension policies be changed to reflect the range of productive activities of women across the life course? Can you think of other seemingly neutral policies with outcomes structured by systems of inequality?

8   Mike LeFevre and Ernesto Galarza were both men and therefore privileged in one system of inequality: gender. But there were differences between these men in the availability of productive activity roles and of the economic rewards associated with these roles. What were these differences? What factors account for the differences?

SUGGESTIONS FOR FURTHER READING

1   Allen, K. R., & Chin-Sang, V. (1990). A lifetime of work: The context and meaning of leisure for aging black women. *The Gerontologist, 30,* 734-740.

For women, productive activity is most often a tapestry of paid and unpaid work throughout the life course. In researching this article, Allen and Chin-Sang interviewed 30 aging African American women about the meanings of leisure within the context of their work histories. "Leisure" for these women most often involved a continuation of their lifetime pattern of hard work and service to others.

2   Stone, R. I. (1989, Spring/Summer). The feminization of poverty among the elderly. *Women's Studies Quarterly, 17,* 20-34.

This article explores a number of issues surrounding increasing risks of poverty for older women. Stone discusses women's economic dependence on men, labor market discrimination, unpaid family labor, and the impact of illness in old age.

3   Calasanti, T. M., & Bonanno, A. (1992). Working overtime: Economic restructuring and retirement of a class. *Sociological Quarterly, 33*(1), 135-152.

In this analysis of retirement adjustment, Calasanti and Bonanno move beyond individual-level characteristics and consider the impact of employment in the primary versus the secondary labor markets. Their analysis is particularly relevant to understanding intersections among systems of inequality, as women and people of color are disproportionately employed in secondary labor market jobs.

4   Terkel, S. (1974). *Working: People talk about what they do all day and how they feel about what they do.* New York: Pantheon.

Studs Terkel interviews a range of working people in the 1950s and 1960s about their work. Listening to the voices of these workers brings to life statistics documenting occupational distribution of the workforce. The interviews demonstrate how the meaning of work is distributed across interlocking systems of privilege and disadvantage.

5   Himes, C. B. (1975). *Black on black: Baby sister and selected writings.* London: Joseph.

What types of productivity roles were available to people disadvantaged by race and class during the Depression of the 1930s? How did this particular historical period shape the opportunity structure, life events, and adaptive resources of African American men as they aged? We recommend, in particular, the selections "Headwaiter" and "Pork Chop Paradise."

6   Clive, A. (1987). The home front and the household: Women, work and family in Detroit. In N. A. Hewitt (Ed.), *Women, families and communities: Readings in American history* (Vol. 2, pp. 188-203). Glenview, IL: Scott, Foresman/Little, Brown.

Dramatic alterations in work and home life for women occurred during World War II. The popular image of Rosie the Riveter symbolized the belief that women could move into industry and become "one of the boys." Clive traces these alterations as they were played out in Detroit, Michigan. He explores changes in the sexual and racial composition of the workforce, attitudes of employers and coworkers toward women, and the impact of federal policies on women's work and family experiences both during and after the war.

7   Lerner, G. (1973). It takes a while to realize that it is discrimination. In *Black women in white America* (pp. 275-281). New York: Vintage.

The historian Gerda Lerner traces the quest of an African American woman for equitable paid work roles. Covering the

Great Depression of the 1930s and World War II of the 1940s, this selection illustrates how sociohistorical time and disadvantaged status in three systems of inequality converged to limit role availability.

8 Singer, I. B. (1988). The hotel. In *The death of Methuselah and other stories*. New York: Farrar, Straus & Giroux.

This story demonstrates how productive activity roles in early life influenced the retirement role chosen by an affluent Jewish man. The meanings Israel Danziger attached to productive activities throughout his life continued to influence his adjustment to retirement.

9 Quadagno, J., & Meyer, M. H. (1990). Gender and public policy. *Generations, 14*(3), 64-66.

This discussion of pension policy illustrates ways in which ostensibly neutral social policies can produce outcomes that are structured by older people's gender, class, and race or ethnicity. The article begs the question of how pension policies might be changed to reflect the range of productive activities of women across the life course.

10 Ostrander, S. (1984). Community volunteer. In *Women of the upper class* (pp. 111-139). Philadelphia: Temple University Press.

Productive activity takes on different meanings for women of the upper class.

11 Gibson, R. C. (1987). Reconceptualizing retirement for black Americans. *The Gerontologist, 27*(6), 691-698.

Productive activity roles in early life shape economic well-being and meanings of work and retirement roles in late life.

PART IV

Family

Variations on "The American Family"

The Diversity of American Families

Our understanding of family, perhaps more than any other institution, is clouded by myth. Masking diversity among contemporary U.S. families is an ideology that describes the American family as "one man who goes off to earn the bacon, one woman who waits at home to fry it, and roughly 2.5 children poised to eat it" (Cole, 1986, p. 11). This image of family dominated U.S. culture during the decades following World War II, a period during which the majority of today's older people experienced at least part of their childrearing years. As described by Betty Friedan (1964) in *The Feminine Mystique*, this ideology told women that caring for their home and family was the path to fulfillment and gratification (Andersen, 1997). The sociologist Talcott Parsons (1955) described the American family as an isolated, nuclear unit in which the husband, wife, and their dependent children live geographically and economically independent from other relatives. Families were viewed as safe havens from the competitiveness of the work place, and both popular images and social scientific treatises emphasized the split between the public sphere of employment and the private sphere of home (Coontz, 1992).

In this section, we will explore the consequences of this idealized image of the American family on our efforts to understand the diversity of family experiences among older people today. Our exploration of older families will ask these questions:

1. How does the myth of the American family mask the diversity of families in which today's cohorts of elderly people grew up and grew old?
2. How do interlocking hierarchies based on gender, race, and class structure the family experiences of today's older Americans?
3. How do definitions of family based on the experiences of the dominant groups in society bias research on other older families?

How the Myth of the American Family Masks the Diversity of Families in Which Today's Cohorts of Elderly People Grew Up and Grew Old

There are a number of problems with the ideological view of the nuclear family as a key to understanding family experiences of older people today. First, not all older people married, and not all married people had children. Of the people who are 65 and older today, 5% never married, 6% divorced or separated, and 20% do not have adult children. Marriage and divorce rates also vary by gender and ethnicity. Older American Indian and Asian American women are slightly less likely to have remained single throughout their lives than are other older people. Rates of divorce and separation for elderly Blacks, Hispanic Americans, American Indians, and Asian Americans are higher than rates for elderly Whites.

Second, the idealized view of the family glorified the role of the full-time housewife, wife, and mother. Married women who did not enter the paid labor force and worked full time at home often found that their lives did not correspond to the image fostered by popular culture. Many full-time mothers were troubled by the isolation of their daily lives, the repetitiveness of household tasks, and the invisibility of their accomplishments (Oakley, 1974). Betty Friedan (1964) labeled the vague, unspoken anxiety experienced by the full-time housewives in her study as "the problem that has no name." According to popular ideology, these women should have been among the most happy and fulfilled. Their families came closest to the idealized American family. Yet Friedan's subjects shared doubts and dissatisfactions. Moreover, they felt responsible for this unease, because the ideology of the feminine mystique shifted the blame to women themselves if they were unsatisfied with their lives. Women were taught that

> [they] could desire no greater destiny than to glory in their femininity. . . . If a woman had a problem in the 1950s and 1960s, she knew that something must be wrong with her marriage and with herself. . . . What kind of woman was she if she did not feel this mysterious fulfillment waxing the kitchen floor? (1964, p. 19)

Not all women who opted for full-time work at home over paid work in the labor market were dissatisfied with their lives. Caring for a home and family offered opportunities for creativity and satisfaction. Because work at home provides freedom from supervision and some flexibility in organizing tasks, many women preferred it to the more alienating conditions they would have encountered in paid positions available to them (Andersen, 1997). Nevertheless, as the 1960s came to a close, the vague discontent described by Friedan began to crystallize into a feminist analysis that defined motherhood as a serious obstacle to women's fulfillment. This strain of feminist thought reflects the race and class position of its creators. In gathering data for *The Feminine Mystique,* Friedan interviewed her former classmates at Smith College, and her results reflect the experiences of these White, middle-class, college-educated women. bell hooks (1984) describes the bias of an analysis developed from the standpoint of this particular group:

> [They] argued that motherhood was a serious obstacle to women's liberation, a trap confining women to the home, keeping them tied to cleaning, cooking, and child care. . . . Had black women voiced their views on motherhood, [motherhood] would not have been

named a serious obstacle to our freedom as women. Racism, availability of jobs, lack of skills or education, and a number of other issues would have been at the top of the list—but not motherhood. Black women would not have said motherhood prevented us from entering the world of paid work, because we have always worked. (p. 133)

As hooks's (1984) critique suggests, not all of today's older women were able to choose whether or not they would stay out of the paid labor force when their children were young, despite the popular and scholarly rhetoric advocating full-time motherhood. Women rearing children alone because of single motherhood, divorce, or widowhood had little choice but to combine the nurturing roles assigned to mothers with the breadwinning responsibilities supposedly reserved for fathers. Furthermore, poor and working-class two-parent families often needed two incomes to survive. Women of color were more likely than White women to find themselves in this situation, as racial oppression denied many of these women sufficient economic resources to maintain nuclear family households (Collins, 1990). Elderly Black women, for example, typically combined childrearing with paid work at a time when employment opportunities for women and for people of color were even more restricted than they are today.

The rigid gender-based division of labor that characterized popular constructions of the American family of the 1950s did not apply across all combinations of race and class. For example, the strict gender role segregation within the domestic sphere applied more to White families than to Black families. Black couples have traditionally been more flexible in allocating family obligations, with parents sharing household tasks and childrearing as well as responsibility for earning a living (McAdoo, 1986). Upper-class women, most of whom were White, retained personal responsibility for managing children and household, but rarely did the actual work themselves (Ostrander, 1984). Rather, they supervised the work of paid domestic workers, who were usually poor or working-class women and often women of color (Cole, 1986).

Upper-class women also had more resources with which to exercise their family responsibilities than less affluent women. Susan Ostrander's (1984) wealthy subjects wanted their children "to develop to their fullest potential, . . . to be 'the best' " (p. 75). They expressed concerns about their children's personal happiness and their future success. Most important, they had resources to facilitate these goals for their children. For example, if their children encountered academic difficulties or adjustment problems, the parents often sent them to private schools. Mrs. Miles, a woman now in her 70s, whose husband had been chairman of the board of a major bank, describes her decision to enroll her teenage daughter in a private boarding school: "She was a very shy child . . . so I thought . . . going away to school would be good for her, would give her some confidence and put her on her feet" (p. 85). As Ostrander explains, "Upper-class children . . .

are not allowed to fail academically or personally. This gives them strong advantages" (p. 84). Parents from other social classes share many of the same dreams and concerns for their children expressed by the women Ostrander interviewed, but they do not share the same resources for helping their children realize these dreams.

Another aspect of the mythic American family that clouds our understanding of the family experiences of today's elderly people is the assumption of the nuclear family as isolated from other relatives. Contrary to this image of independent nuclear households, women have traditionally maintained family relationships across households through visiting, writing letters, organizing holiday gatherings, and remembering birthdays and anniversaries—activities that have been described as "kinship work" (DiLeonardo, 1987; Rosenthal, 1985). The work of "kinkeeping" can produce complex networks of female kin, who entrust confidences, pool resources, and share social activities. Furthermore, as social gerontologists have demonstrated, women are the primary caregivers of frail elderly people in their families.

Strong female-centered networks have also linked families and households among Blacks. Mothering responsibilities have traditionally been shared among women in Black communities. Boundaries distinguishing biological mothers from other women who care for children are less rigid within these communities, and women often feel a sense of obligation for "our children," a term that includes all of the children in their community. Patricia Hill Collins (1991) explains that

> Black communities recognized that vesting one person with full responsibility for mothering a child may not be wise or possible. As a result, 'othermothers,' women who assist bloodmothers by sharing mothering responsibilities, traditionally have been a central part of the institution of Black motherhood. (p. 47)

When children are orphaned, when parents are ill or at work, or when biological mothers are too young to care for their children alone, other women in the community take on child care responsibilities, sometimes temporarily but other times permanently.

These women-centered networks of bloodmothers and othermothers within Black communities have often been described as a reaction to the legacy of slavery and to generations of poverty and oppression. Some scholars have challenged this interpretation. The impact of racial oppression on Black families must be acknowledged, but it is also important to recognize the ways in which today's elderly Blacks evolved new definitions of family from their everyday experiences and cultural legacies. Networks of community-based child care, for example, provided supervision for children while biological parents worked to provide economic support. Alternative definitions of motherhood, emphasizing both emotional support and physical provision of care, were adapted from West African culture, which had been retained as a culture of resistance since slavery

(Sudarkasa, 1981). Building on this cultural heritage, Black women devised strategies for ensuring their children's physical survival within a racist society—ways of ensuring their physical survival without compromising their sense of self-worth (Collins, 1991). The historian Elsa Barkley Brown (1991) describes this approach to mothering by explaining how her mother understood "the need to socialize me to live my life one way and, at the same time, to provide me with the tools I would need to live it differently" (p. 231). Like other Black women writing about family, Brown stresses the contributions of mothers and grandmothers in teaching the "delicate balance between conformity and resistance. . . . Black daughters must learn how to survive in interlocking structures of race, class, and gender oppression while rejecting and transcending these very same structures" (Collins, 1991, p. 54).

Other examples also challenge the myth of self-reliance of isolated, nuclear households. Coontz (1992) points out that working-class and ethnic subcommunities "evolved mutual aid in finding jobs, surviving tough times, and pooling money for recreation" (p. 71). Immigrant groups developed infrastructures of churches, temperance societies, workers' associations, fraternal orders, and cooperatives that provided instrumental and emotional aid beyond the confines of the nuclear household. Godparenting created extrafamilial bonds among Catholic populations, bonds that often cut across social class boundaries, and as Coontz points out, "the notion of 'going for sisters' has long and still thriving roots in black communities" (p. 72). Extended networks of kin also characterize Latino families, in which child care responsibilities are often shared with older siblings, aunts, uncles, and grandparents. Ceremonial events frequently involve close friends linked to the family through *compadrazgo,* a network of kinlike ties among very close friends who exchange tangible assistance and social support (Heyck, 1994).

The idealized image of the American family also assumes a heterosexual couple. Despite more recent attention to gay and lesbian rights, it is important to remember that today's cohorts of elderly gay men and lesbians grew up in a social environment in which they encountered strong pressures to hide their sexual orientation. They lived most of their lives during a historical period characterized by hostility toward homosexuality (Fullmer, 1995). Many kept their relationships secret to avoid discriminatory treatment by their families, their employers, and their communities (D'Augelli & Hart, 1987). Lesbians and gay men who revealed their relationships to others often needed to develop strategies for coping with negative attitudes and discriminatory treatment (Hooyman & Kiyak, 1999). Indeed, there is some evidence that the experience of "coming out" strengthens the adaptive resources for meeting challenges of late life (Quan & Whitford, 1992). Although marriage between gay and lesbian partners is not legally sanctioned, many couples establish long-term relationships (Peplau, 1991). The absence of legal recognition creates a number of obstacles for these couples in late life. Many employers do not extend insurance or retirement benefits to unmarried partners, and social security does not extend survivor's benefits to gay men or lesbians whose partners have died. Although provision of domestic partnership benefits is increasing, these benefits were not available for current cohorts of gay or lesbian elders. Locating assisted living or nursing home environments receptive to gay or lesbian couples can also be difficult. When one partner is hospitalized, the other partner may be denied access to an intensive care unit or other contexts reserved for "next of kin." Without a medical power of attorney, hospital personnel do not recognize the authority of one partner to make health care decisions for his or her incapacitated partner. Gay or lesbian couples can try to protect each other's financial situations in their wills, but other family members sometimes contest the right of the surviving partner to an inheritance.

The short story "The Linden Tree" introduces us to one such couple. Although the two men in this story are relatively isolated, gay and lesbian elders often establish networks of friends who, like family members, exchange emotional and instrumental support (Kimmel, 1992). Lipman (1986) reported that elderly gay men and lesbians tend to have more friends than heterosexuals of similar age. Most of these friends are of the same gender, and many are also gay or lesbian. These friendship networks can serve as surrogate families, supplemented by support from advocacy organizations, such as the Lavender Panthers, Senior Action in a Gay Environment, or Gay and Lesbian Association of Retiring Persons.

Generalizing the image of the American family to all couples masks the complexity of family experiences and resources with which older Americans face the challenges of aging. Uncritically accepting dominant stereotypes of older families is like wearing blinders. Our understanding is limited, because we don't think to ask questions about dimensions of social reality that we overlook. We forget to ask how people who never married develop other relationships to meet their needs for companionship in old age. We forget to ask how gay and lesbian couples activate a support network to care for them when they are ill. We forget to ask how more fluid definitions of family and more flexible divisions of labor both within and beyond nuclear-family households influence strategies used by older Blacks in coping with disability in old age. These oversights are not intentional. They reflect limited views of social reality from particular standpoints. The poet Adrienne Rich (as quoted in West & Fenstermaker, 1995) used the term *White solipsism* to refer to the process of thinking, imagining, and speaking "as if Whiteness described the world," resulting in a "tunnel-vision which simply does not see nonwhite experience or existence as precious or significant" (p. 306).

How Interlocking Hierarchies of Gender, Race, and Class
Structure the Experience of Family Among Older People Today

Families of older people today are continuations of families established by young adults in the 1930s, 1940s, and 1950s. The composition of these families has changed over the intervening decades as new members were added through birth, marriage, adoption, or other alliances; others were lost through death, and the remainder aged and moved through life transitions. Economic and political fluctuations produced changes in opportunities and access to resources available to support family members, and changes in attitudes regarding old age influenced older people's self-esteem and their relationships with kin. Although these demographic, socioeconomic, and political forces impinge on all families, differences in their consequences are grounded in hierarchies based on gender, race or ethnicity, and social class.

Because of sex differences in life expectancy, the tendency of women to marry men older than themselves, and higher remarriage rates among older men, the majority of older men are married and the majority of older women are widowed. For example, only 41% of women age 65 and older are married and living with a spouse, in comparison to 76% for men. Minority elders, particularly those also disadvantaged by social class, have shorter life expectancies than elderly people privileged by race and class, but the sex differential in life expectancy persists across all racial and ethnic groups. Among people 65 to 75 years of age, 80% of White men in comparison to only 55% of White women are married and living with a spouse. Among Blacks the same age, 62% of men but only 35% of women are living with a spouse. Among Hispanic elders the same age, the comparable figures are 71% for men and 46% for women (Quadagno, 1999). Once again, comparing these differences reveals the intersection of gender and race or ethnicity in generating differences in the experiences of late life.

Historical trends in fertility and differences in mortality have also influenced the number of adult children in families of today's older people. Although birthrates have evidenced a long-term decline since the early 1800s, several fluctuations in this trend influence today's elderly families. The oldest-old (i.e., people over 85 years of age) experienced their marriage and childbearing years during the Great Depression of the 1930s, a period when limited economic opportunities reduced marriage and fertility rates. In contrast, older people in their late 60s and 70s experienced their marriage and childbearing years during the prosperous decades following World War II, when as we have seen, dominant ideology emphasized marriage and motherhood as primary goals for U.S. women. This cohort of elders were the parents of the post-World-War-II baby boom. As a result of these demographic shifts, the current cohort of old-old people have, on the average, fewer adult children than do young-old people. This difference will shift, of course, as the parents of the baby boom reach their late 80s and will shift again as people experiencing their childbearing years during the so-called birth dearth of the 1970s enter old age.

Families as well as individuals are shaped by historical context. In her book *The Way We Never Were: American Families and the Nostalgia Trap,* Stephanie Coontz (1992) interprets the so-called traditional middle-class family of the 1950s as a product of a particular historical period. She argues that this family type was a qualitatively new phenomenon, reflecting a "unique and temporary conjuncture of economic, social and political factors" (p. 29): high rates of savings during the war; America's postwar industrial advantage; expansion of middle class management occupations, a honeymoon period between management and organized labor, and a rapid growth in real wages; and expanded government subsidy of education, job training, housing loans, and highway and sewer construction. As she explains, the family arrangements that became the new standard in the 1950s were not a return to traditional patterns established in previous decades. Indeed, early marriages, high birth rates, and declines in the proportion of never-married persons stand in sharp contrast to the rest of the 20th century, in which American families have been characterized by falling birth rates, rising divorce rates, and older ages at first marriage (Skolnick, 1991).

Decisions regarding fertility are also influenced by economic and cultural factors, so it is not surprising that family size varies by social class and by race or ethnicity. In general, more affluent families have had fewer children than poorer families, a tendency that persists across all racial groups. One exception to this negative relationship between social class and number of children occurs at the pinnacle of the class hierarchy, with upper-upper-class families slightly larger than average (Ostrander, 1984). Fertility rates also vary by race or ethnicity. Hispanics have the highest fertility rate of any racial or ethnic group. Fertility rates for Blacks have been consistently higher than fertility rates for Whites, with the difference most pronounced during the 1950s. Differences in mortality, however, reduce the numerical advantage of older Blacks and Hispanic Americans in numbers of adult children implied by these fertility differentials. Children of Black and Hispanic American parents are less likely than children of White parents to survive infancy and childhood, and young men from these groups face higher risks of death from violence. Children of today's young-old elders compose the cohort that participated in the Vietnam War. Besides the gender difference in deaths in combat, studies of wartime mortality documented higher death rates among minority soldiers than among White soldiers, a difference that reflected race and class biases in both the military draft and assignments within the military (Waitzkin, 1974).

Why Women Are Most Often the Providers of Family Care for Frail Older People

Despite the myth that older people are dumped into nursing homes by uninterested relatives too involved in their own careers and activities to care for their frail elderly relatives, gerontologists have demonstrated that family members, particularly spouses and adult children, provide the majority of long-term care to older people in the United States today. A recent study by the National Alliance for Caregiving and the American Association of Retired Persons (1997) estimated that 70% to 80% of all the in-home care for older people with chronic impairments is provided by families. Caring for frail elderly relatives represents a major gender difference in the experience of old age, as provision of this unpaid care is disproportionately women's work. Among elderly couples, the caregiver is most likely the wife, as she is typically younger than her husband. Widowed women most often rely on adult daughters for assistance, because sons are unlikely to provide the personal (or hands-on) care that frail elderly people often require. A preference hierarchy for family caregivers appears to exist. If a spouse or adult daughter is not available, sibling networks become involved. Gerontologists estimate that over 70% of the family members caring for frail elderly relatives are women and that over 50% of all women will provide care to a frail relative at some point in their lives (Pavalko & Artis, 1997).

The research on family caregiving illustrates the intersection of hierarchies based on gender and on class. The majority of people who provide unpaid care to frail elderly people are women, but social class differences mediate the experience of family caregiving. Relatively affluent women have resources to hire supplementary assistance or purchase market alternatives for caregiving tasks or domestic work. These women become care managers, delegating responsibilities to formal providers, most of whom are women who work for minimal wages. They are relieved of some of the drudgery of housework and caregiving by "becoming managers of the drudgery of domestic work done by other women" (Cole, 1986, p. 8). These other women are most often working-class women, frequently members of racial or ethnic minority groups, who return home from performing the personal care and household tasks of more affluent women to their own second shift of unpaid domestic work.

Responsibilities of caring for a frail older relative can discourage labor force participation among women caregivers. With minimal support from either public services or male relatives, these women often experience the obligation to care for a spouse or elderly parent as a necessity rather than a choice (Aronson, 1992; Brubaker & Brubaker, 1992). But not all women faced with caregiving responsibilities are able to reduce demands on their time by withdrawing from paid labor. Poor and working-class women lack the financial resources to retire early, leave the labor force temporarily, or work part-time. For unmarried women who cannot pool resources with a second wage earner, the situation is particularly bleak. Traditional notions of the "maiden aunt" as a provider of care for her frail elderly parents must be tempered by the reality that even lifelong continuous employment in the secondary labor market fails to provide adequate pension benefits or opportunities to accumulate savings (O'Rand, 1996).

As with many transitions in the life course of older families, the transition from adult son or daughter to caregiver is an unscheduled one. Sometimes, the shift occurs suddenly, as when an older parent suffers a stroke. More often, however, the transition begins almost imperceptibly, with caring for an older parent at first entailing more a sense of responsibility than tangible assistance (Lewis & Meredith, 1988). A number of the adult daughters interviewed by Jane Lewis and Barbara Meredith felt they had "just drifted into caring" and were unable to identify the point at which they had assumed a caregiving role. The narrator in Ann Tracy's short story, "Between the Funerals," catches this subtle shift in dependency long before her mother needs concrete assistance.

Methodological Issues in Studying Older Families:
How Definitions Based on Experiences of the
Dominant Group Can Bias Research on Older Families

Exploring the implications of heterogeneity in families in late life reminds us that knowledge is socially constructed. As we have tried to demonstrate in this chapter, definitions of family based on the experience of White, middle-class elders can mask the richness and complexity of family structure and relationships of older people who occupy or have occupied other positions along the intersections of gender, race or ethnicity, and social class.

Research on informal caregiving has highlighted the contribution of spouses and adult children, particularly daughters, as providers of assistance to frail elderly. But these studies have most often focused on the experiences of White middle- or working-class elders. Studies of caregivers often rely on respondents recruited through newspaper advertising or from client rosters of social service agencies. This means that our knowledge of caregiving is based disproportionately on people who have sought some type of outside support. As Sarah Matthews (1988) argues, these strategies for recruiting subjects systematically bias research by emphasizing the experiences of older people with inadequate resources. People who are sharing the responsibility of caring for a frail older relative with an extensive network of kin and friends or who have enough money to hire people to provide some of the care are less likely to participate in support groups or in a study of caregiver burden.

Research on family care of older people can also be biased by researchers' assumptions about definitions of family. Many studies emphasize the relationship between older care recipients and their so-called primary caregiver, a strategy that can overlook the contributions of other people within helping networks—people who provide assistance but do not have the primary responsibility of coordinating care for the disabled person. These secondary caregivers are more likely to be men than women and more likely to be relatives other than spouses or adult children. We shouldn't be surprised, then, that researchers who ask older people to "tell me about the person who helps you the most" are most likely to obtain information about husbands, wives, and adult daughters.

In some older families, this picture of family care may be fairly accurate. But this question will provide only a partial picture of assistance to older people embedded in extensive networks of kin and what can be called fictive kin. For example, we have already seen that definitions of kin have traditionally been more fluid and flexible within Black communities, where "institutions of community-based childcare, informal adoption, [and] greater reliance on othermothers . . . emerge as adaptations to the exigencies of combining exploitive work with nurturing children" (Collins, 1991, p. 49). The result is not a collection of isolated nuclear families but rather "a nurturing female community of grandmothers, aunts, and friends [encircling] their 'daughters' " (Guy-Sheftall, 1991, p. 62). These expanded definitions of family can enhance the resources available to older Blacks for coping with illness and disability. For example, Colleen Johnson and Barbara Barer (1990) studied older Blacks living in the inner city in San Francisco. They concluded that their respondents were

> quite competent in drawing on numerous mechanisms for creating extensions in the kinship system that result in dense and often emotionally supportive networks. Blacks, much more than Whites, are close to relatives on the periphery of the kinship system. They are also able to create fictive kin by redefining their relationships with friends. In doing so, they add members to their networks who function like kin. (p. 732)

Family assistance does not always flow from younger to older generations. Parents continue contributing to their children and grandchildren as long as they are able. One type of assistance from older to younger family members involves grandparents acting as surrogate parents for their grandchildren. Nearly 3.7 million children—5%—live in the same household with their grandparents, an arrangement that has almost doubled over the past decade (Saluter, 1997). This arrangement is more common among Black than among European American households. More than 12% of Black children are living with their grandparents. Nearly 40% of these children are in "skipped generation households," in which neither parent is present in the home. Grandparents have long been a source of child care in the event of death or divorce, but increasingly, grandparents are stepping into the surrogate parent role because of social or economic problems facing their adult children (e.g., unemployment, substance abuse, imprisonment; Burton & DeVries, 1995).

Just as caring for a frail elderly parent can produce feelings of burden among adult daughters, filling an empty nest with young grandchildren can introduce strains on grandparents who may already be coping with declining health and limited resources. Custodial grandparents are 60% more likely to report incomes below the poverty line than are noncustodial grandparents (Minkler & Fuller-Thompson, 1997). Furthermore, the 1996 Welfare Reform Act limited economic benefits for which caregiving grandparents are eligible (Hooyman & Kiyak, 1999).

We have discussed the exchange of support using a linear model—from adult children to frail elderly parents, from custodial grandparents to grandchildren. But this model of family reciprocity best fits the experiences of European American families (Akiyama, Antonucci, & Campbell, 1990). In contrast, the Japanese model of reciprocity emphasizes the role of the middle generation in providing support to both the young and the old. Norms regarding reciprocity among Blacks emphasize sharing resources with kin and fictive kin according to need, a model described as "communal" (Morgan & Kunkel, 1998).

Definitions of family based on the experience of White, middle-class elders can mask the richness and complexity of this fluidity in the boundaries between family and community. If we don't understand how people come to define someone as kin, we will ask the wrong questions. Too often, we try to fit answers to these questions into a conceptual framework built on our own understanding of the world. The result can be inaccurate research conclusions. Elsa Barkley Brown (1991) illustrates this process when she shares her reactions to a study concluding that Black culture emphasized kinship rather than friendships among Southern women:

> All of . . . my mother's closest confidantes, her support network, were her sisters and cousins and aunts. Thus, I initially thought that perhaps the article . . . captured some element of Black women's networks. . . . It was not until I sat down to write this article that I recognized the fallacy in my own thinking, even about my mother's life. Of course my mother's female network consisted almost exclusively of family members—because all those women who had become part of her support network had also become part of her family. . . . So much so that when I had attempted to really think about the female networks in my mother's life I had been unable to separate "friends" from "family" but, knowing them all to be family, had assumed my mother had no need for "friends." (p. 88)

Intergenerational Relationships and Ethnic Culture: Variation in Family Values

When politicians call for a "return to family values," they most often summon up an image of the mythical American family of the 1950s. As we have seen, American families have always exhibited more diversity than that stereotype suggests. Values concerning family relationships also vary by race or ethnicity. Hispanic American families, for example, have been described as highly integrated, intergenerational kin networks sustained by rules of mutual obligation (Hines, Garcia-Preto, McGoldrick, & Weltman, 1992). Traditional Hispanic values emphasize respect for elders (Stanford, Peddecord, & Lockery, 1990). Women assumed caregiving roles in the family, including care of older relatives, and devoted their lives to the welfare of others (Hines et al., 1992), values illustrated in Gerald Haslam's short story, "The Horned Toad."

Traditional Asian American family values also emphasize respect and care of elderly parents. Filial piety, a central value in Chinese, Korean, Japanese, and other Asian societies influenced by Confucian culture, obliges a married son and his wife to serve the husband's parents, providing physical care and social-psychological comfort, consulting parents about important family and personal issues, and honoring parents through achievements and observance of ceremonial occasions (Kim, Kim, & Hurh, 1991). Traditional conceptions of filial piety, institutionalized within a patrilineal, extended family system, defined the tie to one's parents as more important than the tie to one's spouse and emphasized obligations to the husband's rather than the wife's parents. Different expectations about intergenerational assistance also occur among European American families.

> Whereas Italians or Greeks are likely to grow up with the expectation that eventually they will take care of their parents, White Anglo-Saxon Protestant parents' worst nightmare might be that eventually they will have to depend on their children for support. (Hines et al., 1992, p. 323)

Neither extended networks of kin and fictive kin nor traditional values stressing respect for and support of elderly parents are sufficient to guarantee that older relatives will receive the treatment they expect from younger family members. Families disadvantaged by social class often lack the economic resources to support older relatives. Meeting obligations of caring for older relatives is difficult when all adult members of the family must be employed. Unlike affluent families, poor and working-class families lack the financial resources to hire supplemental help or purchase market equivalents for their own unpaid labor. Although celebrating the strength of extended kin networks sustained by values of mutual obligation, planners and policymakers must also evaluate resources available for implementing these expectations. Otherwise, images of minority elders embedded in multigenerational families can serve as rationales for failing to provide needed formal services (Bengtson, Rosenthal, & Burton, 1996).

How Family Relationships and Family Values Can Vary Among Generations Within Families

Variation in definitions of kin and family obligations also occur within ethnic groups and among generations within families. Sometimes, these differences reflect differences in life stage. Elaine Brody and her colleagues (Brody, Johnson, Fulcomer, & Lang, 1983) interviewed three generations of women within the same families and found that the oldest generation were least likely to feel that children should help elderly parents and most likely to prefer hiring formal help than asking family members for assistance. As Gary Lee (1988) concluded, although cultural norms emphasize responsibility for family members, very few people want to be on the receiving end in family relations, especially if they cannot reciprocate for the help they receive.

Other generational differences can reflect cohort effects. For example, an elderly mother who followed the dictates of the feminine mystique and stayed out of the labor force to care for her children may disapprove of a daughter's decision to return to full-time employment while an infant grandchild stays in a day care facility. She also may interpret her daughter's decision as an implicit criticism of the way she handled work and family roles when her daughter was very young. Generational differences within ethnic families can also reflect differences in length of time in the United States. Challenges to traditional values accompanying acculturation of immigrant groups can produce generational differences in expectations about how elders should be treated. The immigrant generation tends to keep to traditional values more closely than either their children or grandchildren. If these immigrants came to the United States as young or middle-aged adults and left their parents behind, they were probably socialized into norms regarding care of elderly parents but never experienced the difficulties that accompany implementation of those norms. As a result, these elderly parents can be more demanding and less appreciative of care provided by their own adult children.

Norms based in one culture can be difficult to implement in another culture. Differences between the dominant culture and elements of ethnic cultures can also produce conflicts between generations. Children and grandchildren who embrace norms and values of the dominant culture can disappoint elderly parents and grandparents by failing to fulfill expectations delineated by traditional ethnic culture. The dominant position of the eldest generation can be undermined by their unfamiliarity with ways of life in the United States, with their children and grandchildren sometimes embarrassed by the "foreign" ways of older relatives. These types of intercultural and intergenerational conflicts are illustrated by Barbara Yee's selection, "Elders in Southeast Asian Refugee Families."

Ethnic culture is not always a source of conflict within multigenerational families. The renewed interest in ethnic cultures over the past several decades provides mechanisms through which cultural differences within families can strengthen intergenerational relationships. Renewed interest in "ethnic roots" among younger generations translates older people's knowledge of ethnic history and culture into an exchange resource. Older people's self-esteem is enhanced, because they are perceived as sources of valuable information (Cool, 1980). They become the experts or the teachers. "Culture camps" through which elderly American Indians teach music, language, crafts, and local history to children and teenagers not only maintain traditional knowledge but also enhance the self-esteem of the elders. Family or local history projects that record memories of elders are two other strategies for translating older people's memories into a valued resource. Joan Weibel-Orlando's selection, "Grandparenting Styles: American Indian Perspectives," illustrates this role of elderly family members as teachers of traditional culture. The selection "Lame Deer: Seeker of Visions" in Part I also illustrates the role of American Indian grandparents in transmitting cultural heritage to their grandchildren.

Key Issues

This discussion and the following readings illustrate the following points:

1. How earlier marriage and childrearing experiences of today's cohorts of elderly Americans differed from the idealized image of the American family
2. How these differences in family experiences as young and middle-aged adults were patterned along hierarchies based on gender, race, and class
3. How interlocking hierarchies of gender, race, and class structure the experience of family among older people today
4. Why women are most often the providers of family care for frail older people
5. How research based on the caregiving experiences of White middle-class families can undermine our understanding of caregiving in other families
6. How family relationships and family values can vary among generations within families

The Readings

Family relationships are one example of adaptive resources on which people can call in coping with particular life events. Black families have provided a source of support against stressors of racism. Black women have developed strategies for ensuring their children's physical survival without compromising their sense of self-worth. Kathleen Slevin and Ray Wingrove weave the life histories of 50 retired Black professional women into an account of surviving and resisting racism, sexism, and classism. In the selection "Survival and Resistance: Early Lessons in the Family," these women remember lessons learned in childhood from both mothers and fathers—lessons that enabled them to turn "stumbling blocks into stepping stones." Dreaming of a better lives for their children than they themselves had experienced, parents struggled to construct safe spaces—what the anthropologist Irma McLaurin-Allen (1990) describes as emotional sanctuaries—for their daughters. At the same time, their parents taught their daughters the skills they would need to navigate institutional racism, individual-level discrimination, and negative imagery.

Ella Leffland describes the two characters in her story, "The Linden Tree," as "just a couple who had grown old together." In many respects, the two elderly men are similar to many couples who are facing aging and death after a lifetime together. They had learned to accept each other's idiosyncrasies and granted each other space to express their uniqueness. They had developed a division of domestic labor that spilled over into their rooming house business. They also monitored and worried over each other's health, confronting not only the pain of a beloved partner but their own impending loss. In the case of George and Guilio, however, their shared memories included discrimination grounded in racism and homophobia. Their experiences contrast with the networks of kin and friends described in some research on elderly gay men and lesbians, but perhaps this reflects patterns of isolation begun in adolescence—Guilio as a young, single immigrant from Italy and George as the son of a poor Black couple isolated in a Finnish farming community in the upper Midwest.

Although the importance of women as providers of care for frail elderly has been well documented empirically, gerontologists have devoted less attention to explaining the caregiving patterns they have described. As Jane Lewis and Barbara Meredith reported, many adult daughters are unable to pinpoint the moment at which they became caregivers for a frail older mother. The shift begins with a sense of responsibility. The selection from the short story, "Between the Funerals," by Ann Tracy provides insight into the subtle ways in which this transition in the mother-daughter relationship can occur. The mother in this story lives independently, and the dependence her daughter senses is more psychological than physical. The narrator is not facing demanding caregiving tasks, but she is confronting aging—both her mother's and her own. She tells us "there's a moment when I can't catch my breath and I want to scream and protest that I'm not ready for this changing of the guard."

Gerald Haslam's story, "The Horned Toad," illustrates family caregiving in a Mexican American family. Described by the author as "fiction based on actual events," with Haslam as the young narrator, the story illustrates the centrality of *la familia* in Chicano culture. None of the boy's relatives question their responsibility for the elderly grandmother. Moving from house to house within the family reflects concerns with her happiness, efforts to "find a place she'd accept." The story also illustrates the importance of place, a lesson the old woman teaches her great-grandson when she exhorted him to return the horned toad "to his own place." As she faced the end of her own life, she, too, focused on the open country in which she had spent most of her life. Last, Haslam's story illustrates the importance of language as both a bridge and barrier within Chicano culture. The young narrator has little facility in the Spanish language, because his Anglo father had decided that learning "that foreign tongue" would hurt the boy's chances in school. Unlike bilingual children of immigrant parents, who serve as bridges between their parents and the anglophone community, Haslam's family had been in the United States since his great-great-grandparents emigrated from Mexico in the 1850s. In this case, the Spanish language proved a barrier, at least initially, between the boy and his *abuelita*. Haslam's story reminds us that Latinos in the United States differ not only by country of origin; they also differ by history of immigration both between and within cultural groups.

Immigration and acculturation can also strain family relationships. Elderly grandparents and great-grandparents adhere more closely than younger generations to traditional culture, and they can be disappointed with behaviors and attitudes of younger family members who adopt patterns of the dominant culture. These types of intercultural and intergenerational conflicts are illustrated in Barbara Yee's selection, "Elders in Southeast Asian Refugee Families." Among these families, elderly relatives' traditional roles as family advisers and decision makers are undermined by their unfamiliarity with the culture and language of their new country. Unfamiliarity with traditional culture among younger generations need not always lead to isolation and lack of respect for elderly relatives. Knowledge of ethnic culture and history can also be a resource that enhances the self-esteem of older people. The selection by Joan Weibel-Orlando, "Grandparenting Styles: Native American Perspectives," presents a typology of grandparenting roles that includes "cultural conservator," a role that can apply to grandparenting within both minority and European American cultures. The Sioux and Muskogean (Creek, Chickasaw, and Choctaw) grandparents that she interviewed sought to teach their urbanized grandchildren about traditional culture. As one respondent explained, her own children were "just too far gone" to respond to efforts to maintain their American Indian heritage. Her grandchildren were "her only hope for effecting both personal and cultural continuity."

The study of "Grandmother Involvement in Child Caregiving in an Urban Community" by Jane Pearson and colleagues explores the involvement of grandmothers in parenting activities. As we discussed earlier, surrogate parenting by grandparents is receiving increased attention. Rather than rely on volunteer or "at risk" samples, Pearson and her associates examined grandparenting among a community-based sample in East Baltimore. Grandmothers' involvement in their grandchildren's lives is related to family structure, particularly to the number of parents in the household, and economic resources. Black grandmothers were more likely to be involved in activities surrounding school, meal, and bedtime preparation, but they were comparable to White grandmothers in setting and enforcing rules and providing emotional support. How can we explain racial differences in the involvement of grandparents in their grandchildren's lives? Are the differences due to family demography, economic resources, or cultural values? This article explores these complex relationships.

The selection by Bebe Moore Campbell is an excerpt from her memoir, *Sweet Summer: Growing Up With and Without My Dad,* her story of growing up as the child of divorced parents. Bebe Moore moved North with her mother but spent the summers in the South with her father, a paraplegic following an automobile accident. As she images herself in the caregiver role for her mother, father, and grandmother, the author demonstrates the strength of familial ties, cultural expectations regarding family care, and the competing demands and resource limitations that constrain adult daughters' ability to care for elderly relatives. The exchanges between the author and her mother also hint at generational differences in preferred care arrangements in late life.

28

Survival and Resistance:
Early Lessons in the Family

Kathleen Slevin
Ray Wingrove

[My parents] were always teaching us to do whatever was right; to be honest. They were anxious that we would complete school as much as we could. They wanted us to be self-reliant and reliable.

—Retired high school math teacher—the youngest child of four and the only girl

Rearing children to understand and to live in two cultural milieus—one Black, one White—presents unique challenges to Black American parents in any time period. In a legally and rigidly segregated setting, however, Black parents had to be even more vigilant and creative in what and how they taught their children. They had to teach them to feel good about themselves and yet to deal with the inevitable contradictions that accompany being a member of an oppressed group formally defined as second-class citizens. These young Black American girls had to learn to appreciate the difference between what was ideal and what was reality. They had to learn to strive for as much education as possible, since education represented the only viable escape from a life of labor in the White man's kitchen. At the same time, they had to learn that, no matter how much education they achieved, their opportunities would still be limited by their race. Thus, the facts of life crucial to their survival had to encompass the inevitability of both institutional racism and personal discrimination. Indeed, the inextricable tensions of race, gender, and class systems shaped a social construction of reality that, while first experienced in the context of early childhood, would be continuously revisited from childhood through old age.

It is thus not surprising that the theme of survival and resistance resonates throughout these women's early childhoods. Their reminiscences make clear that parents and surrogates found ways to teach them self-respect and racial pride even in the face of denigration and racial hatred. One retiree who grew up in poor circumstances recalled her parents' constant advice to "hold your head up. No matter how poor you are, you're as good as anyone else, regardless of color." Another, in describing her close-knit family, said, "We were encouraged to love each other, to protect each other, and to stand by each other."

Learning to think well of themselves and to be the best were integral lessons of their early years. Childhood lessons ran the gamut from the subtle to the obvious, and most reflected the lived experiences of mothers and fathers whose own family lives bore keen memories of slavery and oppression. From the example of their elders, these Black American youngsters learned that the lessons of childhood must form the basis of lifelong learning and that negotiating negative experiences and encounters—"turning negatives into positives," as more than one woman put it—must become, if not second nature, then a practiced art of survival in a hostile world.

"Avoid Hurtful Whites"

As part of their race work, parents and other adults had to protect young children from contact with Whites who might harm them. Most of these women recall how their parents, especially in early childhood, tried to shield them from the harshness of segregation and from racist encounters. A typical comment was, "We were sheltered and protected from a lot of things." The majority who lived in the isolation of heavily segregated communities often had their direct exposure to racism delayed. Those few who grew up in patterns of living arrangements that brought them closer to Whites had constant reminders of racial hierarchy. The importance of physical boundaries is reflected in statements made by a couple of the women. One said, "I lived in a Black world. We did not have White neighbors. I did not have any associations." And another remembered, "I had not been around White people . . . was not around anybody but the nurturing good Black folk. . . . I was living in a Black world. I never thought about it. Just moving along, enjoying my growing and just developing that self-confidence— being nurtured." In this second quote, we also hear how the hindsight provided by age allows for a heightened level of insight.

Some women lived close enough to Whites to have White children as playmates. In such cases, specific incidents of racial bigotry quickly shattered their sense of childhood innocence. A retired school principal recalled an early and particularly hurtful experience. "I was more aware that I was Black, and it was because we . . . lived in such close proximity to Whites in our community. And I had, as a little girl, a friend who was White who went to a different school than I. And I remember the thing that hurt me most is [that] one day I was coming from school (I had to walk by her school to get home), and she was with some of her friends. And I

spoke, and she did not speak to me. . . . I guess that's what really hurt."

In the long run, place of residence and proximity to Whites made little difference in the women's ultimate experiences with prejudice and discrimination in a racist world. Even those youngsters who lived in a separate Black world, with little personal experience of racial prejudice, spoke of their awareness of racial inequality, which came to them through the discussed experiences of others. A woman who grew up in considerable comfort on the outskirts of a sizable Southern town and whose father was employed in a well-paid, skilled job in a racially mixed setting said, "It was only through my dad that we would hear these comments [about racism and prejudice]. . . ." Still, parents tried to protect their young as long as possible and in as many ways as possible. Social class influenced the manner in which some parents tried to offer protection. The comments of a physician's daughter, for example, highlight the advantage of economic resources as an additional shield. She said, "I didn't run into a lot of that [separate facilities] because Daddy had a car by that time, and he was practicing [medicine], so we didn't have to go on the streetcar. We didn't have to do other things, and he took us where we went. And he did his best to make sure we weren't exposed to it [discrimination], if possible."

Hence, we see why Black American parents understood the need to create what the African American anthropologist Irma McClaurin-Allen calls "an emotional sanctuary" as an essential part of self-protection in a world of racial hatred. The ability to create boundaries, whether physical or emotional, to construct safe spaces that were largely restricted to other Black Americans, became something that influenced the lives of these women from early childhood on.

"Be the Best"

Like their parents before them, these women's parents dreamed of a better life for their children. Thus, the ideals of achievement and success so typical of the "American Dream" were an important message conveyed to the women as youngsters. Parental emphasis on excelling was a pervasive one in the stories told to us. Nevertheless, it was understood that Black Americans' successes would have to be realized within the confines of a segregated world. For them, "making it" could never be the same as for Whites. One woman's comment reflects this as she recalled the message her parents gave her: "Do your best whatever you're doing. If it's a garbage man or woman or whatever, be the best."

The demand to do their best went beyond verbal entreaty. Parents, and specifically mothers, who oversaw the running of the household, pushed their daughters. Whether the task at hand was a household chore or a homework assignment, the message was clear that shoddy work was unacceptable and that nothing but the best would pass muster. Indeed, several women specifically recalled being required to re-do a chore until they "got it right."

Excelling—doing one's very best—was recognized as essential in order to reach even minimal levels of success. The specific forms of racism extant in segregation forced Black Americans to use different strategies to fulfill the dream. These strategies reflected their lack of legal recourse in the face of unjust treatment by the White majority and the higher stakes that accompanied being Black. Thus, while the values learned by Black children—education, hard work, honesty, responsibility—appeared to mirror the values of White society, they were often distinctly racialized. In fact, they were frequently taught from a basis of resistance to the dominant society rather than as acquiescence to it. This point is illustrated in a story told by a retiree who had grown up in abject poverty in the rural South and whose parents worked for a local White farmer and his wife. On weekends and holidays, the girls in her family were required to work for the same family. She recollected angrily how deeply resentful all the members of her family felt toward this particular White couple because they so openly and consistently treated them with disrespect. Tearfully, she recounted her parents' instructions to her and her sister about how they should approach their Saturday house cleaning jobs:

They [parents] wanted to be sure that we understood our positions, and they would say to us, "Even if you have to dust around money, leave it laying there. I don't care if it's on the floor. Leave it laying there. Don't give them a chance to think that you'll take a dime." And I would dust around it because I didn't want them to even think that I attempted to move a penny or two pennies or three pennies or whatever. And, yet it would be tempting. But you knew that you didn't do that because . . . you know, I'm going to be honest, what they thought, what we heard that all White folks thought about Black folks is—they stink and they steal. And, you know, our parents were so adamant about the fact that they didn't want us to be in that category.

This narrative suggests that these girls had to live up to standards that would have far exceeded those expected of White children. They had to exceed the norm in an attempt to combat racial stereotypes. They had to be better than the best. It demonstrates also how some values, in this case honesty, were not just an emulation of the dominant culture but rather reactions and resistance to it.

Keep Your Skirt Down and Your Pants Up

Women remembered that parents were much more restrictive of girls' activities than they were of boys'. Parents saw daughters as presenting a special headache. They had an obsessive fear that their girls might become pregnant while young and unmarried. Pregnancy outside the confines of marriage would seriously hinder, if not kill, their daughters' chances of becoming achievers. Although this problem was not race-specific, there were circumstances surrounding it that were particularly racialized. Legal segregation of Black communities created housing patterns that made it difficult for Black parents to control the contacts their daughters had with neighborhood boys of different social classes. Thus, a kind of double jeopardy was created. Parents recognized that most young Black men in their communities were in economically precarious positions that made them unsuitable as early fathers or mates, a fact that stood in contrast to the situations of middle-class Whites. Consequently, African American parents perceived themselves as facing special challenges in managing the sexual encounters of their daughters. Although their issues were different, in this regard they paralleled the gender asymmetry of the dominant society.

Many women in our study recalled parental anxiety and suspicion about their whereabouts, especially after they reached puberty. They mentioned the special role fathers assumed in preaching sexual modesty and abstinence for girls in the family. It was not uncommon for parents across the spectrum of social classes to resort to chaperones or strict parental supervision of daughters when they were dating. A woman who grew up poor told what it was like in her family. As she remembered it, "We could dance, but since couples danced close then, we were not allowed to dance at night. Morning or breakfast dances were held in some nearby community building. Young people would go and parents would serve brunch type food, and we would dance. But we were chaperoned by adults even then." A woman from a more affluent home told a similar story:

[Mother] knew what she had taught me. But Daddy was practicing medicine, and he saw lots of pregnant girls, and he was determined that I wasn't going to be one . . . and in the summer, my daddy would be certain that every month . . . we had a party at my house. And, we'd go on hayrides and

that type of thing. But . . . you had a chaperon. I was seventeen years old and out of high school before I ever went to the movies alone with a fellow.

Another woman who grew up in a sizable Southern city and who was one of thirteen children remembered her father "walking behind her and her friends" when they left teenage social events. She laughed as she recalled how her father constantly preached, "Keep your dress down and your pants up." She went on to recount the effectiveness of her father's admonitions: "I got married a virgin and was scared to death on my wedding night!"

"Pick Your Battles"

Regardless of how protected they might have been as young children, women told us how as children they soon learned the social meaning of race and some of the strategies to resist racism. When asked to identify some major turning points in her life, a retired federal employee said that it was when she first realized "as a small kid" that "Blacks couldn't go certain places or do certain things." Black parents had to teach general principles of resistance because in day-to-day life there was an endless array of unpredictable issues and encounters to face. The context of racism and oppression was constantly changing, so adaptability and creativity were critical tools of survival for all African Americans. The young had to learn how to see racism as external to them, to understand it as something beyond the individual—that it was systemic. At the same time, they had to handle racism and prejudice on a personal level. Even though they understood that *all* Black Americans were treated unequally, they also had to deal with the reality of what that inequality meant for them personally. In other words, they had to be ready to deal with the institutionalized constraints as well as the personal hatred and prejudice.

What were these women taught that helped them face these issues and allowed them to feel in control of their own lives? A key strategy was learning when to fight and when to avoid confrontation—something that became an important lifelong skill in navigating hostile situations. Parents and other adults taught these youngsters how to "pick their battles." Clearly, there was a time to fight, but there were also times when fighting openly was not the best option. If too much was at stake or if, as one woman put it, "they [Whites] had *all* the cards," then protecting one's interests was the pragmatic thing to do. This is illustrated in a story told by the woman who grew up in the Midwest:

My brother was very popular in high school. And so, when he became a senior, the senior class wanted to run him for [the class] presidency. The principal called him in and told him. "Kenny, I understand that there's a move . . . on to elect you as president of the senior class. Well, I want to tell you right now that has never happened in this school, and it's not going to happen this year. So, if you want to graduate, you'd better back out right now." He did. So, my brother backed out. He wanted to graduate.

Sometimes, with a little creativity, a situation could be manipulated to one's advantage. The daughter of an upwardly mobile businessman referred to this as "strategizing." She explained how her father would do that by the way in which he chose his words when putting together a deal with a White man. As she remembered:

He [father] would talk about his business transactions and talk about how he would put over a sale or a transaction without ever being dishonest . . . maybe by answering the way the person wanted him to answer or something. Strategizing. That's the only thing I can think of, and I don't know if that's a good word to use. But I guess he taught that there's more than one way to accomplish your aim—your goal. But you don't ever give up your integrity.

Again, we see that, regardless of the strategy chosen, it was always important to maintain integrity. Sometimes passive resistance might be the route to self-respect and a feeling of integrity. Such was the case of the woman whose mother forbade her to patronize White restaurants that served Blacks through side windows. Her mother said, " 'Don't you ever let me see you do that as long as you live. Don't ever go to a window to get any [food]' . . . because that was another way of putting you down. And she said, 'You don't do that.' So we did not . . . they kept us away from it. That is the way they protected us."

Still, there were times when avoidance, strategizing, passive resistance, and all the other nonviolent tactics were not enough. There were times when the ugliness of racism came crashing down on Blacks and demanded that risks be taken, to preserve not only integrity but, indeed, life itself. There were times when backs were against the wall, and there was no alternative but to stand and fight. Such is the case in the following account, vividly remembered by a woman who grew up in a small town in North Carolina:

I was a little girl, about six, I'd say. And we lived, you know, how the towns were divided. All the Black folk were across the railroad tracks. And it was said in the town . . . some Black boy had been down on the main street where the White high school was, standing across the street looking at the White girls. Well, that evening they were going around trying to find this boy. Fifty White men on horses with big guns and things. So they came to our house, and my father went out to meet them. He said, "Good evening, gentlemen." And they were trampling all over my mother's flowers and prancing all around.

And they said they wanted him to bring my brother out—to take his hat out, his coat out, his little jacket that he wore and everything, to let them see because they had a description. And you know it, that sort of impressed the girls, because he didn't act like he was scared or nothing; he just told them to bring his coat and hat out; and my Daddy went out there, and then my brother faced them. My mother! We were shocked at her. She was loading shotguns. They loved to hunt. We had plenty shotguns. And we were crying, and she said, "Shut up that crying, because we are going to fight! If they get one of us, they're going to get all." And honey, she was loading shotguns and giving us positions, and she said, "All I ask you to do is to get one." And I tell you and from that day forward . . . I've never been afraid of White people ever again. You know I could always face any confrontation that I had. Ah, but she said, "Oh, no, we are going to fight!" Un, un, she said, "Today, if one goes, everybody goes."

So after they looked at him and looked at the jacket and the coat, they decided that he was not the one, and they went on. But boy, I tell you, when me and my sisters were in there, we were crying and wailing. She said, "Shut up! Stop that crying and you get by this window, and you get by that window, and here, Bessie [making motion of receiving a shotgun], and all you got to do is aim it and pull the trigger." Never had a gun in my hand in my life. I said, "Oh Lord, no." But she was a brave little woman. Yeah, she was really a tower.

Some battles were worth fighting. Some battles *had* to be fought. To do anything less would mean the denigration of personal honor and integrity. The words of the speaker's parents after that episode strengthened this message and remain with her to this day. "If you know you're not guilty, if you haven't done anything, don't back down off nobody. You know. Don't back down." And so, she said, "You know, we grew up being strong like that."

"You're as Good as Anybody Else"

Parents taught some forms of resistance that were more subtle and psychological than those already discussed. For example, they taught their daughters to view life with a positive attitude and to build inner strength and self-esteem. In other words, they taught them to develop an armor of resistance to negative messages. Time and time again, women alluded to this armor and how they learned to use it to their advantage.

The lessons in the psychological armor of resistance almost always included the notion that "You are as good as anybody else and don't you ever forget it." Parents and mentors taught that if children did their best, they could compete with anyone, regardless of color. One woman said, "[Mother] always taught us that we could do whatever we wanted to do if we worked hard at it. And I always felt, and again she always emphasized, that we were just as good as everybody else." Echoing the same sentiment, another said:

They [parents] would say, "Look at your achievements in school. All of you can play the piano. You sing well. And, you know, you're a nice kid. And you're very, very important. And don't ever let anyone put you down. If . . . anybody can do anything, you can do it better." And I always kept that in the back of my mind.

Not only mothers but fathers also taught this vital lesson, as one woman made clear in the following remarks:

He really would sit down and talk with us. We would just get together and talk maybe after dinner. And he always told us that, you know, "you have got a brain, so use it." He was saying to us that people just don't think. "They go put their minds in neutral and go where they're pushed. You better stand up for yourself. You've got what it takes, you've got to use it." And you know, he insisted on good manners. He said that good manners would take you to the White House. He said that first it has got to come from inside. You have to believe in yourself. He said that you've got to be strong within yourself, and then you can be strong with whatever that comes.

The positive self-esteem that resulted from such messages helped form an invisible shield of armor that served as a protection in later years when others attempted to demean their abilities and their sense of self worth. They created a kind of emotional sanctuary. A Ph.D. in psychology summarized what her armor of resistance could do for her in these words: "So effective were my parents in making me feel that I was as good as anyone else that later I could find myself in a room of one thousand Whites all telling me that I was not as capable as they, and I would say 'No, you are wrong,' and really believe it."

"Always Be Economically Independent"

Paid labor has long been a part of Black American women's history. The historian Gerda Lerner says that Black women's relationship with work is best characterized not as "a liberating goal, but rather an imposed lifelong necessity." The testimonies of these women reinforce her assertion. All recounted the importance of childhood lessons that emphasized work as a passport to economic independence. Some of their earliest memories are of parents who stressed hard work and the need for economic independence, even for married women.

Work played a dominant role in family life. In most cases survival depended not only on both parents' employment but also on the contributions of the children themselves. But work was more than survival. In a way that was distinct for Black Americans during segregation, work was also resistance. It was a mechanism for teaching children values, such as hard work and responsibility, that would help them survive in a racist world. Parents from all social classes coached their children in this lesson. A retired social worker spoke of being expected as a teenager to look outside the home for a part-time job. Despite the

relative affluence of her family, her need to be employed as a young girl underscores the ways that race and class intersected for Black families, making them more economically precarious than Whites. The jobs she could get as a Black girl filled her with a determination to get an education and to prepare herself for a different type of work:

Well, before I finished high school, I started having little jobs. And most of the jobs that we had were taking care of rich White people's children. And I went to the mountains in the summer, you know, and earned money—that little bit of money they were paying. From Dunville, I would go to Beach Haven and take care of little White children all summer, and that sort of thing. And I knew I didn't want that to be my life work. I said, "Oh no, I got to get above this."

Just as the emphasis on the importance of work cut across all class boundaries, so did the stress on economic independence. Unlike affluent White girls of that time, who were expected to marry well and to become dependent on their husbands, Black girls were taught, regardless of their circumstances, to depend on themselves for economic solvency. As one woman said, "My mom did not stay at home, so it never occurred to me that I was supposed to marry and [have] my husband take care of me. I always saw myself as a working woman." The one physician we interviewed reminisced about the message her physician father gave her.

My daddy used to say, and my husband would tell you [that] when we got married, he swears this is true . . . my daddy took him down to the railroad track and said, "Now, if you can't be nice to my daughter, you send her back home to me." But, in the meantime, when I told him I wanted to get married, he said, "Get married, but finish school. You must be independent." And his example was this, "Suppose something (and he was a great person for thinking about automobile accidents), . . . suppose you have an automobile accident, and he is crippled or maimed for life, who are you going to go to? Will you go on welfare, or are you going to be able to take care of things." He was very practical. But he didn't have to tell me, because I was going to do it anyway. Because those summers I was working, I was saving my money.

Of course, mothers also conveyed the message of economic independence to their daughters. Often, their entreaties were even more specific. A concerned mother is remembered as warning, "Have your children . . . [but] get your education first so that you will be prepared to take care of your children. It's a poor hen that can't scratch for a couple of biddies." Again, mothers, like fathers, did not see marriage as financial security for their daughters. Sometimes, as one retiree recalled, the messages from mothers reflected a tension between men's dominance and women's drive for independence:

My mother used to always tell me, "You always work and have a little something of your own. Don't ever depend on anyone." And she said, "Even when you get married . . . don't ever give all your money—all that you make—to your husband. Always have a bank account of your own and be independent. Stand on your own two feet." And I've always done that.

Family life is important in the development of all children as they grow to become functioning adults in society. That minority families are faced with additional challenges and burdens is illustrated time and time again in the stories of these African American women. Growing up during segregation added additional strains. Yet, despite the hardships, parents demonstrated great creativity and strength in making a positive world for their children. They found ways to encourage their daughters to develop positive self-identities as young Black women who had to take control of their own lives.

Whether the themes highlighted are those that emphasize being the best or those that focus on the need to be economically independent, the accounts provided by the women interviewed underscore how race and gender intertwined to create and reinforce identities that were quite distinct from those of White girls of their generation. Their social class origins also influenced the directions their lives took and the experiences they had. Because they were Black women, they had to excel in order to reach a minimal level of success. They learned, too, from myriad sources, that self-reliance was not an option that they could call on if Prince Charming did not materialize—married or not, economic independence was mandatory. This was not just the lesson learned by *some* of these Black American women as youngsters; this was the lesson learned by *all*. Small wonder, then, that this message, so powerfully learned in childhood, remains a cornerstone of their identities, even in old age.

29

The Linden Tree

Ella Leffland

In the early years there had been passion, but now they were just a couple who had grown old together. The last twenty years they had owned a rooming house, where they lived contentedly on the ground floor with their cat, Baby.

Giulio was a great putterer. You could always see him sweeping the front steps or polishing the doorknobs, stopping to gossip with the neighbors. He was a slight, pruny man of sixty-eight, perfectly bald, dressed in heavy trousers, a bright sport shirt with a necktie, and an old man's sweater-jacket, liver-colored and hanging straight to the knees. He had a thick Italian accent and gesticulated wildly when he was excited.

George was quite different. Everything about him was slow and solid, touched by grandeur. Though he was a Negro from the Midwest, he spoke with an accent that sounded British, yet not exactly. He was seventy-four, but looked much younger, with a hard body and a hard face with only a few deep fissures in it. Giulio was a neat dresser, but George was attired. His perfectly creased trousers, his crisp white shirt, smoothly knotted tie, and gray sleeveless sweater seemed out of place in the stuffy little flat.

A home is usually the wife's creation, and so it was in their case. The doilies, the vases with their wax flowers, the prints of saints hanging among gaudy floral calendars—all these were Giulio's. George's contribution was less concrete but more important. He made their life possible, dealing with the rents and taxes, attending to the heavy chores,

ousting tenants who drank or brawled. If Giulio were to run the building he would soon come to grief, for he had no real sense of work, and as for the rents, it was all he could do to add two digits together. In addition, he was fussy and fault-finding, so that he often took a dislike to perfectly good tenants, yet countenanced glib bullies.

They were a nicely balanced couple, and for years had been happy. When they were young they had had their troubles—living quarters had been hard to find not only because of George's color, but because of their relationship. In those days Giulio had had fetching ways, too obvious to be ignored. But gradually he passed into a fussy dotage, and now people thought of the pair merely as two lonely old men who lived together. George's color no longer represented problems now that he had proved what was not necessarily demanded of those who asked for proof: that he was a responsible man, an asset to the neighborhood. His building was the best kept on the block, his rents reasonable, his tenants, for the most part, permanent. He would not rent to the fly-by-night element that was slowly invading the district.

The tenants consisted of a pair of raddled, gadabout sisters, a World War I veteran with one leg, and a few clerks and students. Giulio regaled George with facts about these people he gleaned by snooping through their rooms in their absence, and George put him down for this, even threatened him, but it did no good. And in any case, the tenants did not seem to care; there was something so simple about Giulio that his spying was like that of a mouse or a bird. They called him Aunty Nellie (his last name being Antonelli), and the younger ones sometimes invited him into their rooms so that his teeth might be enjoyed. These were ill-fitting, too large for his mouth, and clicked through his speech. When he grew excited, they slipped out of place, at which he would pause in a natural, business-like way to jam them back in before going on.

Giulio was forever dragging the carpet sweeper up and down the halls, looking for an ear to gossip in. George, on the other hand, talked very little. Only tenants who had lived there a long time got to know him at all, when, once in a great while, he would invite them in for a glass of sherry when they came to pay the rent.

In his flat, the tenants found George to be a different man, less aloof and forbidding. Sitting there with Giulio and Baby, the cat, he had something patient, indulgent, altogether loving in his face. Giulio looked with pride at him, glancing now and then at the guest, as though to say: Isn't he wonderful? Sometimes he would go so far as to confess, "I no good at the paper work, but George, George, he *smart.*" Or, "We live together fifty years, never a yell, always happy." And George would give him a look to show him that he was saying too much, and then Giulio would sulk and refuse to rejoin the conversation. But the next day he would be the same as ever, whirling creakily around the steps with his broom, or around his garden with a green visor clamped to his head.

He had a shrine in the garden, with statues of the saints standing in sun-blanched profusion. He was an ardent Catholic, and there was no one with a greater collection of religious objects—rosaries and crosses and vestments, which he kept in his bureau drawer and brought out to enjoy their varied glass, wooden, and satin richness. But religious as he was, he would not divest his beloved garden of one fresh bloom for his saints. It was a skimpy garden, heavily bolstered with potted geraniums, and he was so proud of each green shoot that struggled through the hard ground, and attended its subsequent flowering with such worried care, that it was only when a flower had finally begun to wither on the stem that he would pluck it as an offering to his statues.

George understood this attitude and was properly grateful when once a year on his birthday he received a sacrifice of fresh daisies and marigolds. He was amused by Giulio's niggardliness toward the saints. He himself did not care about them. He, too, was a Catholic, but had become one only so that he and Giulio might be buried together. Two fully paid-for plots, side by side, awaited them under a linden tree in Our Lady of Mercy Cemetery just outside town. Whoever was the first to go, George because he was older, Giulio because he was frailer, the other would join him in due time. Giulio had vague visions of an afterlife. The older man did not.

He had had a good life, everything considered, and he would be content to die and be done with when the time came, and have his bones rest by his friend's forever. Sometimes he thought of the linden tree and gave a satisfied nod.

But lately George had noticed something strange about Giulio. His large red ears seemed to have grown less red.

"Giulio," he said one day, "your ears don't seem to be as red as they used to be."

Giulio touched his ear. When he was young he had been sensitive about their largeness. "Nothing wrong with my ears," he said defensively.

"I'm not criticizing you, Giulio. I think it's just strange." And now he realized that some definite change had been taking place in his friend, but he could not put his finger on it. It was as though he were a little smaller. The jacket seemed to hang lower than it had.

Ah, well, he thought, we're both getting old.

A few days later, as Giulio was raking the leaves in the garden, he complained to George of shortness of breath, and there was the faintest touch of blue in his lips.

"Why don't you go to the doctor for a check-up?" George asked as casually as he could.

Giulio shook his head and continued his raking.

That night, as Giulio was turning on the television set, he suddenly stepped back and dropped into a chair with his hand spread across his chest. "Help!" he shouted into the air. "Help!" and when his friend ran to his side, he gasped, "I gotta pain. Here! Here!" And his hand clutched at his heart so hard that the knuckles were white.

The next day George took him to the doctor, and sat by his side through all the tests. Giulio was terrified, but when it was all over and they came out of the doctor's office he seemed restored.

"See," he said, "I'm okay. The doctor he say no worry."

George's face did not reflect Giulio's good spirits. "I know he says not to worry, but . . ."

"He say no worry," Giulio repeated cheerfully.

But from then on Giulio was visited frequently by the paralyzing pains. He would stop what he was doing and crouch over, his eyes darting frenziedly in their sockets. If George was there he would hurry to his friend's side, but at these moments Giulio seemed totally alone even though his hand grasped George's arm. When it was over he would be stripped of his little ways; he would wander slowly around the room or stand for long moments looking at nothing. Patiently George would wait, and eventually the old Giulio returned. Uneasily, fretfully, he would say, "I no understand. Looka me, I never hurt a fly in all my life, and this pain, he come and scare me. It's not right."

"Well," George would venture soothingly, "if you'd just eat fewer starches and stop worrying, these pains would go away. You've got plenty of years ahead of you . . ."

"Plenty years?" Giulio would break in sharply. "I *know*, I *know* I got plenty years ahead. This pain, he no *important*, he just *scare* me."

In an effort to distract him, George broke a lifelong precedent and invited Myrna and Alice Heppleworth, the two aging sisters who lived on the third floor, down to the flat for the evening. He himself did not like women, but Giulio did, in a way that George could not understand. Giulio loved to gossip with them, and afterward delighted in describing their clothes and manners, which he usually found distressing. He was more interested in the Heppleworth sisters than in anyone else in the building, and always pursed his lips when he saw them going out with their rheumy escorts, and could never forget that he once found a bottle of gin in a dresser drawer ostensibly given over to scarves and stockings.

The Heppleworth sisters came, drank all their wine, and turned the television set up as high as it would go. George grew rigid; Giulio went to bed. The sisters were not asked again.

It seemed to George that Giulio failed daily. His ears were as pale as his face, and this seemed particularly significant to George. He found himself suddenly looking at his friend to check his ears, and each time they looked whiter. He never discussed this with Giulio, because Giulio refused to speak about his fears, as though not daring to give them authority by acknowledging them.

And then one morning Giulio gave up this pretense. As he was getting out of bed he had an attack, and when he recovered this time he let out a piercing wail and began to weep, banging his head from side to side. The rest of the day he spent immobile, wrapped from head to foot in a patchwork quilt.

Toward evening George made him get up and walk in the garden with him. George pointed to the flowers, praising them, and gently turned his friend's face to the shrine. The white plaster faces looked peaceful. Even he, George, felt it, and he realized that for weeks he had been in need of some comfort, something outside himself.

"Look," he said, and that was all, fearing to sound presumptuous, because the statues belonged to Giulio and the Church—he himself understood nothing of them.

Giulio looked without interest, and then, forgetting them, he took George's arm and his eyes swam with tears. "What can I do?" he asked. "What will happen?"

As they walked slowly back to the house he drew his lips back from his big false teeth and whispered, "I'm gonna die."

"No, no, don't think that way," George soothed, but he felt helpless, and resentful that his friend must go through this terror. And now that Giulio had said the words, his terror would grow, just as the pain of a bad tooth grows when you finally acknowledge the decay and are plunged into a constant probing of it with your tongue.

When they came back inside Giulio went straight to bed. George stood in the kitchen and looked at his face in the little mirror that hung on the wall. He feared Giulio would die this very minute in the bedroom as he was removing his carpet slippers, and he wanted with every muscle to run to him. But it would not do to become as hysterical as Giulio, and he stood still. Presently the sound of the bedsprings released a sigh from his throat. The flat was silent. He looked again at his face in the mirror. It was as though he were one person and the reflection another, and he was uneasy and embarrassed, and yet could not look away. He felt deeply aware of himself standing there, staring, and it seemed he was out of place, lost. He whirled around, catching his breath. He had felt entirely alone for the first time in fifty years.

The next day he decided to call for Father Salmon, the young priest from the neighborhood church Giulio attended. Father Salmon dropped in for friendly chats now and then, and Giulio liked him very much, so much, in fact, that the priest often had to silence him when he got carried away with intimate gossip.

A few days later the priest knocked on the door. He was horse-faced, with thinning hair and rimless glasses, and he was quiet and pleasant.

Giulio was wrapped up in his quilt in the armchair. He did not greet the priest with his usual beam of pleasure; he did not even smile.

"Well, Giulio," the priest said, "how are you feeling? I haven't seen you at church lately."

Giulio said at once, "Father, I'm dying."

"What is the trouble?" the priest asked gently.

"It's my heart," Giulio shot back, his hand scrounging around his shirtfront and fumbling with the buttons until it was clutching his bare chest. He looked as though he were prepared to pull the heart out for inspection. His eyes pleaded with the priest to set it right. The priest sat down next to him.

"What does your doctor say?" he asked.

"Oh, Father," Giulio moaned, "the doctor is a stupid. He never tell me one real thing. In and out and all around, around the bush. He no understand, but I understand—this heart, he gonna kill me. You think so, Father? What do you think? You think so?"

"Surely, Giulio," the priest replied, "you must accept the doctor's word. If he says there's no reason to fear . . ."

Giulio looked away, black with melancholy.

The priest sat silently for a moment, then began again. "Giulio, death is as natural as birth. Think of your flowers out there in the garden, how they grow from little seeds and then fade and fall—what could be more natural? God has been with you all your life, and He will not forsake you now . . ."

But Giulio, his eyes shutting tighter and tighter as the priest spoke, got up from his chair and crept into the bedroom, dragging his quilt behind him.

Afterward he said to George, "I no wanna see Father Salmon again."

"Father Salmon is trying to help," George told him.

Giulio shook his head, his fingers rubbing the area of his heart.

What a strange person he is, George thought, looking at him closely. All these years he has been immersed in the church, and now, suddenly, the church means nothing to him. He recalled a conversation he had overheard a few days ago as he was fixing a faulty burner in the second floor kitchen. Two of the students were going down the hall, talking. One had commented on Giulio's bad health. The other had replied, "Don't worry, Aunty Nellie could never do anything so profound as to die."

George had bristled, as he always did whenever anyone made fun of his friend—but it was true that Giulio was not profound. He liked pretty things, and the church gave him its rich symbols; he liked intimate conversation, and the church gave him patient Father Salmon; he liked the idea of an afterlife, and the church gave him that, too. He loved the church, but when you came right down to it, he believed only what he could see with his two eyes, and he could see only his blue lips and wasted face in the mirror. This oddly realistic attitude explained his stinginess toward the saints; they were, after all, only plaster. And yet when Baby had once jumped up on the shrine and relieved himself on St. Francis's foot, Giulio had screamed at the animal until the neighbors hung from the windows.

All these amiable contradictions in Giulio had been known to George for fifty years, and he had always believed that they would sustain his friend through everything. Now the contradictions were gone. All that was left in Giulio was the certainty of death. It made George feel forlorn, on the outside. He sensed that nothing could be set right, that Giulio would live consumed by fear until he died consumed by fear, and the linden tree would not mark two intertwined lives, but forever cast its shadow between two strangers.

They had met for the first time in front of the Minneapolis train station in the first decade of the century. George sat in the driver's seat of a Daimler, in his duster and goggles. His employer had gone inside to meet one Giulio Antonelli, just arrived from Calabria, nephew of the head gardener. When he emerged he had in tow a thin boy of eighteen dressed in a shabby suit and carrying a suitcase that looked like a wicker basket. He wore cherry-colored cigar bands on his fingers, and had a shoot of wilted wild flowers stuck

through the buttonhole of his jacket. His eyes were red-rimmed; apparently he had been crying all the way from Calabria. Delicate and terrified, his cigar bands glittering hectically in the sunlight, he crawled into the Daimler and collapsed in a corner.

George had worked as a chauffeur and handyman on his employer's estate for five years, but was originally from an isolated Finnish farming community where God knows what fates had conspired to bring his parents, a bitter, quarreling, aloof, and extremely poor black couple. George became friends with only one thing native to that cold country, the stones that littered the fields. He could not say what attracted him to them, but he felt a great bond with them. When he was ten he built a wall of the stones. It was only a foot high and not very long, and there was nothing in the world for it to guard there in the middle of the empty field, but he knew he had discovered the proper use of the stones, and all his life he had the feeling he was that wall.

In Minneapolis, on the estate, he kept to himself. He liked the Daimler, which he drove with authority, and the appearance of which on the streets caused people to gawk with admiration. He picked up his employer's speech habits, and this, combined with the Finnish accent he had absorbed, gave a peculiar, unplaceable ring to his words, which he relished, because it was his alone.

The Calabrian boy turned out to be a poor gardener, not because he was listless with homesickness, for that soon passed, but because he made favorites of certain flowers and would have nothing to do with the others. The tulips, for instance, he apparently considered stout and silly-looking, and he made disparaging faces at them. He liked the wild flowers that cropped up in odd corners.

George was fascinated by Giulio, although he did not like him. He reminded him of a woman. Women had never respected George's wall, at least a certain type of woman had not—the bold Finnish farm girls, some of the hired women here on the estate.

He was well favored, and maybe there was something in his coloring, too, that attracted women, something tawny, reminiscent of the sun, here, where everyone else looked like a peeled banana. In any case, they were always after him. He was not flattered. He felt they were not interested in him as he knew himself, proud and valuable, but in some small part of him that they wanted for their own use, quickly, in a dark corner.

But Giulio, though girlish, had no boldness in him. He would leave the garden and lean against the garage door where George was polishing the Daimler. "*Bella, bella,*" he would murmur, and his face shone with a kind of radiant simplemindedness. There was no calculation in him—sometimes you could see him cocking his head and singing before the wild flowers in the garden. Watching George, the boy spoke foreign words rich in their tones of admiration, and his quick, glittering fingers—he had bought flashy rings with his pay—seemed anxious to catch the sun and make a present of it to the tall, mute figure in the gloom of the garage.

Two months after his arrival Giulio was fired. George, filled with fear for himself feeling a great chasm opening before him, quit his job, and the two of them, with hardly a word between them, took the train to San Francisco, where Giulio had another uncle. All during the trip George asked himself: "Why am I doing this? Why am I going with him? I don't even like him. He's a silly, ridiculous person; there's something the matter with him."

They got off at the San Francisco depot, and before George was even introduced to the uncle, who stood waiting, he picked up his baggage and, without a word of farewell to Giulio, walked quickly away from him.

First he found odd jobs, and finally he wound up on Rincon Hill with another Daimler. On his half day off each week he would wander around the city, looking at the sights. Whenever he saw a quick, thin figure that reminded him of Giulio his heart would pound, and he would say to himself, "Thank God it's not Giulio, I don't want to see him

again." And then he found that what had begun as a casual walk around the city was turning into a passionate weekly search. The day he caught sight of Giulio sadly and ineffectively constructing a pyramid of cabbages in a vegetable market, he had to restrain himself from throwing his arms around him.

Giulio's face had blanched with surprise when he looked up, and then his eyes had filled with a dazzling welcome, and he had extended his hand to his returned friend with a tenderness George never forgot.

They were together from then on. In time they bought a vegetable stand, and as a result of George's frugality and common sense he was able to save in spite of Giulio's extravagances. They worked and invested, and in thirty years they were able to buy, for cash, the old apartment building they now lived in. Life had always been strangely easy for them. They had been incapable of acknowledging affronts, even when they were refused lodgings or openly stared at on the street, and the last twenty years in the security of their own flat had been free from problems, satisfying in all ways.

Now Giulio moaned, "Oh, I gotta pain, I gotta pain."

George would take his hand and say, "I'm here, Giulio, I'm here."

But Giulio would look through him, as though he did not exist.

"Don't we *know* each other?" George finally exploded one day, causing Baby to speed under a table with his ears laid back. "Are we strangers after all these years?"

Giulio closed his eyes, involved with his fear.

George sighed, stroking his friend's hand, thin and waxy as a sliver of soap. "What are you thinking about now, this very minute, Giulio? You must tell me."

"I'm thinking of my dog," Giulio said, after a silence.

"What dog was that?" George asked softly.

"I had him in Nocera."

"And what about him?"

"He died, and my father he dug a hole and put him in." His lips turned down. "I dug him up later, I was lonely for him."

"What a foolish thing to do, my poor Giulio."

"His own mother wouldn'a wanted him. Bones and worms . . ."

"Hush, Giulio."

"Gonna happen to me."

"But your soul . . ."

"What's my soul look like?" Giulio asked quickly.

"Like you, Giulio . . . it's true . . ."

Giulio cast him a look of contempt George would not have thought him capable of.

"The little hole, the bones and worms," Giulio moaned.

"But you've *had* a life!" George suddenly cried with exasperation. "Do you want to live forever?"

"Yes," Giulio said simply.

From then on George felt a fury. In the past all Giulio's little fears had been bearable because he, George, could exorcise them, like a stevedore bearing a small load away. But this final cowardice excluded him. And there was nothing, no one he could turn to. He went halfheartedly to church, but got nothing from it. He began making small overtures to his tenants, but his sociability was stiff with rust. He looked with curiosity at the black people on the street, and thought there were more of them than there used to be. When a young black couple stopped him on a corner one day he listened attentively as they talked of civil rights. He accepted a pamphlet from them and read it thoroughly. But afterward he threw it out. He felt no connection with the problems it presented.

He cursed Giulio as he had cursed him fifty years ago when he had walked away from him at the train depot, and he wished for the oneness with himself that he had known in the empty fields of his youth.

In the daytime he was angrily helpful, like a disapproving orderly, but at night as they sat in the small living room with Baby flicking his tail back and forth across the blank television screen, he went to Giulio and mutely pleaded with him. Giulio sighed abstractedly; he seemed far away, deep inside himself, listening to every heartbeat, counting every twinge, with a deep frown line between his eyes.

George moved the twin beds together, and Giulio allowed his hand to be held through the night. From then on they slept that way, hand in hand. George slept lightly, waking often. It was almost as if he wished to be awake to enjoy the only hours of closeness he had with his friend as he held his hand. And also, in the back of his mind was the fear that if he drifted off Giulio would be released into the arms of death. And so he lay quietly, listening to Giulio's breathing, to the wind in the trees.

Then gradually the bedroom window would turn from black to gray, and the breeze that ruffled the curtain carried in the scent of early morning. Dawn brought him sleep; the rising sun gave him a sense of security. Bad things never happened in the daytime—at least one felt that way. And so his fingers grew lax in Giulio's hand as he trusted his friend to the kindness of the dawning day.

But when he awoke later it would be with a sharp sense of foreboding. Quickly he would turn to look at Giulio, his eyes narrowed against the possible shock. But Giulio would be breathing evenly, his bluish lips parted over his gums, his teeth grinning from a water glass on the bureau. Giulio's clothes were neatly laid out, his liver-colored jacket hung over the back of a chair. How lifeless the jacket looked. George would shut his eyes, knowing that the sight of that empty jacket would be unbearable when Giulio was gone. He shook the thought from his head, wondering if life could be more painful than this. Then Giulio's eyes would open, George's face take on a formal nonchalance. And so another night had passed. Their hands parted.

"How do you feel?" George would ask shortly.

Giulio would sigh.

They took their breakfast. The sun shone through the kitchen window with a taunting golden light. George snapped at Giulio. Giulio was unmoved.

One summer morning George persuaded Giulio to sit outside in the backyard. He hoped that watching him work in the garden, Giulio might be persuaded to putter around again. He settled his friend into a chair and picked up the rake, but as the minutes wore on and he moved around the garden in the hot sun, raking the leaves together, Giulio showed no sign of interest. George stopped and put the rake down. Not knowing if he wished to please Giulio or anger him, he suddenly broke off the largest marigold in the garden and held it out.

Giulio shaded his watering eyes with his hand; then his eyes drifted away from the flower like two soap bubbles in the air. George flung the flower to the ground, staring at Giulio, then strode to the shrine and stood there with his hands in fists, blindly determined to do something that would shake his friend open, break him in two if need be. He grabbed the arm of the Virgin Mary and lifted the statue high, and heard Giulio's voice.

"George."

"That's right," George growled, replacing the statue and breathing threateningly through his nostrils, "I would have smashed it to bits!"

"Smash what?" Giulio asked indifferently, and George saw that under the awning of his thin hand his eyes were closed.

"Were your eyes closed?" George thundered. "Didn't you *see* me?"

"You no care that I can't open my eyes— this sun, he hurt them. You *mean*, George, make me sit out here. Too hot. Make me feel sick. I wanna go inside."

"I was going to smash your Virgin Mary!" George cried.

Giulio shrugged. "I wanna go inside."

And then George's shoulders hunched, his face twisted up, and he broke into a storm of tears. Turning his head aside with shame, he made for the back door; then he turned around and hurried back, glancing up at the windows, where he hoped no one stood watching him cry. He put his arm around Giulio and helped him up from his chair, and the two old men haltingly crossed the garden out of the sun.

"Humiliating," George whispered when they were inside, shaking his head and pressing his eyes with a handkerchief. He slowly folded the handkerchief into a square and replaced it in his pocket. He gave a loud sniff and squared his shoulders, and looked with resignation at his distant friend.

Giulio was settling himself into the armchair, plucking the patchwork quilt around him. "Time for pills," he muttered, reaching next to him, and he poured a glass of water from a decanter and took two capsules, smacking his lips mechanically, like a goldfish. Sitting back, he looked around the room in his usual blank, uninterested way. Then a puzzled expression came into his eyes.

"Why you cry then, George?"

George shook his head silently.

"I do something you no like?"

"You never talk. It's as though we're strangers." And he broke off with a sigh. "I've told you all that before—what's the use?"

"I got big worry, George. No time to talk."

"It would be better than to think and think. What do you think about all day?"

Giulio slowly raised his eyebrows, as though gazing down upon a scene. "Bones and worms."

"Giulio, Giulio."

"Big worry, George."

"You'll drive yourself mad that way."

"I no mad at you. Just him." He lay one thin finger on his heart, lightly as though afraid of rousing it.

"I don't mean angry . . ."

But Giulio was already tired of talking, and was plucking at the quilt again, ill, annoyed, retreating into sleep.

"Giulio, please, you've talked a little. Talk a little more—stay."

With an effort, his eyes sick and distant, Giulio stayed.

But now that he had his attention, George did not know where to begin, what to say. His mind spun; his tongue formed a few tentative words; then, clubbed by an immense fatigue, he sank into a chair with his head in his hands.

"I'm sick man," Giulio explained tonelessly, closing his eyes. After a silence he opened them and looked over at George, painfully, as though from under a crushing weight. "Tonight I hold your hand in bed again, like always. Hold your hand every night, you know that."

"You hold *my* hand?" George asked softly, lifting his head.

"In daytime," Giulio said slowly, his eyes laboriously fixed on George's attentive face, "in daytime only the bones and worms. But in the night . . . in the night, I see other things, too . . ." He was silent for a moment until a twinge had passed, then spoke again. "See you, George. And I hold your hand. Make you feel better . . ." His eyes still fixed on George's face, he gave an apologetic twitch of the lip as his lids closed, and slowly he nodded off to sleep.

Between the Funerals

Ann B. Tracy

Murphy's getting married. Surprise, surprise! We had him pegged for a lifelong bachelor (no rarity in this undermated family) but he was, it seems, just being frugal with his dating money. Now he's fetched a fiancee back from Winnipeg, where he's been doing graduate study, and my mother and I are giddy with the novelty. We haven't added a family member since Murphy himself was born, and now there'll be a whole new relative, bringing along her own story like a character in a hypertext novel. We're delighted with Zirka from the start: she's bright and agreeable and funny, and comes with a bonus of cultural exoticism—she laughs at our struggle to say her name right, while we find her lapses into Ukrainian consonant sounds no end endearing, and she knows how to cook ethnic things we never heard of. She's at first a bit stunned by the skylarking of the family women, having come from a house where nobody whistles or fools around in front of the icons, but she rallies—she's clearly made of the right stuff. Only a few years from now she'll be wearing black leather skirts and driving a vicious bargain in Tibetan bazaars, and nobody will be surprised.

Her family are somewhat stunned too, at having acquired a hairy American. American popularity in Canada is even lower than usual. Murphy not only isn't Ukrainian, he isn't even Catholic, though at least (as a kind aunt points out) the Baptists have a radio program. But the match is made, and in Winnipeg they welcome us to the most exciting wedding we've ever seen, with gold crowns and book-kissing and exhortations in a tongue as mysteriously religious as glossolalia.

In the half day before our plane leaves, my mother and I go shopping at The Bay. By the time we're through at the regional gifts section we've lost our bearings completely, have no idea which way we came in. I stand around vaguely waiting for my mother to lead, as she has, after all, done for my whole life. In a bit it occurs to me that nothing is happening. I look at her, and she's looking at me, clearly waiting for *me* to lead *her* out, this short, white-haired person that I'm suddenly supposed to be responsible for. I'm appalled. I can't believe that a major transition would happen this way, with no discussion. It's not as though one of us had just turned a milestone age. My mother has never announced, "I'm sixty-five now and retiring from management" or "You have now officially entered middle age and become the leader." What is going on in her head and how did she arrive at this point? She just gives me a trustful, dependent look. There's a moment when I can't catch my breath and I want to scream and protest that I'm not ready for this changing of the guard. But what's the use?

"I think it's over this way," I say, and she follows me.

The Horned Toad

Gerald Haslam

"*Expectoran su sangre!*" exclaimed great-grandma when I showed her the small horned toad I had removed from my breast pocket. I turned toward my mother, who translated: "They spit blood."

"De los ojos," Grandma added. "From their eyes," Mother explained, herself uncomfortable in the presence of the small beast.

I grinned, "Awwwwww."

But my great-grandmother did not smile. "*Son muy toxicos*," she nodded with finality. Mother moved back an involuntary step, her hands suddenly busy at her breast. "Put that thing down," she ordered.

"His name's John," I said.

"Put John down and not in your pocket, either," my mother nearly shouted. "Those things are very poisonous. Didn't you understand what Grandma said?"

I shook my head.

"Well . . ." Mother looked from one of us to the other—spanning four generations of California, standing three feet apart—and said, "Of course you didn't. Please take him back where you got him, and be careful. We'll all feel better when you do." The tone of her voice told me that the discussion had ended, so I released the little reptile where I'd captured him.

During those years in Oildale, the mid-1940s, I needed only to walk across the street to find a patch of virgin desert. Neighborhood kids called it simply "the vacant lot," less than an acre without houses or sidewalks. Not that we were desperate for desert

then, since we could walk into its scorched skin a mere half-mile west, north, and east. To the south, incongruously, flowed the icy Kern River, fresh from the Sierras and surrounded by riparian forest.

Ours was rich soil formed by that same Kern River as it ground Sierra granite and turned it into coarse sand, then carried it down into the valley and deposited it over millenia along its many changes of channels. The ants that built miniature volcanoes on the vacant lot left piles of tiny stones with telltale markings of black on white. Deeper than ants could dig were pools of petroleum that led to many fortunes and lured men like my father from Texas. The dry hills to the east and north sprouted forests of wooden derricks.

Despite the abundance of open land, plus the constant lure of the river where desolation and verdancy met, most kids relied on the vacant lot as their primary playground. Even with its bullheads and stinging insects, we played everything from football to kick-the-can on it. The lot actually resembled my father's head, bare in the middle but full of growth around the edges: weeds, stickers, cactuses, and a few bushes. We played our games on its sandy center, and conducted such sports as ant fights and lizard hunts on its brushy periphery.

That spring, when I discovered the lone horned toad near the back of the lot, had been rough on my family. Earlier, there had been quiet, unpleasant tension between Mom and Daddy. He was a silent man, little given to emotional displays. It was difficult for him to show affection and I guess the openness of Mom's family made him uneasy. Daddy had no kin in California and rarely mentioned any in Texas. He couldn't seem to understand my mother's large, intimate family, their constant noisy concern for one another, and I think he was a little jealous of the time she gave everyone, maybe even me.

I heard her talking on the phone to my various aunts and uncles, usually in Spanish. Even though I couldn't understand—Daddy had warned her not to teach me that foreign tongue because it would hurt me in school, and she'd complied—I could sense the stress. I had been afraid they were going to divorce, since she only used Spanish to hide things from me. I'd confronted her with my suspicion, but she comforted me, saying, no, that was not the problem. They were merely deciding when it would be our turn to care for Grandma. I didn't really understand, although I was relieved.

I later learned that my great-grandmother—whom we simply called "Grandma"— had been moving from house to house within the family, trying to find a place she'd accept. She hated the city, and most of the aunts and uncles lived in Los Angeles. Our house in Oildale was much closer to the open country where she'd dwelled all her life. She had wanted to come to our place right away because she had raised my mother from a baby when my own grandmother died. But the old lady seemed unimpressed with Daddy, whom she called *"ese gringo."*

In truth, we had more room, and my dad made more money in the oil patch than almost anyone else in the family. Since my mother was the closest to Grandma, our place was the logical one for her, but Ese Gringo didn't see it that way, I guess, at least not at first. Finally, after much debate, he relented.

In any case, one windy afternoon, my Uncle Manuel and Aunt Toni drove up and deposited four-and-a-half feet of bewigged, bejeweled Spanish spitfire: a square, pale face topped by a tightly-curled black wig that hid a bald head—her hair having been lost to typhoid nearly sixty years before—her small

white hands veined with rivers of blue. She walked with a prancing bounce that made her appear half her age, and she barked orders in Spanish from the moment she emerged from Manuel and Toni's car. Later, just before they left, I heard Uncle Manuel tell my dad, "Good luck, Charlie. That old lady's dynamite." Daddy only grunted.

She had been with us only two days when I tried to impress her with my horned toad. In fact, nothing I did seemed to impress her, and she referred to me as *el malcriado,* causing my mother to shake her head. Mom explained to me that Grandma was just old and lonely for Grandpa and uncomfortable in town. Mom told me that Grandma had lived over half a century in the country, away from the noise, away from clutter, away from people. She refused to accompany my mother on shopping trips, or anywhere else. She even refused to climb into a car, and I wondered how Uncle Manuel had managed to load her up in order to bring her to us.

She disliked sidewalks and roads, dancing across them when she had to, then appearing to wipe her feet on earth or grass. Things too civilized simply did not please her. A brother of hers had been killed in the great San Francisco earthquake and that had been the end of her tolerance of cities. Until my great-grandfather died, they lived on a small rancho near Arroyo Cantua, north of Coalinga. Grandpa, who had come north from Sonora as a youth to work as a *vaquero,* had bred horses and cattle, and cowboyed for other ranchers, scraping together enough of a living to raise eleven children.

He had been, until the time of his death, a lean, dark-skinned man with wide shoulders, a large nose, and a sweeping handlebar mustache that was white when I knew him. His Indian blood darkened all his progeny so that not even I was as fair-skinned as my great-grandmother, Ese Gringo for a father or not.

As it turned out, I didn't really understand very much about Grandma at all. She was old, of course, yet in many ways my parents treated her as though she were younger than me, walking her to the bathroom at night and bringing her presents from the store. In other ways—drinking wine at dinner, for example—she was granted adult privileges. Even Daddy didn't drink wine except on special occasions. After Grandma moved in, though, he began to occasionally join her for a glass, sometimes even sitting with her on the porch for a premeal sip.

She held court on our front porch, often gazing toward the desert hills east of us or across the street at kids playing on the lot. Occasionally, she would rise, cross the yard and sidewalk and street, skip over them, sometimes stumbling on the curb, and wipe her feet on the lot's sandy soil, then she would slowly circle the boundary between the open middle and the brushy sides, searching for something, it appeared. I never figured out what.

One afternoon I returned from school and saw Grandma perched on the porch as usual, so I started to walk around the house to avoid her sharp, mostly incomprehensible, tongue. She had already spotted me. *"Venga aqui!"* she ordered, and I understood.

I approached the porch and noticed that Grandma was vigorously chewing something. She held a small white bag in one hand. Saying *"Qué deseas tomar?"* she withdrew a large orange gumdrop from the bag and began slowly chewing it in her toothless mouth, smacking loudly as she did so. I stood below her for a moment trying to remember the word for candy. Then it came to me: *"Dulce,"* I said.

Still chewing, Grandma replied, *"Mande?"*

Knowing she wanted a complete sentence, I again struggled, then came up with *"Deseo dulce."*

She measured me for a moment, before answering in nearly perfect English, "Oh, so you wan' some candy. Go to the store an' buy some."

I don't know if it was the shock of hearing her speak English for the first time, or the way she had denied me a piece of candy, but I suddenly felt tears warm my cheeks and I sprinted into the house and found Mom, who stood at the kitchen sink. "Grandma just talked English," I burst between light sobs.

"What's wrong?" she asked as she reached out to stroke my head.

"Grandma can talk English," I repeated.

"Of course she can," Mom answered. "What's wrong?"

I wasn't sure what was wrong, but after considering, I told Mom that Grandma had teased me. No sooner had I said that than the old woman appeared at the door and hiked her skirt. Attached to one of her petticoats by safety pins were several small tobacco sacks, the white cloth kind that closed with yellow drawstrings. She carefully unhooked one and opened it, withdrawing a dollar, then handed the money to me. *"Para su dulce,"* she said. Then, to my mother, she asked, "Why does he bawl like a motherless calf?"

"It's nothing," Mother replied.

"Do not weep, little one," the old lady comforted me, "Jesus and the Virgin love you." She smiled and patted my head. To my mother she said as though just realizing it, "Your baby?"

Somehow that day changed everything. I wasn't afraid of my great-grandmother any longer and, once I began spending time with her on the porch, I realized that my father had also begun directing increased attention to the old woman. Almost every evening Ese Gringo was sharing wine with Grandma. They talked out there, but I never did hear a real two-way conversation between them. Usually Grandma rattled on and Daddy nodded. She'd chuckle and pat his hand and he might grin, even grunt a word or two, before she'd begin talking again. Once I saw my mother standing by the front window watching them together, a smile playing across her face.

No more did I sneak around the house to avoid Grandma after school. Instead, she waited for me and discussed my efforts in class gravely, telling Mother that I was a bright boy, *"muy inteligente,"* and that I should be sent to the nuns who would train me. I would make a fine priest. When Ese Gringo heard that, he smiled and said, "He'd make a fair-to-middlin' Holy Roller preacher, too." Even Mom had to chuckle, and my great-grandmother shook her finger at Ese Gringo. "Oh you debil, Sharlie!" she cackled.

Frequently, I would accompany Grandma to the lot where she would explain that no fodder could grow there. Poor pasture or not, the lot was at least unpaved, and Grandma greeted even the tiniest new cactus or flowering weed with joy. "Look how beautiful," she would croon. "In all this ugliness, it lives." Oildale was my home and it didn't look especially ugly to me, so I could only grin and wonder.

Because she liked the lot and things that grew there, I showed her the horned toad when I captured it a second time. I was determined to keep it, although I did not discuss my plans with anyone. I also wanted to hear more about the bloody eyes, so I thrust the small animal nearly into her face one afternoon. She did not flinch. *"Ola señor sangre de ojos,"* she said with a mischievous grin. *"Qué tal?"* It took me a moment to catch on.

"You were kidding before," I accused.

"Of course," she acknowledged, still grinning.

"But why?"

"Because the little beast belongs with his own kind in his own place, not in your pocket. Give him his freedom, my son."

I had other plans for the horned toad, but I was clever enough not to cross Grandma. "Yes, Ma'am," I replied. That night I placed the reptile in a flower bed cornered by a brick wall Ese Gringo had built the previous summer. It was a spot rich with insects for the toad to eat, and the little wall, only a foot high, must have seemed massive to so squat an animal.

Nonetheless, the next morning, when I searched for the horned toad it was gone. I had no time to explore the yard for it, so I trudged off to school, my belly troubled. How could it have escaped? Classes meant little to me that day. I thought only of my lost pet—I had changed his name to Juan, the same as my great-grandfather—and where I might find him.

I shortened my conversation with Grandma that afternoon so I could search for Juan. "What do you seek?" the old woman asked me as I poked through flower beds beneath the porch. "Praying mantises," I improvised, and she merely nodded, surveying me. But I had eyes only for my lost pet, and I continued pushing through branches and brushing aside leaves. No luck.

Finally, I gave in and turned toward the lot. I found my horned toad nearly across the street, crushed. It had been heading for the miniature desert and had almost made it when an automobile's tire had run over it. One notion immediately swept me: if I had left it on its lot, it would still be alive. I stood rooted there in the street, tears slicking my cheeks, and a car honked its horn as it passed, the driver shouting at me.

Grandma joined me, and stroked my back. "The poor little beast," was all she said, then she bent slowly and scooped up what remained of the horned toad and led me out of the street. "We must return him to his own place," she explained, and we trooped, my eyes still clouded, toward the back of the vacant lot. Carefully, I dug a hole with a piece of wood. Grandma placed Juan in it and covered him. We said an Our Father and a Hail Mary, then Grandma walked me back to the house. "Your little Juan is safe with God, my son," she comforted. We kept the horned toad's death a secret, and we visited his small grave frequently.

Grandma fell just before school ended and summer vacation began. As was her habit, she had walked alone to the vacant lot but this time, on her way back, she tripped over the curb and broke her hip. That following week, when Daddy brought her home from the hospital, she seemed to have shrunken. She sat hunched in a wheelchair on the porch, gazing with faded eyes toward the hills or at the lot, speaking rarely. She still sipped wine every evening with Daddy and even I could tell how concerned he was about her. It got to where he'd look in on her before leaving for work every morning and again at night before turning in. And if Daddy was home, Grandma always wanted him to push her chair when she needed moving, calling, "Sharlie!" until he arrived.

I was tugged from sleep on the night she died by voices drumming through the walls into darkness. I couldn't understand them, but was immediately frightened by the uncommon sounds of words in the night. I struggled from bed and walked into the living room just as Daddy closed the front door and a car pulled away.

Mom was sobbing softly on the couch and Daddy walked to her, stroked her head, then noticed me. "Come here, son," he gently ordered.

I walked to him and, uncharacteristically, he put an arm around me. "What's wrong?" I asked, near tears myself. Mom looked up, but before she could speak, Daddy said, "Grandma died." Then he sighed heavily and stood there with his arms around his weeping wife and son.

The next day my Uncle Manuel and Uncle Arnulfo, plus Aunt Chintia, arrived and over food they discussed with my mother where Grandma should be interred. They argued that it would be too expensive to transport her body home and, besides, they could more easily visit her grave if she was buried in Bakersfield. "They have such a nice, manicured grounds at Greenlawn," Aunt Chintia pointed out. Just when it seemed they had agreed, I could remain silent no longer. "But Grandma has to go home," I burst. "She has to! It's the only thing she really wanted. We can't leave her in the city."

Uncle Arnulfo, who was on the edge, snapped to Mother that I belonged with the other children, not interrupting adult conversation. Mom quietly agreed, but I refused. My father walked into the room then. "What's wrong?" he asked.

"They're going to bury Grandma in Bakersfield, Daddy. Don't let 'em, please."

"Well, son . . ."

"When my horny toad got killed and she helped me to bury it, she said we had to return him to his place."

"Your horny toad?" Mother asked.

"He got squished and me and Grandma buried him in the lot. She said we had to take him back to his place. Honest she did."

No one spoke for a moment, then my father, Ese Gringo, who stood against the sink, responded: "That's right . . ." he paused, then added, "We'll bury her." I saw a weary smile cross my mother's face. "If she wanted to go back to the ranch then that's where we have to take her," Daddy said.

I hugged him and he, right in front of everyone, hugged back.

No one argued. It seemed, suddenly, as though they had all wanted to do exactly what I had begged for. Grown-ups baffled me. Late that week the entire family, hundreds it seemed, gathered at the little Catholic church in Coalinga for mass, then drove out to Arroyo Cantua and buried Grandma next to Grandpa. She rests there today.

My mother, father, and I drove back to Oildale that afternoon across the scorching westside desert, through sand and tumbleweeds and heat shivers. Quiet and sad, we knew we had done our best. Mom, who usually sat next to the door in the front seat, snuggled close to Daddy, and I heard her whisper to him, "Thank you, Charlie," as she kissed his cheek.

Daddy squeezed her, hesitated as if to clear his throat, then answered, "When you're family, you take care of your own."

32

Elders in
Southeast Asian Refugee Families

Barbara W. K. Yee

For the elderly in Southeast Asian refugee families, the experience of aging in America is very different from what they had expected for their second half of life. These elderly Southeast Asian refugees must cope with their rapidly acculturating younger family members, while having to take on different roles and expectations in a frighteningly foreign culture. The gap between the American experience of age, gender, family, and work roles and that of Southeast Asian cultures highlights just a few major differences. Life-course issues such as historical context upon migration, life stage, age at immigration, and acculturation opportunities will have a significant impact upon the adjustment and aging of these immigrants in America. Waves of Southeast Asian refugees who have come to American shores have differed dramatically, for example, in social class or urbanization, and these differences have influenced survival skills and adaptation to American life in predictable ways.

A large majority of middle-aged and elderly Southeast Asian refugees either migrated with their families or joined their relatives through the family reunification program. As a result, there are very few Southeast Asian elders in the United States who have no relatives here. Yet, the large extended family system traditional in Vietnam, has large holes for Southeast Asian families living in America. Family reunification is the major goal for many Southeast Asian families, especially family elders.

As suggested in Gelfand and Yee (1992), the fabric of aging in America will become increasingly complex and diverse. The influences of new cultures will be woven into the American culture by immigrants. These new Americans will, over time, incorporate varying degrees of American culture within themselves and their families. The trend into the year 2000 will be increasing diversity of the aging (Gelfand & Yee, 1992) and general population (Sue, 1991). Our understanding of this diversity will enhance our ability as a society to successfully address the beautiful mosaic of elders in the future.

The purpose of this article is to examine the cultural transformation of the Southeast Asian refugee family as seen from the perspective of the older generation. The story is only beginning to be told. A closer examination of these rapid changes in the Southeast Asian refugee family must be made because they have major implications for elders in these families. Changes in age and gender roles and in intergenerational relationships have occurred within Southeast Asian refugee families after migration to this country. This article will examine the impact of these significant changes on the elder Southeast Asian refugee ("elder" as defined by this cultural group includes both middle-aged and elderly family members).

Age Roles

Many younger Southeast Asian refugee elders may also find that they are not considered elderly by American society. Migration to a new culture changes the timing and definitions of life stages across the life span. For instance, in the traditional Hmong culture, one can become an elder at 35 years of age when one becomes a grandparent. With grandparent status, these elder Hmong can retire and expect their children to take financial responsibility for the family. Retiring at 35 years of age is not acceptable in this country (Yee, 1989).

There is a strong influence of Confucianism in traditional Vietnamese society (Liem & Kehmeier, 1979). Confucius instituted the Cult of Ancestors, which is reflected in filial piety and respect for the family elders. Age roles within society and the family were hierarchical, with strict rules for social interaction. The child was to have total obedience to the father and to venerate him; the same was true for the relationship between a woman and her father—and later her husband—and for the student/teacher relationship. The major discrepancy for refugee families is between the traditional roles of elders in the homeland and those available to them in the United States (Weinstein-Shr & Henkin, 1991).

Weinstein-Shr and Henkin find that because the older refugees lack facility with the English language and American culture, their credibility is decreased when advising younger family members about important decisions. As youngest family members take on primary roles as family mediators within American institutions—the school or legal system and social service agencies, for example—elders gradually lose some of their leadership roles in the eyes of the family and the larger American society (Yee, in press).

Weinstein-Shr and Henkin also recognize that the older refugees try to maintain their role as transmitters of traditional values and customs, but grandchildren often reject their cultural heritage in order to lessen their cognitive dissonance during acculturation to American ways. The majority of refugee families are still struggling to survive in the work and educational arenas so that they can support dependent family members. This translates into very little time left to show respect toward family elders (Detzner, in press).

Some research in other Asian-American groups, however, shows an increased interest in and appreciation of cultural roots during the adolescent and young adult period by some Asian-Americans (see review in Kitano & Daniels, 1988; D. W. Sue & D. Sue, 1990). A so-called search for cultural roots occurs during critical periods of the life span, when people look for components of their identity. During this phase, the family elders may be called upon to help younger family members explore, discover, and appreciate their cultural heritage and family history.

Although older refugees provide child-care assistance and perform household duties for their families (Detzner, in press), they can no longer offer financial support, land, or other material goods as they would have in the homeland. The refugee process strips away the refugee elders' resources, one of the bases for high status and control of inheritance in the family. What is more important, elderly refugees can no longer provide advice and lend their wisdom: Because their counsel is derived from traditional culture and tied to the homeland, it is too foreign to American ways. Older refugees find that they are increasingly dependent upon their children and grandchildren for help rather than the reverse (see review in Yee, 1989). This role reversal between the elder and young generation has created numerous family conflicts in the Southeast Asian refugee communities (Yee, in press).

Intergenerational Roles

Tran (1991) found that elderly refugees who lived within the nuclear or extended family had a better sense of social adjustment than those living outside the family context. Of elderly living in a family context, those living in overcrowded conditions or in homes including children under the age of 16 experienced a poorer sense of adjustment. The relationship between overcrowding and life satisfaction holds regardless of age and across numerous groups. The relationship between living with younger children and poorer adjustment for the Southeast Asian elderly may be, as Tran speculates, a result of more economic pressures and stressors found in households with younger children. Tran's second speculation is that intergenerational conflicts among three generations living under the same roof create great stress because the younger generations are very Americanized. This acculturation gap leads to greater conflicts among the generations and depresses satisfaction with or adjustment to the refugee elders' new life because their general life satisfaction is closely tied to satisfaction with family relationships (Gelfand, 1982; Yee, in press). The age of these refugees was also inversely related to poorer adjustment. Older refugees have poorer adjustment than their younger counterparts (a finding that has been replicated in other studies) because older refugees experience more losses and fewer gains after coming to America than do their younger family members (Yee & Nguyen, 1987).

In a recent study, Rick and Forward (1992) examined the relationship between level of acculturation and perceived intergenerational differences among high school students from Hmong refugee families. These authors found that students perceived themselves to be more acculturated than their parents. Higher acculturation was associated with higher perceived intergenerational differences. Rick and Forward examined three specific acculturation items concerning the elderly: consulting the elderly on life issues, taking care of the elderly, and respecting the elderly. It appears that values concerning relationships with family elders may be the last to change, if at all, following changes in decisions about timing of marriage, having children, appropriate dress, where to live before marriage, ideal family size, or decisions on marriage.

Gender Roles

Refugee elders must cope with the gender role differences practiced in the homeland versus those in the United States. Even before migration, traditional gender roles were changing in Southeast Asia during the Vietnam war. Men of military age were away fighting the war, and their spouses were solely responsible for tasks normally divided along gender lines. When Vietnamese came to this country, changes in traditional gender roles sped up and became more dramatic. This was especially true for middle-aged and employed refugees. There were more employment opportunities for younger refugees and middle-aged refugee women because their employment expectations often fit with the lower status jobs that were among the few opportunities open to refugees with few English skills and little or non-transferable educational credentials. Age bias against older men and women may be operating as well, and many elders could not find gainful employment outside the home. Many middle-aged women and younger refugees of both sexes became family breadwinners. This was a radical change for the male elders, who had been the major breadwinners of the family.

The body of empirical and anecdotal work on adaptation and adjustment of refugee populations suggests that there might be a gender difference in short- versus long-term adaptation (see review in Yee, 1989). It appears that at least for short-term adaptation, which includes the period soon after migration to as long as 15 years, middle-aged and elderly refugee women adapt to life in the new country in a more positive manner than do men of the same age. Several investigators have attributed this gender difference to the continuity of female roles from the homeland to America (Barresi, 1992; Detzner, in press; Yee, 1989). Female refugee elders perform important but not necessarily honorific roles in the family such as household tasks and childcare, whereas male refugee elders, especially the old men, have less clear functional roles in the family. This latter pattern is especially evident for Cambodian men (Detzner, in press).

The ability of refugees to perform work roles outside the family also shows a gender pattern (see review in Yee, in press). There is an expansion of work roles for both young adults and young middle-aged refugee women, which is especially true for the Vietnamese group. The down side is that both groups must also take on roles and responsibilities they had not anticipated for these periods in the life cycle.

By contrast, there is a constriction of work and family roles for refugee men, especially middle-aged and elderly men. Elderly refugee men experience a significant downward mobility. Migration created the loss of high status work, family, and community roles. Many of these refugee men are not able to recover their former status because their job skills may not be transferable to the United States or employers may be unwilling to hire an older worker. In addition, their lack of facility in English may form an insurmountable barrier to recovering their former job status by passing American credentialing tests (Yee, in press). After struggling for many years, these elderly refugees may resign by putting all their hope in the younger generation and giving the responsibility to achieve their lifelong goals to the next generation.

The pattern for long-term adaptation of refugee elders is yet to be determined empirically, but there are indications that the long-term adaptation of female refugee elders may not be so rosy. Middle-aged and elderly refugee women are integrated within the family in the short term. These elderly women provide household and childcare services in order to free younger family from these responsibilities so that they can work one or two jobs and perhaps go to school to ensure economic survival of the family. While these elderly refugee women are helping younger members of the family succeed in America, they themselves are often isolated at home and not learning new skills, English, or knowledge about American society, with which to cope with the new environment (Tran, 1988). After

the family has passed through the stage of meeting basic survival needs, these elderly women may find that they are strangers in their own family and their new country. In other words, their adult children and grandchildren have acculturated to American ways in school and work settings, yet these elderly women have had few opportunities to be exposed to mainstream American culture.

Summary and Conclusions

The elders' place and role in the Southeast Asian family in the years to come are unknown, but there are several indicators that predict increasing difficulty for elderly female refugees. The impact of ethnicity and culture on aging is a dynamic process (Barresi, 1992). It is not unidirectional and unidimensional but bidirectional and multidimensional. The immigrant from another culture is touched and transformed by American culture. This transformation varies across individuals and life contexts. Something not as well recognized, but necessarily true, is that the American culture is forever changed by its association with these new Americans. Our great nation has derived its strength, creativity, and vision from our heritage of immigrants. Let us remember and appreciate this diversity. From within this diversity comes the force that will keep America at the cutting edge in a twenty-first century global society.

References

Barresi, C. M. (1992, Mardi 15). *The impact of ethnicity on aging: A review of theory, research, and issues.* Presentation at the American Society on Aging Annual meeting, San Diego, CA.

Detzner, D. F. (in press). Conflict in Southeast Asian refugee families: A life history approach. In J. Gilgun, K. Daly, & R. Handel (Eds.), *Qualitative methods in family research.* Newbury Park, CA: Sage.

Gelfand, D. E. (1982). *Aging: The ethnic factor.* Boston: Little, Brown.

Gelfand, D., & Yee, B.W.K. (1992). Trends and forces: Influence of immigration, migration, and acculturation on the fabric of aging in America. *Generations, 15*(4), 7-10.

Kitano, H., & Daniels, R. (1988). *Asian Americans.* Englewood Cliffs, NJ: Prentice Hall.

Liem, N. D., & Kehmeier, D. F. (1979). The Vietnamese. In J. R McDermott (Ed.), *Peoples and cultures of Hawaii.* Honolulu: University of Hawaii Press.

Rick, K., & Forward, J. (1992). Acculturation and perceived intergenerational differences among Hmong youth. *Journal of Cross-Cultural Psychology, 23*(1), 85-94.

Sue, D. W., & Sue, D. (1990). *Counseling the culturally different: Theory and practice* (2nd ed.). New York: John Wiley.

Sue, S. (1991). Ethnicity and culture in psychological research and practice. In J. D. Goodchilds (Ed.), *Psychological perspectives on human diversity in America.* Washington, DC: American Psychological Association.

Tran, T. V. (1988). Sex differences in English language acculturation and learning strategies among Vietnamese adults aged 40 and over in the United States. *Sex Roles, 19,* 747-758.

Tran, T. V. (1991). Family living arrangement and social adjustment among three ethnic groups of elderly Indochinese refugees. *International Journal of Aging and Human Development, 32*(2), 91-102.

Weinstein-Shr, G., & Henkin, N. Z. (1991). Continuity and change: Intergenerational relations in Southeast Asian refugee families. *Marriage and Family Review, 16,* 351-367.

Yee, B.W.K. (1989). Loss of one's homeland and culture during the middle years. In R. A. Kalish (Ed.), *Coping with the losses of middle age.* Newbury Park, CA: Sage.

Yee, B.W.K. (in press). Markers of successful aging among Vietnamese refugee women. *Women and Therapy, 12*(2).

Yee, B.W.K., & Nguyen, D. T. (1987). Correlates of drug abuse and abuse among Indochinese refugees: Mental health implications. *Journal of Psychoactive Drugs, 19,* 77-83.

33

Grandparenting Styles:
Native American Perspectives

Joan Weibel-Orlando

Grandparental roles among contemporary North American Indians are expressed across a range of activities, purposes, and levels of intensity. The ways these components fit together are so varied as to be identified as distinct grandparenting styles. These five grandparenting styles are identified below as: cultural conservator, custodian, ceremonial, distanced, and fictive.

Freedom of choice in the creation of one's particular brand of grandparenthood is considerable. Some American Indian grandparents petition their children for the privilege of primary care responsibilities for one or more grandchildren with considerable success. When parents are reluctant to relinquish care of a child to its grandparents, individuals who relish continuing child care responsibilities past their childbearing years activate alternative strategies of both traditional and contemporaneous origin. Establishment of fictive kinship, provision of foster parent care, and involvement in cultural restoration programs in the public schools are among the alternative roles available to older American Indians whose grandchildren, either because of distance or parental reluctance, are not immediately accessible to them.

While custodial, fictive, ceremonial, and distanced grandparenting styles are evidenced cross-culturally, I suggest that the cultural conservator grandparenting style, if not particularly North American Indian, is essentially a phenomenon of general ethnic minority-group membership. Fearing loss of identity as a people because of the relentless assimilationist influences of contemporary life, many ethnic minority members view their elders as cultural resources for their children. Grandparents as cultural conservators constitute both a cultural continuity in that responsibility for the enculturation of the youngest generation was traditionally the role of the grandparents across American Indian tribal groups (Amoss, 1981; Schweitzer, 1987). Cognizant of the heady influences which attract their urbanized, educated, and upwardly mobile children away from tribal pursuits, many contemporary American Indian grandparents understand their roles as conservators and exemplars of a world view and ethos that may well disappear if they do not consistently and emphatically impart it to and enact it for their grandchildren.

Grandparenting Styles

What little literature there is on the role of the North American Indian grandparents in the enculturation of their grandchildren during historic times (sixteenth to nineteenth centuries) tends to be sketchy, ambiguous, and highly romanticized. Grandparents are depicted as storytellers (Barnett, 1955, p. 144), mentors to girls about to become socially acknowledged as women (Elmendorf & Kroeber, 1960, p. 439) and to boys old enough to embark upon the first of many vision quests (Amoss, 1981), and caretakers of children left orphaned by disease, war, or famine (Schweitzer, 1987). In all cases the literature depicts Indian grandparents as protective, permissive, affectionate, and tutorial in their interactions with their grandchildren. Only most recently has Pamela Amoss (1986) offered an intriguing analysis of the ambiguous nature of Northwest Coast Native American myths about grandmothers. In these legends the old women have the power both to protect and to destroy their progeny.

The generally acknowledged model of Indian grandparenting presented above fits most closely the cultural conservator and custodial models. In both cases, such grandparenting styles in contemporary American Indian family life spring from the same conditions and concerns that shaped historical grandparenting modes: practical issues of division of labor and the efficacy of freeing younger women so that they can participate more fully in the economic sector of the tribal community; nurturance of unprotected minors so as to maximize the continuance of the tribe as a social entity; and the belief that old age represents the culmination of cultural experience. Elders are thought to be those best equipped to transmit cultural lore across generations, thus ensuring the cultural integrity of the group.

The Cultural Conservator Grandparent

Being raised by one's grandparents is not an enculturative phenomenon unique to either twentieth-century rural or urban American Indian experience. In fact, grandmothers as primary caretakers of first and second grandchildren is a long-established native American child care strategy. Leo Simmons (1945) tells us that "old Crow grandmothers were considered essential elements in the household, engaged in domestic chores" (p. 84) while helping young mothers who were burdened with work. And Marjorie Schweitzer (1987) explains that "within the framework of the extended family a special relationship existed between grandparents and grandchildren which began at birth and lasted a lifetime.

Children were cared for by grandparents and, in turn, the family cared for the old when they were feeble" (p. 169).

The cultural conservator role is a contemporary extension of this traditional relationship. Rather than accept an imposed role, the conservator grandparents actively solicit their children to allow the grandchildren to live with them for extended periods of time for the expressed purpose of exposing them to the American Indian way of life. Importantly, the cultural conservator is the modal grandparenting style among the families in this study.

Six families are best described by this term. One Sioux woman, who had two of her grandchildren living with her at the time of the interview, exemplifies the cultural conservator grandparenting style. The enthusiasm about having one or more grandchildren in her home for extended periods of time is tempered by the realization that, for her own children who grew up in an urban environment, the spiritual magnetism of reservation life is essentially lost. She regards their disdain for tribal life with consternation and ironic humor and consciously opts for taking a major role in the early socialization of her grandchildren. She views her children as being just "too far gone" (assimilated) for any attempt at repatriation on her part. Her role as the culture conservator grandmother, then, is doubly important. The grandchildren are her only hope for effecting both personal and cultural continuity: "The second- or third-generation Indian children out [in Los Angeles], most of them never get to see anything like . . . a sun dance or a memorial feast or giveaway or just stuff that Indians do back home. I wanted my children to be involved in them and know what it's all about. So that's the reason that I always try to keep my grandchildren whenever I can" (Sioux woman, sixty-seven, Pine Ridge, South Dakota).

She recognizes the primary caretaking aspects of her grandmotherhood as not only as traditionally American Indian, but also as a particularly Lakota thing to do: "The grandparents always took . . . at least the first grandchild to raise because that's just the way the Lakota did it. They [the grandparents] think that they're more mature and have had more experience and they could teach the children a lot more than the young parents, especially if the parents were young. . . . I'm still trying to carry on that tradition because my grandmother raised me most of the time up until I was nine years old."

She remembers her grandparents' enculturative styles as essentially conservative in the sense that those things they passed on to their grandchildren were taken from traditional Sioux lore. The grandparents rarely commanded or required the grandchild's allegiance to their particular world view. Rather, instruction took the form of suggestions about or presentation of models of exemplary behavior. "Well, my grandfather always told me what a Lakota woman wouldn't do and what they were supposed to do. But he never said I had to do anything." She purposely continues to shape her grandmotherhood on the cultural conservator model of her own grandparents. "I ask [my children] if [their children] could spend the summer with me if there isn't school and go with me to the Indian doings so that they'll know that they're Indian and know the culture and traditions. [I'm] just kind of building memories for them."

Those cultural and traditional aspects of Sioux life to which this grandmother exposes her city-born grandchildren include a wide range of ceremonial and informal activities. The children go everywhere with her. An active participant in village life, she and her grandchildren make continual rounds of American Indian church meetings, senior citizens lunches, tribal chapter hearings, powwows, memorial feasts, sun dances, funerals, giveaways, and rodeos. The children attend a tribe-run elementary school in which classes are taught in both English and Lakota. The children actively participate in the ceremonial life of the reservation, dancing in full regalia at powwows and helping their grandmother distribute gifts at giveaways and food

at feas[...] dren who[...] time are im[...] reservation life[...] firm, authoritative[...] by their gentle and a[...] and through the rough-a[...] rural age-group members [...] part, can claim some kinship [...] born visitors, they learn, as did [...] century Sioux children (through obs[...] example, and experimentation), their so[...] core values and interactional style.

Today, however, presenting one's grandchildren with traditional cultural lore has become a critical issue of cultural survival vis-à-vis a new and insidious enemy. Faced by consuming cultural alternatives and unmotivated or inexperienced children, American Indian grandparents can no longer assume the role of cultural conservator for their grandchildren as practiced historically. Rather, grandparents, concerned with continuity of tribal consciousness, must seize the role and force inculcation of traditional lore upon their grandchildren through a grandparenting style best described as cultural conservation.

References

Amoss, R. (1981). Cultural centrality and prestige for the elderly: The Coast Salish case. In C. Fry (Ed.), *Dimensions: Aging, culture and health* (pp. 47-63). Brooklyn, NY: J. F. Bergin.

Barnett, H. (1955). *The Coast Salish of British Columbia.* Eugene: University of Oregon Press.

Elmendorf, W., & Kroeber, A. (1960). *The structure of Twona culture with notes on Yurok culture.* Pullman: Washington State University Press.

Schweitzer, M. (1987). The elders: Cultural dimensions of aging in two American Indian communities. In J. Sokolovsky (Ed.), *Growing old in different societies.* Acton, MA: Copley.

Simmons, L. (1945). *The role of the aged in primitive society.* New Haven, CT: Yale University Press.

...vement in Child Caregiving
...ban Community[1]

...e L. Pearson

...rea G. Hunter

...an M. Cook

...olas S. Ialongo

...ppard G. Kellam

In a community-defined, epidemiologic sample in East Baltimore, we examined grandmother's rates of co-residence and their involvement in four parenting activities. Co-residence rates exceeded the national average. Six types of family households with grandmothers were identified, and their frequency varied by race. Neither grandmother age nor employment was associated with grandmothers' parenting involvement, although family structure was. Grandmothers who were the sole parent (21%) or co-parent with a grandfather (6.5%) were most involved in child care and had the fewest number of helpers. Grandmothers living with single mothers (41%) were the next most involved, while grandmothers in mother/father households (9%) were least involved.

The number of children in the United States who currently live with older adults is substantial. Since 1980 there has been a 44% increase in the number of children living in homes with grandparents (U.S. Bureau of the Census, 1994). In 1990, the rate for all children was 5%. However, rates vary with ethnicity and living context: More than 12% of African American children lived with a grandparent, while 5.8% of Hispanic and 3.6% of White

children lived with a grandparent (U.S. Bureau of the Census, 1991). Grandparents are more likely to co-reside with children in urban settings. The 1990 Census data indicated that for all households with at least one grandchild, 77% were in urban areas (U.S. Bureau of the Census, 1992). Moreover, these cross-sectional estimates substantially underestimate the prevalence for children *ever* living with a grandparent (Hunter & Ensminger, 1992). A recent report by Fuller-Thomson, Minkler, and Driver (1997) found that in a national survey of households, 10.9% of grandparents reported that they had primary responsibility for raising a grandchild for a period of 6 months or more in their lifetimes.

Several factors appear to converge to contribute to the increasing numbers of grandparents living with grandchildren and taking on parent roles: Longer and more active life spans of older persons and, for their offspring, trends in marriage and childbearing, economic disparities and disruptions, and public health problems (e.g., AIDS, substance abuse) (Burton, 1992; McLoyd, 1990; Minkler, Roe, & Price, 1992; Minkler & Roe, 1993; Mullen, 1995). As these demographic trends continue, there is a growing need to better understand grandparents' living circumstances and the extent to which grandparents take on parenting roles.

The grandparenting literature indicates that several factors are related to grandparent co-residence and child care involvement. Race and a child's family structure appear to have the most empirical support, and these studies are described below. Age (Burton & Bengtson, 1985) and financial strain (Presser, 1989) have been described as affecting role satisfaction, but little is known about the degree to which they are associated with co-residence and child care involvement.

Racial Differences

Robertson (1995), in a recent review, described the strengths and shortcomings of grandparenting studies conducted during the past several decades. Among the problems were limitations in the types of samples studied. With regard to research on grandparental child care, studies of White grandmothers have tended to sample healthy volunteers and focus on relationship quality with grandchildren (e.g., Roberto & Stroes, 1992; Thompson & Walker, 1987), rather than direct parenting involvement. Few studies have examined White grandmothers who live with grandchildren; they instead focus on the voluntary roles and the meaning of grandparenthood (e.g., Neugarten & Weinstein, 1964; Robertson, 1977).

In contrast, studies of African American families typically describe high rates of co-residence with grandchildren and extensive child care involvement. Evidence for race effects includes ethnographic studies that have documented how multi-generational interactions and residence sharing are common in African American families, with grandparents playing dominant roles (Apfel & Seitz, 1991; Burton & DeVries, 1992; Martin & Martin, 1978). Other support comes from more quantitative studies that focus on the social problems of early childbearing (Colletta &

Lee, 1983; Furstenberg & Crawford, 1978; Stevens, 1984), single parenthood and poverty (Casper & Hogan, 1990; Chase-Lansdale, Brooks-Gunn, & Zamsky, 1994), and family substance abuse and incarceration crises (Burton, 1992; Minkler & Roe, 1993). Quantitative studies on samples not selected for family crises also indicate substantial involvement by African American grandparents in caring for grandchildren (Hunter, 1997; Kellam, Ensminger, & Turner, 1977; Kivett, 1993; Pearson, Hunter, Ensminger, & Kellam, 1990; Wilson, 1984).

In the few studies comparing adequate numbers of White and African American grandparents, African American grandparents and in particular, grandmothers, are more likely to co-reside with their grandchildren and are more integrally involved in parenting compared with their White counterparts (Burton & Bengtson, 1985; Cherlin & Furstenberg, 1986; Fuller-Thomson, Minkler & Driver, 1997). Differences in cultural background, family demography, and economic circumstances have been proposed to account for these variations (Beck & Beck, 1989; Jackson, 1971; Martin & Martin, 1978; Wilson, 1984).

When economic and living circumstances are comparable among White and African American grandparents, however, the degree of racial differences in co-residence rates and involvement may be less. Kivett's (1993) study of the grandparent role among rural Blacks and Whites indicated that although differences were found, there were more similarities than differences in the grandmother role across race. These similarities may reflect the impact of common values among southern rural families regardless of race, namely strong intergenerational ties, and/or the financial strains of both Black and White families in rural southern areas (Dressler, 1985; Martin & Martin, 1978; Shimkin, Shimkin, & Frate, 1978).

Whether comparable financial status and community context converge to reveal similarities among urban Black and White grandparents remains to be seen.

Family Structure Differences

As described above, one explanation for a higher rate of co-residence between grandmothers and grandchildren in African American families is that there are higher rates of single-mother families where grandparents assist in child care and, in turn, where a large majority of households would be expected to be mother/grandmother families. However, there is evidence that African American grandmothers reside in a variety of household structures and that their parenting involvement varies by the type of household.

Pearson, Hunter, Ensminger, and Kellam (1990) described grandmothers' household presence and parenting patterns in a community-epidemiologically defined population of relatively poor, urban African American families in Chicago in the late 1960s. The co-residence rate between grandmothers and the target child, who was in first grade, was 10%. Grandmothers were the sole primary caregiver in 19% of the grandmother households, co-parent with their husbands in 10% of grandmother households, resided with their husbands and daughters in 16% of cases, and resided with single daughters in 35% of families (Pearson et al., 1990). The remaining 20% of grandmothers lived in households with their daughters and sons-in-law (mother/father, or mother/stepfather family structures).

Woodlawn grandmothers' parenting involvement varied by family structure. Where grandmothers acted as the primary parents (in the absence of mothers and fathers), they were most likely to set rules and enforce them. In mother/father/grandmother households as compared with mother/grandmother households, grandmothers were much less likely to set or enforce rules. Across all family structures, between 30% and 65% of grandmothers engaged in supportive parenting (e.g., reading to children, telling stories, taking children to fun places). Wilson (1984), studying a convenience sample of southern working-class African American families, also found parent and grandmother perceptions of grandmother parenting involvement to vary by co-residence and by the number of parents in the household.

The Present Study

Given the rising rates of grandmother co-residence and the preponderance of studies that rely on convenience samples, more information based on well-defined-populations is needed. The present study sought to determine (a) the rate of grandparent co-residence of a defined, urban population of families; (b) the types of family structures grandparents lived in; (c) the degree of child-care involvement; and (d) the associations of grandparent age, employment, grandchild gender, and household family structure with parenting involvement. The families studied here are from a population in East Baltimore, selected by a child's school membership. The population is diverse with regard to household family structure and income, and consists of both African Americans and Whites. By examining a defined cohort of children and their families, we can provide unbiased rates of the occurrence of co-residence with grandmothers and their parenting involvement within the community. Such community epidemiologic studies complement random or nationally representative samples in that community studies allow for specificity of context and examination of variations within a known population.

The compositions of the grandmother household family structures were defined as follows: (a) mother/grandmother (no grandfather or father); (b) grandmother alone (no mother, father or grandfather); (c) mother/grandmother/grandfather (no father); (d) mother/father/grandmother (can include grandfather); (e) grandmother/grandfather (no mother or father); (f) father/grandmother (no mother, no grandfather, but can include stepmother).

Results

The rate of co-residence of grandmothers with these sixth graders was 16%. Rates did not significantly vary with ethnicity (African American vs. White) in this urban population (χ^2 (1) = 1.08, p = .30). Specifically, 17% of the African American families included grandmothers (n = 99), and 13% of the White families did (n = 24). Grandmothers present without grandfathers was the most common type of grandparent co-residence (70% of the cases).

The order of prevalence for the grandmother types was as follows: mother/grandmother (41%), grandmother (21%), mother/grandmother/grandfather (16%), mother/father/grandmother (9%), grandmother/grandfather (6.5%), and father/grandmother (6.5%). Nearly all grandmothers living with mothers were maternal grandparents, and grandmothers living with fathers were paternal grandmothers. A quarter of the grandparents in the grandmother/grandfather alone families were paternal, the rest maternal. Of the grandmothers who were sole parents, a third were paternal grandmothers.

The distribution of grandmother family types across the five urban areas was considered next. Mother/grandmother households were the most frequent family type and were approximately evenly dispersed across these areas. In contrast, mother/father/grandmother families were not present in Area 2 (public housing), but were equally frequent in the row house neighborhoods—Area 1 (predominantly White) and Area 3 (predominantly African American). Area 3 had a somewhat higher income level and had more males present in grandmother households. Area 4 (racially integrated) had mother/grandmother, grandmother only, and mother/grandmother/grandfather families occurring at nearly similar rates.

In this population, nearly as many White (37%) as African American (40%) mothers were likely to be teen mothers (began childbearing at age 18 or younger). In families where mothers and grandmothers co-resided, teen mothers were most likely to be in mother/grandmother families (63%), followed by mother/grandmother/grandfather families (31%). In terms of teenage motherhood rates across the neighborhoods, there was substantial variation. Twenty percent of the grandmother families in Area 5 (predominantly White) included teen mothers, while in Area 2 (public housing, African American neighborhood) 60% of the grandmother families had teen mothers.

The rates of specific family structures did vary with ethnicity (χ^2 (1,5) = 12, p < 0.3). Mother/father/grandmother families were more common among Whites (25% vs 5% for African Americans), while among African American families, mother/grandmother households were more common (43.4% vs 29.2% for Whites). Father/grandmother households were more likely to occur among White families (12.5% vs 5.1% for African American families).

Although grandmother involvement did not vary by the gender of the target child, interestingly, the child gender varied with family structure (χ^2 (1,5) = 13.9, p < 0.2). Boys were more likely to be in mother/father/grandmother families (73%) and father/grandmother families (75%). Girls were more likely to be in grandmother/grandfather families (88%) and grandmother alone families (69%). Target boys and girls were equally distributed in mother/grandmother/grandfather families, and mother/ grandmother families.

With regard to grandmothers' main work activities, about a third (32%) were employed, 11% were unemployed, 20% were retired, 13% had disabilities, and 22% reported keeping house as their main activity (2 cases refused). The ages of the grandmothers ranged from 41 to 86, with an average age of 58 years. Grandmother age did not vary with family structure (F[1,5] = 1.36, p = .25). All employed grandmothers were age 65 or younger; the majority (68%) of grandmothers reported as having a disability were in the 51–65 age

Table 1 Grandmother Parenting Involvement (ever nominated) by Race, in Percent

Parenting Activities	African American	White
Organize	82	58
Set Rules	69	50
Enforce Rules	68	50
Emotional Support	77	71

NOTE: Chi-square: $\chi^2 (1) = 6.06, p < .01$.

group. The likelihood of grandmothers working varied with family structure, with grandmothers living with their husbands most likely to be working. The median income among these families was $20,000 in 1990 (with a range of less than $5,000 to $60,000). Family income above or below the median did not substantially differ by ethnic group ($\chi^2 (1) = 2.24, p = .13$). However, family income varied across family structures. Families with fathers or grandfathers were more likely to have incomes above the median. Grandmother alone families, followed by mother/grandmother families, were at greatest risk for poverty.

The question of whether African American grandmothers were more involved than their White counterparts was addressed by determining whether the grandmother was nominated (yes or no) for each parenting activity (see Table 1). African American grandmothers were likely to be more involved in organizing the target child, but were comparable to White grandmothers in whether they engaged at all in setting rules, enforcing rules, and providing emotional support.

Discussion

The purpose of this study was to examine, in a community-defined epidemiologic sample, the co-residence rates of grandparents with grandchildren, the types of family struc-

tures the grandparents lived in, the extent to which they took on parenting roles, and possible factors related to their involvement—specifically, their age, employment status, family structure, and grandchild gender. This methodology allowed for the examination of grandparents' parenting roles without the biases of selecting a high-risk sample or the self-selection bias that comes with a volunteer sample.

Among these urban families, we found few grandfathers co-residing with grandchildren without the presence of grandmothers. Thus, the rate of grandparent co-residence was essentially the rate of grandmother co-residence. In this population, the co-residence rate was substantial—about one of every six families. This is about four times the national average and most likely reflects the tendency for co-residence to appear in urban compared to rural contexts. Although co-residence rates might be expected to be higher because the majority of the families are African American (about 70%), the overall rates of coresidence among urban White families were also higher than national estimates. It may be that the convergence in co-resident rates for grandmothers and grandchildren among African American and White families in this community is due to comparable historic patterns of intergenerational co-residence, financial strains, or community values, similar to Kivett's (1993) findings among rural White and African American families.

Six types of family households with grandmothers were defined, and the frequency of grandmother family types varied by neighborhood area and by race. In White families, grandmothers were five times more likely to live in a mother/father household, compared to African American families. Although this pattern was apparent in Area 1, it was not common in Area 5—both predominately White neighborhoods. The grandmother/mother household was the most common family structure, appearing with at least 28% frequency in all neighborhood areas. Overall, it was a family structure more common among African American than

White families. Racial differences in family structure patterns may reflect a number of forces that result in sharing a residence. African American grandmothers may be called upon more often to assist in child rearing due to the higher frequency of single-mother families (Beck & Beck, 1989) compared to White families, while White grandmothers in this urban context may be more likely to co-reside based on their own needs or the advantages of pooling family financial resources (the highest-income family structure was mother/father/grandmother).

Grandmothers' parenting involvement was first examined in the context of the number of helpers for each activity—both in and out of the household—named by the survey respondent. With the exception of emotional support, the number of helpers varied with family structure. In households with two parents and a third adult—either mother/father/grandmother or grandmother/grandfather/ mother—more helpers were named. In households with fewer adults—grandmother-alone families and mother/grandmother families—fewer helpers were described. Grandmother-alone households, in addition to having fewer helpers, were also the most impoverished, highlighting the possible strains of this family context for grandmothers and grandchildren. For emotional support, having two or more helpers was a modal response for all family types, suggesting that this parenting behavior is less specific to household structure.

Grandmothers' degree of parenting involvement varied with family structure. Grandmothers were most likely to engage in all parenting activities if they were the primary parent or co-parent with their husbands (grandmother-only and grandmother/ grandfather families). Grandmothers in single-parent situations (father/grandmother, mother/grandmother families), followed by grandmothers in mother/grandmother/grandfather households, were the next most involved. Grandmothers in mother/father/grandmother households were the least likely to engage in parenting behaviors.

These patterns are consistent with those reported in an earlier community-defined sample (Pearson et al., 1990), as well as a volunteer sample of single- and two-parent family types (Wilson, 1984).

When grandmother race was examined with regard to whether grandmothers were nominated at all for help, African American grandmothers were more likely than their White counterparts to assist in getting their grandchildren organized for school and in feeding and bedtime care. Due to the relatively small number of White grandmothers in this sample, there was insufficient statistical power to examine the rankings of parenting involvement with grandmother race. A larger sample may reveal even more cultural differences with regard to who helps, and in what contexts. Nonetheless, similar to Kivett's (1993) findings that there are more similarities than differences among rural Black and White grandparents, there were many similarities among the urban grandmothers studied—specifically, similar degrees of co-residence, parenting involvement, income level, and likelihood of having a daughter who was a teen mother.

In summary, grandmothers in this defined urban population were found to co-reside at a significant rate with older elementary-school-age children. Depending on the household family structure, grandmothers' involvement was diverse, ranging from caring for children as a parent-surrogate (grandmother-alone families), to assisting, in a secondary or tertiary role, mothers or fathers who are present (mother/father/grandmother families). Financial and extended family resources also varied with the family structure grandmothers find themselves in, with those grandmothers who are without other relatives in the household being at highest risk for having the fewest of these resources.

Note

1. This work was supported by the following NIMH grants: Epidemiologic Prevention Center

for Early Risk Behavior (P50 MH38725); Periodic Outcome of Two Preventive Trials (R01 MH42968); and a Postdoctoral Training Program in Family Process and Psychopathology (T32 MH311109). The authors thank the Baltimore City Public School System and the children and family members who participated, and also Drs. Anne Brodsky and Margaret Ensminger for feedback on the manuscript. The views expressed here are those of the authors; no official endorsement by NIMH is intended or should be inferred. Portions of this article were presented at the 1993 APA Symposium, Grandparenting Roles and Meaning Across Diverse Contexts.

References

Apfel, N. H., & Seitz, V. (1991). Four models of adolescent mother-grandmother relationships in Black inner-city families. *Family Relations, 40,* 421-429.

Beck, R. W., & Beck, S. H. (1989). The incidence of extended households among middle-aged Black and White women: Estimate from a 5-year panel study. *Journal of Family Issues, 10,* 147-168.

Burton, L. M. (1992). Black grandparents rearing children of drug-addicted parents: Stressors, outcomes, and social service needs. *The Gerontologist, 32,* 744-751.

Burton, L. M., & Bengtson, V. (1985). Black grandmothers: Issues of timing and continuity of roles. In V. Bengtson & J. Robertson (Eds.), *Grandparenthood* (pp. 61-78). Beverly Hills, CA: Sage.

Burton, L. M., & DeVries, C. (1992). Challenges and rewards: African American grandparents as surrogate parents. *Generations, 16,* 51-54.

Casper, L. M., & Hogan, D. P. (1990). Family networks in prenatal and post-natal health. *Social Biology, 37,* 84-101.

Chase-Landsdale, P. L., Brooks-Gunn, J., & Zamsky, E. S. (1994). Young African-American multigenerational families in poverty: Quality of mothering and grandmothering. *Child Development, 65,* 373-393.

Cherlin, A. J., & Furstenberg, F. F. (1986). *The new American grandparent.* New York: Basic Books.

Colletta, N. D., & Lee, D. (1983). The impact of support for Black adolescent mothers. *Journal of Family Issues, 4,* 127-143.

Dressler, W. (1985). Extended family relationships: Social support and mental health in a southern Black community. *Journal of Health and Social Behavior, 26,* 39-48.

Fuller-Thomson, E., Minkler, M., & Driver, D. (1997). A profile of grandparents raising grandchildren in the United States. *The Gerontologist, 37,* 406-411.

Furstenberg, G., & Crawford, D. B. (1978). Family support: Helping teenagers to cope. *Family Planning Perspectives, 10,* 322-333.

Hunter, A. G. (1997). Counting on grandmothers: Black mothers' and fathers' reliance on grandmothers for parenting support. *Family Issues, 18,* 251-269.

Hunter, A. G., & Ensminger, M. E. (1992). Diversity and fluidity in children's living arrangements: Family transitions in an urban Afro-American community. *Journal of Marriage and the Family, 54,* 418-426.

Jackson, J. J. (1971). Sex and social class variations in Black and White parent-adult child relationships. *International Journal of Aging and Human Development, 2,* 96-106.

Kellam, S. G., Ensminger, M. E., & Turner, R. J. (1977). Family structure and the mental health of children. *Archives of General Psychiatry, 34,* 1012-1022.

Kivett, V. (1993). Racial comparisons of the grandmother role. *Family Relations, 42,* 165-172.

Martin, E., & Martin, J. M. (1978). *The black extended family.* Chicago: University of Chicago Press.

McLoyd, V. C. (1990). The impact of economic hardship on Black families and children: Psychological distress, parenting, and socioemotional development. *Child Development, 61,* 311-346.

Minkler, M., & Roe, K. M. (1993). *Grandmothers as caregivers: Raising children of the crack cocaine epidemic.* Newbury Park, CA: Sage.

Minkler, M., Roe, K. M., & Price, M. (1992). The physical and emotional health of grandmothers raising grandchildren in the crack cocaine epidemic. *The Gerontologist, 32,* 752-761.

Mullen, F. (1995). *A tangled web: Public benefits, grandparents, and grandchildren.* Washington, DC: American Association of Retired Persons.

Neugarten, B. L., & Weinstein, K. K. (1964). The changing American grandparent. *Journal of Marriage and the Family, 26,* 199-204.

Pearson, J. L., Hunter, A. G., Ensminger, M. E., & Kellam, S. G. (1990). Black grandmothers in multigenerational households: Diversity of family structure and parenting involvement in the Woodlawn community. *Child Development, 61,* 434-442.

Presser, H. B. (1989). Some economic complexities of child care provided by grandmothers. *Journal of Marriage and the Family, 51,* 581-591.

Roberto, K. A., & Stroes, J. (1992). Grandchildren and grandparents: Roles, influences, and relationship. *International Journal of Aging and Human Development, 34,* 227-239.

Robertson, J. F. (1977). Grandmotherhood: A study of role conceptions. *Journal of Marriage and the Family, 39,* 165-174.

Robertson, J. F. (1995). Grandparenting in an era of rapid change. In R. Blieszner & V. H. Bedford (Eds.), *Handbook of aging and the family* (pp. 243-260). Westport, CT: Greenwood Press.

Shimkin, D. B., Shimkin, E. M., & Frate, D. A. (Eds.) (1978). *The extended family in Black societies.* Paris: Mouton.

Stevens, J. H. (1984). Black grandmothers' and black adolescent mothers' knowledge about parenting. *Developmental Psych* 1017-1025.

Thompson, L., & Walker, A. J. (1987). mediators of intimacy between gran and their young adult granddaughter *Family Relations, 36,* 72-77.

U.S. Bureau of the Census. (1991). *Current population reports. Marital status and living arrangements: March 1990* (Series P-20 No. 450). Washington, DC: U.S. Government Printing Office.

U.S. Bureau of the Census. (1992). *General population characteristics: Metropolitan areas, Section 2 of 3* (Series 1990 CP-1-1B). Washington, DC: U.S. Government Printing Office.

U.S. Bureau of the Census. (1994). *Marital status and living arrangements. March 1993.* Current Population Reports, p. XIV, Table H. Washington, DC: U.S. Government Printing Office.

Wilson, M. N. (1984). Mothers' and grandmothers' perceptions of parental behavior in three-generational black families. *Child Developments, 55,* 1333-1339.

35

Sweet Summer:
...ing Up With and Without My Dad

Bebe Moore Campbell

When my father died, old men went out of my life. From the vantage point of my girlhood, he and his peers had always been old to me, even when they were not. In his last years, the reality of his graying head began to hit home. I no longer boogied the weekends away in smoke-clogged rooms that gyrated all night with Motown sounds, where I'd take a breather from the dancing by leaning up against the wall, sipping a sloe gin fizz and spewing out fire-laced rhetoric of "death to the pigs." I was a mature young wife, a mother even, three rungs from thirty, a home owner, a meal planner, who marched for an end to apartheid in front of the South African embassy only often enough to feel guilty. I made vague plans to care for him in his dotage. Care for him on a teacher's salary, in the middle of a marriage that was scratching against the blackboard with its fingernails, in a two-bedroom brick fixer-upper my husband, daughter and I had outgrown the moment we moved in. That was the plan.

When he died in 1977, I suppose, a theoretical weight was lifted, since Daddy was a paraplegic because of a car accident he'd had when I was ten months old. No doubt his senior-citizen years would have been expensive and exhausting for me. And then too, I had other potential dependents. I mused about the future, fantasized about my role as a nurturer of old people, feeling vaguely smug and settled, maybe a little bourgeois.

The afternoon was muggy as only a D.C. summer afternoon can be. The humidity and my afro were duking it out on the tiny sun porch of our home, the ring being the area immediately above the base of my neck, the hair coffee-colored grandmamas laughingly call the "kitchen." It is the hair I hated most as a child. The rest of my head was covered with a wavy-frizzy mixture that proclaimed my black ancestry had been intruded upon. My "kitchen" has always been hard-core naps, straight from the shores of Dahomey. Benin, they call it now. From time to time I'd tug my fingers haphazardly through the tight web of kinks, trying to make my recalcitrant hair obey me and separate into manageable clumps of curls. The hair was simply too dense back there. I would need my big black comb with the wide-spaced prongs, something heavy like that to pry my rebellious locks apart. All I was doing was hurting my fingers. I raised the window higher for more air. The faint smell of roses wafted in on a thin, damp breeze.

"I am not your responsibility, darling," Mommy had said in a brisk, businesslike tone of voice that still managed to sound loving when, on one of my frequent visits to Philly, I broached the subject of my caring for her when she got old. Each word my mother uttered stood at attention, like a soldier doing battle in the war for improved communication. But what should I have expected from a woman who was absolutely savage about enunciation, pronunciation, speaking correctly, so that *they* would approve. My mother viewed speaking impeccably proper English as a strategy in the overall battle for civil rights. "Bebe, we've got to be prepared," she'd say briskly.

When as a child I said, "He be going," my mother's eyes would widen as big as silver dollars and the corners of her mouth would get dry and chalky-looking. She'd clench her throat with wide, splaying fingers and spring into action, like a fireman sniffing a cigarette in a forest and dousing it before flames erupt. "Don't say that." Her voice would be firm and patiently instructive. "That's a Negro colloquialism. Totally incorrect. They'll think you're dumb if you talk like that." They, always they.

She was sitting at her small mahogany desk in the dining room, her glasses propped on her nose, sorting papers into neat little stacks, bundling them together with rubber bands. Glancing down I saw that the papers were related to her church work, Alpha Kappa Alpha sorority, her volunteer work with a senior citizens' group and her membership on the grievance board of Holmesburg Prison, all overwhelmingly dignified pursuits. Although she was no longer a social worker for the city, my dear mother's retirement consisted of running feverishly from one volunteer gig to the next one, all for the uplifting of the race. My mother has always been and will always be a very lift-every-voice-and-sing type of sister, a woman who takes her Christian duty very seriously. Under the desk she crossed her short, brown legs and tapped her foot a little. "Clara and I will probably take a fabulous apartment together, one of those new complexes with everything inside, a laundry, a grocery store, cleaners, everything. Or by that time, my goodness, the church's senior-citizen complex will be ready and I'll just move in there. Or I'll stay here." She smiled serenely at me for a brief moment, her smooth brown face full of sunshine, then excused herself to continue working on the church bulletins.

"Senior citizens' complex!" I let my words explode in the air. "You *want* to live in an old folks' home? Mommy, that's not our culture." I finished, totally disgusted.

Mommy looked at me, her eyes squinched up in laughter, a grin spreading across her face. She loves for me to mess with her, gets a big kick out of my tongue-in-cheek assaults on her dignity. As if anything could ever put a dent in her dignity.

"Here I am, offering you a secure place in your old age, nutritious hot meals, no abuse, make sure you get your high-blood-pressure medicine. All you have to do is sign over the ole pension, SS check, bonds, CDs, deed to your property, and you get the run of the place. Do whatever you want to do. Want to have the AKAs over? The sorors can come. You get to have a boyfriend. All the sex you want! I'm talking about the best the black extended family has to offer. And you want to go . . ."

"I don't have high blood pressure," my mother said, chuckling and dabbing at her eyes.

"Yet, yet . . ."

My mother whooped.

"What about your arthritis?" I asked in an aha! kind of tone, truly alarmed at the notion of my aged mother hobbling to a dingy basement laundromat, sorting faded bras and well-worn girdles while her ancient sidekick, Clara, threw her yellowed undies into the motley heap.

Doris looked at me as if the word "lunatic" had suddenly become emblazoned on my forehead. Her shoulders and her full upper lip went stiff; the nostrils in her wide nose flared slightly. "What are you talking about, girl? I don't have any arthritis. If you're referring to the occasional stiffness in my knees, I've had that since I was a young girl and it's not going to get any worse. Darling," she said, her tone softening a little, her hands still busily sorting, stacking, writing, "you have your family to look after. A baby. Don't worry about me. I'll go right on, the same as always."

So that was that; my mother was immortal. However, if by some fluke lightning struck or the rapture came and my divine mother was sent soaring away from this earth on diaphanous wings, merrily pumping her way to heaven with stiff knees, then, then I'd be duty-bound to take in Nana.

My feisty grandmother could talk the naps out of any black child's kitchen. Mouth all mighty. Mouth's mammy. I was Nana's sole choice for a caretaker, since her only other children, my Aunt Ruth and my namesake, Aunt Bebe, were dead and her only other grandchild, my cousin Michael, was engaged in a perennial search—finding himself—that made his life-style suspect. Nana wasn't into living with anyone whose phone was on one day and off the next. "Hell, I might as well have stayed in Virginia and picked cotton if I didn't want to do any better," she told me with a snort, referring to her and her parents' migration from the grips of the sharecropping South, aeons ago when she was a baby. For the record, Nana had never picked cotton a day in her life, but all the same, she was fervent about black economic progress and she found Michael's gypsy ways appalling. What was worse, what was intolerable was that her only grandson didn't have a job, at least not a steady one.

"The boy is mad," she said one day as we were snapping string beans in her kitchen. Her large almond-shaped eyes flashed. Nana's eyes were bright, the white part startlingly clear. She was small and plump, the color of a lemon wafer. "Gorgeous in my day, honey," she'd tell you in a minute. "I had all the men frothing at the mouth." Gold hoop earrings dangled at her ears. She gave off subtle whiffs of Estée Lauder, and when she spoke I could smell Doublemint chewing gum. "Smart boy like that. Nice-looking," she said disgustedly. "They need to put him in some government work camp or something." Nana's "they" was different from my mother's. More all-encompassing. Whoever made the rules, set the tone, that was Nana's "they."

"The depression is over, sweetheart. There are no work camps anymore."

"Well, then they should put his ass in the Army!" she snapped.

"Who is 'they'?" I asked, just for fun. Nana laughed. "Anyway, you can't force someone to be in the Army. And besides, he's too old."

Nana put down her beans. Her fingers were motionless in front of her. "You think he's ever gonna get himself together?" Nana's eyes were brimming with concern.

"What do you think?"

Nana sighed and began rubbing at her temples, where her hair was mostly gray, with the base of her thumbs so as to keep her fingers clean. Her eyes stared right into mine as she pulled her hands away from her hair and reached across the table and grabbed my wrist, squeezing it tightly with her thick fingers. "If anything happens to your mother you'll have to take me, Bebe," she whispered.

I simply nodded, too surprised at the sudden serious turn her outburst about Michael had taken. If I had been thinking, I would have said flippantly, "Nuh unh, honey. Sending your butt straight to the old folks' home with your daughter. Come see you every Tuesday." I could have lightened the moment a little, but I chose not to, probably because deep inside I didn't think Nana would outlive Mom. She didn't want to. Nana was seventy-five when we had this little talk and was beginning to show unmistakable signs of disenchantment with life. Her old folks' blues would become increasingly more sorrowful as she approached her eighties. The older she got, the clearer it was that she was ready to "pass."

At seventy-nine, she called me one late afternoon and wailed into the telephone. "I don't like it anymore. I can't even go out in the winter; I'm so scared I'll fall on the ice and break my ass. And I don't even have a boyfriend," she cried, her voice high and piercing, plaintive. "What kind of life is that?"

A life with no rustling taffeta dresses, no fire-engine-red toes and fingers, no mambo nights, no baritones calling on the phone. For my jazzy grandmother (I still thought of her that way), no life. No life at all.

Whatever frailties owned her, she still possessed the strength to will herself right on out of this world. Seven years after my father's death, I believe she did just that. Only days after her eightieth birthday and a few weeks before the first Philadelphia snowstorm of 1984 could trap her for yet another season, Nana slipped off her red velvet bedroom slippers, lay down on the sofa in the living room of the house I grew up in, and fell into a dreamless, endless sleep.

1   bell hooks challenges the idea that motherhood and family are sources of women's oppression. How might the women interviewed by Slevin and Wingrove respond to this argument? What about Elsa Barkley Brown? What parallels do you see between the images of the adult daughter-older mother relationship described in this chapter and that developed by Alice Walker (in "In Search of Our Mothers' Gardens" in Part I)?

2   Official definitions of kin are based on blood and legal ties. How do these official definitions affect the lives of older gay men and lesbians? In what ways, if any, do you think changing attitudes toward homosexuality will produce differences between current cohorts and future cohorts of elderly gay men and lesbians?

3   Ann Tracy's story is told from the standpoint of the adult daughter. How might this account have been different had Tracy told the story from the mother's perspective?

4   The predominance of women as family caregivers of frail elderly should not mask the contributions of men. Male caregivers are most often older husbands caring for their wives. What differences would you predict between older women caring for their husbands and older men caring for their wives? Consider the meaning of care, changes in a couple's daily life, changes in their relationship, and sources of both burden and satisfaction.

5   Project yourself forward in time to the point at which your surviving parent is struggling to maintain independence in the face of increasing frailty. How do you visualize your role as caregiver? What other demands will compete for your time? If you have sisters or brothers, what factors will determine the division of parent care responsibilities among you and your siblings? How will the plans for care you devise be influenced by your social class?

6   Several of the readings in this book illustrate the role of grandparents as cultural conservators as described by Weibel-Orlando (see, for example, Lame Deer and Haslam). What evidence do you see in your own family that the oldest generation fulfills the role of "cultural conservator" or "family historian"?

1 West, D. (1995). *The wedding.* New York: Doubleday.

Dorothy West, a Harlem Renaissance writer who died in 1998, traces the history of an African American family. Her novel vividly illustrates the impact of historical time, changing opportunities, and the intersections of gender, race, and class.

2 Bell-Scott, R., Guy-Sheftall, B., Jones Royster, J., Sims-Wood, J., DeCosta-Willis, M., & Fultz, L. (1991). *Double stitch: Black women write about mothers and daughters.* Boston: Beacon.

The editors use quilting as a metaphor for mother-daughter relationships among African American women. The stories, poems, and essays in this anthology elaborate on the material on mothers, daughters, and extended female networks introduced in this part. The editors are members of the editorial collective of *SAGE: A Scholarly Journal on Black Women.*

3 Tan, A. (1989). *The joy luck club.* New York: G. P. Putnam.

In her first novel, Amy Tan explores the bond among four Chinese American women and their adult daughters. Like the central character in the novel, Amy Tan is the daughter of Chinese parents who emigrated to California from China after the Red Army took over China. The stories of these four families bring to life the relationships between two cultures within one family.

4 Erdrich, L. (1984). *Love medicine.* Bloomington: Indiana University Press.

Louise Erdrich's first novel introduces us to an extended Chippewa family in North Dakota. In the nonlinear tradition of Native American writing, we see the Kapshaw family at various times during the 50 years between 1934 and 1984. Louise Erdrich is a Turtle Mountain Chippewa who grew up in North Dakota.

5 Allen, K. R. (1989). *Single women/family ties: Life histories of older women.* Newbury Park, CA: Sage.

As the author explains, women are socialized to structure their lives around an orderly sequence of marital and parental roles. Using a life course perspective, Katherine Allen explores the events and processes that characterize the family lives of never-married, childless women. Her work is based on in-depth, unstructured interviews with 30 women from the 1910 birth cohort.

6   Dwyer, J. W., & Coward, R. T. (Eds.). (1992). *Gender, families and elder care.* Newbury Park, CA: Sage.

This volume explores the gendered nature of family caregiving. In exploring the way gender structures the social context of caregiving, the authors of the 13 chapters explore the structure of specific caregiving relationships (spouse-spouse, parent-child, sibling-sibling), the link between theory and research, and implications for policy and practice.

7   Kimmel, D. C. (1992, Summer). The families of older gay men and lesbians. *Generations, 16,* 37-38.

Kimmel's review of the limited research available illustrates the ways in which older gay men and lesbians maintain family relationships and create networks of close friends that provide the same type of supports we typically associate with families. Kimmel also describes some of the adaptive resources elderly gay men and lesbians have developed in coping with discrimination based on sexual orientation.

8   Coontz, S. (1992). *The way we never were: American families and the nostalgia trap.* New York: Basic Books.

Coontz's historical study of American family life demonstrates that the "traditional nuclear family" was neither traditional nor nuclear. Her demythologizing of American families enriches our understanding of the family contexts in which current cohorts of elderly people grew up and grew old.

9   Gates, H. L., Jr. (1994). *Colored people, a memoir.* New York: Random House.

Described as a story "of a family, of a village, and of a special time and place in American history," Gates's memoir revisits his childhood in Piedmont, West Virginia (population 2,565). His description of a "small, intimate, middle-class colored community" provides a glimpse into the context in which many elderly African Americans experienced their early adulthoods.

PART V

Health and Mortality

Inequalities

Inequalities in Health and Mortality: Gender, Race, and Class

Poor health and disability are among the most feared aspects of old age (Kart, 1997). As we get older, the risk of health problems increases. More than 80% of people 65 years of age and older have one or more chronic conditions (National Center for Health Statistics, 1991). Only about 45% of these people report limitations in their desired activities, however, and only about 2% are confined to bed. As with other resources, health is distributed unevenly across the elderly population. People who are disadvantaged by systems of inequality have more chronic conditions, greater disability, and shorter life expectancy than their more privileged counterparts. As we have seen throughout this book, social structure imposes conditions on members of disadvantaged groups that reduce their life chances. These limited opportunities result in inadequate health care and greater exposure to risk factors for disease and mortality at each life stage. The poorer health experienced by disadvantaged people in old age reflects the cumulative effects of a lifetime of blocked opportunities for healthy lifestyles and adequate health care. Here, we explore ways in which people's positions on hierarchies based on gender, race, and class affect their health status in old age and the resources available for coping with illness and disability. Our discussion addresses the following questions:

1. How does position on hierarchies based on gender, race, and class influence the likelihood of poor health and mortality?
2. Are disadvantaged elderly people more likely than their privileged counterparts to be exposed to risk factors for disease and death?
3. How do these systems of inequality affect the quantity and quality of health care available to older people?
4. What strategies do people use to manage illness on their own?

How Does Position on Hierarchies Based on Gender, Race, and Class Influence the Likelihood of Poor Health and Mortality?

All three of the systems of inequality we have discussed structure the health status of older people. In most cases, people occupying more privileged positions enjoy better health, less disability, and longer life than their more disadvantaged counterparts. The strongest of these links is between social class and health. Universally, the poor, the poorly educated, and those on the lower rungs of the occupational ladder are sicker, more functionally limited and more likely to die earlier than people with higher levels of wealth, income, occupation, and education (Williams, 1990). Heart disease, cancer, and stroke—the leading causes of death for all elderly people—are more prevalent among people with less than 8 years of formal schooling, family incomes below $14,000 a year, and a lifetime of employment in working-class occupations. Social class differences in subjective health assessments are also large. Lower-strata individuals consistently report worse health than their more privileged counterparts. This greater prevalence of illness and disability in the lower strata is not confined to old age. People in the lowest social classes experience poorer health throughout their lives, and they encounter chronic disease and disability earlier in life than people occupying more privileged positions. Furthermore, evidence is accumulating that socioeconomic position in early life influences health status in old age (Joseph & Kramer, 1996; Lynch, Kaplan, & Salonen, 1997). Increasingly, health policy experts underscore the importance of equalizing income and occupational and educational opportunities earlier in life so as to equalize the chances for good health in old age (House et al., 1990).

Disadvantaged minority group status is also associated with poor health. This is particularly true of older Black and American Indian elderly. The current cohort of elderly Blacks have more chronic disease, higher levels of disability, and higher mortality rates than White Americans (Markides & Wallace, 1996). This disadvantage holds for all three leading causes of death in old age: heart disease, cerebrovascular disease, and cancer. The mortality for elderly Blacks from heart disease and stroke is 1.5 times higher than for comparable Whites, and cancer mortality is 1.35 times higher (Manton & Stallard, 1997). Elderly Blacks also experience more difficulties with activities of daily living (e.g., eating, bathing, dressing, using the toilet, getting in and out of a bed or chair, walking, and getting outside) and with instrumental activities of daily living (e.g., preparing meals, shopping for personal items, managing money, using the telephone, and doing housework; Clark & Gibson, 1997). Not a surprise, given these differences in disease and disability, Blacks are about twice as likely as Whites to assess their health as poor (Cohen, Van Nostrand, & Suzman, 1995).

American Indians also encounter higher rates of disease and disability across the life course. Life expectancy for American Indians has improved over the past 50 years, an improvement largely attributable to the efforts of the Indian Health Service to combat infectious disease and improve maternal and child health (John, 1997). American Indians are less likely than Whites to die from heart disease, cancer, stroke, and chronic obstructive pulmonary disease (the four leading causes of mortality), but they are more likely to die from influenza, pneumonia, diabetes, accidental injuries, and kidney and liver disease. Alcohol-related mortality among elderly American Indians is consistently 3 times higher than among White elders (John, 1997). For elderly American Indians, a lifetime of poverty translates into poor nutrition, substandard living conditions, and inadequate medical care, all of which undermine the likelihood of living to old age.

The prevalence rates for most chronic diseases among Hispanic elders are comparable or even lower than rates among elderly Whites for most causes of death. The major exception is diabetes, with a prevalence rate of 1.5 to 2 times higher among Mexican American elders (Hazuda & Espina, 1997). High rates of diabetes are of special concern, because researchers have shown that diabetes undermines people's ability to manage basic physical activities (Strawbridge, Cohen, Shema, & Kaplan, 1996). Diabetes frequently leads to other health problems, including heart attack, stroke, vision problems, and kidney disease.

Looking at limitations in activities of daily living among the major Hispanic groups yields some interesting comparisons. Middle-aged Hispanics, except for Puerto Rican Americans, exhibit lower levels of activity limitations than middle-aged Whites. However, Hispanic elders, except for Cuban Americans, are more likely to report limitations in activities of daily living. How can we explain this reversal in the pattern of ethnic disability rates? Angel and Angel (1997) suggest that we consider the role of migration history and the availability of social networks. As they explain, social networks seem to have a protective function against disability, and people who migrate later in life have more difficulty forming social networks in their new environments. Over 98% of Cuban and Puerto Rican American elders were born outside the U.S. mainland, in comparison to only 42% of Mexican American elders. Cuban American elderly, however, in comparison to Puerto Rican elderly, seem to be protected against this negative impact of migration, because they become part of well-established ethnic enclaves that provide them with social support. Their interpretation demonstrates the ways in which social resources can buffer the potential negative effects of health risks.

Generalizing about health status of Asian and Pacific Island American (APIA) elders is complicated by diversity of national origin, culture, and immigration history. Aggregate statistics indicate that APIA elders are healthier than other Americans their age. Mortality rates are lower than for any other group of elders. Part of this advantage relates to immigration history. Foreign-born APIA elders have lower mortality rates than their American-born counterparts (Elo & Preston, 1997). APIA elders suffer from the major three mortality risks of the general population (heart disease, cancer, and stroke), although prevalence rates are generally lower than for the general American population. But aggregate statistics mask the diversity among this heterogeneous population category. Significant differences exist, however, with respect to particular diseases. Non-insulin-dependent diabetes rates among Japanese Americans are twice as high as the rate among the White population and 4 times the rate among Japanese in Japan (Kagawa-Singer, Hikoyeda, & Tanjasiri, 1997). This difference has been attributed to U.S. dietary patterns.

Liver cancer rates are 12 times higher among Asians Americans than among Whites; Japanese Americans experience stomach cancer and Chinese Americans experience nasopharyngeal cancer at rates 7 times higher than the general U.S. population (Kagawa-Singer et al., 1997).

Although it is true that up to about age 85, Blacks and American Indians are more likely than nonminority elders to have poorer objective and subjective health, more functional limitations, and a higher probability of death, something very curious happens in old age. When people 65 years and older are disaggregated by age, health, and mortality, differentials appear that do not always favor White Americans. The disadvantage in health and mortality observed in younger age groups of the elderly population narrows, disappears, or even turns into a minority group advantage among the oldest old. Among Blacks, the crossover occurs after age 85 (Gibson, 1994), and for American Indians, the crossover appears after age 75 (John, 1997). This trend is evident in morbidity data and in both all-cause and cause-specific mortality data (Gibson, 1994). This crossover effect is often attributed to the "survival of the fittest," suggesting that adverse conditions faced by minority elders at earlier ages lead to high mortality with only the strongest and most robust people surviving to old age. Another possible explanation is the poor quality of statistics used to estimate age at death for minority elders. For example, many Black elders were born in the South, where many births were never registered (Elo & Preston, 1997). However, the age at which the crossover occurs varies by cause of death, and there is no reason to expect that age misreporting would be associated with specific diseases (Manton & Stallard, 1997). The selection by Rose Gibson explores the relationship between race and health—a relationship that is more complicated than it first appears.

Gender is also related to health status and risk of mortality, but the relationship between privilege and positive outcome is less clear cut. Men in all age groups over 65 are more likely than women to die (Van Nostrand, Furner, & Suzman, 1993). This gender difference holds for two of the three leading causes of death in old age: heart disease and cancer. The exception to female advantage in mortality occurs with cerebrovascular disease: The death rate for women 85 years and older for cerebrovascular disease is higher than it is for men. Despite their lower likelihood of dying, women report more non-life-threatening chronic conditions and more functional limitations than men (Lorber, 1997). Elderly women in all age groups are more likely than older men to report difficulties with both activities of daily living and instrumental activities of daily living (Cohen et al., 1995).

Women over 65 years old are also more likely than men to be living in nursing homes. This disparity increases with age until, by age 85 and over, women are almost twice as likely to be living in nursing homes than men. Part of this gender difference might reflect the fact that women have more non-life-threatening conditions that cause disability (Van Nostrand et al., 1993). Inability to function in the community is a significant predictor of institutionalization. Another reason for higher rates of institutionalization among older women might be that they are more likely to be living alone. As we saw in Part IV on family, women are more likely than men to be widowed in old age. Having a spouse who can serve as caregiver is an important deterrent to nursing home entry among disabled older people.

In summary, although women are more advantaged than men in terms of life expectancy, they are more disadvantaged in terms of non-life-threatening chronic diseases that limit their functioning. Some gerontologists have captured this phenomenon with the idea that "women get sick, but men die." Perhaps because women are advantaged on measures of mortality and men are advantaged on measures of functional capacity, there are no gender differences in subjective health. Women and men are about equally likely to rate their health as excellent or poor throughout old age.

Although gender, race, and social class are each linked with health status in old age, the three systems of inequality often interlock to produce more complicated patterns of disease, disability, and death. For example, it is not just men who live shorter lives, but Black men in particular. It is not just women who are likely to live out their final days in institutions, but White women in particular. It is not just those in lower strata who are sicker and who die sooner but, in particular, lower-strata Blacks. In understanding the health status of older people, it is important to be aware not only of the individual effects of class, race, and gender but of their interlocking effects as well.

Are Disadvantaged Elderly People More Likely Than Their Privileged Counterparts to Be Exposed to Risk Factors for Disease and Death?

One explanation for the uneven distribution of disease, disability, and death within the elderly population is differences in exposure to risk factors across the life course. Public health campaigns in the media have devoted considerable attention to behaviors that increase our risk of disease in late life, including smoking, poor diets, sedentary lifestyles, and inadequate strategies for dealing with stress. The U.S. Surgeon General, in fact, estimated that only 20% of mortality can be attributed to genetic factors, only 20% to environmental factors, and only 10% to inadequate medical care, but fully 50% can be attributed to individual health behaviors and lifestyles (Williams, 1990). Bruce Link and Jo Phelan (1995) call these individual-level risk factors "proximate causes" of disease. Focusing on these proximate risk factors reflects a belief system that emphasizes the ability and responsibility of the individual for controlling his or her own fate (Becker, 1993). Many of these risk-related behaviors are more common among people who are disadvantaged than among people who are privileged, and public health officials have designed interventions aimed at altering these behaviors. With a focus on individual responsibility, it is easy to blame the victim for disease and disability—if only people would stop smoking, get more exercise, or cut down on the amount of fat in their diet, they would live longer and stay healthier. Link and Phelan (1995) stress the importance of "contextualizing" risk factors, that is, attempting to understand what it is about people's life circumstances that shape their exposure to risk factors, such as poor diet, lack of exercise, or a stressful home life. As we shall see, sometimes these proximate causes are a direct product of a person's social environment; in other times, they also involve limited access to resources. The greater prevalence of risk factors for disease and mortality among people who are disadvantaged in systems of inequality is related to the social structure. People's behaviors are a response to the reduced life chances imposed by the social conditions under which they have lived.

Health researchers classify risk factors into three broad categories: biomedical, social, and psychological. Diabetes and hypertension are two conditions that illustrate the distribution of biomedical risk factors along systems of inequality. Diabetes is associated with vascular changes involving many organ systems, including eyes, kidneys, peripheral nervous system, and the heart. Hypertension is an important risk factor for coronary heart and cerebrovascular disease (National Center for Health Statistics, 1991). Among people 65 and older, both diabetes and hypertension are more prevalent among women, Blacks, and those in lower socioeconomic strata (National Center for Health Statistics, 1991). American Indians also exhibit high rates of diabetes. But this is only part of the story. Race and gender interact with both diabetes and hypertension. Although White women are less likely than White men to have diabetes, Black women are more likely than Black men to develop this disease. In fact, elderly Black women are the most likely of these four race-gender groups to have diabetes.

A similar interaction pattern occurs with hypertension. Hypertension is more prevalent among elderly White than among elderly Black men but more prevalent among older Black women than among older White women. Black women are the most likely among these groups to have hypertension. Once again, we see how looking at one hierarchy at a time presents an overly simplistic picture. To get a valid picture of biomedical risk factors for disease and dying among the older population, it is important to examine the interrelationships among systems of inequality.

The second class of risk factors for disease and mortality is social. Social risks include both environmental stress and lifestyles that lead to nonhealthful behaviors. Environmental stress includes greater lifetime exposure to crime, air and water pollutants, accidents, hazardous wastes, pesticides, and industrial chemicals. People living in inner-city neighborhoods face greater exposure to many of these risk factors. Others are related to a lifetime of dangerous occupational conditions. High mortality rates from motor vehicle accidents among American Indians have been attributed to the greater need for automobiles in areas of low population density, poor road conditions on rural reservations, and high rates of alcohol use (John, 1997).

Lifestyles that lead to nonhealthful behaviors are another type of social risk factor that is more prevalent among disadvantaged elders. Obesity, smoking, and alcohol abuse illustrate this category of behavioral risks. Being severely overweight is associated with increased risks of hypertension, non-insulin-dependent diabetes, and certain cancers (National Center for Health Statistics, 1991). Excess weight is more prevalent among women, among people in lower socioeconomic strata, and among disadvantaged minorities, particularly Mexican Americans, Puerto Rican Americans, and Blacks (Tucker, Falcon, & Bermudez, 1997). Again, however, there is a race-gender interaction. Among disadvantaged minorities, excess weight is more prevalent among women than men. Among nonminorities, the pattern is reversed. As with interactions among biomedical risk factors, elderly Black women are the people most likely to be overweight (National Center for Health Statistics, 1991).

Thousands of people die each year from the consequences of smoking. Smoking is a major risk factor for lung cancer, cardiovascular disease, and chronic obstructive pulmonary disease. Gender, race, and class differences in mortality from these diseases reflect lifelong smoking patterns in the older population. Cigarette smoking has been more prevalent among today's older Blacks, American Indians, and Puerto Rican Americans than among Whites; more prevalent among Whites than among Asian Americans; more prevalent in the lower than middle classes; and more prevalent among men than among women. In general, people with higher educations are less likely to smoke—and more likely to quit if they did smoke—than people with lower educations (Berkman & Mullen, 1997). Indeed, social class differences explain a significant portion of the racial gap in smoking behavior. Once again, an interaction emerges between gender and social class. Men with lower education, income, and occupational status are more likely to smoke than higher-status men. Among women, however, the opposite pattern has been documented. Women with higher levels of education, income, and occupational status were more likely to smoke than lower-status women. Some of these patterns may change with future cohorts of elderly people, however, if people with higher levels of education stop smoking at higher rates than people with lower levels of education.

Alcohol consumption also varies along dimensions of gender, race, and class. George Maddox (1988), who studied use of alcohol among older people, estimated that about 5% of older Americans can be classified as problem drinkers. However, alcohol problems are distributed unevenly across systems of inequality. Men are about 4 times as likely as women to report problem drinking. Alcohol-related problems are also inversely related to social class (Maddox, 1988). Studies that find a racial difference in alcohol consumption among elderly people report higher drinking rates among Whites than Blacks (Berkman & Mullen, 1997). A number of researchers have emphasized problems of alcohol abuse among American Indians (Markides & Mindel, 1987).

The third set of risk factors is more psychological in nature: high stress, weak feelings of personal control and mastery, and weak perceived or actual social ties. All three of these psychological risk factors are more prevalent among people disadvantaged along hierarchies based on race and class. High levels of stress are associated with a number of disease outcomes (Williams, 1990). Older people disadvantaged by race and class have been exposed to more stressors throughout their lives than their more privileged counterparts. They are more likely to experience divorce, unemployment, and the death of someone close to them. They more often struggle with substandard housing and unpaid bills and report being more troubled by the everyday annoyances researchers call "daily hassles." As we saw in Part I, "The Life Course Perspective," surviving in a racist society is another source of chronic stress. Blacks have learned to live "in a react mode" (White, 1991, p. 190). Harriet McAdoo (1986) described this type of stress as a "mundane extreme environment," highlighting the pervasiveness of coping with racism as a daily reality. White Americans rarely think about the consequences of being White. In fact, part of race privilege is the luxury of ignoring the implications of race in one's daily life (McIntosh, 1988).

Several types of adaptive resources can buffer the effects of stress. Strong feelings of personal control, in contrast to feelings of powerlessness, seem to enhance health and soften the impact of stress. A sense of control is molded by the conditions under which people live and work. For example, corporate executives and professionals have more opportunities to exercise their authority, to use their expertise to solve problems, and to control the pace of their work than do industrial workers on an assembly line. The accumulation of these stress-inducing experiences over the life course contributes to a sense of control over one's life. In contrast, low-status jobs are more often characterized by a combination of high demands but low decision latitude (Schnall, Schwartz, Landsbergis, Warren, & Pickering, 1992). Some women also experience stress resulting from overload as they work and shoulder family responsibilities within a context of limited personal power (Rosenfield, 1989). Accumulation of these feelings of powerlessness undermines people's confidence and feelings of mastery.

Strong social ties are another resource that often predict better health and lower mortality (Berkman & Mullen, 1997). Social ties can enhance health status in several ways. Close friends and relatives can provide emotional support and advice in times of trouble. Social networks can also help shape healthy lifestyles, link members to formal health services, and affirm people's self-esteem. People sometimes assume that extended kin networks of poor and minority elders mean that they enjoy an advantage over more privileged groups in social support resources. But social ties and social support are not necessarily equivalent. Sometimes, networks lack the resources to provide support to members. Relationships with other people can be sources of stress as well as sources of support. Older parents can be upset, for example, by an adult child's divorce or loss of a job. Problems of alcoholism and drug addiction reverberate throughout a family. Given the higher prevalence of negative life events among more disadvantaged segments of the population, the conclusion that social networks of poor and minority elders provide stress and support in roughly equal doses should come as no surprise (Williams, 1990).

In summarizing the impact of risk exposure on health outcomes in late life, we return to Link and Phelan's (1995) emphasis on contextualizing risk factors:

> Why is it so important that we strive to contextualize risk factors? One reason is that efforts to reduce risk by changing behavior may be hopelessly ineffective if there is no clear understanding of the process that leads to exposure. . . . Without an understanding of the context that leads to risk, the responsibility for reducing the risk is left with the individual, and nothing is done to alter the more fundamental factors that put people at risk. (p. 85).

How Do Systems of Inequality Affect the Quantity and Quality of Health Care Available to Older People?

Another reason older people who are disadvantaged in systems of inequality experience more disease, disability, and mortality than their more privileged counterparts is that they receive poorer health care. Although medicare and medicaid have increased the quantity of health care for the elderly and the poor, it is less clear that the quality of that care has increased.

Health care quantity is most often measured by number of contacts with the health care system. Currently, the number of physician contacts per person does not differ by gender, race, or social class (Van Nostrand et al., 1993). Health care quality is assessed using several types of indicators, including use of services aimed at disease prevention, accessibility of care, availability of health care resources, and the doctor-patient relationship. People who are more disadvantaged in systems of inequality are less likely to have full access to the health care system, less likely to receive preventive services, more likely to have problems paying for health care, and less likely to enjoy high-quality relationships with physicians.

The health care received by disadvantaged elders is more oriented toward treatment of existing disease than toward prevention of future problems. Disadvantaged elders enter the medical care system later and are sicker on diagnosis than more privileged elders. For example, elderly Blacks with cancer are usually diagnosed at a more advanced stage of the disease than are elderly Whites. Once hospitalized, average lengths of stay are longer for elderly Blacks and for elderly people with lower incomes.

Restricted access to high-quality medical care results from a range of both perceived and actual barriers. Limited financial resources limit access for many near-poor and working-class elderly people. Without private insurance, they have difficulty paying for medicare deductibles and copayments and for costs not covered by medicare, such as medications, dental checkups, and nursing home care. Many people also have difficulty paying the premiums for Medicare's Supplemental Medical Insurance (Part B), which reimburses some physician and related services. Coverage under medicaid, the program of medical assistance designed for the poor, has also decreased over the past decade as states have attempted to control rising costs by limiting services and restricting eligibility. As a result, only one third of the elderly poor are covered by medicaid (Nathan, 1990).

More affluent elderly can afford to purchase private "medicap" insurance to supplement medicare coverage. Older people who were employed in jobs in the primary labor market are also more likely to have access to health plans that extend coverage to retired workers. Almost 70% of the elderly population had some private insurance, either privately purchased supplementary policies or employer-related coverage. But access to this additional protection is not distributed evenly across the elderly population As we saw in Part III, "Productive Activity," older workers of color are less likely to have found employment in the primary labor market, so they are less likely to have access to these benefits. Older women are also less likely to have worked in primary labor market jobs, but women married to affluent men are often covered through spousal benefits. This provides yet another example of the interface of privilege and disadvantage. As with other financial resources in late life, a lifetime of limited financial benefits translates into limited medical coverage in old age. This situation is compounded by minority status. Among low-income elderly, fully one third of ethnic minorities but only one quarter of Whites rely exclusively on medicare for paying for health care (Nathan, 1990).

Finding a source of medical care can also be difficult. Some physicians will not accept medicaid patients. The availability of physicians also varies by geographic setting. The ratio of physicians to patients is lower in low-income and minority areas, and the cost and difficulty of travel can reduce access, particularly for people with mobility problems. The mismatch of patient characteristics with the values of a predominantly White middle-class health care system further limits access to quality medical care. This gap can create psychological barriers that undermine the quality of health care for minority and poor elderly, barriers that include fear of loss of personal control and self-esteem and fear of class, gender, or racial discrimination. Discriminatory practices of practitioners and medical institutions often make encounters with the medical system a dehumanizing experience for lower-class and minority elders (Williams, 1990). The selection by Zora Neale Hurston, titled "My Most Humiliating Jim Crow Experience," illustrates such discriminatory treatment of a woman of color by a White physician.

The doctor-patient relationship is likely to be of poorer quality for disadvantaged individuals. Systematic and regular visits to private physicians' offices result in more thorough delivery of care and foster better patient-physician relationships. Encounters with physicians, however, are less systematic and regular in disadvantaged groups. For example, minority elders and elders with annual incomes below $25,000 have longer intervals between physician visits than do Whites and people with higher incomes. Where the physician contact takes place also differs by minority and socioeconomic status. Whites and people with higher family incomes are more likely to see physicians in their offices, whereas Blacks and people with lower incomes are more likely to see physicians in hospital outpatient departments, emergency rooms, and nonhospital clinics (National Center for Health Statistics, 1991). In these settings, there is small likelihood of seeing the same physician over time, and patients have limited choice in who provides their care.

Despite greater functional limitations, minority elders at almost all ages are less likely than older Whites to be living in nursing or personal care homes (Wallace & Villa, 1997). One study reports that about 26% of non-Hispanic Whites aged 85 and over lived in nursing homes, in comparison to only 17% of Blacks, 11% of Hispanics, and 12% of Asian Americans in the same age category (Damron-Rodriguez, Wallace, & Kingston, 1994). Hispanic elders also use community-based long-term care facilities at lower rates than other groups (Hazuda & Espino, 1997). The extent of these ethnic differences in nursing home use also varies by age. Rose Gibson and James Jackson (1992) report that, under age 75, Whites are only slightly less likely than Blacks to be living in nursing and personal care homes, but the percentage of Whites who are institutionalized is larger than the percentage of Blacks after age 75. Whites between 75 and 84 years are about 1.5 times more likely than Blacks that age to be institutionalized. At ages 85 and over, Whites are almost twice as likely to be institutionalized, with the ratio increasing to Whites being about 4 times as likely after age 100.

What accounts for these disparities in long-term care among elders of color? More limited financial resources means that minority elders are more likely to rely on medicaid—or to spend down to medicaid in a shorter period of time—than White elders. Medicaid reimburses nursing homes below the rate charged to private-pay patients, so patients with the resources to pay for their care are more attractive to long-term care facilities. The geographic distribution of nursing homes is another explanatory factor. For example, Jacqueline Angel and Ronald Angel (1997) explain that in Texas, the elderly Mexican American population is concentrated in the southern and western parts of the state, whereas long-term care facilities are concentrated in the northern and eastern parts. Nursing homes are also rare in American Indian communities (John, 1997). Ethnic differences in family values and attitudes toward long-term care have also been cited as potential explanations. Chapleski (1997) reports that key informants in the Great Lakes region reported that "long-term care is foreign to the American Indian lexicon and way of thinking—families and tribal members take care of one another just because 'it is the Indian way.'" (p. 377). Studies explaining low rates of long-term care use among Hispanic elders also cite norms regarding children's responsibilities for care of aging parents (Hazuda & Espina, 1997). An unfamiliar physical and cultural environment coupled with cultural differences between providers of care and minority elders, unpalatable food, and difficulty with English also reduces the appeal of nursing homes among Hispanic elders. Similarly, Chapleski (1997) found that nursing homes were the least preferred option for long-term care but,

> if absolutely necessary and given no other choice, 70% of urban Indians would prefer to go further away in order to be with other American Indian residents. Furthermore, nearly three-fourths . . . acknowledged that the presence of American Indian staff at such a facility was somewhat or very important. (p. 383)

Racial prejudice, among staff or among other residents or patients, has also been mentioned as a contributing factor. Clearly, gerontologists have more to learn about ethnic differences in use of long-term care services.

What Strategies Do People Use to Manage Illness on Their Own?

Physicians are not the only source of information for managing symptoms of illness. Health surveys suggest that the majority of symptoms are evaluated and treated outside the formal medical care system and that a large proportion of people who seek medical care have treated themselves before seeking medical advice. Lay treatment strategies include use of medications, including both over-the-counter medications purchased on their own or prescription medications prescribed previously for managing ongoing chronic conditions; use of appliances, such as thermometers, enemas, heating pads; use of homemade preparations, such as certain foods, herb teas, salves, and gargles; changes in activity, such as bed rest or changes in exercise level; avoidance behaviors, such as not stooping or lifting, not smoking or drinking, avoiding stressful situations, avoiding drafts; or changes in diet, such as increasing fluids or increasing bulk. Recent reviews of research on self-care strategies used by older people suggest that self-care decisions are generally appropriate and self-treatment generally helpful (Stoller, 1998).

As with family care of frail elderly relatives, women are most often the providers of lay health care. Women are more likely than men to serve as lay consultants in matters of health and illness (Stoller, 1993). They are more likely to practice health-enhancing behaviors, to exhibit more knowledge about health matters, and to monitor their own health. Spouses reportedly talk about most health problems, but these discussions focus more frequently on the husband's health than on the wife's (Dean, 1986). Debra Umberson (1992) found that wives are more likely than husbands to try to modify their spouses' behavior to reduce their chances of illness.

Some of the health-related information shared within these informal networks parallels current medical care practices. People develop lay understandings of disease from multiple sources. These repertoires of lay knowledge and beliefs are created from people's own experience with illness, the vicarious experience of other people shared through the telling and retelling of personal illness narratives, observation of specific cases of disease in both personal networks and the public arena, and information gained over the years from professional practitioners and from the media (Davison, Frankel, & Smith, 1992; Segall & Goldstein, 1989; Stoller, Forster, & Pollow, 1994). Some of these beliefs and practices are based on traditional or folk medical practices that are part of ethnic, regional, or immigrant cultures.

Wilkinson (1987) studied folk medicine among American Indians, Appalachian Whites, Blacks, and Mexican Americans. In all of these groups, she stressed the role of elders, particularly older women, as lay healers. In his novel, *Bless Me, Ultima*, Rudolfo Anaya (1982) describes the character La Grande as a *curandera*, or healer, "a woman who knew the herbs and remedies of the ancients, a miracle-worker who could heal the sick." Curanderas treat illness with food and herbs, massages and manipulations of the body, and use of religious or magical objects (Twaddle & Hessler, 1987). These practices reflect beliefs about causation that emphasize imbalances between hot and cold within the body, dislocation of bodily organs, emotional disturbances, and magic or witchcraft. The narrator in Anaya's novel alludes to beliefs in magic within traditional Mexican healing systems when he refers to La Grande's power "to lift the curses laid by brujas [witches]." In this part, the Mexican curandera in González's story, Doña Toña, also exhibits beliefs in magic to cure disease.

American Indian healers also mix medications and mechanical interventions with the use of religious symbols and spiritual interventions. American Indian practitioners developed stimulants, anesthetics, astringents, cathartics, emetics, antibiotics, and herbal contraceptives, many of which were borrowed by Western practitioners (Twaddle & Hessler, 1987). They also employed sweat baths, poultices, surgery, and quarantines. These physical interventions were supplemented with incantations, singing, and use of symbols, including ceremonial masks, rattles, drums, and pipes. Healing practices reflect American Indian beliefs that emphasize harmony or balance among everything in the universe.

Historically, lack of economic resources and institutional racism have limited access of many Blacks to formal health care and increased the importance of self-care practices (Davis & Wykle, 1998). Lay etiologies of disease among Blacks emphasize individual responsibility for health and attention to harmony, balance, and moderation (Davis & McGadney, 1993). Folk beliefs also emphasized the importance of "overcoming," "surviving," and accommodating oneself to the situation (Segall & Wykle, 1988-89), a theme we emphasized in our discussion in Part II. Lay explanatory models of disease also incorporate beliefs that illness can be spiritual in nature, a finding consistent with the involvement of clergy and religious organizations in health ministries (Wood & Wan, 1993).

Self-care practices are not limited to ethnic minorities or immigrant subcultures. Indeed, self-care is the predominant form of health care among all elderly Americans. Only about 10% to 25% of illness episodes actually result in contacts with professional health care providers, and a large proportion of the people who seek medical care have treated themselves before seeking professional advice (Konrad, 1998). In a study of a sample of elderly European Americans in upstate New York, Stoller and colleagues (1993) identified a range of lay treatments, including cranberry drinks for urinary problems; heating pads and liniments for joint or muscle pain; camphor oil, mustard plasters, and various gargles (water with salt, baking soda, vinegar, or whiskey) for sore throats; and leisure activities and prayer for depression.

The extent to which lay understandings of disease coincide with medical explanations used by health care professionals remains an empirical question, but available literature suggests that the fit is less than perfect. For example, rural Blacks and poor Whites in Appalachia complain of "high blood," "sugar," "fallin' out," and "nerves" (Kleinman, 1988). But even explanations couched in medical terms do not always reflect tenets of scientific medicine. Hypertension is the most widely cited example. Although hypertension is an asymptomatic condition, patients often believe that they can monitor their own blood pressure by referring to their body's signs or symptoms. For example, one study found that 80% of a sample of patients in treatment for hypertension agreed that people in general cannot tell when their blood pressure was elevated, but 90% of the same set of patients believed they themselves could tell when their pressure went up. This type of misinterpretation can have detrimental effects on adherence to treatment regimens, because differences in disease representations suggest different treatment goals. As the health psychologist Howard Leventhal explains,

> Successful treatment for patients meant the amelioration of symptoms, while for physicians it meant lowering the blood pressure reading. Thus, the physicians were asking the patients to begin and sustain a treatment which basically made no sense from the patient's perspective. (Leventhal, Diefenbach, & Leventhal, 1992, p. 156). Not surprisingly, Leventhal and his colleagues found that patients who believed they could monitor their own blood pressure were less likely to follow prescribed treatments.

The anthropologist Suzanne Heurtin-Roberts (1993), who studied lay understandings of hypertension among lower-class elderly Black women, discovered that her subjects were experiencing two chronic folk illnesses ("high-pertension" and "high blood") rather than the biomedical condition "hypertension." "High-pertension" is understood as primarily a disease of the "nerves." "High blood," a condition in which excessively "hot," "thick," or "rich" blood rises up in the body, is most often caused by salty, highly seasoned, or greasy foods but can also be exacerbated by heredity, hot temperatures, or stress. This confusion has strong implications for treatment. If hypertension is considered a disease stemming from nervousness (as in "high-pertension"), adherence to a medication or dietary regimen designed to improve cardiovascular fitness may be seen as irrelevant.

Miscommunication can also result from fragmentation in the health care system and inadequate patient education by health care professionals. Without a primary care physician integrating medical care, elders with multiple conditions can have difficulty synthesizing messages from various specialists. Lucille Davis and May Wykle (1998) describe the experience of a 70-year-old Black female who had recently been diagnosed with glaucoma and hypertension:

> On her clinic day, she had an appointment in the glaucoma clinic and the doctor told her that her pressure was fine. In the afternoon, when visiting the high blood pressure clinic, she was told that her pressure was "up." Not recognizing the distinction between pressure in the eye and in the vascular system, she decided not to come back to the clinic. She stated: "The doctors don't know anything—one says my pressure is up and the other one that it is OK—I think I will be better off taking care of myself." (p. 175)

Key Issues

This discussion and the following readings illustrate several key points:

1. How hierarchies based on gender, race or ethnicity, and class influence the meaning and distribution of disease, disability, and mortality
2. The distribution of risk factors among people occupying different positions in systems of inequality
3. How systems of inequality affect the quantity and quality of health care available to older people
4. Use of lay care strategies and folk medicine among older people and the role of women as lay providers of health care

The Readings

The following readings provide several illustrations of the ways in which interlocking hierarchies structure the experience and interpretation of disease, disability, and mortality. In the Introduction to this book, we emphasized differences in the meanings people attach to old age. Maya Angelou's poem, "On Aging," returns to this theme by reminding us that the same symptoms or disabilities can be interpreted very differently by different people. Angelou's narrator acknowledges the physical changes that often accompany old age: stiff and aching bones, loss of hair, "a lot less lungs and much less wind." But she cautions against interpreting these changes within the context of negative stereotypes. She may have changed in physical appearance and physical abilities, but she's still "the same person I was back then." Angelou's poem thus stresses continuity over the life course: The physical losses that people experience in late life do not erase or diminish the essence of who they are.

For some people, age-related decrements challenge their understanding of quality of life. Older people and their families sometimes confront this dilemma near the end of life when deciding whether or not to use complicated surgical techniques or life support systems to extend the life of a terminally ill patient. The older couple in Arna Bontemps's story, "A Summer Tragedy," face a similar decision far from the high-tech environment of a hospital ICU. The Pattons were poor Black sharecroppers in the rural South, who were living independently when the story begins. But their ability to maintain this independence is threatened by poor health and minimal resources, and they plan to wrest control over their future in one of the few ways open to them.

Other choices regarding health care also require us to evaluate what gives meaning to life. The series of poems, "A Place for Mother," by Joanne Seltzer illustrates nursing home placements for two generations of women from a middle-class family. The series begins with the narrator, the adult daughter, confronting nursing home placement for her older mother. The poems describing her search for a nursing home for her mother illustrate several dilemmas faced by families: the struggle to find a suitable placement, the guilt caregivers feel when they must finally resort to institutionalization, the acute medical crises that demand an immediate decision, the impact of death of a parent, the continuity of a mother-daughter bond throughout life, and the resolve never to be a burden to one's children.

The Zora Neale Hurston selection, "My Most Humiliating Jim Crow Experience," also illustrates how poor patient-physician relationships are brought about by discriminatory practices of practitioners and how both perceived and actual discriminatory treatment can dampen the patient's enthusiasm for seeking future medical care. This selection also illustrates the interlocking nature of systems of inequality. Zora Neale Hurston was a Black woman who completed graduate study in anthropology at Columbia University, but this class advantage was not sufficient to deflect the racist response of the White physician.

Hierarchies based on race, class, and gender are reflected in the organization of the medical care system, as well as in the performance of individual practitioners. The percentage of health workers who are women and people of color increases as we move down the medical hierarchy from highly paid physicians and administrators, most of whom are White men, to lowly paid aides and assistants. From the consumer's perspective, affluent patients receive the best care that money can buy, whereas poor and minority patients have disproportionately served the medical care system as teaching and research material (Waitzkin, 1974). Perhaps nowhere has this bias been more dramatically illustrated than in the 40-year Tuskegee Syphilis Study described in the selection by Stephen Thomas and Sandra Quinn. Under the guise of medical research, the Black men in this study, many poor men who welcomed the government's offer of free medical checkups and burial insurance, were denied treatment without their permission for a curable yet ultimately fatal disease.

Louie the Foot González's story, "Doña Toña of Nineteenth Street," also illustrates the ways in which different positions on systems of inequality influence the strategies people use to manage illness outside the formal medical care system. The Mexican American *curandera* in his story uses traditional Mexican folk medicine—magic objects, herbs, and massage—to treat illness after other healing techniques have failed. The curandera is a shamanistic wise woman who is revered and respected but also feared because of her powers and associations with the supernatural.

The next two selections, by Amy Tan and by Wilma Mankiller and Michael Wallis, provide two different perspectives on the relationship between traditional medical beliefs and practices and Western scientific medicine. Novelist Amy Tan describes the reluctance of an adult daughter to disclose an illness diagnosis to her mother. This hesitation emerges from an unwillingness to engage in a dialogue based on her mother's beliefs surrounding illness. "According to my mother," the daughter explains, "nothing is an accident. . . . Everything could have been prevented." The discrepancy in lay etiologies of disease between this Chinese mother and her American-born daughter reminds us of the value differences between elderly

Southeast Asian immigrants and their Americanized children, described in Part IV by Barbara Yee.

Wilma Mankiller describes a blending of traditional Cherokee and allopathic medical practices in her own life as she relates the events surrounding an automobile accident in which she suffered serious injuries and her close friend died. Mankiller describes the long healing process during which she "fell back on my Cherokee ways and adopted what our elders call a Cherokee approach to life." She did not substitute Cherokee healing traditions for Western medicine. Rather, she blended the two traditions, crafting a recovery strategy that synthesized elements of both traditions. Wilma Mankiller is Principal Chief of the Cherokee Nation.

Taken together, these readings provide a range of examples of how interlocking hierarchies structure the experience and interpretation of disease, disability, and mortality. The final selection by Rose Campbell Gibson reports an analysis of how age and race combine to affect health, disability, and mortality. Subdividing the age group 65 and over into finer age groups unmasks race differentials in morbidity and mortality that often favor Blacks in the older age groups. There are varying opinions as to the nature and meaning of this narrowing race gap in mortality at older ages. For example, Elo and Preston (1997) suggest that the racial mortality crossover is simply due to the seriously flawed way in which Black death rates are currently constructed. In regard to morbidity, Schoenbaum and Raidmann (1997) demonstrate that much of the difference in the prevalence of chronic conditions and functional limitations between Blacks and Whites aged 70 and older is attributable to differences in socioeconomic status between these two groups.

On Aging

Maya Angelou

When you see me sitting quietly,
Like a sack left on the shelf,
Don't think I need your chattering.
I'm listening to myself.
Hold! Stop! Don't pity me!
Hold! Stop your sympathy!
Understanding if you got it,
Otherwise I'll do without it!
When my bones are stiff and aching
And my feet won't climb the stair,

I will only ask one favor:
Don't bring me no rocking chair.
When you see me walking, stumbling,
Don't study and get it wrong
'Cause tired don't mean lazy
And every goodbye ain't gone.
I'm the same person I was back then,
A little less hair, a little less chin,
A lot less lungs and much less wind.
But ain't I lucky I can still breathe in.

A Summer Tragedy

Arna Bontemps

Old Jeff Patton, the black share farmer, fumbled with his bow tie. His fingers trembled and the high stiff collar pinched his throat. A fellow loses his hand for such vanities after thirty or forty years of simple life. Once a year, or maybe twice if there's a wedding among his kinfolks, he may spruce up; but generally fancy clothes do nothing but adorn the wall of the big room and feed the moths. That had been Jeff Patton's experience. He had not worn his stiff-bosomed shirt more than a dozen times in all his married life. His swallow-tailed coat lay on the bed beside him, freshly brushed and pressed, but it was as full of holes as the overalls in which he worked on weekdays. The moths had used it badly. Jeff twisted his mouth into a hideous toothless grimace as he contended with the obstinate bow. He stamped his good foot and decided to give up the struggle.

"Jennie," he called.

"What's that, Jeff?" His wife's shrunken voice came out of the adjoining room like an echo. It was hardly bigger than a whisper.

"I reckon you'll have to he'p me wid this heah bow tie, baby," he said meekly. "Dog if I can hitch it up."

Her answer was not strong enough to reach him, but presently the old woman came to the door, feeling her way with a stick. She had a wasted, dead-leaf appearance. Her body, as scrawny and gnarled as a string bean, seemed less than nothing in the ocean of frayed and faded petticoats that surrounded her. These hung an inch or two above the tops of her heavy unlaced shoes and showed lit- tle grotesque piles where the stockings had fallen down from her negligible legs.

"You oughta could do a heap mo' wid a thing like that'n me—beingst as you got yo' good sight."

"Looks like I oughta could," he admitted. "But ma fingers is gone democrat on me. I get all mixed up in the looking glass an' can't tell wicha way to twist the devilish thing."

Jennie sat on the side of the bed and old Jeff Patton got down on one knee while she tied the bow knot. It was a slow and painful ordeal for each of them in this position. Jeff's bones cracked, his knee ached, and it was only after a half dozen attempts that Jennie worked a semblance of a bow into the tie.

"I got to dress maseff now," the old woman whispered. "These is ma old shoes an' stockings, and I ain't so much as un- wrapped ma dress."

"Well, don't worry 'bout me no mo', baby," Jeff said. "That 'bout finishes me. All I gotta do now is slip on that old coat 'n ves' an' I'll be fixed to leave."

Jennie disappeared again through the dim passage into the shed room. Being blind was no handicap to her in that black hole. Jeff heard the cane placed against the wall beside the door and knew that his wife was on easy ground. He put on his coat, took a battered top hat from the bedpost and hobbled to the front door. He was ready to travel. As soon as Jennie could get on her Sunday shoes and her old black silk dress, they would start.

Outside the tiny log house, the day was warm and mellow with sunshine. A host of wasps were humming with busy excitement in the trunk of a dead sycamore. Gray squirrels were searching through the grass for hickory nuts and blue jays were in the trees, hopping from branch to branch. Pine woods stretched away to the left like a black sea. Among them were scattered scores of log houses like Jeff's, houses of black share farmers. Cows and pigs wandered freely among the trees. There was no danger of loss. Each farmer knew his own stock and knew his neighbor's as well as he knew his neighbor's children.

Down the slope to the right were the cultivated acres on which the colored folks worked. They extended to the river, more than two miles away, and they were today green with the unmade cotton crop. A tiny thread of a road, which passed directly in front of Jeff's place, ran through these green fields like a pencil mark.

Jeff, standing outside the door, with his absurd hat in his left hand, surveyed the wide scene tenderly. He had been forty-five years on these acres. He loved them with the unexplained affection that others have for the countries to which they belong.

The sun was hot on his head, his collar still pinched his throat, and the Sunday clothes were intolerably hot. Jeff transferred the hat to his right hand and began fanning with it. Suddenly the whisper that was Jennie's voice came out of the shed room.

"You can bring the car round front whilst you's waitin'," it said feebly. There was a tired pause; then it added, "I'll soon be fixed to go."

"A'right, baby," Jeff answered. "I'll get it in a minute."

But he didn't move. A thought struck him that made his mouth fall open. The mention of the car brought to his mind, with new intensity, the trip he and Jennie were about to take. Fear came into his eyes; excitement took his breath. Lord, Jesus!

"Jeff . . . O Jeff," the old woman's whisper called.

He awakened with a jolt. "Hunh, baby?"

"What you doin'?"

"Nuthin. Jes studyin'. I jes been turnin' things round'n round in ma mind."

"You could be gettin' the car," she said.

"Oh yes, right away, baby."

He started round to the shed, limping heavily on his bad leg. There were three frizzly chickens in the yard. All his other chickens had been killed or stolen recently. But the frizzly chickens had been saved somehow. That was fortunate indeed, for these curious creatures had a way of devouring "Poison" from the yard and in that way protecting against conjure and black luck and spells. But even the frizzly chickens seemed now to be in a stupor. Jeff thought they had some ailment; he expected all three of them to die shortly.

The shed in which the old T-model Ford stood was only a grass roof held up by four corner poles. It had been built by tremulous hands at a time when the little rattletrap car had been regarded as a peculiar treasure. And, miraculously, despite wind and downpour it still stood.

Jeff adjusted the crank and put his weight upon it. The engine came to life with a sputter and bang that rattled the old car from radiator to taillight. Jeff hopped into the seat and put his foot on the accelerator. The sputtering and banging increased. The rattling became more violent. That was good. It was good banging, good sputtering and rattling, and it meant that the aged car was still in running condition. She could be depended on for this trip.

Again, Jeff's thought halted as if paralyzed. The suggestion of the trip fell into the machinery of his mind like a wrench. He felt dazed and weak. He swung the car out into the yard, made a half turn and drove around to the front door. When he took his hands off the wheel, he noticed that he was trembling violently. He cut off the motor and climbed to the ground to wait for Jennie.

A few minutes later she was at the window, her voice rattling against the pane like a broken shutter.

"I'm ready, Jeff."

He did not answer, but limped into the house and took her by the arm. He led her slowly through the big room, down the step and across the yard.

"You reckon I'd oughta lock the do'?" he asked softly.

They stopped and Jennie weighed the question. Finally she shook her head.

"Ne' mind the do'," she said. "I don't see no cause to lock up things."

"You right," Jeff agreed. "No cause to lock up."

Jeff opened the door and helped his wife into the car. A quick shudder passed over him. Jesus! Again he trembled.

"How come you shaking so?" Jennie whispered.

"I don't know," he said.

"You mus' be scairt, Jeff."

"No, baby, I ain't scairt."

He slammed the door after her and went around to crank up again. The motor started easily. Jeff wished that it had not been so responsive. He would have liked a few more minutes in which to turn things around in his head. As it was, with Jennie chiding him about being afraid, he had to keep going. He swung the car into the little pencil-mark road and started off toward the river, driving very slowly, very cautiously.

Chugging across the green countryside, the small battered Ford seemed tiny indeed. Jeff felt a familiar excitement, a thrill, as they came down the first slope to the immense levels on which the cotton was growing. He could not help reflecting that the crops were good. He knew what that meant, too; he had made forty-five of them with his own hands. It was true that he had worn out nearly a dozen mules, but that was the fault of old man Stevenson, the owner of the land. Major Stevenson had the odd notion that one mule was all a share farmer needed to work a thirty-acre plot. It was an expensive notion, the way it killed mules from overwork, but the old man held to it. Jeff thought it killed a good many share farmers as well as mules, but he had no sympathy for them. He had always been strong, and he had been taught to have no patience with weakness in men. Women or children might be tolerated if they were puny, but a weak man was a curse. Of course, his own children—

Jeff's thought halted there. He and Jennie never mentioned their dead children any more. And naturally he did not wish to dwell upon them in his mind. Before he knew it, some remark would slip out of his mouth and that would make Jennie feel blue. Perhaps she would cry. A woman like Jennie could not easily throw off the grief that comes from losing five grown children within two years. Even Jeff was still staggered by the blow. His memory had not been much good recently. He frequently talked to himself. And, although he had kept it a secret, he knew that his courage had left him. He was terrified by the least unfamiliar sound at night. He was reluctant to venture far from home in the daytime. And that habit of trembling when he felt fearful was now far beyond his control. Sometimes he became afraid and trembled without knowing what had frightened him. The feeling would just come over him like a chill.

The car rattled slowly over the dusty road. Jennie sat erect and silent, with a little absurd hat pinned to her hair. Her useless eyes seemed very large, very white in their deep sockets. Suddenly Jeff heard her voice, and he inclined his head to catch the words.

"Is we passed Delia Moore's house yet?" she asked.

"Not yet," he said.

"You must be drivin' mighty slow, Jeff."

"We might just as well take our time, baby."

There was a pause. A little puff of steam was coming out of the radiator of the car. Heat wavered above the hood. Delia Moore's house was nearly half a mile away. After a moment Jennie spoke again.

"You ain't really scairt, is you, Jeff?"

"Nah, baby, I ain't scairt."

"You know how we agreed—we gotta keep on goin'."

Jewels of perspiration appeared on Jeff's forehead. His eyes rounded, blinked, became fixed on the road.

"I don't know," he said with a shiver. "I reckon it's the only thing to do."

"Hm."

A flock of guinea fowls, pecking in the road, were scattered by the passing car. Some of them took to their wings; others hid under bushes. A blue jay, swaying on a leafy twig, was annoying a roadside squirrel. Jeff held an even speed till he came near Delia's place. Then he slowed down noticeably.

Delia's house was really no house at all, but an abandoned store building converted into a dwelling. It sat near a crossroads, beneath a single black cedar tree. There Delia, a cattish old creature of Jennie's age, lived alone. She had been there more years than anybody could remember, and long ago had won the disfavor of such women as Jennie. For in her young days Delia had been gayer, yellower and saucier than seemed proper in those parts. Her ways with menfolks had been dark and suspicious. And the fact that she had had as many husbands as children did not help her reputation.

"Yonder's old Delia," Jeff said as they passed.

"What she doin'?"

"Jes sittin' in the do'," he said.

"She see us?"

"Hm," Jeff said. "Musta did."

That relieved Jennie. It strengthened her to know that her old enemy had seen her pass in her best clothes. That would give the old she-devil something to chew her gums and fret about, Jennie thought. Wouldn't she have a fit if she didn't find out? Old evil Delia! This would be just the thing for her. It would pay her back for being so evil. It would also pay her, Jennie thought, for the way she used to grin at Jeff—long ago when her teeth were good.

The road became smooth and red, and Jeff could tell by the smell of the air that they were nearing the river. He could see the rise where the road turned and ran along parallel to the stream. The car chugged on monotonously. After a long silent spell, Jennie leaned against Jeff and spoke.

"How many bale o' cotton you think we got standin'?" she said.

Jeff wrinkled his forehead as he calculated.

"'Bout twenty-five, I reckon."

"How many you make las' year?"

"Twenty-eight," he said, "How come you ask that?"

"I's jes thinkin'," Jennie said quietly.

"It don't make a speck o' difference though," Jeff reflected. "If we get much or if we get little, we still gonna be in debt to old man Stevenson when he gets through counting up agin us. It's took us a long time to learn that."

Jennie was not listening to these words. She had fallen into a trance-like meditation. Her lips twitched. She chewed her gums and rubbed her gnarled hands nervously. Suddenly she leaned forward, buried her face in the nervous hands and burst into tears. She cried aloud in a dry cracked voice that suggested the rattle of fodder on dead stalks. She cried aloud like a child, for she had never learned to suppress a genuine sob. Her slight old frame shook heavily and seemed hardly able to sustain such violent grief.

"What's the matter, baby?" Jeff asked awkwardly. "Why you cryin' like all that?"

"I's jes thinkin'," she said.

"So you the one what's scairt now, hunh?"

"I ain't scairt, Jeff. I's jes thinkin' 'bout leavin' eve'thing like this—eve'thing we been used to. It's right sad-like."

Jeff did not answer, and presently Jennie buried her face again and cried.

The sun was almost overhead. It beat down furiously on the dusty wagon-path road, on the parched roadside grass and the tiny battered car. Jeff's hands, gripping the wheel, became wet with perspiration; his forehead sparkled. Jeff's lips parted. His mouth shaped a hideous grimace. His face suggested the face of a man being burned. But the torture passed and his expression softened again.

"You mustn't cry, baby," he said to his wife. "We gotta be strong. We can't break down."

Jennie waited a few seconds, then said, "You reckon we oughta do it, Jeff? You reckon we oughta go 'head an' do it, really?"

Jeff's voice choked; his eyes blurred. He was terrified to hear Jennie say the thing that had been in his mind all morning. She had egged him on when he had wanted more than anything in the world to wait, to reconsider, to think things over a little longer. Now she was getting cold feet. Actually there was no need of thinking the question through again. It would only end in making the same painful decision once more. Jeff knew that. There was no need of fooling around longer.

"We jes as well to do like we planned," he said. "They ain't nothin' else for us now—it's the bes' thing."

Jeff thought of the handicaps, the near impossibility, of making another crop with his leg bothering him more and more each week. Then there was always the chance that he would have another stroke, like the one that had made him lame. Another one might kill him. The least it could do would be to leave him helpless. Jeff gasped—Lord, Jesus! He could not bear to think of being helpless, like a baby, on Jennie's hands. Frail, blind Jennie.

The little pounding motor of the car worked harder and harder. The puff of steam from the cracked radiator became larger. Jeff realized that they were climbing a little rise. A moment later the road turned abruptly and he looked down upon the face of the river.

"Jeff."

"Hunh?"

"Is that the water I hear?"

"Hm. Tha's it."

"Well, which way you goin' now?"

"Down this-a way," he said. "The road runs 'long 'side o' the water a lil piece."

She waited a while calmly. Then she said, "Drive faster."

"A'right, baby," Jeff said.

The water roared in the bed of the river. It was fifty or sixty feet below the level of the road. Between the road and the water there was a long smooth slope, sharply inclined. The slope was dry, the clay hardened by prolonged summer heat. The water below, roaring in a narrow channel, was noisy and wild.

"Jeff."

"Hunh?"

"How far you goin'?"

"Jes a lil piece down the road."

"You ain't scairt, is you, Jeff?"

"Nah, baby," he said trembling. "I ain't scairt."

"Remember how we planned it, Jeff. We gotta do it like we said. Brave-like."

"Hm."

Jeff's brain darkened. Things suddenly seemed unreal, like figures in a dream. Thoughts swam in his mind foolishly, hysterically, like little blind fish in a pool within a dense cave. They rushed, crossed one another, jostled, collided, retreated and rushed again. Jeff soon became dizzy. He shuddered violently and turned to his wife.

"Jennie, I can't do it. I can't." His voice broke pitifully.

She did not appear to be listening. All the grief had gone from her face. She sat erect, her unseeing eyes wide open, strained and frightful. Her glossy black skin had become dull. She seemed as thin, as sharp and bony, as a starved bird. Now, having suffered and endured the sadness of tearing herself away from beloved things, she showed no anguish. She was absorbed with her own thoughts, and she didn't even hear Jeff's voice shouting in her ear.

Jeff said nothing more. For an instant there was light in his cavernous brain. The great chamber was, for less than a second, peopled by characters he knew and loved. They were simple, healthy creatures, and they behaved in a manner that he could understand. They had quality. But since he had already taken leave of them long ago, the remembrance did not break his heart again. Young Jeff Patton was among them, the Jeff Patton of fifty years ago who went down to New Orleans with a crowd of country boys to the Mardi Gras doings. The gay young crowd, boys with candy-striped shirts and rouged-down girls in noisy silks, was like a picture in his head. Yet it did not make him sad. On that very trip Slim Burns had killed Joe Beasley—the crowd had been broken up. Since then Jeff Patton's world had been the Greenbriar Plantation. If there had been other Mardi Gras carnivals, he had not heard of them. Since then there had been no time; the years had fallen on him like waves. Now he was old, worn out. Another paralytic stroke (like the one he had already suffered) would put him on his back for keeps. In that condition, with a frail blind woman to look after him, he would be worse off than if he were dead.

Suddenly Jeff's hands became steady. He actually felt brave. He slowed down the motor of the car and carefully pulled off the road. Below, the water of the stream boomed, a soft thunder in the deep channel. Jeff ran the car onto the clay slope, pointed it directly toward the stream and put his foot heavily on the accelerator. The little car leaped furiously down the steep incline toward the water. The movement was nearly as swift and direct as a fall. The two old black folks, sitting quietly side by side, showed no excitement. In another instant the car hit the water and dropped immediately out of sight.

A little later it lodged in the mud of a shallow place. One wheel of the crushed and upturned little Ford became visible above the rushing water.

38

A Place for Mother

Joanne Seltzer

Preliminary Advice

Remember how you once went shopping
for the right nursery school
and when the teacher asked you if your
      child was toilet trained
you lied and said she was.

Use the same strategy
in shopping for a nursing home.

Later—when you are told
of Mother's incontinence—
you will clench your fist and shout:
"What have you done to my mother?"

More Advice

Have a daughter-to-mother talk.
Ask her what she wants.
If she doesn't know
ask her if she's happy.
She will either say
she doesn't know
or she will be silent.
Tell her how much you love her.
Promise you won't forsake her.

A Checklist

Place One has an eight-year waiting list.
Place Two has a nursing home odor.
Place Three is in a bad neighborhood.
Place Four is in another city.
Place Five won't take medicaid.
Place Six takes only terminal cases.

Place Seven doesn't offer therapy.
Place Eight puts three in a room.
Place Nine requires a hike to the dining
      room.
Place Ten demands Mother's money up
      front.
Place Eleven decides Mother won't fit in.

The Search

Though Mother says
she won't fit in anywhere
you keep on looking.

You learn about levels of care,
levels of caring.

The Jewish Home offers
a night in the Rabbi's room
when the Rabbi isn't there

to newly matched couples
who hanker after
geriatric sex.

A Sudden Illness

When Mother is discharged
from the hospital
you accompany her down
on the same elevator
with a young couple
bringing Baby home.

They call to mind
the Holy Family
until you realize

that every family is holy.

You feel holier-than-thou.

Confusion

While you ponder your choices
Mother continues to slip.

She thinks she will go to jail
for being a dope addict.

She thinks there's a conspiracy
against the family.

She worries about the poison
in the drinking water.

Though people call her *lady*
she isn't sure if she's a woman
or a man.

Platitudes

Mother is with God.
Mother is at rest.
Mother is with Dad.

Mother was ready to go.
Mother has paid her dues.
Mother is still with us.

Mother loved life.
Mother lived a full life.

Time heals all wounds.
You will mourn Mother
the rest of your life.

The Orphan

There's no umbrella now
to separate you
from eternity.

Meanwhile an army
marches behind you
in the rain.

Your friends are dead
or dying.

You're a survivor
with all the loneliness
of survivorship.
Life Must Go On

Your hair has turned white.
Your skin is parchment.
You have a bulldog's jowls.

You ask yourself
what Mother's face is doing
in the mirror.

She sticks out her tongue.

You wonder where the years went
and with horror
realize you forgot to flush
the toilet.

In Conclusion

Not wanting to be a burden
on your children
you sign yourself into
a nursing home.

You become active
in every group
and serve on every committee.

You are voted
resident-of-the-month,
a role model.
Mother would be proud of you.

My Most Humiliating Jim Crow Experience

Zora Neale Hurston

My most humiliating Jim Crow experience came in New York instead of the South as one would have expected. It was in 1931 when Mrs. R. Osgood Mason was financing my researches in anthropology. I returned to New York from the Bahama Islands ill with some disturbances of the digestive tract.

Godmother (Mrs. Mason liked for me to call her Godmother) became concerned about my condition and suggested a certain white specialist at her expense. His office was in Brooklyn.

Mr. Paul Chapin called up and made the appointment for me. The doctor told the wealthy and prominent Paul Chapin that I would get the best of care.

So two days later I journeyed to Brooklyn to submit myself to the care of the great specialist.

His reception room was more than swanky, with a magnificent hammered copper door and other decor on the same plane as the door.

But his receptionist was obviously embarrassed when I showed up. I mentioned the appointment and got inside the door. She went into the private office and stayed a few minutes, then the doctor appeared in the door all in white, looking very important, and also very unhappy from behind his rotund stomach.

He did not approach me at all, but told one of his nurses to take me into a private examination room.

The room was private all right, but I would not rate it highly as an examination room. Under any other circumstances, I would have sworn it was a closet where the soiled towels and uniforms were tossed until called for by the laundry. But I will say this for it, there was a chair in there wedged in between the wall and the pile of soiled linen.

The nurse took me in there, closed the door quickly and disappeared. The doctor came in immediately and began in a desultory manner to ask me about my symptoms. It was evident he meant to get me off the premises as quickly as possible. Being the sort of objective person I am, I did not get up and sweep out angrily as I was first disposed to do. I stayed to see just what would happen and further to torture him more. He went through some motions, stuck a tube down my throat to extract some bile from my gall bladder, wrote a prescription and asked for twenty dollars as fee.

I got up, set my hat at a reckless angle and walked out, telling him that I would send him a check, which I never did. I went away feeling the pathos of Anglo-Saxon civilization.

And I still mean pathos, for I know that anything with such a false foundation cannot last. Whom the gods would destroy, they first made mad.

Public Health Then and Now:
The Tuskegee Syphilis Study, 1932 to 1972

Stephen B. Thomas
Sandra Crouse Quinn

How Did It Go on for So Long?

The Tuskegee study of untreated syphilis in the Negro male is the longest nontherapeutic experiment on human beings in medical history. Numerous factors contributed to the continuation of this experiment over a period of 40 years. However, almost from the outset, its scientific merit was questionable.

The Alabama state health officer and the Macon County Board of Health extracted a promise from the PHS that all who were tested and found to be positive for syphilis, including those selected for the study, would receive treatment. It was understood by all, except the subjects, that the treatment given was less than the amount recommended by the PHS to cure syphilis. By the late 1930s some physicians began to raise concerns regarding the scientific merit of a study about untreated syphilis when it was clear that some subjects had received some form of treatment. In 1938, removal of these men from the experiment was briefly considered, but it was decided that in the interest of maintaining esprit de corps among the participants and in order to avoid suspicion, those men who had received minimal treatment would remain in the experimental group.

The ultimate tragedy of the Tuskegee experiment was exemplified by the extraordinary measures taken to ensure that subjects in the experimental group did not receive effective treatment. During World War II, approximately 50 of the syphilitic cases received letters from the local draft board ordering them to take treatment. At the request of the PHS, the draft board agreed to exclude the men in the study from its list of draftees needing treatment. According to Jones:

[Preventing] the men from receiving treatment had always been a violation of Alabama's public health statutes requiring public reporting and prompt treatment of venereal diseases.... Under the auspices of the law health officials conducted the largest state-level testing and treatment program in the history of the nation [but] state and local health officials continued to cooperate with the study. (p. 178)

In 1943, the PHS began to administer penicillin to syphilitic patients in selected treatment clinics across the nation. The men of the Tuskegee Syphilis Study were excluded from this treatment for the same reason other drugs had been withheld since the beginning of the study in 1932—treatment would end the study. Once penicillin became the standard of treatment for syphilis in 1951, the

PHS insisted that it was all the more urgent for the Tuskegee study to continue because "it made the experiment a never-again-to-be-repeated opportunity" (p. 179).

In 1952, in an effort to reach subjects who had moved out of Macon County, the PHS utilized its entire national network of state and local health departments for the first time in its history in order to bring subjects in for examination. Over the next 20 years, state and local health departments cooperated in keeping the men in the study, yet denying treatment.

According to Jones, the ultimate reason why the Tuskegee Syphilis Study went on for 40 years was a minimal sense of personal responsibility and ethical concern among the small group of men within the PHS who controlled the study. This attitude was reflected in a 1976 interview conducted by Jones with Dr. John Heller, Director of Venereal Diseases at the PHS from 1943 to 1948, who stated, "The men's status did not warrant ethical debate. They were subjects, not patients; clinical material, not sick people" (p. 179).

Jones details the following chronology of events leading to the end of the Tuskegee Syphilis Study:

November 1966. Peter Buxtun, a venereal disease interviewer and investigator with the PHS in San Francisco, sent a letter to Dr. William Brown, Director of the Division of Venereal Diseases, to express his moral concerns about the experiment. He inquired whether any of the men had been treated properly and whether any had been told the nature of the study.

November 1968. Buxtun wrote Dr. Brown a second letter, in which he described the current racial unrest prevalent in the nation. Buxtun made the point that "the racial composition of the study group [100% Negro] supported the thinking of Negro militants that Negroes have long been used for medical experiments and teaching cases in the emergency wards of county hospitals . . ." (p. 193). Dr. Brown showed this letter to the Director of the Centers for Disease Control. For the first time, health officials saw the experiment as a public relations problem that could have severe political repercussions.

February 1969. The CDC convened a blue-ribbon panel to discuss the Tuskegee study. The group reviewed all aspects of the experiment and decided against treating the men. This decision ended debate on the Tuskegee study's future: It would continue until "end point." The committee also recommended that a major thrust be made to upgrade the study scientifically.

In the final analysis, it was Peter Buxtun who stopped the Tuskegee Syphilis Study by telling his story to a reporter with the Associated Press. On July 25, 1972, the *Washington Star* ran a front-page story about the experiment. It is important to note that the PHS was still conducting the experiment on the day when the story broke.

41

Doña Toña of Nineteenth Street

Louie the Foot González

Her name was Doña Toña and I can't help but remember the fear I had of the old lady. Maybe it was the way all the younger kids talked about her:

"Ya, man. I saw her out one night and she was pulling some weeds near the railroad tracks and her cat was meowing away like it was ready to fight that big black dog and, man, she looked just like a witch, like the Llorona trying to dig up her children."

"Martin's tellin' everybody that she was dancin' aroun' real slow and singin' some witch songs in her backyard when it was dark and everybody was asleep."

Doña Toña was always walking somewhere . . . anywhere . . . even when she had no particular place to go. When she walked, it was as though she were making a great effort because her right leg was kind of funny. It dragged a little and it made her look as if her foot were made of solid metal.

Her face was the color of lightly creamed coffee. The wrinkles around her forehead and eyes were like the rings of a very old tree. They gave her age as being somewhere around seventy-five years old, but as I was to discover later, she was really eighty-nine. Even though her eyes attracted much attention, they always gave way to her mouth. Most of the people that I had observed looking at her directed their gaze at her mouth. Doña Toña had only one tooth to her name and it was the strangest tooth I had ever seen. It was exceptionally long and it stuck out from her upper gum at a forty-five degree angle. What made it even stranger was that it was also twisted. She at one time probably had an overabundance of teeth, until they began to push against each other, twisting themselves, until she had only one last tooth left. It was the toughest of them all, the king of the hill, 'el mero chingón.'

Doña Toña was born in 1885 in one of the innumerable little towns of México. The Mexican Revolution of 1910 drove her from her little-town home when she was twenty-seven years old. She escaped the mass bloodshed of the Revolution by crossing the border into the United States and living in countless towns from Los Angeles to Sacramento, where she became the most familiar sight in Barrio Cinco. She was one of the barrio's landmarks; when you saw her, you knew that you were in the barrio. She had been there longer than anyone else and yet no one, except perhaps her daughter Maria, knew very much about her. Some people said that was the way she wanted it. But as far as I could see, she didn't show signs of wanting to be alone.

Whenever Doña Toña caught someone watching her during one of her never-ending strolls, she would stop walking and look at that person head-on. No one could keep staring at her once she had started to stare back. There was something in Doña Toña's stare that could make anybody feel like a child. Her crow-black eyes could hypnotize almost anybody. She could have probably put an owl to sleep with her stare.

* * *

Doña Toña was Little Feo's grandmother. She lived with her daughter, Maria, who was Little Feo's mother. All of Little Feo's ten years of life had passed without the outward lovingness that grandmothers are supposed to show. But the reason for it was Little Feo's own choice.

Whenever Little Feo, who was smaller, thinner, and darker than the rest of the barrio ten years olds, was running around with us (Danny, Fat Charlie, Bighead, Joe Nuts, and a few other guys that lived close by) nobody would say anything about his "abuelita." Before, whenever anybody used to make fun of her or use her for the punchline of a joke, Little Feo would get very quiet; his fists would begin to tighten and his face would turn a darker shade as all his blood rushed to his brain. One time when Fat Charlie said something like, "What's black and flies at night? Why . . . it's Feo's granny," Little Feo pounced on him faster than I had ever seen anybody pounce on someone before. Fat Charlie kicked the hell out of Little Feo, but he never cracked another joke like that again, at least not about Doña Toña.

Doña Toña was not taken very seriously by very many people until someone in the barrio got sick. Visits to Doctor Herida when someone got sick were common even though few people liked to go to him because he would just look at the patient and then scribble something on a prescription form and tell the sick one to take it next door to McAnaws Pharmacy to have it filled. Herida and the pharmacist had a racket going. When the medicine Herida prescribed didn't have the desired effect, the word was sent out in the barrio that Doña Toña was needed somewhere. Sometimes it was at the Osorio house, where Jaime was having trouble breathing, or the Canaguas place, where what's-her-name was gaining a lot of weight. Regardless of the illness, Doña Toña would always show up, even if she had to drag herself across the barrio to get to where she was needed and, many times, that's exactly what she did. Once at the place of need, she did whatever it was she had to and then she left asking nothing of

anyone. Usually, within a short time of her visit—hours (if the illness were a natural one) or a day or two (if it were supernatural)—the patient would show signs of improvement.

Doña Toña was never bothered about not receiving any credit for her efforts.

"You see, comadre, I tol' you the medicina would estar' to work."

"Ándale, didn't I tell you that Doctor Herida knew what he was doing?"

"I didn't know what that stupid old lady thought she was going to accomplish by doing all the hocus-pocus with those useless herbs and plants of hers. Everybody knows that an old witch's magic is no match for a doctor's medicine. That crazy old WITCH."

And that's how it was. Doña Toña didn't seem to mind that they called on her to help them and, after she had done what she could, they proceeded to badmouth her. But that's the way it was and she didn't seem to mind.

I remember, perhaps best of all, the time my mother got sick. She was very pale and her whole body was sore. She went to see Doctor Herida and all he did was ask *her* what was wrong and, without even examining her, he prescribed something that she bought at McAnaws. When all the little blue pills were gone the soreness of her bones and the paleness of her skin remained. Not wanting to go back to Herida's, my mother asked me to go get Doña Toña. I would have never gone to get the old lady, but I had never before seen my mother so sick. So I went.

On the way to Little Feo's house, which was only three blocks from my own, I saw Doña Toña walking towards me. When she was close enough to hear me, I began to speak but she cut me off, saying that she knew my mother was sick and had asked for her. I got a little scared because there was no way that she could have known that my mother had asked for her, yet she knew. My head was bombarded with thoughts that perhaps she might be a witch after all. I had the urge to run away from her but I didn't. I began to think that if she were a witch, why was she always helping people? Witches were bad people. And Doña Toña wasn't. It was at this point that my fear of her disappeared and, in its place, sprouted an intense curiosity.

Doña Toña and I reached my house and we climbed the ten steps that led to the front door. I opened the door and waited for her to step in first, but she motioned with her hand to me to lead the way.

Doña Toña looked like a little moving shadow as we walked through the narrow hallway that ended at my mother's room. Her leg dragged across the old faded linoleum floor making a dull scraping sound. I reached the room and opened the door. My mother was half-asleep on the bed as Doña Toña entered. I walked in after her because I wanted to see what kind of magic she was going to have to perform in order to save my mother; but as soon as Doña Toña began taking some candles from her sack, my mother looked at me and told me to go outside to play with the other kids.

I left the room but had no intentions of going outside to play. My mother's bedroom was next to the bathroom and there was a door that connected both of them. The bathroom could be locked only from the inside, so my mother usually left it unlocked in case some unexpected emergency came up. I went into the bathroom and, without turning on the light, looked through the crack of the slightly open door.

My mother was sprawled on the bed, face down. Her night gown was open exposing her shoulder blades and back. Doña Toña melted the bottoms of two candles and then placed one between the shoulder blades and the other at the base of the spine. Doña Toña began to pray as she pinched the area around the candles. Her movements were almost imperceptible. The candlelight made her old brown hands shine and her eyes looked like little moons. Doña Toña's voice got louder as her hands moved faster across my mother's back. The words she prayed were indecipherable even with the increase in volume. The scene reminded me of a priest praying in Latin during Mass, asking God to save us from damnation while no one knew what he was saying. The wax from the candles slid down onto my mother's back and shoulder blades, forming what looked like roots. It looked as though there were two trees of wax growing out of her back.

About a half an hour went by before the candles had burned themselves into oblivion, spreading wax all over my mother's back. Doña Toña stopped praying and scraped the wax away. She reached into the sack and pulled out a little baby food jar half-filled with something that resembled lard. She scooped some of the stuff out with her hand and rubbed it over the areas that had been covered by the wax. Next, she took from the sack a coffee can filled with an herb that looked like oregano. She sprinkled the herb over the lardlike substance and began rubbing it into the skin.

When she was almost finished, Doña Toña looked around the room and stared straight into the dark opening of the bathroom. I felt that she knew I was behind the door but I stayed there anyway. She turned back to face my mother, bent down, and whispered something in her ear.

Doña Toña picked up all her paraphernalia and returned it to its place in the sack. As she started to leave, she headed for the bathroom door. The heart in my chest almost exploded before I heard my mother's voice tell Doña Toña that she was leaving through the wrong door.

I hurried from the bathroom and ran through the other rooms in the house so that I could catch Doña Toña to show her the way out. I reached her as she was closing the door to my mother's room and led her to the front of the house. As she was making her way down the stairs I heard her mumble something about "learning the secrets" then she looked up at me and smiled. I couldn't help but smile back because her face looked like a brown jack-o-lantern with only one strange tooth carved into it. Doña Toña turned to walk down the remaining four stairs. I was going to ask her what she had said, but by the time I had the words formed in my mind, she had reached the street and was on her way home.

I went back inside the house and looked in on my mother. She was asleep. I knew that she was going to be all right and that it was not going to be because the "medicina" was beginning to work or because Doctor Herida knew what he was doing.

42

The Kitchen God's Wife

Amy Tan

I meant to tell her. There were several times when I planned to do exactly that. When I was first diagnosed, I said, "Ma, you know that slight problem with my leg I told you about. Well, thank God, it turned out *not* to be cancer, but—"

And right away, she told me about a customer of hers who had just died of cancer, how long he had suffered, how many wreaths the family had ordered. "Long time ago I saw that mole growing on his face," she said. "I told him, Go see a doctor. No problem, he said, age spot—didn't do anything about it. By the time he died, his nose and cheek—all eaten away!" And then she warned me sternly, "That's why you have to be careful."

When Cleo was born, without complications on my part or hers, I again started to tell my mother. But she interrupted me, this time to lament how my father was not there to see his grandchildren. And then she went into her usual endless monologue about my father getting a fate he didn't deserve.

My father had died of stomach cancer when I was fourteen. And for years, my mother would search in her mind for the causes, as if she could still undo the disaster by finding the reason why it had occurred in the first place.

"He was such a good man," my mother would lament. "So why did he die?" And sometimes she cited God's will as the reason, only she gave it a different twist. She said it must have been because my father was a minister. "He listened to everyone else's troubles," she said. "He swallowed them until he

made himself sick. Ai! *Ying-gai* find him another job."

Ying-gai was what my mother always said when she meant, I should have. *Ying-gai* meant she should have altered the direction of fate, she should have prevented disaster. To me, *Ying-gai* meant my mother lived a life of regrets that never faded with time.

If anything, the regrets grew as she searched for more reasons underlying my father's death. One time she cited her own version of environmental causes—that the electrician had been sick at the time he rewired our kitchen. "He built that sickness right into our house," she declared. "It's true. I just found out the electrician died—of cancer, too. *Ying-gai* pick somebody else."

And there was also this superstition, what I came to think of as her theory of the Nine Bad Fates. She said she had once heard that a person is destined to die if eight bad things happen. If you don't recognize the eight ahead of time and prevent them, the ninth one is always fatal. And then she would ruminate over what the eight bad things might have been, how she should have been sharp enough to detect them in time.

To this day it drives me crazy, listening to her various hypotheses, the way religion, medicine, and superstition all merge with her own beliefs. She puts no faith in other people's logic—to her, logic is a sneaky excuse for tragedies, mistakes, and accidents. And according to my mother, *nothing* is an accident. She's like a Chinese version of Freud, or worse. Everything has a reason. Everything could have been prevented. The last time I was at her house, for example, I knocked over a framed picture of my father and broke the glass. My mother picked up the shards and moaned, "Why did this happen?" I thought it was a rhetorical question at first, but then she said to me, "Do you know?"

"It was an accident." I said. "My elbow bumped into it." And of course, her question had sent my mind racing, wondering if my clumsiness was a symptom of deterioration.

"Why this picture?" she muttered to herself.

So I never told my mother. At first I didn't want to hear her theories on my illness, what caused this to happen, how she should have done this or that to prevent it. I did not want her to remind me.

And now that so much time has gone by, the fact that I still haven't told her makes the illness seem ten times worse. I am always reminded, whenever I see her, whenever I hear her voice.

Mary knows that, and that's why I still get mad at her—not because she trips over herself to avoid talking about my medical condition. I'm mad because she told *her* mother, my Auntie Helen.

"I had to tell her," she explained to me in an offhand sort of way. "She was always saying to me, Tell Pearl to visit her mother more often, only a one-hour drive. Tell Pearl she should ask her mother to move in with her, less lonely for her mother that way. Finally, I told my mother I couldn't tell you those things. And she asked why not." Mary shrugged. "You know my mother. I couldn't lie to her. Of course, I made her *swear* not to tell your mother, that you were going to tell her yourself."

"I can drive," I told Mary. "And that's not the reason why I haven't asked my mother to live with me." And then I glared at her. "How could you do this?"

"She won't say anything." Mary said. "I made her promise." And then she added a bit defiantly, "Besides, you should have told your mother a long time ago."

Mary and I didn't exactly have a fight, but things definitely chilled between us after that. She already knew that was about the worst possible thing she could have done to me. Because she had done it once before, nine years ago, when I confided to her that I was pregnant. My first pregnancy had ended in a miscarriage early on, and my mother had gone on and on about how much coffee I drank, how it was my jogging that did it, how Phil should make sure I ate more. So when I became pregnant again, I decided to wait, to tell my mother when I was in my fourth month or so. But in the third month, I made the mistake of confiding in Mary. And Mary slipped this news to her mother. And Auntie Helen didn't exactly tell my mother. But when my mother proudly announced my pregnancy to the Kwongs, Auntie Helen immediately showed my mother the little yellow sweater she had already handknit for the baby.

I didn't stop hearing the laments from my mother, even after Tessa was born. "Why could you tell the Kwongs, not your own mother?" she'd complain. When she stewed over it and became really angry, she accused me of making her look like a fool: "Hnh! Auntie Helen was pretending to be so surprised, so innocent. 'Oh, I didn't knit the sweater for Pearl's baby,' she said, 'I made it just in case.' "

So far, Auntie Helen had kept the news about my medical condition to herself. But this didn't stop her from treating me like an invalid. When I used to go to her house, she would tell me to sit down right away, while she went to find me a pillow for my back. She would rub her palm up and down my arm, asking me how I was, telling me how she had always thought of me as a daughter. And then she would sigh and confess some bit of bad news, as if to balance out what she already knew about me.

"Your poor Uncle Henry, he almost got laid off last month," she would say. "So many budget cuts now. Who knows what's going to happen? Don't tell your mother. I don't want her to worry over us."

And then "I" would worry that Auntie Helen would think her little confessions were payment in kind, that she would take them as license to accidentally slip and tell my mother: "Oh, Winnie, I thought you knew about your daughter's tragedy."

And so I dreaded the day my mother would call and ask me a hundred different ways, "Why did Auntie Helen know? Why did you never tell me? Why didn't you let me prevent this from happening to you?"

And then what answer could I give?

43

A Chief and Her People

Wilma Mankiller
Michael Wallis

Sherry and I were about the same age, but other than that simple fact, there were very few similarities between us—at least on the surface. For example, Sherry came from the Deep South, a totally different background, lifestyle, and culture than mine. A strikingly beautiful woman, she had been concerned with her physical looks as a girl and young woman. But even though she was a former beauty queen and had been a first runner-up for Miss Mississippi, we hit it right off when we met. Sherry became one of my best friends.

Sherry was just beginning to come into her own as a person. She had finally stopped being so concerned with her physical self, and was starting to turn inside as well as looking beyond at the world around her. Over time, rural health-care issues and early child development became her primary interests. She also was so great with Meagan, her exceptional three-year-old daughter. It was good to see how Sherry nurtured her child. As someone who had experienced my own evolution into a more independent woman, I felt privileged to be able to watch Sherry grow and find her own path.

Then something happened. Something beyond tragedy occurred. It took place on November 8, 1979, a Thursday. A sign, an omen that calamity was approaching had showed up at my house the night before.

That evening, my second cousin Byrd Wolfe and his wife, Paggy, came to visit me at Mankiller Flats. Byrd was very active at the Flint ceremonial grounds in our community, and Paggy was a shell shaker at our ceremonial dances. We sat and talked of the world of Cherokee medicine—a special world that few outsiders realize still exists to this day. The Cherokee Nation and our people have a well-known reputation for being able to adapt to the non-Indian world and of running a well-organized tribal government. But what people do not realize is that we live within two realities, and the two are very different. One reality is the acceptance of and ability to deal with the non-Indian world around us, and the other reality is our being able to hold onto and retain our ancient Cherokee belief systems, values, customs, and rituals.

An essential part of our belief system in some communities is the belief in the power of medicine people. That evening at my home, we discussed those practitioners. We sat around the fire burning in my stove, and we talked about how medicine people usually practice two kinds of old medicine. One type requires the use of herbs, roots, and other gifts of creation for curing, for something as simple as a headache or as complex as a blood ailment. The other type draws on ancient tribal rituals and customs, which sometimes include songs, incantations, and other thoughts or acts. Many of the prescriptions and rituals are preserved in medicine books written in Cherokee and passed down from medicine person to medicine person.

That November evening, our conversation turned to the use of medicine to settle disputes or cause harm. As time passed, the gist of our talk centered on how, even in contemporary Cherokee society, some of our people still use medicine to "settle scores."

As the three of us sat near the fire and continued to talk about medicine, we became aware of a presence outside my house. We heard sounds coming from the darkness, and we looked out the windows into the night. There were movements in the trees. Then we saw the owls—some were in flight, and others were sitting in the branches. We heard their voices.

Some Cherokee, including my own family, are taught to beware of owls. We were told that a *dedonsek*, "one who makes bad medicine," could change into an owl and travel through the night skies to visit Cherokee homes. That usually brought bad luck. I had heard stories that if owls came close to the house, it often meant bad news was coming. Just the hooting of an owl could make some people wary. In eastern Oklahoma, there are still Cherokee tales of *Estekene*, the Owl, who can change shape to appear in almost any form. Other native peoples also consider the owl to be a powerful figure of death in their tribal legends. They throw rocks and sticks at owls that gather near their homes.

That November evening, my house was surrounded by owls. They were everywhere. Despite what I had been taught as a child, owls normally do not bother me as long as they keep some distance. But these owls did not do that. They came very close to my house, and made all sorts of loud noises. All of the owl activity, coupled with our conversation, made me feel very uneasy. Later, after my cousin and his wife had left and I was alone with my two daughters, the owls were still there.

The Indian knows his village and feels for his village as no white man for his country, his town, or even his own bit of land. His village is not the strip of land four miles long and three miles wide that is his as long as the sun rises and the moon sets. The myths are the village, and the winds and rains. The rain is the village, and . . . the talking bird, the owl, who calls the name of the man who is going to die.

—Margaret Craven
I Heard the Owl Call My Name, 1973

I am not someone who experiences premonitions or visions. But even though I did not have a feeling that something bad was going to happen, a kind of uneasiness did wash over me. It was very unsettling.

The next morning, I arose and prepared to go to Tahlequah. I had not missed any classes prior to that time, so I planned to take the day off from college to speak to the personnel director at the Cherokee Nation about working on a study to pick up some extra cash. At the time, I was living on about three hundred dollars per month from my graduate assistantship, a few grants, and food given to me by my Cheyenne friend, Jerri Warledo. I needed the extra money for necessities.

Just as I headed out the front door, something on the television caught my eye, and I stopped for a few minutes to watch. I cannot even recall exactly what it was. The hostage crisis in Iran had just erupted, so perhaps it was a newscast that made me stop. Much later, I thought about how my stopping to watch television threw my routine off and changed my timing slightly, although it did not cause me to hurry.

I left my home and got on the road. As I always did, I drove my station wagon up the backcountry roads until I reached Highway 100. Everything seemed perfectly normal. I was only about three miles from my house, going up a slight grade. On the other side of the hill, a car headed for Stilwell pulled out to pass two other cars that were going slowly. There was a blind spot at that point, and the driver of that other car did not see me. I did not see the other car until it was too late. I came up to the top of the hill, and there was that car in my lane bearing down on me. In a split second, I realized we were about to collide. I tried to veer to the right, but it did no good. Our automobiles crashed head-on.

I have little recollection of what happened after the collision. I faintly remember people screaming at each other, trying to figure out how to extract me from the wreckage of my car. The front of my auto was pushed back so far that the edge of the hood cut into my neck. My face was literally crushed. My right leg was very severely crushed, and my left leg and ankles were broken. So were many of my ribs. There was blood all over the place, pouring from cuts and abrasions. Death was very near. I felt it.

Two ambulances tore down the two-lane asphalt highway to the scene of the crash. Of course, I had no way of knowing it at the time, but there was only one person from the other vehicle involved in the accident. Only much later would I find out that the other victim was also a woman. Her car was much smaller than my station wagon, and sustained even more damage. She lived only a short time. Unbelievably, she was someone I knew. She was my friend—my very good friend. The woman who died was Sherry Morris.

The odds of two friends crashing into each other on a rural road had to be quite low. I had seen Sherry earlier that week. We had made plans to go together to Arkansas to hunt for antiques. She was anxious to find an oak table. Her husband, Mike, was away at an educational conference. Fortunately, their daughter, Meagan, was not with Sherry on that fateful ride when our cars collided.

One of the ambulances carried Sherry to Tahlequah, but her neck was broken, and they knew she was dead before arrival at the hospital. I was taken to Stilwell, where I was stabilized. From there, they quickly transported me to a larger hospital in Fort Smith. I faded in and out of consciousness. As the ambulance sped down the highway, I believe I was really trying to die. It was such a wonderful feeling! That is the best way to describe what I felt. I was dying, yet it was all so beautiful and spiritual. I experienced a tremendous sense of peacefulness and warmth. It was probably the most profound experi-

ence I have ever had. All these years later, I can still recall how it felt, but it is difficult to explain. It was overwhelming and powerful. It was a feeling that was better than anything that had ever happened to me. It was better than falling in love.

I had this feeling all the while the ambulance raced me to the hospital. There was a woman there in the ambulance. I later learned she straddled me and tried to stop me from dying. She fought to keep me alive. But there was this tremendous pull toward what seemed to be an overpowering love. The woman was pulling me back toward life. I recall that while I was in that condition, Felicia and Gina came into my mind. Then I made an unconscious choice to return to life. I did not see any tunnels or white lights. There was none of that. It was more as if I came to fully understand that death is beautiful and spiritual. It is part of life, and when I finally came out of it, I vowed to hang onto that experience. I wished to retain that feeling, and I did so. As a result, I have lost any fear of death. I began to think of death as walking into spirit country rather than as a frightening event. Even though more brushes with death were ahead, the idea of dying no longer frightened me.

That first day, right after the accident, I was in surgery for six hours. Then I was taken into intensive care. Some of the people who were at the scene of the accident told me later that when I was pulled from the car, I was so badly mutilated they did not know if I was a man or a woman. I did not really wake up until a couple of days later. Then I realized I had been in an accident, and immediately I asked if there had been others involved, and my friends and family assured me that everything was OK. They wanted to shield me from the news about Sherry. For three weeks, I did not know what had happened. People would come into my hospital room, and I would ask about the other driver.

Friends and relatives came to visit, including Mike Morris, but I did not see Sherry, and I thought that was odd. I asked about her and was told that she was busy with something or other, but that did not seem to make much sense. She and Mike were close friends of mine, and I wondered why she was not with me. Then one day Mike spoke to my family and the doctors, and he asked to visit with me alone. He wanted to tell me the truth. Mike came into my room and said he had something to tell me. I thought it was going to be about his work or the mysterious project that was keeping Sherry away. But it was not. Instead he told me that the woman in the other car was Sherry, and that she was dead.

It was awful—truly awful. I do not remember much of what happened after that, but Mike says the shock and emotional pain were so severe that I began to cry uncontrollably, and then I began to hemorrhage from the many wounds in my face. Nurses and doctors rushed to the room to stop the bleeding.

My sister, who was waiting in the hall outside my room, said that a few minutes after Mike went into my room, she heard me scream. Much later that day, she visited me, but I did not acknowledge her presence for several hours. When she left, I asked her, "Did you go to her funeral?" She said, "Yes." I returned to my silent mourning.

Having to deal with the shock of Sherry's death, coupled with my own physical pain, made the suffering almost unbearable. For a very long time, I carried around my share of survivor's guilt. My relationship with Mike was difficult, but he had little or no emotional support, so I tried to be there for him and his daughter. He had a very hard time moving forward and escaping his deep depression.

Finally, Mike did get on his feet. There were bumpy times, but our friendship survived. He and little Meagan stayed on in Oklahoma for several years. Ultimately, they moved to Maine, where Mike became a dean at the University of New England. Later, he moved to New Mexico to pursue his career as a professional educator and to launch a multicultural university. Meagan joined her father in Albuquerque. She has grown into a bright, energetic young woman. During the George Bush years, Meagan was right there at Kennebunkport, picketing the Bush residence to protest the so-called Gulf War of 1991. That was a very brave thing for her to do, but Meagan is as socially conscious and as involved with issues as her mother was. Mike is proud of her, and I know Sherry is too.

Meanwhile, I had to keep moving forward. My own struggle with the many debilitating injuries was difficult, to say the least. My initial stay in the hospital lasted for more than eight weeks. During that time, there were many surgeries to put my face and shattered bones back together. Before it was all over, I would have to endure seventeen operations, mostly on my right leg. At one point, the doctors thought I would not walk again, and they even considered amputation. The pain was unbelievable, and I had to wear full casts on both legs. I was confined to a wheelchair for some time, and would be somewhat incapacitated for almost a year. I could not even go to the bathroom or brush my teeth without assistance. To this day, I am not sure how I managed to regain mobility.

But throughout the entire ordeal, I never allowed myself to become depressed—not once. I had faced death, and I had survived. I would not permit myself to sink into a negative state. Recovering at my home, I had the time to examine my life in a new way—to reevaluate and refocus. The entire family was a big help to me during those troubled times. My sister Linda came to my house every day for about six months. I will always be indebted to her. Mother also helped to care for my daughters, and our friends pitched in to see that our basic needs were fulfilled. I was so proud of my girls. They rolled with the punches. They did not allow the chaos in our lives to best them.

During the long healing process, I fell back on my Cherokee ways and adopted what our elders call "a Cherokee approach" to life. They say it is "being of good mind." That means one has to think positively, to take what is handed out and turn it into a better path. At the beginning of some Cherokee traditional prayers and healing ceremonies, everyone is asked to remove all negative things from the mind, to have a pure mind and heart for the prayer and the ceremony ahead. I tried to do that in the process of healing.

That accident changed my life. I had experienced death, felt its presence, touched it, and then let it go. It was a very spiritual thing, a rare natural gift. From that point on, I have always thought of myself as the woman who lived before and the woman who lives afterward.

Throughout the recuperation process, I made steady progress. I read and made plans and worked very hard at improving my physical self. I was determined not to have to wear leg braces. My goal was to get out and walk a quarter of a mile to the mailbox and back. At first, I could not even get out of my yard without tumbling onto the ground. I would become frustrated and angry at my helplessness, but I went back the next day and tried again. I started to make some real progress. Week by week, I got a little farther.

But my trials were far from over. I was to experience even more physical woes before I could even become weaned off the crutches from the automobile accident. All of this came just a few months after my first encounter with death. It was in early 1980, and I began to experience muscle problems. At first, it was relatively minor. For instance, I had a little trouble peeling a grapefruit and holding a pencil. Then it became worse. I dropped my hairbrush constantly and lost my grip. Before long, I could not even hold my toothbrush. Then I started to experience severe double vision. My sister Linda took me to several physicians, including an optometrist and neurologist. They did not help. They could not confirm any specific disease or ailment.

My strength was leaving me. I was growing weaker and weaker. Before too long, I lost control of my fingers, my hands, my arms. Then I could no longer stand up, even on my crutches. I would rise and then crumble and fall. I could speak only for short periods of time because my throat muscles would give out. My breathing became labored, and I could not hold my head up. I lost the ability

to chew except for very short periods of time. Soon, I had lost forty pounds. I was afraid to drink water because it would come out of my nose. Some days I could not keep my eyes open for very long, so I would just lie down and keep my eyes closed. That became my existence.

For someone who absorbed life visually, loved to read, and was always on the go, the inability to see things around me and to move about freely was particularly difficult. During that terrible period, Linda took me to Oklahoma City to visit Mary Barksdale, an activist lawyer and good friend. I lay on the back seat of the car all the way there to conserve my strength. When we drove up to Mary's house, Linda helped me out of the car with my crutches. As I started to walk toward the front door, my muscles suddenly gave out and I fell straight forward on the sidewalk. I broke my nose again, and blood gushed all over me. I began to choke. It was so awful.

After that experience, I came to the conclusion that I was destined to continue to erode until death took me. I clearly remember one night at my house when I was lying there on the couch and several of my brothers and sisters had come to visit. My breathing became more and more strained. I felt my old friend death approach me. Somehow, I knew what to do. I found that if I relaxed and closed my eyes, everything would get better, and that is what I did that night. I lay there absolutely still, and the moment passed.

Almost ten months after the automobile accident and seven months after my muscle problems started, I found out what was causing my condition. This revelation came on Labor Day in 1980. I was watching the television, and switched on the "Jerry Lewis Muscular Dystrophy Telethon." A woman appeared and described her muscle problems, and how she had come to be dependent on a respirator. As she talked, I began to think that her symptoms sounded so familiar. She spoke of subtle signs such as the drooping of an eyelid, difficulty with chewing, and immobility. Then it struck me—"My God! That is what I have!" The woman was describing myasthenia gravis, a form of muscular dystrophy that can lead to paralysis. Finally, I knew what was causing my awful problems.

The following week, Linda took me to Tulsa, and I met with the staff at the local Muscular Dystrophy Association and their physicians, and they conducted tests. My fears were well founded. I was immediately diagnosed with systemic myasthenia gravis.

I went to my sister's car and wept quietly. I was spent. I needed to collect my thoughts before proceeding. I thought about how I had somehow managed to get through the trauma of the automobile accident and Sherry's death, and then had faced the continuing problems with my legs and regaining use of my limbs. Now this had happened to me. I was stricken with a disease that most people had never even heard of. I was very discouraged, but I knew I could not give in. I went home and prepared to battle this latest assault on my physical self and spirit. I could feel the anger running through my body. I was determined to win. I drew on the strength of my ancestors and of present-day Cherokee medicine people, and on my own internal resolve to remove all negative factors from my life so I could focus on healing.

In November of 1980, I checked into a hospital in Tulsa and went through more tests and procedures. I quit smoking and worked very hard to prepare my body and mind for what lay ahead of me. The physicians presented me with various treatment options, including chest surgery to remove my thymus. I also understood that I would need to endure further treatment through high doses of steroids. Although this approach seemed drastic, it made complete sense. I did not want merely to cope with this disease—*I wanted to beat it.* I wanted to rid myself of it. I wanted it to go into total remission. That is why I opted for surgery.

The operation was successful. I felt a surge of strength when I woke up on a respirator after the surgery. Within less than a week after my surgery, I was up. I wanted to wash my hair and take care of myself. I was anxious to get on with living and my work. The surgery and the intensive drug program truly worked miracles. Although the drugs had side effects, such as causing a significant weight gain, the worst of my symptoms were completely gone within four to six weeks after the operation. I continued to experience moderate muscle dysfunction, but even that was under control in less than two years after the surgery. The drug therapy continued until late in 1985, yet I was able to return to my post with the Cherokee Nation in January of 1981.

Within only a very few years, I would became first of all deputy chief and then principal chief of the Cherokee Nation. That vision of the spiritual leader would come true. But none of that would have happened if it had not been for the ordeals I had survived in the first place. After that, I realized I could survive anything. I had faced adversity and turned it into a positive experience—a better path. I had found the way to be of good mind.

44

The Age-by-Race Gap in Health and Mortality in the Older Population: A Social Science Research Agenda[1]

Rose C. Gibson

Subdividing the age group 65 and over into finer age groups unmasks race differentials in mortality and morbidity that often favor blacks in the older age groups. This article describes the unusual phenomena and proposes a systematic research program to explain them.

Differentials that favor white Americans in the elderly population have been observed since health and mortality data have been collected. This black health and mortality disadvantage is not apparent in all age groups of the elderly, however. When the group 65 and over is subdivided, the black handicap in younger age groups narrows and frequently disappears in older age groups. These age-by-race differences are observed in all-cause and cause-specific mortality statistics and in certain health status data. Explanations of these unusual age-by-race disparities in mortality and health status should not be ignored if health prevention and health care programs are to accurately target needy groups of the elderly.

We first present evidence of age-by-race differentials in mortality and health status data. Next we discuss potential explanations of the differentials. We follow with a research agenda for identifying factors associated with the age-by-race irregularities.

Age-by-Race Differences in Mortality Data

When the age group 65 and over is examined as a whole, blacks are more disadvantaged in mortality than whites. dividing the group into finer age categories, however, uncovers race differentials in the older groups that do not always favor whites. Lower death rates for whites before about age 75 and lower rates for blacks after that age have been observed in U.S. vital statistics as far back as 1900 (Wing, Manton, Stallard, Haynes, & Tyroler, 1985) and in more recent data (Kasl & Berkman, 1981; Manton, 1982; Manton, Patrick, & Johnson, 1987; Manton & Soldo, 1985; Markides, 1983, 1989; Nam, Weatherby, & Ockay, 1978; Spiegelman, 1967; Thornton & Nam, 1968; Wing et al., 1985).

This unexplained reversal of the probability of dying in older age groups appears in a variety of studies and samples: for example, in a community-based longitudinally followed population (Wing et al., 1985); in period and cohort data (Hambright, 1969; Kitagawa & Hauser, 1973; Klebba, Maurer, & Glass, 1973; Zelnick, 1969) in a regional sample (Ford, Haug, Jones, Roy, & Folmar, 1990); and in a national probability sample (House, 1986, Americans Changing Lives [ACL]. In the ACL data, blacks in the youngest age

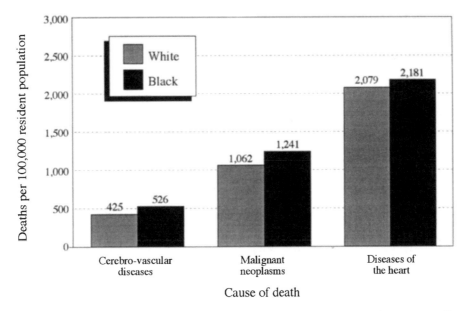

Figure 1. Deaths per 100,000 resident population for the three leading causes, for persons 65 years of age and over, according to race: United States, 1988.
SOURCE: National Vital Statistics System, and U.S. Bureau of the Census, Current Population Surveys.
NOTE: Numbers of deaths are rounded.

groups, 55–64 and 65–74, were more likely than comparable whites to die out of the sample between the first and second data collections. However, blacks in an older age group, 75–79, were less likely than their white agemates to die.

The age-by-race differences also are observed in cause-specific mortality data (National Center for Health Statistics, 1992). Examining the age group 65 and over without subdividing, blacks have higher death rates than whites for the three leading causes. In 1988, heart disease was the leading cause of death for both blacks and whites ages 65 and over, followed by malignant neoplasms and cerebrovascular diseases (Figure 1). Heart disease mortality for blacks was about 5% higher than for whites; cancer mortality was 17% higher for blacks, and cerebrovascular disease mortality 24% higher for blacks.

Disagreggating the 65 and over group, however, a black disadvantage is not apparent in every age group. Blacks in older age

groups gain the advantage over whites. The same phenomenon of black gain is illustrated by Manton's work (1982). Analyzing black-white relative mortality risk ratios for heart disease, cancer, stroke, generalized arteriosclerosis, and pneumonia in 1962, 1969, and 1975, he identified racial mortality crossovers in all five diseases in all three time periods. For example, among men in 1975, the ages of crossover for cancer, heart disease, stroke, generalized arteriosclerosis, and pneumonia mortality respectively were: 81, 76, 80, 79, and 79.

In this chapter we make a more recent comparison of 1960 and 1988 vital statistics which verifies Manton's earlier observations. The age-by-race differentials are evident and persisted over time. In 1960, death rates for men from diseases of the heart were higher for blacks than whites only in the youngest age groups, 55–64. After that age, rates were lower for black men (Figure 2). This black advantage widened considerably until at ages 85 and over, white men were about 1.7 times as likely as black men to die of heart

	1960					1988			
Age Group	White Men	Black Men	White Women	Black Women	Age Group	White Men	Black Men	White Women	Black Women
55-64	1,056	1,237	383	952	55-64	565	833	213	471
65-74	2,298	2,281	1,230	1,680	65-74	1,349	1,617	656	1,060
75-84	4,840	3,534	3,630	2,927	75-84	3,258	3,436	2,102	2,626
85+	10,136	6,038	9,281	5,650	85+	8,072	6,166	6,957	5,648

Figure 2. Deaths per 100,000 resident population for diseases of heart according to sex, race, and age: United States, 1960 and 1988.

SOURCE: Vital Statistics of the United States, Vol. 11, Mortality, Part A, for data years 1950–1988. National Center for Health Statistics.

NOTE: Rates are rounded.

	1960					1988			
Age Group	White Men	Black Men	White Women	Black Women	Age Group	White Men	Black Men	White Women	Black Women
55-64	451	580	329	443	55-64	509	750	372	454
65-74	887	938	562	542	65-74	1,050	1,434	660	728
75-84	1,414	1,053	939	696	75-84	1,840	2,344	984	1,063
85+	1,791	1,155	1,305	729	85+	2,533	2,720	1,300	1,288

Figure 3. Deaths per 100,000 resident population for malignant neoplasms according to sex, race, and age: United States, 1960 and 1988.

SOURCE: Vital Statistics of the United States, Vol. 11, Mortality, Part A, for data years 1950–1988. National Center for Health Statistics.

NOTE: Rates are rounded.

disease (the ages of crossover are boxed). By 1988, death rates were constantly higher for black than white men in all age groups except 85 and older.

For women in 1960, there was a black disadvantage in the two youngest groups, ages 55–64 and 65–74, but a black advantage in the two older groups, ages 75–84 and 85 and over. This edge of black women widened in the very oldest group. White women became more than 1.5 times as likely as black women to die of heart disease. By 1988, black women had higher rates than white women until

about age 85, when black women gained the mortality advantage.

Death rates for men from cancer (all sites) were higher in 1960 for blacks than whites up to about age 74 (Figure 3). After that age, rates were higher for white men. By 1988, however, this crossover had disappeared and death rates were higher for black than white men in all age groups. For women in 1960, the black advantage in cancer deaths began at about age 65, and widened steadily in the older age groups. In 1988, black women gained the advantage later, at about age 85.

	1960					1988			
Age Group	White Men	Black Men	White Women	Black Women	Age Group	White Men	Black Men	White Women	Black Women
55-64	139	440	103	452	55-64	50	146	37	106
65-74	501	899	383	830	65-74	164	326	125	265
75-84	1,565	1,475	1,445	1,413	75-84	591	796	513	701
85+	3,735	2,700	3,796	2,579	85+	1,667	1,303	1,767	1,518

Figure 4. Deaths per 100,000 resident population for cerebrovascular diseases according to sex, race, and age: United States, 1960 and 1988.

SOURCE: Vital Statistics of the United States, Vol. 11, Mortality, Part A for data years 1950–1988. National Center for Health Statistics.

NOTE: Rates are rounded.

As indicated in Figure 4, men and women did not differ on ages of the racial crossover in death rates from cerebrovascular disease either in 1960 or 1988. For both men and women in 1960, death rates were higher for blacks than whites up to about age 75, when rates became higher for whites. By 1988, the crossover had moved for both men and women to about age 85.

Thus, the unusual age-by-race differentials in mortality appear to be persisting over time. They are found in all-cause and cause-specific mortality data, among both men and women, and in a variety of samples and studies. Although the crossover is there in different time periods, it seems to be advancing to later ages. The important point is that failure to subdivide the age group 65 and over masks differentials in mortality that sometimes favor blacks. This leads to the question of whether there are comparable age-by-race differentials in health status data.

Age-by-Race Differences in Health Status Data

Some evidence suggests that, as in the mortality data, a black disadvantage in health status in younger age groups of the elderly narrows or even disappears in older age groups. This may be due to a stronger relationship between age and health in the white than black elderly population. For example, the strong increase in rheumatoid arthritis with age holds only for whites. Although blacks have higher rates until age 64, whites have higher rates in the 65 and older age group. Similarly, prevalence rates for diabetes are much higher among blacks than whites until age 65, when the rates become almost identical (cf. Kasl & Berkman, 1981).

Recent work is beginning to support this idea of a closer correspondence of advancing age to poor health in the white than black elderly population and attributes it to less decline (Ford et al., 1990) or more "recovery" (Rogers, Rogers, & Belanger, 1992) in health and functioning among blacks than whites in the very oldest age groups. Thus, a narrowing of the health gap with age.

Ford et al. (1990), for example, examined health changes between 1975 and 1984 and found that although deterioration in Activities of Daily Living (ADLs) and Instrumental Activities of Daily Living (IADLs) occurred for both very old blacks and whites, greater percentages of whites than blacks declined.

Clark and Maddox (1993) examined data over a 6-year period and found that declines in functional health among the elderly were

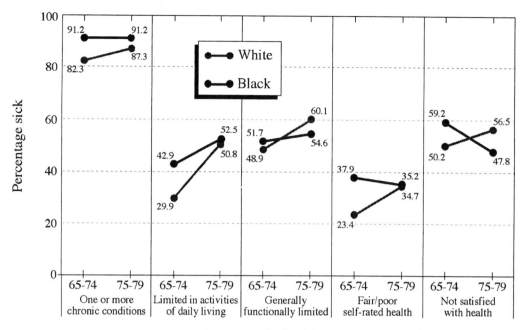

Figure 5. Percentage differences on five health measures: Americans' Changing Lives, Wave 1 data, by race and age.

similar among blacks and whites in the younger age groups, but greater for whites than blacks among the oldest old. Blacks ages 85 and over were less likely than whites that age to decline in functioning.

Rogers and colleagues (1992) examined transitions in functional health from 1984 to 1986 using the Longitudinal Study on Aging data. Two of their findings are relevant here:

(1) Although the odds of becoming disabled over the 2-year period were greater for blacks than whites, the odds also were greater for blacks than whites for moving back from a disabled to an able state. This suggests that the unusual age-race disparities in functional health we found are due to a greater tendency for blacks to "recover" with age.

(2) Age was a significant predictor of becoming disabled for black women but not for black men. This suggests that the weak association of age and functional health in the older black population may be more characteristic of men than women.

Gibson (1991a) similarly found a narrowing of the black health detriment moving from a younger to an older group of the elderly population. She identified two pervasive trends in multiple sources of heath data (objective, subjective, physiological, clinical, and functional). First, comparing the health status of blacks and whites in the older population, the black health handicap was greater in a younger (65–74) than older (75–79) group. Second, on some measures, blacks in the more robust 75 to 79-year-old group actually had the health advantage over whites in proportions who were healthy.

An analysis of the Americans' Changing Lives (ACL) data performed for this article was consistent with these trends. Figure 5 shows that in the first data collection, the black health handicap on five measures of self-reported health (chronic conditions, activities of daily living, general functional limitation, self-rated health, and satisfaction with health) was larger in the 65 to 74-year-

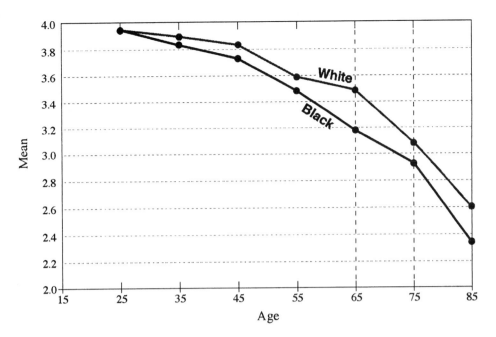

Figure 6. Mean values of functional health: Americans' Changing Lives, Wave 1 data, by age and race (1 = poor, 4 = good).

old group than in the older group aged 75 to 79. On two of the measures, general functional limitation and satisfaction with health, the black detriment more than narrowed in the age group 75 to 79; blacks actually gained the health advantage over whites in percentages who were healthy. Figure 5 also indicates that this narrowing of the black health disadvantage moving from a younger to an older group is due to sharper increases among whites than blacks in proportions of the morbid.

Interestingly, the trend is still evident in the ACL data when mean values instead of percentages are graphed (Figure 6). The black-white inequality in mean values of functional health is widest at about age 65 and narrows considerably by about age 75.

Three years later, at the time of the second ACL data collection, the black-white disparity did not narrow at age 75, but later at age 78 (Figure 7). However, superimposing the vertical lines in Figures 6 and 7 to adjust for the sample's aging 3 years, the Time 1 and 2 curves between the dotted lines become more

similar. In other words, the odd race differentials seemed to have moved along with the groups 65–74 and 75–79 as they aged 3 years. This implies that the age-by-race differences in health status are cohort—rather than aging—related.

All of these findings suggest that age and health are more strongly related in the white than black elderly population, and health differentials favor whites in younger age groups but favor blacks in older age groups. What are some factors that might account for these peculiar age-by-race inequalities in health status?

Potential Explanations of the Age-by-Race Differences in Health Status

As intimated in the Ford et al. (1990) and ACL analyses in this article, one explanation of the unusual age-by-race disparities in health status could be adverse mortality se-

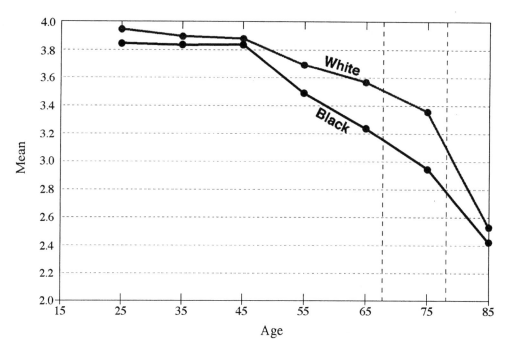

Figure 7. Mean values of functional health: Americans' Changing Lives, Wave 2 data, by age and race (1 = poor, 4 = good).

lection processes. In these processes, a young morbid group of a disadvantaged population dies out rapidly, leaving an older, more select group of survivors (Manton, 1980, 1982; Manton et al., 1987; Markides, 1989; Wing et al., 1985).

A second explanation could be age-by-race differences in susceptibilities to certain diseases. For example, Manton (1982) suggests that blacks are more susceptible to the early onset chronic diseases, but more insulated in some way from the late onset diseases. In support of this, he found that relative risk ratios for heart disease mortality favored white men at younger ages, but favored black men at older ages. His argument was that (a) blacks were more prone to heart disease and other circulatory events of hypertensive origin, and (b) early heart disease death is more likely to be a product of hypertension and constitutional endowment for circulatory failure. He argued further that white men develop arteriosclerosis more rapidly and are more susceptible to arterioscle-

rotic forms of heart disease; and late heart disease death is more likely due to degenerative circulatory changes, mainly arteriosclerosis.

The age-by-race differences, of course, could be due to time of measurement or cohort effects, as suggested by the ACL analyses.

A fourth explanation could be greater prevalences of certain risk factors for disease and functioning in some age-race groups than others. A final explanation could be age-by-race differences in the way that elderly persons perceive and report their health status.

Age-by-Race Differences in Self-Reported Health

No work has been done to date on age-by-race differences in the way that older individuals report their health. A little work, however, has been done on race differences. Gibson (1991b) analyzed race differences in the meaning and measurement of six indicators widely used in health research. She found that subjective interpretations portrayed actual health status as worse for blacks than whites. Nonhealth concerns were more likely to be expressed in the subjective reports of blacks. Thus, different pictures of race differences in health status could emerge depending on whether objective or subjective measures were used. Such differences in the way that elderly blacks and whites interpret their health bear careful scrutiny. They raise the question of whether age-by-race differences in the meaning of self-reported health could help explain the peculiar age-by-race differences in health status.

Age-by-Race Differences in Psychosocial Risk Factors for Disease

A growing body of health research is identifying inadequate social relations and nonhealthful personal behaviors such as poor diet, smoking, excessive alcohol consumption, and lack of physical activity as risk factors for disease and mortality (Berkman & Breslow, 1983; Berkman, Singer, & Manton, 1989; Blazer, 1982; Cohen & Syme, 1985; House, Landis, & Umberson, 1988; Kasl & Berkman, 1981; Rowe & Kahn, 1987; Satariano & Syme, 1981; Sauer & Coward, 1985).

Social relations and health behaviors seem to influence health through a complicated process (Berkman & Breslow 1983; Broadhead et al., 1983; Cohen, 1988; Kaplan, Cassel, & Gore, 1977; Wallston, Alagena, DeVellis, & DeVellis, 1984). Part of this complexity seems due to the dimensionality of each of the constructs—social support, health behaviors, and health. The dimensions of social support are structure, function, and quality. Structure is the vehicle through which support is exchanged, whereas function is that which is actually exchanged. Social support quality is more subjective and involves individuals' perceptions of whether their social support networks are satisfying, adequate, or meet their needs (Antonucci, 1985). The dimensions of health behaviors are formal service use and personal health habits (cf. Andersen & Newman, 1973). By com-

mon agreement, three major dimensions of health are disease, disability, and subjective health (Andersen, Mullner, & Cornelius, 1987; Ferraro, 1987; Gibson, 1991b; Liang, 1986; Newcomb & Bentler, 1987; Whitelaw, 1989; Whitelaw & Liang, 1991; Wolinsky, Coe, Miller, & Prendergast, 1984).

These various dimensions of social support, health behaviors, and health seem to affect each other differently (Funch & Metlin, 1982; House, 1981). Although each dimension of social support and health behaviors influences health and mortality in its own right (Antonovsky, 1979; Cohen & Syme, 1985; House et al., 1988), the effects seem to be of unequal force. For example, functional and qualitative aspects of social support seem to have more powerful effects on health than structural aspects (Blazer, 1982; Broadhead et al., 1983; Donald, Ware, & Brook, 1978). Structural aspects, on the other hand, especially the mere existence of social support, appear to have more influence on physiological processes and disease appraisals of health (Bovard, 1962; Cassel, 1976; Cohen & Syme, 1985; Kasl & Berkman, 1981). Subjective appraisals of health status, rather than health status itself, seem to be directly influenced by formal service use (Wolinsky et al., 1984), structural (Kaplan & Camacho, 1983), and functional aspects of social support (Minkler, Satariano, & Langhauser, 1983). Formal service use also appears to directly influence health status (Newcomb & Bentler, 1987).

Adding to this complexity, perceived need for and perceived availability of social support appear to critically intervene between social support and health in the process (Cohen & Syme, 1985; House & Kahn, 1985; Kaplan et al., 1977; Rowe & Kahn, 1987). Perceived availability, in fact, seems to organize and provide meaning and coherence to other dimensions of social support as they affect health (Antonovsky, 1979). Furthermore, *perceptions* of need and availability are more influential on health than *actual* need and availability (Cohen & Syme, 1985; Kahn & Antonucci, 1980).

Health behaviors also seem to intervene in the relationship between social support and health. While larger numbers of helpers (structural components) promote health by putting individuals in touch with formal health services (Berkman, 1985; Ward, Sherman, & La Gory, 1984; Wills, 1985); informational and instrumental aid (functional components) promote health by changing personal health habits (Antonucci et al., 1986; Berkman, 1984; Langlie, 1977; Umberson, 1987).

Age and race may individually change the process among risk factors, health, and mortality. For example, in the case of age, while the relationship between blood pressure and coronary event seems to strengthen with age, the relationship between cigarettes, relative weight, and coronary events seems to attenuate (Kasl & Berkman, 1981; Rowe & Kahn, 1987).

Although no work has systematically investigated black-white differences in the health-risk factor process, some sparse and fragmented findings emerge from a few studies that examined pieces of the process:

1. Race differences in the effects of functional aspects of social support on health lie more in their operation than in their amount (Gibson, 1982; Gibson & Jackson, 1987; 1993; Mindel, Wright, & Starrett, 1986; Mutran, 1985).

2. The effects of functional aspects of social support on health habits and health are stronger for blacks than whites (Gibson, 1982).

3. The norm of larger networks statistically reduces the effects of structural components of social support on the health and mortality of blacks (House et al., 1988).

4. Older black persons' formal service use may be reduced because they tend to substitute informal for formal networks (Cafferata, 1987).

5. Blacks' lack of information about, and more limited access to, services makes need a less important intervening variable between their social support and formal service use (Ford, 1994; Mindell & Wright, 1982).

6. Perceived social support is less influential on health than actual support for blacks (Ostrow, Fisher, Fraiser, & Whitaker, 1990), while perceived support is more influential than actual support for whites (George, 1986).

These findings together imply that (a) social relations and healthful behaviors are important to health status; (b) the process by which these factors influence health is not simple; and (c) the patterning of the process differs by age and by race. Such disparate findings could be juxtaposed to investigate age-by-race differences in the risk factor health process. Moreover, age-by-race differences in the meaning and measurement of self-reported health and in the risk factor-health process hold special promise as explanations of the unusual age-by-race differentials in health status. A systematic research agenda is required to investigate these relationships.

A Research Agenda for Identifying Causes of the Age-by-Race Differences in Health Status

1. Verify the age-by-race differences in a variety of health data.

2. Identify time of measurement, cohort, and aging effects.

3. Identify age-by-race differences in the meaning and measurement of health.

4. Identify age-by-race differences in the distribution of psychosocial risk factors for disease.

5. Identify age-by-race differences in the process by which psychosocial risk factors affect health status.

6. Investigate adverse mortality selection processes.

Since the age-by-race differentials in health status could be mere coincidences of some kind or unexplainable inflections in the data, the first step in the social science research agenda (the adverse mortality explanation aside) is to verify the peculiar health inequalities. The second step is to identify time of measurement, cohort, or aging effects. Steps 1 and 2 should be done in a variety of cross-sectional and longitudinal data and on both objective and subjective health measures. Longitudinal data can provide information on whether the age-by-race disparities appear in the same age groups over time or whether they follow groups as they age. Answers to such questions will begin to shape thinking on whether the age-race differences are cohort or age-related phenomena.

The third step in the research program is to rule out the possibility that the age-by-race irregularities are due to age-by-race differences in the meaning and measurement of self-reported health.

The fourth step is to identify specific aspects of risk factors, such as social relations and health behaviors, that have different distributions in the age-by-race groups. Identifying differences in distributions of lifetime and current psychosocial risk factors for health and functioning in black and white survivor groups actually can initiate inquiry into differential mortality selection processes.

The final step in the social science part of the research agenda is to identify age-by-race group differences in the process by which risk factors affect health status. This final step should address both theoretical and empirical health change in multiple waves of data to identify:

1. Age-by-race differences in the complex chains through which psychosocial factors go to affect health status.
2. Age-by-race differences in effects of changes in psychosocial factors on changes in health status that may not be observable until they diffuse across the disease, disability, and subjective dimensions of health.
3. Age-by-race differences in effects of changes in psychosocial factors on changes in health status that may be cumulative and observable only above a certain threshold value.
4. Age-by-race differences in different conjunctions and disjunctions of changes in health status and changes in psychosocial factors over time.
5. Age-by-race differences in propitious times for the different dimensions of psychosocial factors to affect the different dimensions of health.

These five theoretical-empirical issues suggest a conceptual frame work for analyzing age-by-race differences in how health affects and is affected by psychosocial factors in dynamic models.

Note

1. This research was supported by the National Institute on Aging (Grant PO1 AGO5561). The data utilized in this publication were made available by the Inter-university Consortium for Political and Social Research, the University of Michigan. The data for "Americans' Changing Lives": 1986–1988 were originally collected by James S. House. Neither the collector of the original data nor the Consortium bears any responsibility for the analyses of interpretations presented here.

References

Andersen, R., M., Mullner, R. M., & Cornelius, L. J. (1987). Black-white differences in health status: Methods or substance? *The Milbank Quarterly, 65*(Suppl.1), 72–99.

Andersen, R. & Newman, J. (1973). Societal and individual determinants of medical care in the United States. *The Milbank Quarterly, 51,* 95–124.

Antonovsky, A. (1979). *Health, stress, and coping.* San Francisco: Jossey-Bass.

Antonucci, T. C. (1985). Personal characteristics, social support, and social behavior. In R. H. Binstock & E. Shanas (Eds.), *Handbook of aging and the social sciences* (2nd ed.; pp. 94–128). New York: Van Nostrand Reinhold.

Antonucci, T. C., Kahn, R. L., Van Harrison, R., & Payne, B. C. (1986). Cancer symptoms in the elderly: Support and responses. Final report to the National Cancer Institute, 5R01 CA 36580. Bethesda, MD: National Institutes of Health.

Berkman, L. (1985). The relationship of social networks and social support to morbidity and mortality. In S. Cohen & S. L. Syme (Eds.), *Social support and health.* New York: Academic Press, 241–259.

Berkman, L. F. (1984). Assessing the physical health effects of social networks and social support. *Annual Review of Public Health, 5,* 413–432.

Berkman, L., & Breslow, L. (1983). *Health and ways of living: Findings from the Alameda County study.* New York: Oxford University Press.

Berkman, L., Singer, B., & Manton, K. (1989). Black/white differences in health status and mortality among the elderly. *Demography, 26,* 661–678.

Blazer, D. G. (1982). Social support and mortality in an elderly community population. *American Journal of Epidemiology, 115,* 684–694.

Bovard, E. W. (1962). The balance between negative and positive brain system activity. *Perspective Biological Medicine, 6,* 116–127.

Broadhead, E. W., Wagner, S., Schoenbach, J. E., Gromson, V. J., Hayden, R., Tibblin, S., & Gehlbach, S. H. (1983). The epidemiologic evidence for a relationship between social support and health. *Journal of Epidemiology, 117,* 521–537.

Cafferata, G. L. (1987). Marital status, living arrangements, and the use of health services by elderly persons. *Journal of Gerontology, 42,* 613–618.

Cassel, J. (1976). The contribution of social environment to host resistance. *American Journal of Epidemiology, 104,* 107–123.

Clark, D., & Maddox, G. (1993). Race, aging, and functional health: Evidence of selective survival? *Journal of Aging and Health, 54,* 536–557.

Cohen, S. (1988). Psychological models of the role of social support in the etiology of physical disease. *Health Psychology, 7,* 269–297.

Cohen, S. & Syme, L. (Eds.). (1985). *Social support and health.* New York: Academic Press.

Donald, C. A., Ware, J. E., & Brook, R. H. (1978). Conceptualization and measurement of health for adults in the health insurance study. *Social Health, Vol, IV.* Washington, DC: U.S. Dept. Health, Education and Welfare.

Ferraro, K. F. (1987). Double jeopardy to health for black older adults? *Journal of Gerontology, 42,* 528–533.

Ford, M. (1994). Personal autonomy and use of health care resources. In R. C. Gibson & J. S. Jackson (Eds.), *Health in black America.* Thousand Oaks, CA: Sage Publications.

Ford, A. B., Haug, M. R., Jones, P. K., Roy, A. W., & Folmar, S. J. (1990). Race-related differences among elderly urban residents: A cohort study, 1975–1984. *Journal of Gerontology: Social Sciences, 45,* S163–S171.

Funch, D. P., & Mettlin, C. (1982). The role of support in relation to recovery from breast surgery. *Social Science and Medicine, 16,* 91–98.

George, L. K. (1986). Easing caregiver burden: The role of informal and formal supports. In R. A. Ward & S. S. Tobin (Eds.), *Health in aging.* New York: Springer.

Gibson, R. C. (1982). Blacks at middle and late life: Resources and coping. *Annals of the American Academy of Political and Social Science, 464,* 79–90.

Gibson, R. C. (1991a). Age-by-race differences in the health and functioning of elderly persons. *Journal of Aging and Health, 3,* 335–351.

Gibson, R. C. (1991b). Race and the self-reported health of elderly persons. *Journal of Gerontology: Social Sciences, 46,* S235–S242.

Gibson, R. C., & Jackson, J. S. (1987). Health, functioning, and informal support among the black elderly. *The Milbank Quarterly, 65*(Supp. 2), 421–454.

Gibson, R. C., & Jackson, J. S. (1993). The black oldest old. In R. Suzman, D. Willis, & K. Manton (Eds.), *The oldest old.* Oxford University Press.

Hambright, T. Z. (1969). Comparison of information on death certificates and matching 1960 census records: Age, marital status, race, nativity, and county of origin. *Demography, 6,* 413–423.

House, J. S. (1981). Work, stress, and social support. Reading, MA: Addison Wesley.

House, J. S. (1986). *Americans' changing lives* (computer file). Producer: Survey Research Center. Ann Arbor, MI: Inter-university Consortium for Political and Social Research, distributor.

House, J. S., & Kahn, R. L. (1985). Measures and concepts of social support In S. Cohen & S. L. Syme (Eds.), *Social support and health.* New York: Academic Press, 83–105.

House, J. S., Landis, K. R., & Umberson, D. (1988). Social relationships and health. *Science, 241,* 540–544.

Kahn, R. L., & Antonucci, T. C. (1980). Convoys over the life course: Attachment, roles and social support. In P. B. Baltes & O. G. Brim (Eds.), *Lifespan development and behavior* (Vol. 3). New York: Academic Press.

Kaplan, B. H., Cassel, J. C., & Gore, S. (1977). Social support and health. *Medical Care, 15*(5), 47–58.

Kaplan, G. A., & Camacho, T. (1983). Perceived health and mortality: A nine-year follow-up of the Human Population Laboratory cohort. *American Journal of Epidemiology, 117,* 292–304.

Kasl, S. V., & Berkman, L. (1981). Some psychosocial influences on the health status of the elderly: The perspective of social epidemiology. In J. L. McGaugh & S. B. Kiesler (Eds.), *Aging, biology and behavior.* New York: Academic Press.

Kitagawa, E. M., & Hauser, P. M. (1973). *Differential mortality in the U.S.: A study in socioeconomic epidemiology.* Cambridge, MA: Harvard University Press.

Klebba, A. J., Maurer, J. D., & Glass, E. J. (1973). Mortality trends: Age, color, and sex, United States, 1950–69. *Vital and Health Statistics.* Series 20, no. 15. Washington, DC: U.S. Government Printing Office.

Langlie, J. K. (1977). Social network, health beliefs, and preventive behavior. *Journal of Health and Social Behavior, 18,* 244–260.

Liang, J. (1986). Self-reported physical health among aged adults. *Journal of Gerontology, 41,* 248–260.

Manton, K. (1980). Sex and race specific mortality differentials in multiple cause of death data. *The Gerontologist, 20,* 480–493.

Manton, K. G. (1982). Temporal and age variation in United States black-white cause-specific mortality differentials: A study of the recent changes in the relative health status of the United States black population. *The Gerontologist, 22,* 170–179.

Manton, K. G., Patrick, C. H., & Johnson, W. K. (1987). Health differentials between blacks and whites: Recent trends in mortality and morbidity. *Milbank Memorial Fund Quarterly, 65*(Suppl. 1), 129–199.

Manton, K. G., & Soldo, B. J. (1985). Dynamics of health changes in the oldest old: New perspectives and evidence. *Milbank Memorial Fund Quarterly Health and Society, 63,* 206–285.

Markides, K. S. (1983). Minority aging. In M. W. Riley. B. B. Hess. & K. Bond (Eds.), *Aging in society: Selected reviews of recent research* (pp. 115–137). Hillsdale, NJ: Erlbaum.

Markides, K. S. (Ed.). (1989). *Aging and health.* Newbury Park, CA: Sage Publications.

Mindel, C. H., & Wright, R. (1982). The use of social services by black and white elderly: The role of social support systems. *Journal of Gerontological Social Work, 4*(¾), 107–125.

Mindel, C. H., Wright, R., & Starrett, R. A. (1986). Informal and formal health and social support systems of black and white elderly: A comparative cost approach. *The Gerontologist, 26,* 279–285.

Minkler, M. A., Satariano, W. A., & Langhauser, C. (1983). Supportive exchange: An exploration of the relationships between social contacts and perceived health status in the elderly. *Archives of Gerontology and Geriatrics, 2,* 211–220.

Mutran, E. (1985). Intergenerational family support among blacks and whites: Responses to culture or to socioeconomic differences. *Journal of Gerontology, 40,* 382–389.

Nam, C. B., Weatherby, N. L., & Ockay, K. A. (1978). Causes of death which contribute to the mortality crossover effect. *Social Biology, 25,* 306–314.

National Center for Health Statistics. (1992). *Health, United States, 1990.* Hyattsville, MD: NCHS.

Newcomb, M. D., & Bentler, P. M. (1987). Self-report methods or assessing health status and health service utilization: A hierarchical confirmatory analysis. *Multivariate Behavioral Research, 2,* 415–436.

Ostrow, D., Fisher, E., Fraiser, K., & Whitaker, R. (1990). Pilot study of psychological symptomatology in a biracial cohort of seripositive inner city gay and bisexual men.

Bethesda, MD: National Institute of Mental Health.

Rogers, R. G., Rogers, A., & Belanger, A. (1992). Disability-free life among the elderly in the United States: Sociodemographic correlates of functional health. *Journal of Aging and Health, 4,* 19–42.

Rowe, J. W., & Kahn, R. L. (1987). Human aging: Usual and successful. *Science, 237,* 143–149.

Satariano, W. A., & Syme, S. L. (1981). Life changes and disease in elderly populations: Coping with change. In J. McGaugh & S. B. Kiesler (Eds.), *Aging, biology, and behavior* (pp. 311–317). New York: Academic Press.

Sauer, W., & Coward, R. (1985). *Social support networks and the care of the elderly: Theory, research, practice and policy.* New York: Springer.

Spiegelman, M. (1967). Why do these mortality curves cross? *New York Statistician, 18*(8).

Thornton, R. G., & Nam, C. B. (1969). The lower mortality rates of nonwhites at the older ages: An enigma in demographic analysis. *Research Report of the Social Sciences, 11* (1), 359–373.

Umberson, D. (1987). Family status and health behaviors: Social control as a dimension of social integration. *Journal of Health and Social Behavior, 28,* 306.

Wallston, B. S., Alagena, S. W., DeVellis, B. M., & DeVellis, R. F. (1984). Social support and physical health. *Health psychology, 2,* 367–393.

Ward, R. A., Sherman, S. R., & La Gory, M. A. (1984). Informal networks and knowledge of services for older persons. *Journal of Gerontology, 39,* 216–223.

Whitelaw, N. A. (1989). *Subjectively rated health among older men and women.* Unpublished doctoral dissertation, University of Michigan, Ann Arbor.

Whitelaw, N. A., & Liang, J. (1991). The structure of the OARS physical health measures. *Medical Care, 29,* 332–347.

Wills, J. (1985). Supportive functions of interpersonal relationships. In S. Cohen & s. L. Syme (Eds.), *Social support and health* (pp. 61–82). New York: Academic Press.

Wing, S., Manton, K., Stallard, E., Haynes, C. G., & Tyroler, H. A. (1985). The black/white mortality crossover: Investigation in a community-based study. *Journal of Gerontology, 40,* 78–84.

Wolinsky, F. D., Coe, R. M., Miller, D. K., & Prendergast, J. M. (1984). Measurement of the global and functional dimensions of health status in the elderly. *Journal of Gerontology, 39,* 88–92.

Zelnick, M. (1969). Age patterns of mortality of American Negroes: 1900–02 to 1959–61. *Journal of the American Statistical Association, 64,* 433–451.

1 How might the meaning of illness and dying be different for Jennie and Jeff Patton than for an urban, more affluent couple? How might exposure to social and psychological risk factors for disease have shaped the situation the Pattons are facing in Bontemps's story?

2 Imagine that you are attending a conference in which a physician in private practice presents a paper lamenting the tendency of elderly African Americans to delay seeking medical care and their low rates of compliance with recommended treatment. How might you use a life course perspective to respond to this physician?

3 Imagine that the president invites you to join a task force charged with minimizing risks of disease and disability in future cohorts of elderly Americans. Outline a plan of action that not only would reduce average levels of disease and disability but would also reduce gaps based on gender, race, and social class.

4 Joanne Seltzer's poem series "A Place for Mother" portrays nursing home decisions from the standpoint of an adult daughter placing an elderly mother and later as an elderly woman needing nursing home care. Rewrite these poems (in narrative form, if you prefer) from the standpoints of the narrator's elderly mother and her adult children.

5 Folk medicine is defined literally as "medicine of the people." People often think of folk medicine as exotic practices of isolated minorities, but folk medicine includes a vast range of self-care practices. Indeed, self-care is the predominant form of primary care in the United States. Most people practice some form of lay diagnosis and treatment prior to, instead of, or after consulting health care professionals. What self-care practices are part of your "lay repertoire" for treating everyday illnesses? Where did you learn these practices?

SUGGESTIONS FOR FURTHER READING

---

1 Belgrave, L. (1990). The relevance of chronic illness in the everyday lives of elderly women. *Journal of Aging and Health,* 2(4), 475-500.

This qualitative study explores the experience of chronic illness in the everyday lives of 29 elderly women suffering from chronic health problems. Belgrave's analysis provides insight into what it is like to live with chronic illness. She explores the ways older women talk about their illness, its impact on their self-concept, and its effect on lifestyle and relationships with others.

2   Jones, J. (1991). *Bad blood: The Tuskegee Syphilis Experiment.* New York: Free Press.

A detailed history of the infamous experiment in which 399 African American men with syphilis were denied treatment for "science's sake." Begun in the 1930s, the experiment continued for 40 years.

3   Wilkinson, D. (1987). Traditional medicine in American families: Reliance on the wisdom of elders. *Culture, Medicine, and Psychiatry, 11,* 65-76.

Wilkinson discusses the social history and prevalence of folk medicine among Native Americans, Appalachian Whites, African Americans, and Mexican Americans. Mothers and grandmothers have played central roles as traditional healers within African American, Mexican American, and Appalachian White communities. Wilkinson concludes with a discussion of the relationships between traditional and Western scientific medicine.

4   Naylor, G. (1989). *Mama Day.* New York: Vintage.

This novel is set on a sea island off the coast of South Carolina and Georgia. Although health care and traditional medicine are not the focus of her story, the title character is Mama Day, a family matriarch and traditional healer. Naylor illustrates the relationship between traditional and Western scientific medicine in this community, where people still practice herbal medicine and honor ancestors brought from Africa as slaves.

5   National Resource Center on Health Promotion and Aging and AARP Health Advocacy Services. (1990). *Healthy aging: Model health promotion programs for minority elders* [½-in. videocassette/ 46 min./color]. (Distributed by National Resource Center on Health Promotion and Aging and AARP, Washington, DC, 202-434-2277)

This video illustrates five specially tailored programs for elderly target populations: Hispanic Americans, Pacific/Asian Americans, Native Americans, African Americans, and multicultural groups. The programs are designed on the premise that each group has its own set of health characteristics and issues. All groups face barriers of discrimination, oppression, and social and economic inequities. Thus the best health promotion efforts for minorities should emphasize advocacy, assertiveness, affirmative action, and the rights of individuals as both citizens and patients.

6 Markides, K., & Manuel Miranda, M. (1997). *Minorities, aging, and health*. Thousand Oaks, CA: Sage.

A comprehensive anthology with review articles written by leading scholars in the field of minority health and aging. In addition to reviews of chronic disease, disability, and mortality among Black, American Indian, Hispanic, and Asian and Pacific Islander elders, the articles explore nutrition, mental health, and use of a range of long-term care service options.

Sources and Permissions

INTRODUCTION

Text of "Nikki Rosa" from *Black Feelings, Black Talk, Black Judgement* by Nikki Giovanni. Copyright © 1968, 1970 by Nikki Giovanni. Used by permission of William Morrow & Company, Inc.

PART 1

Reading 1: Excerpted from "Hard Times in Women's Lives: Historical Influences Across Forty Years" by Glen H. Elder, Jr., & Jeffrey K. Liker. *American Journal of Sociology, 88*(2), 241-269, 1982. Chicago: University of Chicago Press. Reprinted with permission of the University of Chicago Press and the authors.

Reading 2: Excerpted from *Farewell to Manzanar* by Jean Wakatsuki Houston & James D. Houston. (1983). Boston: Houghton Mifflin. Copyright © 1973 by James D. Houston. Reprinted by permission of Houghton Mifflin Company. All rights reserved.

Reading 3: "Puerto Rican Paradise" by Piri Thomas. Excerpted from P. Thomas, *Down These Mean Streets*, 1967. Copyright © 1967 by Piri Thomas. Reprinted by permission of Alfred A. Knopf, Inc.

Reading 4: "In Search of Our Mothers' Gardens" by Alice Walker. Excerpted from *In Search of Our Mothers' Gardens: Womanist Prose*, copyright © 1974 by Alice Walker. Reprinted by permission of Harcourt, Inc. "Women" from *Revolutionary Petunias & Other Poems*, copyright © 1970 by Alice Walker. Reprinted by permission of Harcourt, Inc.

Reading 5: Reprinted with the permission of Simon & Schuster from *Lame Deer: Seeker of Visions* by John Fire/Lame Deer and Richard Erdoes. Copyright © 1972 by John Fire/Lame Deer and Richard Erdoes.

Reading 6: "The World of Our Grandmothers" by C. Young Wu, from *Making Waves*, by Asian Women United of California, copyright © 1989 by Asian Women United of California. Reprinted by permission of Beacon Press, Boston.

Reading 7: "Dear Tía," from *Cuban American Writers: Los Atrevidos*, Carolina Hospital, editor. Copyright © 1988 Ediciones Ellas/Linden Lane Press. Used with permission.

PART 2

Reading 8: "After Sixty" by M. Zuckerman, from *Ourselves, Growing Older*, edited by P. Doress and D. Ziegel, 1987. New York: Simon & Schuster. Reprinted with permission of the author.

Reading 9: From *The Last Gift of Time* by Carolyn G. Heilbrun. Copyright © 1997 by Carolyn Heilbrun. Used by permission of The Dial Press/Dell Publishing, a division of Random House, Inc.

Reading 10: From *Collected Poems* by Langston Hughes. Copyright © 1994 by the Estate of Langston Hughes. Reprinted by permission of Alfred A. Knopf, Inc.

Reading 11: "If I Had My Life to Live Over" by N. Stair. Reprinted in *If I Had My Life to Live Over, I Would Pick More Daisies*, edited by Sandra Haldeman Martz. Watsonville, CA: Papier-Mache Press, 1992.

Reading 12: "Warning" from *Selected Poems*, by J. Joseph, published by Bloodaxe Books Ltd. Copyright © 1992 by Jenny Joseph. Reprinted with permission of John Johnson Limited.

Reading 13: "How It Feels to Be Colored Me" by Z. Neale Hurston. Reprinted in *Speculations: Readings in Culture, Identity and Values*, edited by Charles Schuster and William Van Pelt. Englewood Cliffs, NJ: Prentice Hall, 1992.

Reading 14: "Father Cures a Presidential Fever," from *Father and Glorious Descendant*, by P. Lowe, 1943. Boston: Little, Brown. Copyright renewed 1971 by author. Reprinted by permission of the author.

Reading 15: Excerpts from "When a House Is Not a Home," Christopher J. Elias & Thomas S. Inui, *The Gerontologist, 33*(3), 396-402, 1993. Used by permission of The Gerontological Society of America, 1030 15th Street, NW, Suite 250, Washington, DC 20005 via the Copyright Clearance Center, Inc.

Reading 16: Excerpts from "The Big Boys" in *Coming of Age* by Studs Terkel, 1995, pp. 9-14. New York: The New Press. Reprinted by permission.

PART 3

Reading 17: Excerpted from "I Didn't Have No Family Before I Was Married" by A. Walser, as told to Victoria Byerly in *Hard Times Cotton Mill Girls: Personal Histories of Womanhood and Poverty in the South* (pp. 74-86), 1986. Ithaca, New York: ILR Press. Reprinted by permission of the author.

Reading 18: "I Want You Women Up North to Know" by T. Olsen, originally published in *The Partisan* (March 1934) under Tillie Lerner. Copyright Tillie Olsen. All rights reserved. Reprinted with permission of the author.

Reading 19: Studs Terkel, "Mike LeFevre, Steelworker," from *Working: People Talk About the Work They Do All Day and How They Feel About What They Do*, pp. 520-525. New York: Pantheon Books, a division of Random House, Inc., 1972. Used by permission of Studs Terkel.

Reading 20: "From Homemaker to Housing Advocate: An Interview With Mrs. Chang Jok Lee," by N. Diao, from *Making Waves*, by Asian Women United of California, copyright © 1989 by Asian Women United of California. Reprinted by permission of Beacon Press, Boston.

Reading 21: Excerpted from "Esse Quam Videri" by S. Williams from *Hope and Dignity, Older Black Women of the South* edited by E. Herring Wilson, 1983, Philadelphia: Temple University Press. Copyright © 1983 by Temple University. Reprinted by permission.

Reading 22: Excerpted from "Women's Work and Caregiving Roles: A Life Course Approach," P. Moen et al., 1994, from *Journal of Gerontology: Social Sciences 49*(4), S176-S186. Copyright © 1994 by The Gerontological Society of America. Reprinted with permission.

Reading 23: "The Day the Crows Stopped Talking" by Harvest Moon Eyes, from *Earth Song, Sky Spirit: Short Stories of the Contemporary Native American Experience*, edited by C. Trafzer, 1992. Copyright © 1992 by Harvest Moon Eyes. Harvest Moon Eyes lives and writes in Taos, New Mexico. She has recently finished her first novel, from which this story is an excerpt. Reprinted by permission.

Reading 24: "On the Edge of the Barrio" by Ernesto Galarza, from *Barrio Boy*, E. Galarza, 1971. Copyright © 1971 by the University of Notre Dame Press. Reprinted by permission.

Reading 25: "At the Burns-Coopers'" by Gwendolyn Brooks, from *Maud Martha*, Chicago: Third World Press, 1993. Reprinted by permission of the author.

Reading 26: Excerpted from Alice Childress, *Like One of the Family: Conversations From a Domestic's Life.* Boston: Beacon Press, 1986, pp. 1-3. Used by permission.

Reading 27: Excerpted from "Race inequities in Men's Retirement by M. D. Hayward, S. Friedman, & H. Chen from *Journal of Gerontology: SOCIAL SCIENCES, 51B*(1), S1-S10, 1996. Reprinted by permission.

PART 4

Reading 28: Excerpts from "Survival and Resistance: Early Lessons in the Family" by Kathleen F. Slevin & C. Ray Wingrove in *From Stumbling Blocks to Stepping Stones: The Life Experiences of Fifty Professional African American Women.* New York: New York University Press, 1998, pp. 11-31. Used by permission of the publisher and the authors.

Reading 29: "The Linden Tree" by Ella Leffland, from *Last Courtesies and Other Stories*, Ella Leffland, 1980. Copyright © 1972, 1980 by Ella Leffland. Reprinted by permission of the Wallace Literary Agency.

Reading 30: Excerpted from "Between the Funerals" by A. Tracy, 1992. Reprinted with permission of the author.

Reading 31: "The Horned Toad" by Gerald Haslam, from *Growing Up Chicana/o*, edited by Tiffany Ana López, 1993. New York: Avon Books. Copyright 1993 by Gerald Haslam. Reprinted by permission of the author.

Reading 32: "Elders in Southeast Asian Refugee Families" by B. W. K. Yee, from *Generations*, Summer 1992, pp. 24-27. Reprinted with permission from *Generations*, 833 Market Street, Suite 512, San Francisco, CA 94103. Copyright 1992, ASA.

Reading 33: Excerpts from "Grandparenting Styles: Native American Perspectives" by J. Weibel-Orlando from *The Cultural Context of Aging: Worldwide Perspectives*, edited by Jay Sokolvsky, 1990 (pp. 109-125). Reproduced by permission of Greenwood Publishing Group, Inc., Westport, CT.

Reading 34: Excerpts from "Grandmother Involvement in Child Caregiving in an Urban Community," by Jane L. Pearson, A. G. Hunter, J. M. Cook, N. S. Ialongo, & S. G. Kellam, *The Gerontologist, 1997, 37*(5), 650-657. Used by permission of The Gerontological Society of America, 1030 15th Street, NW, Suite 250, Washington, DC 20005 via the Copyright Clearance Center, Inc.

Reading 35: From *Sweet Summer: Growing Up With and Without My Dad* by Bebe Moore Campbell. Copyright © 1989 by Bebe Moore Campbell. Used by permission of G. P. Putnam's Sons, a division of Penguin Putnam Inc.

PART 5

Reading 36: From *And Still I Rise* by M. Angelou. Copyright © 1978 by Maya Angelou. Reprinted by permission of Random House, Inc.

Reading 37: "A Summer Tragedy" by A. Bontemps. Copyright 1933 by Arna Bontemps, renewed. Reprinted by permission of Harold Ober Associates Incorporated.

Reading 38: "A Place for Mother" by Joanne Seltzer in *When I Am an Old Woman I Shall Wear Purple*, edited by Sandra Martz. Watsonville, CA: Papier-Mache Press, 1987. Used by permission of Joanne Seltzer.

Reading 39: "My Most Humiliating Jim Crow Experience" by Zora Neale Hurston, reprinted in *I Love Myself When I Am Laughing: A Zora Neale Hurston Reader*, edited by Alice Walker. Oldwestbury, NY: The Feminist Press, 1979.

Reading 40: Excerpted from "The Tuskegee Syphilis Study, 1932 to 1972: Implications for HIV Education and AIDS Risk Education Programs in the Black Community," by S. Thomas and S. Quinn, from *American Journal of Public Health, 81*(11), November 1991. Copyright © 1991 by the American Public Health Association. Reprinted by permission.

Bibliography

Abbott, J. (1977). Socioeconomic characteristics of the elderly: Some black/white differences. *Social Security Bulletin, 40,* 16-42.

Aging Health Policy Center. (1985). *The homeless mentally ill elderly* (Working paper). San Francisco: University of California.

Akiyama, H., Antonucci, T., & Campbell, R. (1990). Rules of support exchange among two generations of Japanese and American women. In Jay Sokolovsky (Ed.), *The Cultural Context of Aging* (pp. 127-138). New York: Bergin & Garvey.

Alba, R. (1990). *Ethnic identity: The transformation of white identity.* New Haven, CT: Yale University Press.

Allen, K. R. (1989). *Single women/family ties: Life histories of older women.* Newbury Park, CA: Sage.

Allen, K. R., & Chin-Sang, V. (1990). A lifetime of work: The context and meanings of leisure for aging black women. *The Gerontologist, 30,* 734-740.

Amoss, P. (1981). Cultural centrality and prestige for the elderly: The Coast Salish case. In C. Fry (Ed.), *Dimensions: Aging, culture and health* (pp. 47-63). Brooklyn, NY: J. F. Bergin.

Amoss, P. (1986). *Northwest coast grandmother myths.* Paper presented at the 84th Annual Meeting of the American Anthropological Association, Philadelphia.

Anaya, R. (1982). Uno. In *Bless me, Ultima: A novel.* Berkeley, CA: Tonatiuh International.

Andersen, M. L. (1993). *Thinking about women: Sociological and feminist perspectives.* New York: Macmillan.

Andersen, M. L. (1997). *Thinking about women: Sociological perspectives on sex and gender* (4th ed.). Boston: Allyn & Bacon.

Andersen, M. L., & Collins, P. H. (1998). *Race, class, and gender: An anthology* (3rd ed.). Belmont, CA: Wadsworth.

Angel, R., & Angel, J. (1997). Health service use and long-term care among Hispanics. In K. Markides & M. Miranda (Eds.), *Minorities, aging, and health* (pp. 343-366). Thousand Oaks, CA: Sage.

Angelou, M. (1969). *I know why the caged bird sings.* New York: Random House.

Angelou, M. (1992). On aging. In M. W. Secundy (Ed.), *Trials, tribulations and celebrations: African-American perspectives on health, illness, aging and loss* (p. 150). Yarmouth, ME: Intercultural Press.

Arendell, T., & Estes, C. L. (1991). Older women in the post-Reagan era. *International Journal of Health Services, 21,* 59-73.

Aronson, J. (1992). Women's sense of responsibility for the care of old people: But who else is going to do it? *Gender and Society, 6,* 8-29.

Atchley, R. C. (1997). *The social forces in later life: An introduction to social gerontology* (7th ed.). Belmont, CA: Wadsworth.

Bandura, A. (1977). Self-efficacy: Toward a unifying theory of behavioral change. *Psychological Review, 84,* 191-215.

Barnett, H. (1955). *The Coast Salish of British Columbia.* Eugene: University of Oregon Press.

Barresi, C. M. (1992, March 15). *The impact of ethnicity on aging: A review of theory, research and issues.* Paper presented at the American Society on Aging Annual Meeting, San Diego, CA.

Baxandall, R., Gordon, L., & Reverby, S. (1976). *Factory girls: America's working women: A documentary history 1600 to the present.* New York: Vintage.

Becker, M. (1993). A medical sociologist looks at health promotion. *Journal of Health and Social Behavior, 34,* 1-6.

Belgrave, L. (1990). The relevance of chronic illness in the everyday lives of elderly women. *Journal of Aging and Health, 2*(4), 475-500.

Bell, L. P. (1989). The double standard: Age. In J. Freeman (Ed.), *Women: A feminist perspective* (4th ed., pp. 236-244). Mountain View, CA: Northfield.

Bell-Scott, P. (1982). Debunking sapphire: Toward a non-racist and non-sexist social science. In G. T. Hull, P. Bell-Scott, & B. Smith (Eds.), *But some of us are brave.* Old Westbury, NY: Feminist Press.

Bell-Scott, P., Guy-Sheftall, B., Jones Royster, J., Sims-Wood, J., DeCosta-Willis, M., & Fultz, L. (1991). *Double stitch: Black women write about mothers and daughters.* Boston: Beacon.

Bengtson, V., Rosenthal, C., & Burton, L. (1996). Paradoxes of families and aging. In R. Binstock & L. George (Eds.), *Handbook of aging and the social sciences* (4th ed.; pp. 253-282). San Diego, CA: Academic Press.

Berg, R. R., & Cassells, J. S. (Eds.). (1990). *The second fifty years: Promoting health and preventing disability.* Washington, DC: National Academy Press.

Berkman, L. F., & Mullen, J. M. (1997). How health behaviors and the social environment contribute to health differences between Black and White older Americans. In L. Martin & B. Soldo (Eds.), *Racial and ethnic differences in the health of older Americans* (pp. 163-182). Washington, DC: National Academy Press.

Bogue, D. J. (1983). *Skid row in American cities.* Chicago: University of Chicago Press.

Bohrnstedt, G. W. (1969). Observations on the measurement of change. In E. F. Borgatta (Ed.), *Sociological methodology.* San Francisco: Jossey-Bass.

Bond, J., Galinsky, E., & Swanberg, J. (1997). *The 1997 national study of the changing work force.* New York: Families and Work Institute.

Bontemps, A. (1992). A summer tragedy. In M. W. Secundy (Ed.), *Trials, tribulations, and celebrations: African-American perspectives on health, illness, aging and loss* (pp. 153-161). Yarmouth, ME: Intercultural Press. (Original work published 1933)

Bowlby, J. (1980). *Loss: Sadness and depression* (Vol. 3). New York: Basic Books.

Brenner, M. H. (1973). *Mental illness and the economy.* Cambridge, MA: Harvard University Press.

Breslau, N., Salkever, D., & Staruch, K. S. (1982). Women's labor force participation and responsibilities for disabled dependents: A study of families with disabled children. *Journal of Health and Social Behavior, 23,* 169-183.

Brody, E. M. (1990). *Women in the middle: Their parent-care years.* New York: Springer.

Brody, E. M., Johnson, R., Fulcomer, M., & Lang, A. (1983). Women's changing roles and help to elderly parents: Attitudes of three generations of women. *Journal of Gerontology, 38,* 597-607.

Brody, E. M., Kleman, M. H., Johnston, P. T., Hoffman, C., & Schoonover, C. B. (1987). Work status and parent care: A comparison of four groups of women. *The Gerontologist, 27*, 201-208.

Brooks, G. (1953). At the Burns-Cooper's. In *Maud Martha.* New York: Harper.

Brown, E. B. (1991). Mothers of mind. In P. Bell-Scott, B. Guy-Sheftall, J. Jones Royster, J. Sims-Wood, M. DeCosta-Willis, & L. Fultz (Eds.), *Double stitch: Black women write about mothers and daughters* (pp. 74-93). Boston: Beacon.

Brubaker, E., & Brubaker, T. (1992). The context of retired women as caregivers. In M. Szinovacz, D. Ekerdt, & B. Vinick (Eds.), *Families and retirement* (pp. 222-235). Newbury Park, CA: Sage.

Bullard, S. (1993). Free at last. In V. Cyrus (Ed.), *Experiencing race, class and gender in the United States* (pp. 269-272). Mountain View, CA: Mayfield. (Original work published 1989)

Burton, L. & DeVries, C. (1995). Challenges and rewards: Black grandparents as surrogate parents. In L. Burton (Ed.), *Families and aging* (pp. 101-108). Amityville, NY: Baywood.

Burton, L., Dilworth-Anderson, P., & Bengtson, V. (1991, Fall-Winter). Creating culturally relevant ways of thinking about diversity and aging. *Generations, 15*, 67-72.

Butler, R. N. (1975). *Why survive? Being old in America.* New York: Harper & Row.

Byerly, V. (1986). *Hard times cotton mill girls: Personal histories of womanhood and poverty in the South.* Ithaca, NY: ILR.

Calasanti, T. (1996). Incorporating diversity: Meanings, levels of research, and implications for theory. *The Gerontologist, 36*(2),147-156.

Calasanti, T. M., & Bonanno, A. (1992). Working overtime: Economic restructuring and retirement of a class. *Sociological Quarterly, 33*(1), 135-152.

Cantor, M. H. (1979). Neighbors and friends: An overlooked resource in the informal support system. *Research on Aging, 1*, 434-463.

CBS Fox Video. (1990). *Come see the paradise* [Film]. New York.

Chapleski, E. (1997). Long-term care among American Indians: A broad lens perspective on service preference and use. In K. Markides & M. Miranda (Eds.), *Minorities, aging, and health* (pp. 367-396). Thousand Oaks, CA: Sage.

Cheung, M. (1989). Elderly Chinese living in the United States: Assimilation or adjustment? *Social Work, 14*, 457-461.

Clark, D. O., & Gibson, R. C. (1997). Race, age, chronic disease and disability. In K. Markides & M. Miranda (Eds.), *Minorities, aging, and health* (pp. 107-126). Thousand Oaks, CA: Sage.

Clausen, J. A. (1993). *American lives.* New York: Free Press.

Clive, A. (1987). The home front and the household: Women, work and family in Detroit. In N. A. Hewitt (Ed.), *Women, families and communities: Readings in American history* (Vol. 2, pp. 188-203). Glenview, IL: Scott, Foresman/Little, Brown.

Cohen, C. I., Teresi, J., Holmes, D., & Roth, E. (1988). Survival strategies of older homeless men. *The Gerontologist, 28*(1), 58-65.

Cohen, M. (1998). *Culture of intolerance: Chauvinism, class, and racism in the United States.* New Haven, CT: Yale University Press.

Cohen, R. A., Van Nostrand, J., & Suzman, R. (Eds.). (1995). *Trends in the health of older Americans/1994.* Hyattsville, MD: U.S. Department of

Health and Human Services, Public Health Service, Centers for Disease Control and Prevention, National Center for Health Statistics.

Cohn, R. M. (1978). The effect of employment status on self-attitudes. *Social Psychology Quarterly, 41,* 81-93.

Colby, A. (1998). Crafting life course studies. In J. Giele & G. H. Elder, Jr. (Eds.), *Methods of life course research: Qualitative and quantitative approaches* (pp. viii-xii). Thousand Oaks, CA: Sage.

Cole, J. (1986). *All American woman: Lives that divide, ties that bind.* New York: Free Press.

Collins, P. H. (1990). *Black feminist thought: Knowledge, consciousness, and the politics of empowerment.* Boston: Unwin Hyman.

Collins, P. H. (1991). The meaning of motherhood in black culture and black mother-daughter relationships. In P. Bell-Scott, B. Guy-Sheftall, J. Jones Royster, J. Sims-Wood, M. DeCosta-Willis, & L. Fultz (Eds.), *Double stitch: Black women write about mothers and daughters* (pp. 42-60). Boston: Beacon.

Conzen, K., Gerber, D., Morawska, E., Pozzetta, G., & Vecoli, R. (1992). The invention of ethnicity: A perspective from the U.S.A. *Journal of American Ethnic History, 12,* 3-41.

Cool, L. E. (1980). Ethnicity and aging: Continuity through change for elderly Corsicans. In C. Fry (Ed.), *Aging in culture and society* (pp. 149-169). New York: Praeger.

Coontz, S. (1992). *The way we never were: American families and the nostalgia trap.* New York: Basic Books.

Cornman, J., & Kingson, E. (1996). Trends, issues, perspectives and values for the aging of the baby boom cohorts. *The Gerontologist, 36*(1),15-26.

Coward, R. T., & Dwyer, J. W. (1990). The association of gender, sibling network composition, and patterns of parent care by adult children. *Research on Aging, 12,* 158-181.

Coward, R. T., Horne, C., & Dwyer, J. W. (1992). Demographic perspectives on gender and family caregiving. In J. W. Dwyer & R. T. Coward (Eds.), *Gender, families, and elder care.* Newbury Park, CA: Sage.

Cowgill, D. O. (1986). Economic systems and economic roles of the aged: Ascendancy and continuity. In *Aging around the world* (pp. 108-119). Belmont, CA: Wadsworth.

Crystal, S., & Shea, D. (1990). Cumulative advantage, cumulative disadvantage, and inequality among elderly people. *The Gerontologist, 30,* 437-443.

Crystal, S., Shea, D., & Krishnaswami, S. (1992). Educational attainment, occupational history, and stratification: Determinants of later life economic outcomes. *Journal of Gerontology: Social Sciences, 47,* S213-S221.

Cyrus, V. (Ed.). (1993). *Experiencing race, class, and gender in the United States.* Mountain View, CA: Mayfield.

D'Augelli, A., & Hart, M. M. (1987). Gay women, men and families in rural settings: Toward the development of helping communities. *American Journal of Community Psychology, 15*(1), 79-93.

Damron-Rodriguez, J., Wallace, S., & Kingston, R. (1994). Service utilization and minority elderly: Appropriateness, accessibility and acceptability. *Gerontology & Geriatrics Education, 15*(1), 45-63.

Danigelis, N., & Cutler, S. (1991). An inter-cohort comparison of change in racial attitudes. *Research on Aging, 13*(3), 383-404.

Davis, L., & McGadney, B. (1993). *Social factors in the health of black urban elders: Final report* (NIA IR2/GD7). Chicago: Chicago Northwestern University.

Davis, L., & Wykle, M. (1998). Self-care in minority and ethnic populations: The experience of older Americans. In M. G. Ory & G. DeFriese (Eds.), *Self-care in later life: Research, program and policy issues* (pp. 170-179). New York: Springer.

Davison, C., Frankel, S., & Smith, G. D. (1992). The limits of lifestyle: Reassessing "fatalism" in the popular culture of illness prevention. *Social Science and Medicine, 34,* 675-685.

Dean, K. (1986). Lay care in illness. *Social Science and Medicine, 22,* 275-284.

Delany, S., & Delany, E. (with A. H. Heart). (1993). *Having our say: The Delany sisters' first 100 years.* New York: Kodansha America.

Detzner, D. F. (in press). Conflict in southeast Asian refugee families: A life history approach. In J. Gilgun, K. Daly, & F. Handel (Eds.), *Qualitative methods in family research.* Newbury Park, CA: Sage.

Diao, N. (1987). From homemaker to housing advocate: An interview with Mrs. Chang Jok Lee. *Signs: Journal of Women in Culture and Society, 12,* 440-453.

DiLeonardo, M. (1987). The female world of cards and holidays: Women, families, and the work of kinship. *Signs: Journal of Women in Culture and Society, 12,* 440-453.

Dorris, M. (1987). *A yellow raft in blue water.* New York: Warner.

Duncan, G., & Morgan, J. (1980). The incidence and some consequences of major life events. In G. Duncan & J. Morgan (Eds.), *Five thousand American families* (Vol. 8, pp. 183-240). Ann Arbor: University of Michigan, Institute for Social Research.

Dwyer, J., & Coward, R. T. (Eds.). (1992). *Gender, families and elder care.* Newbury Park, CA: Sage.

Elder, G. H., Jr. (1974). *Children of the Great Depression.* Chicago: University of Chicago Press.

Elder, G. H., Jr., & Liker, J. K. (1982). Hard times in women's lives: Historical influences across forty years. *American Journal of Sociology, 88*(2), 241-269.

Elder, G. H., Jr., & Rockwell, R. C. (1978). Economic depression and postwar opportunity: A study of life patterns and health. In R. A. Simmons (Ed.), *Research in community and mental health* (pp. 249-303). Greenwich, CT: JAI.

Elder, G. H., Jr., Shanahan, M. J., & Clipp, E. C. (1994). When war comes to men's lives: Life-course patterns in family, work and health. *Psychology of Aging, 9*(5), 5-16.

Elder, G. H., Jr., Shanahan, M. J., & Clipp, E. C. (1997). Linking combat and physical health: The legacy of World War II in men's lives. *American Journal of Psychiatry, 154,* 330-336.

Ellison, R. (1952). *Invisible man.* New York: Random House.

Elmendorf, W., & Kroeber, A. (1960). *The structure of Twona culture with notes on Yurok culture.* Pullman: Washington State University Press.

Elo, I., & Preston, S. (1997). Racial and ethnic differences in mortality at older ages. In L. Martin & B. Soldo (Eds.), *Racial and ethnic differences in the health of older Americans* (pp. 10-42). Washington, DC: National Academy Press.

Erdrich, L. (1984). *Love medicine.* Bloomington: Indiana University Press.

Feagin, J. (1991). The continuing significance of race: Antiblack discrimination in public places. *American Sociological Review, 56,* 101-116.

Fischer, L. R. (with Hoffman, C.). (1984). Who cares for the elderly: The dilemma of family support. In M. Lewis & J. Miller (Eds.), *Research in social problems and public policy, a research annual* (Vol. 3, pp. 169-215). Greenwich, CT: JAI.

Foner, A. (1986). *Aging and old age: New perspective.* Englewood Cliffs, NJ: Prentice Hall.

Ford, A., Haug, M. R., Jones, R. K., Roy, A. W., & Folman, S. J. (1990). Race-related differences among elderly urban residents: A cohort study, 1975-1984. *Journal of Gerontology: Social Sciences, 45,* S163-S171.

Friedan, B. (1964). *The feminine mystique.* New York: Norton.

Fullmer, E. M. (1995). Challenging biases against families of older gays and lesbians. In G. C. Smith, S. Tobin, E. A. Robertson-Tchabo, & P. Power (Eds.), *Strengthening aging families: Diversity in practice and power.* Thousand Oaks, CA: Sage.

Galarza, E. (1971). On the edge of the barrio. In *Barrio boy.* Notre Dame, IN: University of Notre Dame Press. (Original work published 1905)

Gates, H. L., Jr. (1994). *Colored people, a memoir.* New York: Random House.

Gelfand, D. E. (1982). *Aging: The ethnic factor.* Boston: Little, Brown.

Gelfand, D. E., & Yee, B. (1992). Trends and forces: Influence of immigration, migration, and acculturation on the fabric of aging in America. *Generations, 15*(4), 7-10.

Gibson, R. C. (1987). Reconceptualizing retirement for black Americans. *The Gerontologist, 27*(6), 691-698.

Gibson, R. C. (1994). The age-by-race gap in health and mortality in the older population. *The Gerontologist, 34*(4), 454-462.

Gibson, R. C., & Jackson, J. S. (1992). The black oldest old. In R. Suzman, K. Manton, & D. Willis (Eds.), *The oldest old* (pp. 321-340). New York: Oxford University Press.

Giddings, P. (1984). *When and where I enter: The impact of black women on race and sex in America.* New York: Bantam.

Gilkes, C. T. (1985). Together and in harness: Women's traditions in the sanctified church. *Signs: Journal of Women in Culture and Society, 10,* 678-699.

Giovanni, N. (1979). *Black feeling, black talk, black judgement.* New York: Morrow Quill.

Goldsmith, R., & Heims, R. (1992). Subjective age: A test of five hypotheses. *The Gerontologist, 32*(3), 312-317.

Grant, J. (1982). Black women and the church. In G. T. Hull, R. Bell-Scott, & B. Smith (Eds.), *But some of us are brave: Black women's studies* (pp. 141-152). Old Westbury, NY: Feminist Press.

Guemple, L. (1983). Growing old in Inuit society. In J. Sokolovsky (Ed.), *Growing old in different cultures* (pp. 24-28). Belmont, CA: Wadsworth.

Guy-Sheftall, B. (1991). Piecing blocks: Identities—introduction. In R. Bell-Scott, B. Guy-Sheftall, J. Jones Royster, J. Sims-Wood, M. DeCosta-Willis, & L. Fultz (Eds.), *Double stitch: Black women write about mothers and daughters* (pp. 61-63). Boston: Beacon.

Gwaltney, J. L. (Ed.). (1980). *Drylongso: A self-portrait of black America.* New York: Random House.

Hacker, A. (1992). *Two nations: Black and white, separate, hostile, unequal.* New York: Scribner.

Hardy, M., & Quadagno, J. (1995). Satisfaction with the early retirement decision: Making choices in the auto industry. *Journal of Gerontology, 50,* S217-S228.

Harvest Moon Eyes. (1992). The day the crows stopped talking. In C. Trafzer (Ed.), *Earth song, sky spirit: Short stories of the contemporary Native American experience.* New York: Doubleday.

Haslam, G. (1993). The horned toad. In T. A. López (Ed.), *Growing up Chicana/o*. New York: Avon Books.

Haug, M. (1995). Elderly power in the 21st century. *Journal of Women and Aging, 7*(4), 3-10.

Hazuda, H. P., & Espino, D. V. (1997). Aging, chronic disease, and physical disability in Hispanic elderly. In K. Markides & M. Miranda (Eds.), *Minorities, aging, and health* (pp. 127-148). Thousand Oaks, CA: Sage.

Herzog, A. R., Kahn, R. L., Morgan, J. N., Jackson, J. S., & Antonucci, T. C. (1989). Age differences in productive activities. *Journal of Gerontology, 44*(4), 129-138.

Hess, B. (1990). Beyond dichotomy: Drawing distinctions and embracing differences. *Sociological Forum, 5*(1), 75-93.

Heurtin-Roberts, S. (1993). High-pertension: The uses of a chronic folk illness for personal adaptation. *Social Science & Medicine, 37*(3), 285-294.

Heyck, D. L. D. (1994). *Barrios and borderlands: Cultures of Latins and Latinas in the United States*. New York: Routledge.

Higginbotham, E. (1989). *Privilege and the inclusive curriculum*. Paper presented at the annual meeting of the American Sociological Society, San Francisco.

Hill, L., Colby, A., & Phelps, E. (1983). *Coping and adaptation to aging in a sample of black women leaders*. Unpublished manuscript, Cambridge, MA.

Himes, C. B. (1975). Headwaiter. In *Black on black: Baby sister and selected writings* (pp. 144-160). London: Joseph.

Himes, C. B. (1975). Pork chop paradise. In *Black on black: Baby sister and selected writings* (pp. 161-175). London: Joseph.

Hines, R. N., Garcia-Preto, M., McGoldrick, R. A., & Weltman, S. (1992). Intergenerational relationships across cultures. *Families in Society: The Journal of Contemporary Human Services* (CEU Article No. 23), pp. 323-338.

Hochschild, A. (1989). *The second shift: Working parents and the revolution at home*. New York: Viking Penguin.

Hondagneu-Soleto, P. (1996). Domestic workers and their employers. In P. Dubeck & K. Borman (Eds.), *Women and work: A reader* (pp. 44-47). New Brunswick, NJ: Routledge.

Hong, M. (Ed.). (1993). *Growing up Asian American: An anthology*. New York: William Morrow.

hooks, b. (1984). *Feminist theory from margin to center*. Boston: South End Press.

Hooyman, N. R., & Gonyea, J. (1995). *Feminist perspectives on family care: Policies for gender justice* (Family Caregiver Application series, Vol. 6). Thousand Oaks, CA: Sage.

Hooyman, N., & Kiyak, H. A. (1999). *Social gerontology: A multidisciplinary perspective* (5th ed.). Boston: Allyn & Bacon.

Horowitz, A. (1985). Family caregiving to the frail elderly. In M. P. Lawton & G. L. Maddox (Eds.), *Annual Review of Gerontology and Geriatrics, 5*, 194-256.

Hospital, C. (Ed.). (1988). *Cuban American writers: Los atrevidos*. London: Lane.

House, J. S., Kessler, R. C., Herzog, A. R., Mero, R., Kinney, A., & Breslow, M. (1990). Age, socioeconomic status, and health. *Millbank Quarterly, 68*(3), 383-406.

Hughes, L. (1926). Mother to son. In *Selected poems of Langston Hughes*. New York: Knopf. Reprinted (1991) in M. H. Washington (Ed.), *Memory of kin: Stories about family by black writers* (p. 165). New York: Anchor.

Hummert, M. L., Garstka, T., Shaner, J., & Strahm, S. (1994). Stereotypes of the elderly held by young, middle-aged and elderly adults. *Journal of Gerontology, 49,* P240-P249.

Hurston, Z. N. (1992a). How it feels to be colored me. In C. Schuster & W. Van Pelt (Eds.), *Speculations: Readings in culture, identity and values.* Englewood Cliffs, NJ: Prentice Hall.

Hurston, Z. N. (1992b). My most humiliating Jim Crow experience. In M. G. Secundy (Ed.), *Trials, tribulations and celebrations: African-American perspectives on health, illness, aging and loss.* Yarmouth, ME: Intercultural Press. Reprinted in A. Walker (Ed.), *I love myself when I am laughing: A Zora Neale Hurston reader* (pp. 163-164). Old Westbury, NY: Feminist Press.

Jackson, J. J. (1988, May-June). Aging black women and public policies. *Black Scholar,* pp. 31-43.

Jackson, J. S. (1989). Race, ethnicity and psychological theory and research. *Journal of Gerontology: Psychological Sciences, 41*(1), P1-P2.

Jackson, J. S., Antonucci, T. C., & Gibson, R. C. (1993). Cultural and ethnic contexts of aging productively over the lifecourse: An economic network framework. In S. A. Bass, F. G. Caro, & Y. Chen (Eds.), *Achieving a productive aging society* (pp. 249-268). Westport, CT: Auburn House.

Jackson, J. S., McCullough, W., Gurin, G., & Broman, C. (1991). Race identity. In J. S. Jackson (Ed.), *Life in black America* (pp. 238-253). Newbury Park, CA: Sage.

Jen, G. (1991). *Typical American.* Boston: Houghton Mifflin.

John, R. (1997). Aging and mortality among American Indians: Concerns about the reliability of a crucial indicator of health status. In K. Markides & M. Miranda (Eds.), *Minorities, aging, and health* (pp. 79-106). Thousand Oaks, CA: Sage.

Johnson, C. L., & Barer, B. M. (1990). Families and networks among older inner-city blacks. *The Gerontologist, 39*(6), 726-733.

Jones, J. (1991). *Bad blood: The Tuskegee syphilis experiment.* New York: Free Press.

Jones, S. W. (1983). Esse quam videri. In E. H. Wilson (Ed.), *Hope and dignity: Older black women of the South* (pp. 59-65). Philadelphia: Temple University Press.

Jöreskog, K. G., & Sörbom, D. (Eds.). (1979). *Advances in factor analysis and structural equation models.* Cambridge, MA: Abt.

Joseph, J. (1987). Warning. In S. Martz (Ed.), *When I am an old woman I shall wear purple.* Watsonville, CA: Papier-Mache.

Joseph, K. S., & Kramer, M.S. (1996). Review of the evidence on fetal and early childhood antecedents of adult chronic disease. *Epidemiological Review, 18,* 158-187.

Juster, F. T. (1965). *Time, goods and well-being.* Ann Arbor: University of Michigan, Survey Research Institute, Institute for Social Research.

Kagawa-Singer, M., Hikoyeda, N., & Tanjasiri, S. P. (1997). Aging, chronic conditions, and physical disabilities in Asian and Pacific Islander Americans. In K. Markides and M. Miranda (Eds.), *Minorities, aging, and health* (pp. 149-180). Thousand Oaks, CA: Sage.

Kaplan, B. H., Cassel, J. C., & Gore, S. (1977). Social support and health. *Medical Care, 15*(5), 47-58.

Kart, C. S. (1997). *The realities of aging: An introduction to gerontology* (4th ed.). Boston: Allyn & Bacon.

Kasl, S. V. (1979). Changes in mental health status associated with job loss and retirement. In American Psychopathological Association (Ed.), *Stress and mental disorder* (pp. 179-200). New York: Raven.

Kasl, S. V., & Berkman, L. F. (1985). Some psychosocial influences on the health status of the elderly: The perspective of social epidemiology. In J. L. McGaugh & S. B. Kiesler (Eds.), *Aging: Biology and behavior* (pp. 345-385). New York: Academic Press.

Kaufman, S. R. (1986). *The ageless self.* Madison: University of Wisconsin Press.

Kim, K. C., Kim, S., & Hurh, W. M. (1991). Filial piety and intergenerational relationship in Korean immigrant families. *International Journal of Aging and Human Development, 33*(3), 233-245.

Kimmel, D. C. (1992, Summer). The families of older gay men and lesbians. *Generations, 16,* 37-38.

Kitagawa, E. M., & Hauser, P. M. (1973). *Differential mortality in the United States: A study in socioeconomic epidemiology.* Cambridge, MA: Harvard University Press.

Kitano, H., & Daniels, R. (1988). *Asian Americans.* Englewood Cliffs, NJ: Prentice Hall.

Kleinman, A. (1988). *The illness narratives: Suffering, healing, and the human condition.* New York: Basic Books.

Kohn, M. L. (1972). Class, family and schizophrenia: A reformulation. *Social Forces, 50,* 295-304.

Kohn, M. L. (1977). *Class and conformity.* Chicago: University of Chicago Press.

Konrad, T. R. (1998). The patterns of self-care among older adults in western industrialized societies. In M. G. Ory & G. DeFriese (Eds.), *Self-care in later life: Research, program and policy issues* (pp. 1-23). New York: Springer.

Langner, T. S., & Michael, S. T. (1963). *Life stress and mental health.* New York: Free Press.

Lee, G. (1988, March). *Family caregiving for the rural elderly.* Paper presented at the conference, "The Rural Elderly in 1988: A National Perspective," sponsored by the U.S. Department of Agriculture and the University of Arizona, San Diego, CA.

Lee, G. (1992). Gender differences in family caregiving: A fact in search of a theory. In J. W. Dwyer & R. T. Coward (Eds.), *Gender, families, and elder care.* Newbury Park, CA: Sage.

Leffland, E. (1992). The linden tree. In *Last courtesies and other stories.* New York: Harper Collins.

Lerner, G. (1973). *Black women in white America.* New York: Vintage.

Leventhal, H., Diefenbach, M., & Leventhal, E. (1992). Illness cognition: Using common sense to understand treatment adherence and affect cognition interactions. *Cognitive Therapy and Research, 16*(2), 143-163.

Lewis, J., & Meredith, B. (1988). *Daughters who care: Daughters caring for mothers at home.* London: Routledge & Kegan Paul.

Liem, N. D., & Kehmeier, D. (1979). The Vietnamese. In J. R. McDermott (Ed.), *Peoples and cultures of Hawaii.* Honolulu: University of Hawaii Press.

Link, B., & Phelan, J. (1995). Social conditions as fundamental causes of disease. *Journal of Health and Social Behavior* [Extra Issue], 80-94.

Lipman, A. (1986). Homosexual relationships. *Generations, 10*(4), 51-54.

Lorber, J. (1997). *Gender and the social construction of illness.* Thousand Oaks, CA: Sage.

Lowe, P. (1943). Father cures a presidential fever. *In Father and glorious descendant*. Boston: Little, Brown. Reprinted (1993) in M. Hong (Ed.), *Growing up Asian American: An anthology*. New York: Morrow.

Lynch, J. W., Kaplan, G.A., & Salonen, J.T. (1997). Why do poor people behave poorly? Variation in adult health behaviors and psycho-social characteristics by stages of the socioeconomic life course. *Social Science and Medicine, 44,* 809-820.

Maas, H. S., & Kuypers, J. A. (1974). *From thirty to seventy: A forty-year longitudinal study of adult life styles and personality*. San Francisco: Jossey-Bass.

Macfarlane, J. W. (1938). Studies in child guidance: I. Methodology of data collection and organization. *Monographs of the Society for Research in Child Development, 3,* 1-254.

Maddox, G. (1988). Aging, drinking, and alcohol abuse. *Generations, 12*(4), 14-16.

Malbin-Glazer, N. (1976). Housework. *Signs, 1,* 905-922.

Manton, K. G., Patrick, C. H., & Johnson, K. W. (1987). Health differences between blacks and whites: Recent trends in mortality and morbidity. *Milbank Quarterly, 65,* 129-199.

Manton, K., & Stallard, E. (1997). Health and disability differences among racial and ethnic groups. In L. Martin & B. Soldo (Eds.), *Racial and ethnic differences in the health of older Americans* (pp. 43-104). Washington, DC: National Academy Press.

Markides, K. S., Liang, J., & Jackson, J. J. (1990). Race, ethnicity and aging: Conceptual and methodological issues. In R. Binstock & L. George (Eds.), *Handbook of aging and the social sciences*. New York: Academic Press.

Markides, K. S., & Mindel, C. H. (1987). *Aging and ethnicity*. Newbury Park, CA: Sage.

Markides, K. S., & Wallace, S. (1996). Health and long-term care needs of ethnic minority elders. In J. Romeis, R. Coe, & J. Morley (Eds.), *Applying health services research to long-term care* (pp. 23-42). New York: Springer.

Martz, S. H. (Ed.). (1987). *When I am an old woman I shall wear purple*. Watsonville, CA: Papier-Mache.

Martz, S. H. (Ed.). (1992). *If I had my life to live over, I would pick more daisies*. Watsonville, CA: Papier-Mache.

Matthews, S. H. (1988). The burden of parent care: A critical assessment of the recent literature. *Journal of Aging Studies, 2,* 158-165.

McAdoo, H. (1986). Societal stress: The black family. In J. Cole (Ed.), *All American women: Lines that divide, ties that bind* (pp. 187-197). New York: Free Press.

McClaurin-Allen, I. (1990). Incongruities: Dissonance and contradiction in the life of a black middle-class woman. In F. Ginsburg & A. L. Tsing (Eds.), *Uncertain terms: Negotiating gender in American culture*. Boston: Beacon.

McIntosh, P. (1998). White privilege and male privilege: A personal account of coming to see correspondences through work in women's studies. In M. L. Andersen & P. H. Collins (Eds.), *Race, class, and gender: An anthology* (3rd ed.). Belmont, CA: Wadsworth.

Mechanic, D. (1972). Social class and schizophrenia: Some requirements for a plausible theory of social influence. *Social Forces, 50,* 305-309.

Meyer, M. (1988). Implications for assessment: Characteristics of rural families in crisis. *Journal of Rural Community Psychology, 9,* 12-15.

Mills, C. W. (1959). *The sociological imagination.* New York: Oxford University Press.

Minkler, M. (1989). Gold in gray: Reflections on business; discovery of the elderly market. *The Gerontologist, 29*(1), 17-23.

Minkler, M., & Fuller-Thompson, E. (1997). Depression in grandparents raising grandchildren. *Archives of Family Medicine,* 445-452.

Moen, P. (1992). *Women's two roles: A contemporary dilemma.* New York: Auburn House.

Moen, P., Dempster-McClain, D., & Williams, R. M., Jr. (1989). Social integration and longevity: An event history analysis of women's roles and resilience. *American Sociological Review, 54,* 635-647.

Moen, P., Dempster-McClain, D., & Williams, R. M., Jr. (1992). Successful aging: A life course perspective on women's multiple roles and health. *American Journal of Sociology, 97,* 1612-1638.

Morgan, L., & Kunkel, S. (1998). *Aging: The social context.* Thousand Oaks, CA: Pine Forge Press.

Morrison, T. (July 4, 1975). A slow walk of trees. *New York Times Magazine.*

Moses, Y. (1992). *Diversity in the undergraduate curriculum.* Plenary address at "Rethinking the Major," conference sponsored by the Association of American Colleges, Philadelphia.

Moynihan, D. P. (1965). *The Negro family: The case for national action.* Washington, DC: Government Printing Office.

Nagel, J. (1997). *American Indian ethnic revival.* Oxford, UK: Oxford University Press.

Nathan, J. (1990). Public policy issues and the minority elder. In *Minority aging.* Washington, DC: U.S. Public Health Services.

National Center for Health Statistics. (1991). *Health, United States, 1990.* Hyattsville, MD: Public Health Service.

National Film Board of Canada. (1991). *Strangers in good company* [Film]. Burbank, CA: Buena Vista Home Video.

National Resource Center on Health Promotion and Aging and AARP Health Advocacy Services. (1990). *Healthy aging: Model health promotion programs for minority elders* [½-in. videocassette/46 min./color]. (Distributed by National Resource Center on Health Promotion and Aging and AARP, Washington, DC, 202-434-2277)

Naylor, G. (1989). *Mama Day.* New York: Vintage.

Neal, M. B., Chapman, N. J., Ingersoll-Dayton, B., & Emlen, A. C. (1993). *Balancing work and caregiving for children, adults and elders.* Newbury Park, CA: Sage.

Neugarten, B. L. (1970). Dynamics of transition of middle age to old age: Adaptation and the life cycle. *Journal of Geriatric Psychiatry, 4,* 71-89.

Novas, H. (1994). *Everything you need to know about Latino history.* New York: Penguin.

O'Rand, A. (1996). The cumulative stratification of the life course. In R. Binstocke & L. K. George (Eds.), *Handbook of aging and social sciences* (4th ed.; pp. 188-207). San Diego, CA: Academic Press.

O'Rand, A. (1998). The craft of life course studies. In J. Giele & G. H. Elder, Jr. (Eds.), *Methods of life course research: Qualitative and quantitative approaches* (pp. 52-74). Thousand Oaks, CA: Sage.

Oakley, A. (1974). *The sociology of housework.* Oxford: Martin Robertson.

Olsen [Lerner], T. (1934, March). I want you women up north to know. *Partisan, 1*. Reprinted (1990) in J. Zandy (Ed.), *Calling home: Working-class women's writings, an anthology*. New Brunswick, NJ: Rutgers University Press; and in D. Rosenfelt (1981), From the thirties: Tillie Olsen and the radical tradition. *Feminist Studies, 7*(3), 367-369.

Ostrander, S. (1984). Community volunteer. In *Women of the upper class* (pp. 111-139). Philadelphia: Temple University Press.

Parsons, T. (1955). The American family: Its relations to personality and the social structure. In T. Parsons & R. Bales (Eds.), *Family socialization and interaction process* (pp. 3-21). Glencoe, IL: Free Press.

Pavalko, E., & Artis, J. E. (1997). Women's caregiving and paid work: Causal relationships in late life. *Journals of Gerontology, 52B*, S170-S179.

Pearlin, L. I., & Johnson, J. S. (1977). Marital status, life strains, and depression. *American Sociological Review, 42*, 704-715.

Peplau, L. A. (1991). Lesbian and gay relationships. In J. C. Gonsiorek & J. D. Weinrich (Eds.), *Homosexuality: Research implications for public policy*. Newbury Park, CA: Sage.

Peterson, C. (1980, October 5-6). *The sense of control over one's life: A review of recent literature*. Paper prepared for the Social Science Research Council Meeting, "Self and Personal Control Over the Life Span," New York.

Quadagno, J. (1999). *Aging and the life course: An introduction to social gerontology*. Boston: McGraw-Hill.

Quadagno, J., & Meyer, M. H. (1990). Gender and public policy. *Generations, 14*(3), 64-66.

Quan, J. K., & Whitford, G. (1992). Adaptation and age-related expectations of older gay and lesbian adults. *The Gerontologist, 32*, 367-374.

Quinn, J., & Smeeding, T. (1993). The present and future economic well-being of the aged. In R. Burkhauser & D. Salisbury (Eds.), *Pensions in a changing economy* (pp. 5-18). Washington, DC: Employee Benefit Research Institute.

Rainwater, L., & Yancey, W. (1967). *The Moynihan Report and the politics of controversy*. Cambridge: MIT Press.

Renzetti, C., & Curran, D. (1997). *Women, men and society* (3rd ed.). Boston: Allyn & Bacon.

Rick, K., & Forward, J. (1992). Acculturation and perceived intergenerational differences among youth. *Journal of Cross-Cultural Psychology, 23*(1), 85-94.

Riley, M. W. (1998). *Sociological lives*. Thousand Oaks, CA: Sage.

Riley, M. W., & Riley, J. W., Jr. (1989). The lives of olde people and changing social roles. *Annals of the American Academy of Political and Social Science, 503*, 14-28.

Rodeheaver, D., & Stohs, J. (1991). The adaptive misperception of age in older women: Sociocultural images and psychological mechanisms of control. *Educational Gerontology, 17*, 141-156.

Rollins, J. (1985). *Between women: Domestics and their employers*. Philadelphia: Temple University Press.

Rosenfield, S. (1989). The effect of women's employment: Personal control and sex difference in mental health. *Journal of Health and Social Behavior, 30*, 77-91.

Rosenthal, C. J. (1985). Kinkeeping in the familial division of labor. *Journal of Marriage and the Family, 47*, 965-974.

Rowe, J., & Kahn, K. (1997). *Successful aging*. New York: Pantheon.

Saluter, A. (1997). *Marital status and living arrangements*. Washington, DC: U.S. Bureau of the Census.

Schecter, S. (Producer & director). (1985). *The homefront* [Film]. PBS.

Schmidt, D., & Boland, S. (1986). Structure of perceptions of older adults: Evidence for multiple stereotypes. *Psychology and Aging, 1*, 255-260.

Schnall, P., Schwartz, J., Landsbergis, P., Warren, K., & Pickering, T. (1992). Relation between job strain, alcohol and ambulatory blood pressure. *Hypertension, 19*, 488-494.

Schoenbaum, M., & Raidmann, T. (1997). Race, socioeconomic status, and health: Accounting for race differences in health [Special issue]. *Journals of Gerontology, Series B, Psychological Sciences, 52*, 61-73.

Schuman, H., & Scott, J. (1989). Generations and collective memories. *American Sociological Review, 54*, 359-381.

Schweitzer, M. (1987). The elders: Cultural dimensions of aging in two American Indian communities. In J. Sokolovsky (Ed.), *Growing old in different societies*. Acton, MA: Copley.

Seccombe, K. (1992). Employment, the family, and employer-based policies. In J. W. Dwyer & R. T. Coward (Eds.), *Gender, families, and elder care*. Newbury Park, CA: Sage.

Segall, A., & Goldstein, J. (1989). Exploring the correlates of self-provided health care behavior. *Social Science and Medicine, 29*(2), 153-161.

Segall, L. M., & Wykle, M. (1998-89). The black family's experience with dementia. *Journal of Applied Social Sciences, 13*, 170-191.

Seltzer, J. (1987). A place for mother. In S. Martz (Ed.), *When I am an old woman I shall wear purple*. Watsonville, CA: Papier Mache.

Shurkin, J. N. (1992). *Terman's kids: The groundbreaking study of how the gifted grow up*. Boston: Little, Brown.

Silko, L. M. (1981). Lullaby. In *The storyteller*. New York: Seaver. Reprinted (1991) in B. R. Rico & S. Mano (Eds.), *American mosaic: Multicultural readings in context* (pp. 587-594). Boston: Houghton Mifflin.

Simmons, L. (1945). *The role of the aged in primitive society*. New Haven, CT: Yale University Press.

Singer, I. B. (1988). The hotel. In *The death of Methuselah and other stories*. New York: Farrar, Straus & Giroux. Reprinted (1991) in M. Fowler & P. McCutcheon (Eds.), *Songs of experience: An anthology of literature on growing old* (pp. 165-175). New York: Ballantine.

Skolnick, A. (1991). Changes of heart: Family dynamics in historical perspective. In P. Cowan, D. Field, D. Hansen, A. Skolnick, & G. Swanson (Eds.), *Family, self and society: Towards a new agenda for family research*. Hillsdale, NJ: Lawrence Erlbaum.

Slevin, K., & Wingrove, R. (1998). *From stumbling blocks to stepping stones: The life experiences of fifty professional African American women*. New York: New York University Press.

Smeeding, T. (1990). Economic status of the elderly. In R. Binstock & L. George (Eds.), *Handbook of aging and the social sciences*. New York: Academic Press.

Smith, B. (Ed.). (1983). *Home girls: A black feminist anthology*. Albany, NY: Kitchen Table.

Smith, D. E. (1987). *The everyday world as problematic: A feminist sociology*. Toronto: University of Toronto Press.

Sone, M. (1953). Pearl Harbor echoes in Seattle. In *Nisei daughter*. Boston: Little, Brown. Reprinted (1991) in B. R. Rico & S. Mano (Eds.), *American mosaic: Multicultural readings in context* (pp. 335-346). Boston: Houghton Mifflin.

Speas, K., & Obenshain, B. (1995). *AARP Images: Aging in America: Final Report.* Washington, DC: American Association of Retired Persons.

Srole, L. (1978). *Mental health in the metropolis: The midtown Manhattan study* (rev. and enlarged ed.). New York: New York University Press.

Stack, C. (1974). *All our kin.* New York: Harper & Row.

Stair, N. (1992). If I had my life to live over. In S. Martz (Ed.), *If I had my life to live over, I would pick more daisies.* Watsonville, CA: Papier-Mache.

Stanford, E. P., Peddecord, M., & Lockery, S. (1990). Variations among the elderly in black, Hispanic, and white families. In T. Brubaker (Ed.), *Family relations in later life* (2nd ed.). Newbury Park, CA: Sage.

Stanford, E. P., & Yee, D. (1991, Fall-Winter). Gerontology and the relevance of diversity. *Generations, 15,* 11-14.

Steinitz, L. Y. (1981). The local church as support for the elderly. *Journal of Gerontological Social Work, 4,* 43-53.

Steuve, A., & O'Donnell, L. (1989). Interactions between women and their elderly parents: Constraints of daughters' employment. *Research on Aging, 11,* 331-353.

Stoller, E. P. (1983). Parental caregiving by adult children. *Journal of Marriage and the Family, 45,* 851-858.

Stoller, E. (1993). Why women care: Gender and the organization of lay care. *Journal of Aging Studies, 7*(2), 151-170.

Stoller, E. P. (1998). Dynamics and processes of self-care in old age. In M. G. Ory & G. DeFriese (Eds.), *Self-care in later life: Research, program and policy issues* (pp. 24-61). New York: Springer.

Stoller, E., Forster, L., & Pollow, R. (1994). Older people's recommendations for treating symptoms: Repertoires of lay knowledge about disease. *Medical Care, 32*(8), 847-862.

Stoller, E., Forster, L., & Portugal, S. (1993). Self-care responses to symptoms by older people. *Medical Care, 30,* 24-42.

Stone, R. I. (1989, Spring & Summer). The feminization of poverty among the elderly. *Women's Studies Quarterly, 17,* 20-34.

Stone, R. I., Cafferata, G., & Sangl, J. (1987). Caregivers of the frail elderly: A national profile. *The Gerontologist, 27,* 616-626.

Stone, R. I., & Short, P. F. (1990). The competing demands of employment and informal caregiving to disabled elders. *Medical Care, 28,* 513-526.

Strawbridge, W. J., Cohen, R. D., Shema, S. J., & Kaplan, G. A. (1996, July). Successful aging: Predictors and associated activities. *American Journal of Epidemiology, 144*(2), 135-141.

Sudarkasa, N. (1981). Interpreting the African heritage in Afro-American family organizations. In H. McAdoo (Ed.), *Black families* (pp. 37-53). Beverly Hills, CA: Sage.

Sue, D. W., & Sue, D. (1990). *Counselling the culturally different: Theory and practice* (2nd ed.). New York: John Wiley.

Sue, S. (1991). Ethnicity and culture in psychological research and practice. In J. D. Goodchilds (Ed.), *Psychological perspectives on human diversity in America* (pp. 51-85). Washington, DC: American Psychological Association.

Tan, A. (1989). *The joy luck club.* New York: G. P. Putnam.

Taylor, R. J., & Chatters, L. M. (1986). Church-based informal support among elderly blacks. *The Gerontologist, 26*(6), 637-642.

Taylor, S. (1982). Religion as a coping mechanism for older black women. *Quarterly Contact, 5*(4), 2-3.

Terkel, S. (1974). Mike LeFevre. In *Working: People talk about the work they do all day and how they feel about what they do*. New York: Pantheon. Reprinted (1992) in C. Schuster & W. Van Pelt (Eds.), *Speculations: Readings in culture, identity and values* (pp. 520-524). Englewood Cliffs, NJ: Prentice Hall.

Terkel, S. (1995). *Coming of age*. New York: The New Press.

Thomas, E. M. (1959). *The harmless people*. New York: Knopf.

Thomas, R. (1967). Puerto Rican paradise. In *Down these mean streets* (pp. 268-272). New York: Knopf.

Thone, R. R. (1992). *Women and aging: Celebrating ourselves*. New York: Haworth.

Torres-Gil, F. M., & Hyde, J. C. (1990). The impact of minorities on long-term care policy in California. In P. Kiebig & W. Lammers (Eds.), *California policy choices for long-term care* (pp. 31-52). Los Angeles: University of Southern California Press.

Tracy, A. (1992). *Between the funerals: Measuring*. Unpublished manuscript.

Tran, T. V. (1988). Sex differences in English language acculturation and learning strategies among Vietnamese adults aged 40 and over in the United States. *Sex Roles, 19*, 747-758.

Tran, T. V. (1991). Family living arrangement and social adjustment among three ethnic groups of elderly Indochinese refugees. *International Journal of Aging and Human Development, 32*(2), 91-102.

Treas, J. (1977). Family support systems for the aged: Some social and demographic considerations. *The Gerontologist, 17*, 486-491.

Tucker, K. L., Falcon, L., & Bermudez, O. (1997). Nutrition among Hispanic elders in the United States. In K. Markides & M. Miranda (Eds.), *Minorities, aging, and health* (pp. 235-270). Thousand Oaks, CA: Sage.

Twaddle, C. A., & Hessler, R. (1987). *A sociology of health* (2nd ed.). New York: Macmillan.

Uhlenberg, P., & Miner, S. (1996). Life course and aging: A cohort perspective. In R. Binstock & L. George (Eds.), *Handbook of aging and the social sciences* (4th ed.; pp. 208-228). San Diego, CA: Academic Press.

Umberson, D. (1992). Gender, marital status and the social control of health behavior. *Social Science and Medicine, 34*, 907-917.

U.S. Bureau of the Census. (1987). Pensions: Worker coverage and retirement income. *Current Population Reports* (Series P-70, No. 12). Washington, DC: Government Printing Office.

U.S. Bureau of the Census. (1989). Projections of the population of the United States, by age, sex, and race: 1988 to 2080. *Current Population Reports* (Series 25, no. 1018). Washington, DC: Government Printing Office.

Van Nostrand, J. F., Furner, S., & Suzman, R. (Eds.). (1993). Health data on older Americans: United States, 1992. *Vital Health Statistics, 3*(77). Hyattsville, MD: National Center for Health Statistics.

Verbrugge, L., Gruber-Baldini, A. C., & Fozard, J. L. (1996). Age differences and age changes in activities: Baltimore Longitudinal Study of Aging. *Journals of Gerontology, 51B*, S30-S41.

Waitzkin, H. (1974). *The exploitation of illness in capitalist society*. Indianapolis, IN: Bobbs-Merrill.

Walker, A. (1983). In search of our mothers' gardens. In *In search of our mothers' gardens: Womanist prose* (pp. 231-243). San Diego, CA: Harcourt Brace Jovanovich.

Wallace, S. (1965). *Skid row as a way of life*. Totowa, NJ: Bedminister.

Wallace, S. P., & Villa, V. M. (1997). Caught in hostile cross-fire: Public policy and minority elders in the United States. In K. Markides & M. Miranda (Eds.), *Minorities, aging, and health* (pp. 397-420). Thousand Oaks, CA: Sage.

Walls, C. T., & Zarit, S. H. (1991). Informal support from black churches and the well-being of elderly blacks. *The Gerontologist, 32*(4), 490-495.

Walser, A. (1986). I didn't have no family before I was married. In V. Byerly (Ed.), *Hard times cotton mill girls: Personal histories of womanhood and poverty in the South*. Ithaca, NY: ILR. Reprinted (1990) in J. Zandy (Ed.), *Calling home: Working-class women's writings, an anthology* (pp. 21-26). New Brunswick, NJ: Rutgers University Press.

Weibel-Orlando, J. (1989). Elders and elderlies: Well-being in Indian Old Age. *American Indian Culture and Research Journal, 13*(3-4), 149-170.

Weibel-Orlando, J. (1990). Grandparenting styles: Native American perspectives. In J. Sokolovsky (Ed.), *The cultural context of aging: Worldwide perspectives* (pp. 109-125). New York: Bergin and Garvey.

Weinstein-Shr, G., & Henkin, N. Z. (1991). Continuity and change: Intergenerational relations in southeast Asian refugee families. *Marriage and Family Review, 16*, 351-367.

West, C., & Fenstermaker, S. (1995). Doing difference. *Gender and Society, 9*(1), 8-37.

White, A. J. (1991). Dyad/triad. In P. Bell-Scott, B. Guy-Sheftall, J. Royster, J. Sims-Wood, M. DeCosta-Willis, & L. Fultz (Eds.), *Double stitch: Black women write about mothers and daughters* (pp. 188-195). Boston: Beacon.

Wilkinson, D. (1987). Traditional medicine in American families: Reliance on the wisdom of elders. *Culture, Medicine, and Psychiatry, 11*, 65-76.

Williams, D. R. (1990). Socioeconomic differentials in health: A review and redirection. *Social Psychology Quarterly, 53*(2), 81-99.

Wilson, E. H., & Mullalley, S. (Eds.). (1983). *Hope and dignity: Older black women of the South*. Philadelphia: Temple University Press.

Woo, D. (1989). The gap between striving and achieving: The case of Asian American women. In Asian Women United of California (Eds.), *Making waves: An anthology of writings by and about Asian American women* (pp. 185-194). Boston: Beacon.

Wood, J. B., & Wan, T. (1993). Ethnicity and minority issues in family caregiving to rural black elders. In C. M. Baressi & D. E. Stull (Eds.), *Ethnic elderly and long-term care* (pp. 39-57). New York: Springer.

Wray, L. (1991). Public policy implications of an ethnically diverse elderly population. *Journal of Cross-Cultural Gerontology, 6*, 243-257.

Wright, R. (1991). The ethics of living Jim Crow. In H. L. Gates, Jr. (Ed.), *Bearing witness: Selections from African-American autobiography in the twentieth century*. New York: Pantheon. (Original work published 1937)

Wu, C. (1989). *Making waves: The world of our grandmothers*. Boston: Beacon.

Yee, B. W. K. (1989). Loss of one's homeland and culture during the middle years. In R. A. Kalish (Ed.), *Coping with the losses of middle age* (pp. 281-300). Newbury Park, CA: Sage.

Yee, B. W. K. (in press). Markers of successful aging among Vietnamese refugee women. *Women and Therapy, 12*(2).

Yee, B. W. K., & Nguyen, D. (1987). Correlates of drug abuse and abuse among Indochinese refugees: Mental health implications. *Journal of Psychoactive Drugs, 19,* 77-83.

Zsembik, B. A., & Singer, A. (1990). The problem of defining retirement among minorities: The Mexican Americans. *Gerontologist, 30*(6), 749-757.

Zuckerman, M. (1987). After sixty. In P. Doress & D. Ziegel (Eds.), *Ourselves, growing older.* New York: Simon & Schuster.

Author Index

Aging Health Policy Center, 106
Akiyama, H., 214
Alagena, S. W., 319
Alba, R., 3
Amoss, P., 249, 250
Anaya, R., 281
Andersen, M. L., xiii, 7, 10, 25, 77, 78,
    79, 203, 204
Andersen, R. M., 319
Angel, J., 271, 280
Angel, R., 271, 280
Angelou, M., 12, 284, 287
Antonovsky, A., 319
Antonucci, T. C., 124, 126, 128, 130, 214,
    319, 320
Apfel, N. H., 253
Arendell, T., 174
Aronson, J., 211
Artis, J. E., 211
Atchley, R. C., 75

Bandura, A., 35
Barer, B., 213
Barnett, H., 249
Barresi, C. M., 246, 247
Baxandall, R., 133
Beck, R. W., 253, 257
Beck, S. H., 253, 257
Becker, M., 273
Belanger, A., 315, 316
Bell, L. P., 78
Bengston, V., 76, 216, 253
Bentler, P. M., 319
Berg, R. R., 166
Berkman, L., 312, 315, 319, 320
Berkman, L. F., 275, 276
Bermudez, O., 275
Berson, A., 106
Blazer, D. G., 319
Bogue, D. J., 106
Bohrnstedt, G. W., 35
Boland, S., 75
Bonanno, A., 127, 135
Bond, J., 127
Bontemps, A., 284, 288-293
Bound, J., 191, 194
Bovard, E. W., 319
Bowlby, J., 34
Brenner, M. H., 36
Breslau, N., 165
Breslow, L., 319
Breslow, M., 270
Brickner, P. W., 106
Broadhead, E. W., 319
Brody, E. M., 165, 216

Broman, C., 87
Brook, R. H., 319
Brooks, G., 138, 139, 140, 187-188
Brooks-Gunn, J., 253
Brown, E. B., 132, 207, 214
Brubaker, E., 211
Bullard, S., 26
Burton, L. M., 76, 214, 216, 252, 253
Butler, R. N., 34
Byerly, V., 131, 138, 142-145

Cafferata, G., 165
Cafferata, G. L., 320
Calasanti, T. M., 2, 4, 127, 135, 137
Camacho, T., 319
Campbell, B. M., 220, 260-263
Campbell, R., 214
Cantor, M. H., 129
Casper, L. M., 253
Cassel, J., 319
Cassel, J. C., 319
Cassells, J. S., 166
Chapleski, E., 280
Chapman, N. J., 174
Chase-Landsdale, P. L., 253
Chatters, L. M., 8
Chen, H., 141, 191-196
Cherlin, A. J., 253
Cheung, M., 82
Childress, A., 141, 189-190
Clark, D. O., 270, 315
Clipp, E. C., 21
Clive, A., 25
Clogg, C. C., 192
Coe, R. M., 319
Cohen, C. I., 107
Cohen, M., 2, 3
Cohen, R. A., 270, 272
Cohen, R. D., 271
Cohen, S., 319
Cohm, R. M., 36
Colby, A., 19, 23, 29
Cole, J., xiv, xv, 7, 8, 129, 130, 139, 203,
    205, 211
Colletta, N. D., 253
Collins, P. H., xiii, 7, 23, 79, 82, 205, 206,
    207, 213
Conanan, B. A., 106
Conzen, K., 3
Cook, J. M., 220, 252-259
Cool, L. E., 217
Coontz, S., 203, 207, 210
Cornelius, L. J., 319
Cornman, J., 85
Coward, R., 319

Hoffman, C., 165
Hogan, D. P., 253
Holmes, D., 107
Hong, M., 84
hooks, b., 204, 205
Hooyman, N. R., 15, 207, 214
Horne, C., 166, 174
Horowitz, A., 126
Hospital, C., 31, 66
House, J. S., 270, 319, 320
Houston, J. D., 26, 30, 40-43
Houston, J. W., 26, 30, 40-43
Huertin-Roberts, S., 283
Hughes, L., 77, 87, 92
Hull, G., 83
Hummert, M. L., 75
Hunter, A. G., 220, 252, 252-259
Hurh, W. M., 215
Hurston, Z. N., 82, 87, 95-97, 279, 285,
    296
Hyde, J. C., 15

Ialongo, N. S., 220, 252-259
Ingersoll-Dayton, B., 174
Institute of Medicine, 106
Inui, T., 88, 106-113

Jackson, J. J., 4, 80, 81, 253
Jackson, J. S., xiii, 87, 124, 126, 128, 130,
    279, 320
John, R., 270, 272, 275, 280
Johnson, C., 213
Johnson, J. S., 34
Johnson, K. W., 191
Johnson, R., 216
Johnson, W. K., 312, 318
Johnston, P. T., 165
Jones, P. K., 312, 315, 317
Joreskog, K. G., 34, 35
Joseph, J., 78, 87, 94
Joseph, K. S., 270
Juster, F. T., 126

Kagawa-Singer, M., 271, 272
Kahn, R. L., 76, 124, 126, 130, 319, 320
Kaplan, G. A., 270, 271, 319
Kart, C. S., 269
Kasl, S. V., 37, 312, 315, 319, 320
Kaufman, S. R., 78
Kehmeier, D., 245
Kellam, S. G., 220, 252-259
Kessler, R. C., 270
Kim, K. C., 215
Kim, S., 215
Kimmel, D. C., 208
Kingson, E., 85
Kingston, R., 279
Kinney, A., 270
Kitagawa, E. M., 312
Kitano, H., 245
Kivett, V., 253, 256, 257
Kiyak, H. A., 207, 214
Klebba, A. J., 312
Kleman, M. H., 165
Kohn, M. L., 33, 35

Konrad, T. R., 282
Kramer, M.., 270
Krishnaswami, S., 134, 135
Kroeber, A., 249
Kunkel, S., 14, 214
Kuypers, J. A., 34, 37

LaGory, M. A., 320
Lame Deer (John Fire), 30, 54-61, 217
Landis, K. R., 319, 320
Landsbergis, P., 276
Lang, A., 216
Langhauser, C., 319
Langlie, J. K., 320
Langner, T. S., 33
Lee, D., 253
Lee, G., 165, 216
Leffland, E., 218, 229-237
Leventhal, E., 283
Leventhal, H., 283
Lewis, J., 11, 212, 218
Liang, J., 4, 319
Liem, N. D., 245
Liker, J. K., 24, 29, 33-39
Link, B., 273, 274, 277
Linn, L. S., 106
Lipman, A., 208
Lockery, S., 215
Lowe, P., 84, 87, 98-105
Lynch, J. W., 270

Maas, H. S., 34, 37
Macfarlane, J. W., 34
Maddox, G., 275, 276, 315
Malbin-Glazer, N., 126
Mankiller, W., 285, 286, 306-311
Manton, K. G., 191, 270, 272, 312, 313,
    318, 319
Markides, K. S., 4, 85, 270, 276, 312, 318
Martin, E., 253
Martin, J. M., 253
Matthews, S., 212
Maurer, J. D., 312
Mayer-Oakes, S. A., 106
McAdoo, H., 21, 205, 276
McClaurin-Allen, I., 218, 222
McCullough, W., 87
McGadney, B., 282
McGoldrick, R. A., 215
McIntosh, P., 5, 276
McLoyd, V. C., 252
Mechanic, D., 34
Meredith, B., 212, 218
Mero, R., 270
Mettlin, C., 319
Meyer, M., 21
Michael, S. T., 33
Miller, D. K., 319
Mills, C. W., 1
Mindel, C. H., 276, 320
Miner, S., 21, 27
Minkler, M., 86, 124, 214, 252, 253, 319
Mitchell, L., 131, 138
Moen, P., 139, 165-175
Morawska, E., 3

Speas, K., 75
Spiegelman, M., 312
Srole, L., 33
Stack, C., 129
Stair, N., 77, 87, 93
Stallard, E., 270, 272, 312, 318
Stanford, E. P., xiv, 215
Starrett, R. A., 320
Staruch, K. S., 165
Steinitz, L., 8
Steuve, A., 165
Stevens, J. H., 253
Stohs, J., 78
Stoller, E. P., 165, 166, 281, 282
Stone, R. I., 125, 126, 133, 165, 166
Strahm, S., 75
Strawbridge, W. J., 271
Stroes, J., 253
Sudarkasa, N., 207
Sue, D., 245
Sue, D. W., 245
Sue, S., 244
Suzman, R., 270, 272, 277
Swanberg, J., 127
Syme, L., 319
Syme, S. L., 319

Tan, A., 285, 303-305
Tanjasiri, S. P., 271, 272
Taylor, R. J., 8
Taylor, S., 7
Teresi, J., 107
Terkel, S., 26, 114-116, 131, 139, 149-
    152
Thomas, E. M., 124
Thomas, P., 26, 30, 44-47
Thomas, S. B., 285, 297-298
Thompson, L., 253
Thone, R. R., 76, 79
Thornton, R. G., 312
Tibblin, S., 319
Toomer, J., 48, 49
Torres-Gil, F. M., 15
Tracy, A. B., 212, 218, 238
Tran, T. V., 245, 247
Treas, J., 166
Trilling, L., 90
Tucker, K. L., 275
Turner, R. J., 253
Twaddle, C. A., 281, 282
Tyroler, H. A., 312, 318

U.S. Bureau of the Census, 14, 86, 173,
    252, 313
Uhlenberg, P., 21, 27
Umberson, D., 281, 319, 320

Van Harrison, R., 320
Van Nostrand, J., 270, 272, 277
Vecoli, R., 3

Verbrugge, L., 126
Villa, V. M., 85, 279

Wagner, S., 319
Waidmann, T., 191, 194
Waitzkin, H., 210, 285
Walker, A., 30, 48-53
Walker, A. J., 253
Wallace, S., 270, 279
Wallace, S. E., 106
Wallace, S. P., 85, 279
Wallis, M., 306-311
Walls, C. T., 8
Wallston, B. S., 319
Walser, A., 138, 142-145
Wan, T., 282
Ward, R. A., 320
Ware, J. E., 319
Warren, K., 276
Weatherby, N. L., 312
Weber, E., 106
Weibel-Orlando, J., 79, 217, 219, 249-251
Weinstein, K. K., 253
Weinstein-Shr, G., 245
Welch, F., 191, 192
Weltman, S., 215
West, C., xiii, 208
Whitaker, R., 320
White, A. J., 21, 276
Whitelaw, N. A., 319
Whitford, G., 207
Wilkinson, D., 281
Williams, D. R., 270, 273, 276, 277, 279
Williams, R. M., 166
Willis, J., 320
Wilson, E. H., 159-164
Wilson, M. N., 253, 254, 257
Wilson, W. J., 191, 192
Wing, S., 312, 318
Wingrove, R., 10, 218
Wolinsky, F. D., 319
Woo, D., 81
Wood, J. B., 282
Woolf, V., 50, 52, 91
Wray, L., 14
Wright, J. D., 106
Wright, R., 13, 22, 320
Wu, C., 31, 62-65
Wykle, M., 282, 283

Yee, B. W. K., xiv, 217, 219, 244-248, 286

Zamsky, E. S., 253
Zarit, S. H., 8
Zelnick, M., 312
Zsembek, B. A., 136
Zuckerman, M., 76, 86, 89

Subject Index

Adaptive resources/strategies, xiv, 9-10, 19, 34
   aging, negative images and, 78-79
   Black experience and, 21-23, 48-53, 82-84, 206, 207, 218, 221-228
   direct instrumental coping, 23
   family relationships, 218
   loss, coping, 38
   racism and, 82-84
   stress and, 276-277
Advantage, cumulative, 27-28, 34, 88, 114-116, 127-128
   See also Disadvantage
African Methodist Episcopal Church, 7-8
Age-by-race gap in health/mortality, 286, 312
   analysis, 317-320
   causes, identification of, 320-321
   health status data, 315-317, 316-318 (figures)
   mortality data, 312-315, 313-315 (figures)
Aging:
   Black experience of, 21-23, 76-77, 92, 284, 288-293
   cohort membership and, 20-21
   continuity within, 87, 90-91, 284, 287
   crossover effect, 272
   direct instrumental coping, 23
   inclusive study of, 14
   loss in, 38
   opportunity of, 86, 89, 94
   race gap in health/mortality and, 286, 312-324, 313-318 (figures)
   success in, 75-77
   See also Cultural images of aging; Life course perspective
Alcohol consumption, 275-276
American Dilemma, 87
American Indians. *See* Native Americans
Angel Island. *See* Chinese immigrant experience
Asian Americans:
   Chinese immigrant experience, 62-65, 87-88, 98-105, 139, 153-158, 272, 285-286, 303-305
   disease/disability and, 271-272
   family values of, 215, 244-248
   Japanese relocation, 25-26, 40-43
   model minority myth, 81-82
   racism and, 84

Berkeley Study, 34, 35

Biological characteristics, 1-2
   skin color, 2-3
   social hierarchies and, 3-4
Black experience:
   adaptive resources/strategies, 21-23, 48-53, 82-84, 206, 207, 218, 221-228
   aging, images of, 76-77, 79-81, 92
   discrimination, 4-5, 21, 22-23, 132-133, 285, 296
   disease management, 281, 282-283, 284, 285, 288-293, 296
   disease/disability, 270, 272, 274, 275
   fertility rates, 210
   grandparenting, 253-254, 256
   health and employment, 141, 191-196
   integration, 13
   Jim Crow, 12-13, 77, 83, 285, 296
   kinship, 206-207, 214
   occupational roles, 131-133, 138, 140-141, 187-190
   productivity and, 128-130
   religion in, 7-8
   retirement and, 136-137, 141, 191-196
   segregation, xiv, 12-13, 77, 83
   social construct and identity, 87, 95-97
   Tuskegee Syphilis Study, 285, 297-298
   women's creativity, 50-53
   See also Civil Rights Movement; Discrimination; Racism
Black Women's Oral History Project, 23
Brown v. Board of Education of Topeka (1954), 12
Bureau of Indian Affairs (BIA), 59-61

Caregiving, paid/unpaid work, 139-140, 165-175, 167 (figure), 168 (table), 169 (figure), 171-172 (tables), 173 (figure)
Categorization of populations, 3-4
Chinese immigrant experience, 62-65, 87-88, 98-105, 139, 153-158, 272, 284-285, 303-305
Civil Rights Act of 1964, 133
Civil Rights Movement, 8, 12, 21, 26-27, 83
Class, xiii, 1
   aging, cultural images and, 84-86
   caregiving/employment and, 140, 165-175
   disease and, 274-275, 282, 283

Great Depression, 21
  cohorts of, 23-24
  health links and, 37-38
  loss, adaptation to, 33-34
  women's resources in, 35-36

Health/mortality:
  adaptive resources, 276-277
  care, availability of, 277-280
  diabetes, 274, 275
  education and, 274, 275
  gender and, 272-273
  generational differences, 285-286,
    303-311
  Great Depression, influence of, 37-38
  hypertension, 274, 275, 282-283
  inequality, systems of, 269, 273
  minority group status and, 270-272
  obesity, 275
  race gap in, 141, 191-196, 286,
    312-324, 313-318 (figures)
  readings, 287-324
  risk, exposure to, 273-277
  self-management, 280-283, 285,
    299-302
  social connectedness, 276-277
  socioeconomic position and, 33-34,
    269-270, 274-275
  stress, 276-277
  See also Elderly population; Risk
    factors in disease
Heterogeneity, 2-3
Hierarchies, intersecting, xiii, xiv, 3-4, 88
  disadvantage/privilege and, 4-5, 6-7
  families and, 209-210
  gender, 2
  Great Depression adversity, 36-37
  health care system and, 285, 297-298
  health/mortality and, 269-273, 274,
    275, 285-286, 303-311, 312-324,
    313-318 (figures)
  productivity and, 139, 159-164
  See also Inequality
Hispanic Americans:
  Cuban immigration experience, 66
  disease/disability and, 271, 275, 281
  family values of, 215, 239-243
  fertility rates, 210
  Mexican folk medicine, 281, 285,
    299-302
  productivity and, 128-130, 138-139,
    140, 146-148, 181-186
  Puerto Rican experience, 44-47
Historical context, xiv, 33
  age of individuals and, 28
  family configuration and, 209-210
  subcohorts and, 21-22
  See also Life course perspective
Homelessness, 88, 106-113
Hypertension, 274, 275, 282-283

Individuals:
  biological difference, 2
  ecological fallacy and, 81
  heterogeneity/diversity, 2-3

history of, 1
  social constructs and, 2, 87, 95-97
Inequality:
  advantage/disadvantage,
    cumulative, 4, 7, 27-28, 34, 88,
    114-117, 127-128
  Civil Rights Movement and, 26-27
  dominanat group perspective, 10-11,
    137
  economic, 9
  Great Depression and, 23-24
  health care availability, 277-280, 285,
    299-302
  Japanese relocation, 25-26
  pension coverage, 27-28
  social, 9-10
  subcohorts/historical time and,
    21-23
  systems of, intersecting, 19-20, 88,
    130, 274
  work roles and, 130-133, 140,
    176-180, 181-186
  World War II, impact of, 24-26
  See also Hierarchies, intersecting
Integration, 13
Interaction hypothesis, 36-37

Japanese experience:
  disease, 271-272
  family reciprocity, 214
  relocation, 25-26, 40-43
Jim Crow, 12-13, 77, 83, 285, 296

Kinship, 11, 213, 214
  Black communities and, 206-207
  nuclear families and, 206
  support in, 9, 215-216

Labor force participation rates (LFPRs),
  191-195
Lesbians. *See* Gay/lesbian couples
Life course perspective, 11-14
  advantage/disadvantage,
    cumulative, 27-28, 34
  caregiving/employment roles,
    165-175
  civil rights era, 26-27
  cohort effect, 20-21
  defined, 19-21
  Great Depression and, 23-24
  period effect, 20
  premises of, 19
  readings, 33-66
  subcohorts/historical time, 21-22
  World War II and, 24-26

MacArthur Foundation Study of
  Successful Aging, 76
Marriage, survival of, 36
Men:
  health status and, 272-273
  job/income loss, 36
  productivity patterns, 126-127,
    134-135, 139, 149-152
Meritocracy, xiii, 6, 82

Social constructs, xiii, xv, 1
  adaptive resources/strategies and, xiv, 9-10, 19
  gendered reality as, 2
  individuals and, 2
  race as, 3-4, 87, 95-97
  skin color and, 2-3
Social gerontology, 1, 10
Social policy. *See* Public policy
Social problems approach, xiv
Social process, 3-4
Social Security, 80, 85, 86
Socioeconomic factors in health, 3-34, 37-38
Stress, 276-277
Surrogate parenting, 213-214, 220, 252-259
Survival lessons, 206-207, 218, 221-228

Tuskegee Syphilis Study, 285, 297-298
Tweeners, 86

Underground economy, 128-129

Welfare, 80, 84
Well-being and employment, 133-135
Wheatley, Phyllis, 49-50, 51

White experience:
  aging and, 80
  health and, 274, 275, 281, 282
  privilege in, 5-6, 276
Women, xiii
  Black, adaptive strategies of, 48-53
  caregiving, paid/unpaid work, 139-140, 165-175
  economic deprivation and, 34-35
  eldercare, 211-212, 218-219, 238
  Great Depression, survival resources, 35-36
  health status and, 272-273
  loss, adaptation to, 33-34
  productivity patterns, 125-127, 133, 134, 138, 142-145
  wartime labor force, 25
  wellbeing/hardship balance, 36-37
  See also Black experience; Families
Women's Political Council, 83
Work. *See* Productivity
World War II, 21
  Black employment after, 26
  cohorts of, 24-25
  female labor force, 25
  Japanese relocation, 25-26